Settlement Houses Under Siege

Settlement Houses Under Siege

*The Struggle to Sustain Community
Organizations in New York City*

Michael B. Fabricant and Robert Fisher

COLUMBIA   UNIVERSITY   PRESS   NEW   YORK

COLUMBIA UNIVERSITY PRESS
Publishers Since 1893
New York   Chichester, West Sussex
Copyright © 2002 Columbia University Press
All rights reserved

Library of Congress Cataloging-in-Publication Data

Fabricant, Michael.
  Settlement houses under siege : the struggle to
sustain community organizations in New York City /
Michael B. Fabricant and Robert Fisher.
    p. cm.
  Includes bibliographical references and index.
  ISBN 0-231-11930-5 (cloth : alk. paper)
  ISBN 0-231-11931-3 (pbk. : alk. paper)
    1. Human services—United States. 2. Human
services—Contracting out—United States. 3. Social
settlements—United States. 4. Social settlements—
New York (State)—New York. I. Fisher, Robert,
1947– II. Title.

HV91 .F29 2002
362.5′57′0973—dc21

                                        2001047218

Casebound editions of Columbia University Press books
are printed on permanent and durable acid-free paper.
Printed in the United States of America

c 10 9 8 7 6 5 4 3 2 1
p 10 9 8 7 6 5 4 3 2 1

Contents

   a Social Services Future   198

              Part 3.   Rethinking the Purposes and Practices of Not-
              for-Profit Social Services

8. From Corporatized Contracting to Community Building   233

              Appendix   Methodology of the Qualitative Inquiry   291

              Notes   301

              References   313

              Index   343

To Dave Bramhall, Frank Caro, and David Houston whose mentoring promoted understanding of the demands of rigorous scholarship and the responsibilities of political activism.

To former colleagues and students in political social work at the University of Houston School of Social Work, who taught me what social work could be and shared in the critical project of reconnecting social work and social activism.

Acknowledgments

A number of organizations and individuals have been essential to the development of this book. To begin with, the financial support of the DeWitt Wallace–Readers Digest Fund provided the basis for the early data collection and analysis. The Hunter College School of Social Work lent secretarial and other support to the project. More than that, our coauthorship was facilitated by Bob's appointment as the Henry and Lucy Moses Distinguished Professor at Hunter College School of Social Work for 1999–2000, for which we are both grateful. Equally important, the Moses professorship enabled him to devote most of his time to this book project. We hope the benefactors of the chair and supporters at the school of social work are pleased with the results.

Barbara Simon, Clarke Chambers, Stanley Aronowitz, and Steve Burghardt read early drafts of the manuscript and offered important feedback. Simon was especially generous with research and reference materials. John Herrick and Roger Lohmann also provided valuable material and references. Maria Helena Reis invested imagination and energy in developing the format for parts of the appendix. Early conversations with Irwin Epstein and Esther Robison influenced the development of the research guide. The project interviewers Jack Levine, Rachel Grob, Molly Woeffler, Dennis Redmond, Lisa Rose, Esther Robison, and Eileen Barrett through skillful questioning and development of rapport with respondents were able to generate a rich body of qualitative data. Paul Graziano was instrumental in converting over 1,500 pages of interviews into data strips and transferring this text onto the Martin software program. The Columbia University Press offered both editorial and substantive comments that were consistently valuable. Sabine H. Seiler meticulously edited the manuscript. John L. Michel, a senior executive editor at the Press, was especially important in steadily moving the project forward. It should be noted that an earlier version of chapters 1 and 2 will appear in the *Journal of Sociology and Social Welfare* (June 2002). Finally, we want to thank our respective families, Betsy, Niki, and Matt for their patience and support, Juliet, Ian and Ace for encouraging and enabling Bob to go off to Hunter.

Settlement Houses Under Siege

Introduction: Social Services in an Unstable Privatized Context

During the last decades the American economy has experienced rapid transformation. Information and biotechnology are changing the lives of more and more citizens in much the same way the technologies of the industrial era—for example, railroad and telegraph—transformed small isolated communities in the late nineteenth century. This change has brought enormous wealth and capital creation as well as a deeper belief in the efficacy of the private sector. Many commentators (Kuttner 1997; Sclar 2000; Starr 1987; Fisher and Karger 1997) suggest that the logic of the market is penetrating a variety of institutions in many areas, including higher education, government, and nonprofit social services. Proponents argue that this change is long overdue and propose that "privatization" will greatly benefit public and nonprofit organizations by making them more business-like, efficient, and productive. Others, however, such as Peter Drucker, believe that the privatization/corporatization of the public and nonprofit sphere represents a profound threat to the enterprise of creating collective goods (Drucker 1994) The corporate sector, it is argued, produces an organizational culture structured to emphasize individual consumption and benefit. Nonprofit agencies, however, must depend on government contracts that increasingly demand social service provision shaped by best business practices.[1] The drive to privatize every aspect of American life conflicts with the demands associated with sustaining the polity, creating civic engagement, and building community and social cohesion. This conflict lies at the center of the re-creation of organizational life for nonprofit social services.

The rapid capital creation of this boom period destabilized service provision. On the one hand, expanded wealth potentially has offered the benefits of an enlarged endowment (for those nonprofits that are vested in the stock market) and greater contributions from patrons or board members. On the other hand, increasing income inequality since 1980 has created an ever greater gulf in resources between the poorest and wealthiest communities (Schor 1997; Reich 2001). Wages have declined dramatically during this period. Although income disparity improved modestly between 1995 and 2000, recent data suggest that these trends should not be overstated. They have almost exclusively benefited the southern region of the country (Uchitelle 1999). Furthermore, capital has also become more mobile in its search for profit. The job market requires ever greater flexibility, information, and hi-tech skills if employees want to avoid low-end wages and extended periods of unemployment. This set of circumstances has particular implications for the poorest communities. The labor market isolation and underperforming public schools of these neighborhoods often leaves residents underprepared to compete in the new economy. Additionally, living on these modest salaries and remaining employed produces various forms of strain (Edin and Lein 1997). For instance, the dismantling of AFDC in favor of workfare and low-wage, private-sector employment has left many poor, single women without the child care and health benefits essential to sustaining employment and developing the new skills necessary for upward mobility. These changing dynamics inside and outside the marketplace have direct consequences for the consumers of social services. They increasingly come to agencies with problems stemming from threatened, reduced, or eliminated benefits and with difficulties associated with their transition to low-wage, private-sector work.

The decline of community or communal networks represents yet another environmental stressor for nonprofit social service agencies.[2] Robert Putnam (2000) notes that "the decline in neighborhood and social capital is one important feature of the inner city crisis . . . in addition to purely economic factors." William Julius Wilson, Robert Sampson, and others concur that very poor communities are experiencing a crisis of social capital formation or social network. (Wilson 1987; Sampson, Raudenbush, and Earls 1997; Anderson 1990) Residents are less and less likely to participate in communal activities or have any membership identification with formal organizations, voluntary associations, or the block on which they live. Poor people are more apt to find themselves isolated in the communities where they live and work.

This matters, for social ties and the consequent accumulation of social capital contribute both subtly and overtly to the health of a community.³ Social capital is most easily understood as the breadth and depth of social networks and communal capacity. In the past the stock of a community's social capital was perhaps most visible in the daily, informal contacts between residents. To Jane Jacobs "the sum of such casual contact at a local level—most of it fortuitous, most of it associated with errands, all of it metered by the person concerned and not thrust upon him by anyone—is a feeling of public identity of people, a web of public respect and trust, and a resource for . . . personal and neighborhood need." (Putnam 2000:308) On the other hand, the decline of a neighborhood's social capital often translates into spiraling breakdowns in education, physical safety, health, and child care. The contemporary ethos of privatization expects nonprofit social service agencies to address these strains as problems of individuals, not of the collective. This growing crisis of community and its translation into intensifying and expanding individual needs represents yet another claim on the often limited resources of nonprofit agencies in a privatized, corporate-driven context.

In the midst of these changes Putnam and others have suggested that we must look to voluntary associations and organizations to regenerate the social ties that undergird strong communities. To renew community Putnam proposes that "some of the innovations of the . . . Progressive Era like the settlement house . . . could inspire twenty-first century equivalents." (Putnam 2000:410) In most of the literature, however, little attention is paid to the actual practice of agency-based community building. Likewise, the public sector is rarely mentioned as a venue for such work. Government and its attendant welter of bureaucratic rules and regulations are increasingly perceived as contributing to the depletion of local social capital. It is argued, at times quite persuasively, that social ties cannot be created through large, distant, unresponsive units of government that are frequently out of touch with the current needs of a locality. Instead, organizations embedded in and reflective of the neighborhood are viewed as a more appropriate fit for the work of community building.⁴ Accordingly, grassroots nonprofit social service agencies, such as settlement houses, due to their relative flexibility in responding to local problems, mission, size, and historic relationship to a neighborhood are a potentially critical locus for significant community-building work.

Of central importance to this book is the nexus between delivering services, community building, and social change. The connection between service delivery and community building is especially critical to the historic mission of nonprofit service agencies, such as the settlement houses, and to the development of innovative responses to the present crisis of social capital in poor neighborhoods. Equally important, a service design that makes such a connection correctly acknowledges the dynamic relationship between individual and collective experience in both the formation and resolution of social problems. Finally, communities are not isolated islands. Poor neighborhoods are affected by economic and political decisions made elsewhere. The capacity of poor neighborhoods to mount a political response to damaging trends and/or policies is in direct proportion to its stock of social capital. More to the point, the effectiveness of social change initiatives depends as much on residents having better resources and information as on strong networks of social solidarity. Only by struggling to integrate individual social services, community building, and social change initiatives can nonprofit social service agencies contribute to arresting and reversing the decline of very poor communities. The opportunities and difficulties associated with such work form a core element of the following analysis.

Settlements and the Building of Community

The settlement house at the turn of the century engaged in various kinds of community-building projects. Its work extended from small groups or clubs to coalitions, all intended to help members through promotion of community and broader social change in housing, health, employment, and public space. Much of the landmark legislation of the Progressive Era can be traced to the work of settlement leaders such as Jane Addams, Lillian Wald, and Florence Kelly. This broad effort for social change rested on the deep and extended social networks that evolved from settlement social service work. The best settlements' work of this period organized social services to promote both individual and collective benefits. Delivery of services, building community, and promoting social change were intertwined. Fragmented communities needed services, but effective services required communal supports. Citizen development required both. Clearly, not all houses were equally inclusive of all neighborhood residents or interested in promoting collective or social capital projects. However, the premier settlements of the Progressive Era are generally regarded as quintessential social service community-building agencies and social change organizations.

A century later the settlement house and other nonprofit multiservice agencies continue to be viewed as central to the work of strengthening very poor communities. Now they are frontline, grassroots institutions with a mission to respond to the immediate crises (AIDS, homelessness, delinquency, drugs, etc.) and chronic problems (underemployment and unemployment, deficient housing, underperforming schools) of very poor areas. For a variety of reasons, however, these agencies often emphasize delivery of individual, not collective, services. Problems are addressed mostly one-on-one, neglecting network development and broader change initiatives. Some authors have charged that social service agencies and social work have abandoned their more collective or community building role (Specht and Courtney 1994). This is especially disappointing when a large number of very poor communities desperately need of strengthened social networks. We argue that the structure of government contracts, on which settlement houses and not-for-profit social services have increasingly become dependent, represents a large obstacle to creating such relationships and networks.

Contemporary government contracting with nonprofit agencies promotes a corporate or business approach to the provision of services. Agencies efficiency, productivity, and outputs receive greater and greater attention. Activity that can be quantified and analyzed in terms of cost per unit gets priority. The intention is to create analogs of corporate measures of productivity in the nonprofit world. The resulting conflict for nonprofit social service agencies, however, is not only that such structural constraints limit an agency's service provision and autonomy but that they do not even consider the qualitative demands and process requirements of forming relationships with community residents. This aspect of service provision gets short shrift because it is more complex, less amenable to quantification, and relatively inefficient. For instance, it is far easier to document the number of children served or to calculate test scores for participants in an enriched component of a school program than to assess social networks and/or the relationships that evolve from such services. And yet it is precisely the latter outcomes that are most central to replenishing the social capital of neighborhoods and to enabling people to capitalize on the services they receive.

As Smith and Lipsky note, contemporary changes in the structure of government financing of nonprofit services extend beyond the redefinition of performance measures (Smith and Lipsky 1993). Agencies are being required by contract to do more with fewer resources. Consequently, encounters between workers and consumers are increasingly rushed, circumscribed, and harried. Neither the needs of the worker nor those of the service user can be met under such conditions. More important, the intensifying demands on the service exchange inevitably increase the distance between consumers and the agency and often lead to staff burnout. Additionally, agency infrastructure and staff benefits and salaries are systematically underfinanced in government contracting. The gulf between levels of funding and agency needs requires that administrators cut corners or juggle funding streams to make do with less. For instance, part-time or less educated staff may replace more expensive full-time, certified counterparts. Furthermore, limited reimbursements for agency infrastructure and overhead costs may result in a more decayed physical plant, limited staff access to phones, and broken photocopy machines that cannot be replaced. Individually, these contract demands and constraints tend to estrange both workers and consumers from the agency and each other. Cumulatively, these externalities of contracting further undermine the ability of settlements and nonprofit social services to build the kinds of relationships with and between neighborhood residents that are an intrinsic property of social networks.

We propose that community building may well be the most important social service work of the next generation. At least it must be understood as integral to effective social service provision. Yet, the very structure of government contracting limits the capacity of not-for-profit agencies to engage in such work. This is especially detrimental for settlement houses whose historic record and present mission is synonymous with the work and intention of community building. The intersection between government contracting, the shifting meaning of social services, and the centrality of community building remains relatively underexplored. This dynamic set of relationships, however, is essential to understanding the historic contribution, present circumstances, and future possibility of nonprofit social services. The core of this book is devoted to exploring these themes.

This Inquiry

Settlement Houses Under Siege: The Struggle to Sustain Community Organizations in New York City will focus on the past, present, and future of the settlement house and, by implication, nonprofit community-based services. Why have settlements been selected as the locus for this inquiry? To begin with, they have occupied a special place in the development of community-based social services. At the turn of the century settlements were instrumental in establishing a legitimacy and presence for social services in the poorest neighborhoods. Equally important, as noted earlier, in a number of the most inventive of these agencies—those that took the most risks—the provision of services for individuals was linked to community building and work for broader social change. The settlement remains a historic reference point for the broadest intentions of social services to meet individual needs while simultaneously working to advance the collective interests of poor communities.

Over time the settlement house evolved into a multiservice agency. Increasingly, services in settlement houses differed little from those offered in a range of other community-based agencies. The earliest intentions of the settlement house to use services to build a basis for social networks and broader social change was at best muted and at worst silenced. Some part of the change can be traced to the shifting financing of services and altered social climate. What is offered in this book and often missing from other works is an exploration of the complexity of developing and implementing a service-based community-building agenda. This discussion is tethered to the interplay between macro-context, not-for-profit capacity and the development of social cohesion and solidarity networks. It also describes agencies' specific struggles with the development of social relationships and networks. Too often the conversation regarding community building ends at precisely the point where these matters of practice surface.

As a historical exemplar of community building, the settlement house offers an especially important prism through which to view the findings of a contemporary inquiry. We propose that it provides a benchmark in the evolution of social services as an instrument to strengthen social capital or networks of poor neighborhoods. This is also the first study in two decades to provide an update on settlements.[5] The discussion of the settlement house rarely addresses present circumstances. Instead, the settlement house appears as artifact, its only significance, like that of a dinosaur bone, located in the past. This analysis is intended as a partial corrective, thus providing an important, independent contribution to the literature on social services.

One hundred agency administrators and the program staff of ten settlements were interviewed in the course of this study.[6] Approximately 75 percent of the study sample was drawn from the ranks of program directors. This particular subgroup was targeted because of the breadth of the subjects' practice roles. The program directors of settlement houses daily juggle administrative functions and the provision of direct services. They are uniquely situated to comment on the broadest range of practice experiences and conflicts salient to settlement house life and community-based nonprofit service provision.

The study, conducted between 1995 and 1996, reveals a particularly critical moment for social services nationally and in New York City in particular. The Contract with America promulgated by Republicans in Congress during this period endorsed wholesale cuts in social services and entitlement programs. This neoconservative agenda trickled down to New York State and New York City during the mid-decade gubernatorial and mayoral elections of George Pataki and Rudy Giuliani, respectively. Consequently, nonprofit social services in general, and New York settlements specifically, were faced with the triple threat of reduced funding from every level of government—city, state, and federal. This broad attack left agencies in an essentially untenable position; they had no sector of government to appeal to for relief. This public abandonment offers a particularly vivid example of how not-for-profit social services fare during an era of cutbacks, retrenchment, and heightened administrative supervision. Surviving in highly conservative private eras has been an integral part of settlement house history. Once again the settlements' flexibility and persistence had to carry them through a difficult time. But the data and results of this study are not limited to that time and series of events. The privatization trend of the mid-1990s has not slowed. Both George Pataki and Rudy Giuliani remained in office through the 1990s and into the new millennium. Moreover, the contracting climate that not-for-profits in New York City continue to face reflects the national trend. Therefore, lessons can be drawn from this analysis that extend beyond the boundaries of New York City and the time frame of the mid-1990s. The settlement house remains under siege, and the era of privatization and corporatization continues virtually unchanged and unchallenged.

Critically, the findings of this study have implications not just for settlement houses. The social services provided by the ten agencies in this study reach tens of thousands of service users annually. These settlement house services, consumers, and contracting arrangements differ little from the broader experience of not-for-profit social services and are therefore representative. Consequently, not only the settlement houses are under siege. The themes and findings of this analysis apply to settlement houses but must also be viewed in the wider context of the vast number of other nonprofit social service agencies struggling to serve poor communities.

Throughout this book we maintain an essentially favorable stance toward social services. It is presumed that services can and do make a difference in the lives of low-income people. The book focuses on the external difficulties of service workers and agencies in shaping services that promote relationships and change. The analysis emphasizes the consequences of recent conservative social policy for agencies. More specifically, it considers how the present political environment influences services through contracting and other forms of privatization. These contextual sources of change deserve independent attention. However, it is equally apparent that the problems of social service agencies can also be traced to internal organizational dynamics. Centralization of administrative authority, monopolization of expertise by professionals, systematic distancing of agencies from the community, and an emphasis of tasks over processes are but a few aspects of agencies' internal choices that can limit their contribution to the development of individual and collective resources. Clearly, not-for-profit agencies must address these internal structural limitations if they are to have any hope of providing social services that meet the needs of individuals and serve as instruments of community building. However, these internal limitations, although critical, are of secondary importance to this inquiry.[7] In this study, inevitably, we had to make choices regarding emphasis. The broad and unabated attack on the very premise of social services and the use of a corporate logic to reshape its meaning has a special significance for contemporary agencies. It is within this context that we chose to explore the interplay between external change and the internal practices of not-for-profit social service agencies.

A number of books have been written on government contracting and social services, most notably *Nonprofits for Hire* by Steven Smith and Michael Lipsky (1993). These books have addressed how the contracting calculus of heightened demand and decreasing resources affects nonprofit agencies. What they have not considered, however, is the lived experience of agency staff in these ever more pressured environments. This book examines the experience of contracting through the eyes of social service providers. It also represents both a deepening and extension of themes that were explored in *The Welfare State Crisis and the Transformation of Social Service Work* (Fabricant and Burghardt 1992) and *Social Work and Community in a Private World* (Fisher and Karger 1997). At the core of the analysis are five qualitative chapters that capture the organizational life of settlements through the voices of executive directors and program personnel of ten New York City agencies. The empirical chapters offer anecdotal data that individually and cumulatively describe how staff struggle daily with the consequences of contracting policies.

This qualitative inquiry is not supported with quantitative data. The purpose of this analysis is to explore and develop the perspective of settlement staff. It seeks to examine the complexity of delivering social services from the perspective of the actors who are caught daily in the cross fire of contract demands and community needs. We use the language of staff throughout the book, with only minor grammatical changes. As noted earlier, the sample of respondents includes staff who are engaged in frontline work as well as administrators who direct the agencies. Both groups of personnel offer unique insights into the condition of settlements. The executive and associate directors can discuss a cross section of programs or the general state of the agency. Alternatively, line staff/program directors are particularly able to comment on the details of daily practice. It is one of our intentions to offer thick descriptions in this book. Clearly, a qualitative inquiry best fits such an intention. The authors understand that quantitative measures would have offered other insights regarding recent program and agency experience. However, a coherent narrative that reflects the complexity and richness of the staff's perspectives has independent merit. Staff perspectives on present agency experience informs behavior in regard to services, consumers, and the agency itself. The prospect for social services is therefore powerfully influenced by such dynamics. For this reason a choice was made to develop a qualitative inquiry to present staff perspectives on present agency experience.

The dialogue regarding the decline of community led by William Julius Wilson and Robert Putnam presumes that mediating institutions, such as not-for-profit social service agencies, will help to strengthen the social capital of poor neighborhoods (Putnam 2000; Wilson 1987). This expectation is rarely joined to an exploration of these settings' present circumstances. More to the point, little attention is paid to the preparedness of specific agencies for such a project. This book offers a particular angle of insight into the world of not-for-profit social services and their present capacity to build the networks and relationships necessary for empowered communities and citizens.

The first and second chapters of the book provide a context for understanding the later empirical chapters. The first chapter broadly describes the evolution of the settlement house from the late nineteenth century through the mid-1970s. Of particular interest are the practices, social contributions, and financing arrangements that defined settlement life during specific epochs. The analysis emphasizes the role of contextual factors, especially the political economy and its impact on social investment. For example, the Progressive Era's investment in a range of programs that benefited the poor marks it as more concerned with the public good and public relationships. Alternatively, the 1920s were marked by a retreat from collective and social justice investment and embraced business practices to meet social needs; this resembles our own era with its focus on the private context of social problems and their solution. The chapter contends that the dynamic interaction between settlement houses and political economic context has both historical and contemporary significance. The second chapter explores the evolving contractual relationship between the state and not-for-profit social services in the increasingly privatized world dominated by corporate globalization as it has emerged in the past few decades. The structure of such financing arrangements and their benefits as well as costs are explored. The intensifying difficulties associated with contracting in the late 1980s and early 1990s—on the one hand, restricting autonomous practice of agencies and, on the other, creation of ever greater financial instability—are discussed as a segue to the qualitative chapters.

Chapters 3 through 8 describe the layers of organizational life associated with both contracting and the current condition of not-for-profit social services. Chapter 3 is broadest in scope and provides social workers' perspectives on the threat and impact of unstable government funding. It explores the widespread perception that social services are under attack and are being devalued. Chapter 4 discusses infrastructure, the surface or most visible aspect of agency operations affected by contracting. It covers topics such as physical plant, supplies, secretarial support, and equipment. The ways in which infrastructure insinuates itself into the workers' relationship to their agency, services, and consumers are described. Chapter 5 reveals another layer of organizational life, the pressures shaping the rhythm of the workday and the social connectedness of workers. Increasingly, line staff have to do more and more with fewer resources or support. As the work quotas expand, speed and pressures intensify. Declining supports impoverish the workers' experience. They find themselves increasingly alone and unable to put their individual stamp on their work. This chapter also explores the resulting morale problems. The burdens of declining infrastructural support and increasing work pressures stand in the way of the basic intention of social services, namely, the building of relationships. Chapter 6 considers the impact of unstable, underfunded, and increasingly demanding contracting on the content of social services and the processes of relationship building. This discussion addresses how contracting contributes to a redefinition of the meaning of nonprofit social services. In chapter 7 nonprofit social service agencies are described by workers as being at a crossroads. On the one hand, the culture of agencies is increasingly defined by business practices and priorities. On the other hand, line staff and administrators are struggling to incorporate practices that promote relationship building and a collective life. These tendencies frequently conflict. The nature of this tension and the present imbalance in favor of business practices are also considered.

The final chapter presents the implications of the study's findings. It places the inquiry within a broader context and reviews the forces driving the changes analyzed earlier and the concomitant threats to building and rebuilding a larger collective life. The bulk of the concluding chapter is devoted to presenting a practice framework for community building.[8] This structure offers a way to think holistically about the practice and demands of community building. Throughout this discussion illustrations are drawn from a wide range of practice literature. This is by no means a final statement regarding the development of a community-building practice in social services. Rather, it represents a preliminary effort that, it is hoped, will stimulate a lively discussion. The chapter also identifies the dilemmas associated with implementing this practice framework. This book intends to connect the best past practices of settlements with their present difficulties and opportunities. As noted earlier, this exploration is not limited to settlements. It has much broader implications for community-based, not-for-profit social services. As communities continue to collapse, institutions need to be transformed to perform critical functions that facilitate the development of social networks and social solidarity. Current tendencies in contracting limit such possibilities. On the basis of their mission and day-to-day experience, social service agencies are particularly well suited to play an important role in rebuilding communities. The practice of community building can help shape a more effective and significant future for social services. Equally important, it can help to blunt and reverse present political attacks. The future course of community building must be charted through our uncertain and challenging present. This book provides some of the information necessary to map such a path.

Part 1

History Matters: Settlements and Not-for-Profit Social Service Financing

1 The Settlement House in Context: From Henry Street to Head Start

History is important to social settlements. The very mention of social settlements evokes a time when settlements and settlement leaders were at the center of a national movement for social reform. Certainly contemporary settlements are very different from their predecessors. Today they are nonprofit multiservice centers heavily tied to centralized structures of programming and support; they can no longer claim to be unique social welfare or neighborhood institutions. Nevertheless, settlement houses are inextricably tied to a past that still provides a collective memory of purpose and mission and serves as a yardstick for measuring present performance (Berry 1986). While there is always a tendency to romanticize history by elaborating accomplishments or downplaying errors and failures, the interest in settlement history harks back to a glorious heyday when the leading houses served as free spaces of social activism and midwives of modern social services in the United States. In his influential study of the recent decline of American community and social cohesion, Putnam (2000) concludes that our society desperately needs a twenty-first-century equivalent of the settlement house.[1]

This chapter tracks historically the direct connection and evolving relationship between financing and nonprofit social service provision. While this critical linkage has been explored historically for other nonprofit institutions, such as schools and hospitals, it has not been fully examined for settlement houses, arguably the quintessential voluntary service agency (Hammack 1998; Hall

1992; Crocker 1992; Lohmann 1991; Carson 1990; Trolander 1975). Critically, an exploration of the history of financing social settlements represents an opportunity to discover and evaluate historic shifts in the relationship between financing and agency programs. To this end, the analysis focuses not only on changes in the financial arrangements but also on shifts in the larger political economy. Within this metastatement the study proposes a cyclical theory of social investment and periodicity regarding settlement financing and political economy. This historical analysis has contemporary significance, exploring how contemporary contracted financing impacts the capacity of neighborhood-based social agencies to deliver community-based services and to engage in the historically and presently critical work of community building.

Accordingly, this book begins with a brief overview of the history of settlements that links the past to the contemporary study of settlement life and work conditions. It does not provide a full history of the settlements as the literature on settlement history is voluminous; rather, it seeks to contextualize the study of contemporary social settlements.[2]

Contextualizing Settlements

Settlements have been a favorite subject of historians dating back to the 1960s when Allen Davis (1967) published his *Spearheads for Reform: The Social Settlements and the Progressive Movement, 1890–1914*. Like Clarke Chambers's *Seedtime of Reform: American Social Service and Social Action, 1918–1933* (1963), which addressed the period following the Progressive Era, Davis situated the history of settlements and social reform in a debate about the nature of the Progressive movement. And, like Chambers, he found settlements inhabited by extraordinary individuals and social activists, significant leaders, and reformers. Since then historians and social work academics interested in the history of social work have written widely on the settlement houses, each from a different perspective, asking different questions, looking at different settlements, and often arriving at different evaluations (Barbuto 1999; Trolander 1991; Tobin 1988; Boris 1992).

Context influences interpretation. The era in which the historian writes changes the questions asked, as each era confronts present and past with different issues. Davis and Chambers, writing in the early and mid-1960s, wanted to know about the origins and nature of successful, innovative liberal reform. They wanted to know whether progressive reform could exist in a conservative era. Later historians, more suspicious of liberal reform, both in the Progressive Era as well as in their own time, criticized settlements for being less democratic than they professed, for being racist and exclusionary, for engaging more in social control and class mediation than in social change and social reform (Crocker 1992; Fisher 1994; Karger 1987a; Lasch-Quinn 1993; Philpott 1978). Crocker (1992), for example, finds most settlement houses, aside from a few progressive exemplars like Hull-House and Henry Street, much less than "spearheads for reform." She argues that to read the history of settlements as one of decline from a golden age of reform is to overlook the fundamental conservatism of most settlements and the limits of most Progressive Era reforms. More recently, historians such as Kathryn Kish Sklar (1995) have found a rich history of social feminist activism running through the lives of settlement leaders such as Florence Kelley. As noted earlier, the literature on settlements is voluminous, significant, and contradictory, with the various sources, perspectives, politics, and contexts of the respective historians informing their research and interpretations. Our study is no different.

Of course, context affects those who make history at least as much as it does those who write it. Stanford (1994:27) suggests that, "The context of an action is the whole environment—social, physical (or natural), and cultural—within which it occurs." Because practices and texts are always specific to particular times, places, and individuals, history must be situated in the varied sites that generate it. Historian E. P. Thompson (1971) refers to history as "the discipline of context." This study focuses on the interpenetration between national political economy and the lived experience of community-based settlement work. Contextualizing settlements means understanding that all strands of social life, on the national and the local level, are intertwined (Fisher and Karger 2000). In order to put continuities and changes in the settlement experience "in context," this chapter discusses broad patterns in American history which provide a better understanding of the transformation of the settlement house over time.

Cycles of History

American social welfare and political history in the past century has been described as a series of cyclical shifts between eras with a more public-centered focus and those with a more private-centered one (Schlesinger Jr. 1986). Piven and Cloward (1972, 1999) discuss the shifts in terms of periods of consensus and dissensus politics. Most recently, Putnam (2000:25) iden-tifies cyclical shifts in terms of ups and downs in "civic engagement." Helen Hall, head worker at the Henry Street Settlement from 1933 until 1967, saw a related trend, "As I look back, I do see the years divided by different overriding problems. And, except for the four years of war, the problems of most concern to the people of slum neighborhoods such as mine have seemed to last approximately a decade, with each ten years producing a new concern" (Hall 1971:xv).

Our version of the model proposes that the dominant political economy and historical events of each era help shape and profoundly influence almost all aspects of society, including social investment. Developments affect and are in turn affected by national electoral politics, social struggles, the nature of social welfare, and even community-based efforts such as social settle-ments. In more liberal or public eras, the model asserts, the social welfare state expands, activism on the left increases, as does social investment for reform-oriented service programs such as social settlements. In more private eras, conservative policymakers dominate, corporate prerogatives are asserted with greater openness and are less challenged, right-wing movements gain currency, social welfare systems become increasingly privatized and timid, which reduces both interest in and funding for organizations such as the settlement house.

Clearly, all models have limits; they reduce historical complexity and conflate historical specificity, and thus risk becoming merely mechanical rather than accurate pictures of lived experience. Regarding our own model, we recognize that historical change usually comes slowly and incrementally rather than in sudden shifts. The dates offered are not absolute. They are designed to emphasize a general change in the national political atmosphere and a shift in the climate for social change. Equally important, continuities in American history, such as a broad consensus on private property and individualism, the persistence of class and racial domination, and the he-gemony of capitalist development, are certainly as significant as the changes this model tends to overemphasize (Hofstadter 1948; Dowd 1974; Crocker 1992; Walkowitz 1999). Acknowledging these and other caveats, we will in subsequent stages of this discussion provide a fuller and more graphic de-piction of the shifts in support for social investment and their influence on the development of settlement houses.

Most histories of social welfare and social work utilize, explicitly and implicitly, this model. This is true for mainstream histories, such as Trattner's

From Poor Law to Welfare State (1999), and radical critiques, such as John Ehrenreich's *The Altruistic Imagination* (1985). Social work begins with the charitable friendly visitors of the Charity Organization Society (COS), focused on individual character and business efficiency. The Progressive Era advances liberal social change efforts, most notably the social settlements. Settlement houses served the immigrant poor and the working class while offering a social analysis of individual problems, helping people to build their communities and engage in social action. In the twenties social work sought professional legitimacy, a knowledge base, and a practice in keeping with the "return to normalcy" (Addams 1930; Lundblad 1995). Accordingly, it incorporated psychology as its intellectual core, case work as its method, and a focus, more or less, on the individual needs of clients and the advancement of social workers (Lubove 1975). During the Great Depression and the New Deal, the micro-focus, that is, the psychological orientation of the profession, gave way to a reemphasis on larger policy issues, the macro-perspective. The needs of individuals had to be met, but an economy in which 40 percent of the people in key industries were unemployed exposed the limits of such a private focus. The postwar era, on the other hand, reemphasized individual over collective needs. Professional concerns, certainly an issue before the twenties, were given greater weight than social change initiatives (Walkowitz 1999).[3] Concern with policy and practice overall also declined. In keeping with such trends, technique and narrow method triumphed over politics as social work sought greater scientific legitimacy and professional standing. Repression of social reform and public life accompanied these changes in the postwar era. The 1960s fostered the reemergence of social, political, and economic justice issues, social policy, community-based practice, and the connection of social work with the public-focused social reform of the day, such as the civil rights movement. In the mid-1970s, social work again turned away from its public role to an individual, private-oriented, psychological emphasis, what Specht and Courtney (1994) deride as social work's "worshiping at the church of individual repair."

Ehrenreich (1985:12–13) describes the model thus:

The history of social work and of social policy is one long account of pendulum swings between the two poles—between a focus on individual treatment and a focus on social reform. Very crudely, in the last decades of the nineteenth century, the 1920s, the 1940s and 1950s,

and the present time [1985], the more individual orientation has pre-
dominated (and along with it, despair as to the possibility of reform
and disdain for social action). Conversely, in the years before World
War I, the 1930s, and the 1960s, community action and social reform
dominated the attention of social workers and planners, and casework
fell into a degree of disrepute. . . . The Progressive Era, the 1930s, and
the 1960s were all periods of massive social unrest, in which broad-
based movements of social change accelerated large-scale expansions
of the role of government. Conversely the interim periods have been
characterized by the repression and decline of social movements, retreat into political apathy and acquiescence, and, to a degree, the
rolling back of earlier reforms.

Historians and social scientists disagree on the causes of change in the
support for social investment and activism (Schlesinger Jr. 1986; Putnam
2000; Piven and Cloward 1971).[4] It is our contention that these changes in
opportunity structures result from the dynamic interaction between the national political economy and the nature of social struggle in any given period. On the one hand, national developments help produce and shape local
activities and efforts. On the other, social change at the local level helps
influence national developments. For example, eras with a stronger focus
on the public sphere tend to emerge when social movements and social
disorder exert pressures, when people begin to doubt the legitimacy of the
existing order, when contradictions between the theory and the reality of
America's democratic promise become part of the daily discourse, and when
as a result increasing demands are placed on society. Given the extent of
social struggle, society may then create a public response to the problems
heretofore ignored or accepted. In this regard, the Progressive Era, which
helped advance the settlement movement and bring it to prominence, is
interpreted differently by historians. Hays (1957) sees the era as a response
to industrialization and the excesses of laissez-faire capitalism that characterized the Gilded Age. Wiebe (1967) sees it as a "search for order" by the
emerging middle class in response to the disorder and chaos of the Gilded
Age. Weinstein (1968) suggests that progressive reform was an effort by corporate liberals to establish greater economic stability in order to maximize
profits. All agree, however, that without the demands of organized labor as
well as farmer and immigrant groups, without the opposition by emerging
professional associations to the divisive and mean-spirited politics and cul-

ture of the Gilded Age, and without the response to these challenges by economic elites who knew they could benefit from a more stable economic order, a spirit and climate of progressivism would not have emerged. Similarly, the 1930s and 1960s, though certainly different from the Progressive Era, represent a comparable time of liberal and left reaction to the excesses, inequities, and contradictions of American economic, political, and social life. Periods of reaction seek to roll back these changes. Conservative leaders try to check the power of the public, reinstate the hegemonic power of business, push people out of the public realm into the private, reassert conservative values and theories, and benefit from right-wing social movements, which further legitimate conservative issues and discourse. These trends push political visions, discourse, and policies much further to the right. The Gilded Age, the 1920s, the 1950s, and our contemporary era fit this description.

Usually the national context appears immutable and hegemonic. The task of building a movement, especially one that successfully challenges the dominant hegemony of a private context, often seems impossible. But the historical model we use asserts that contexts shift. Even in periods of reaction, people plant seeds for change. Clearly, the contradictions of any given context—especially around issues of class, race, gender, and culture— give rise to organized and unorganized resistance. Instead of proposing an overdetermined model of stasis and domination, we propose filtering the history and the contemporary circumstances of settlements through a lens that clarifies how social change is embedded in and develops from the contradictions of contemporary life and the human agency of activists and organizations struggling to effect change (Lipsitz 1988).

Historical Change in the Financing and Administration of Settlement Houses

The history of financing social settlements closely approximates the social investment model. In general, settlement ideals, programs, and progressive practice find more support in public eras; more quiescent, private contexts occasion antagonism to activist practice and settlement house ideals. Public eras resulted in support for the settlement house's core values, goals, and financing. Even during the Great Depression, despite funding instability, settlements revived in response to the heightened public awareness of social problems and social change. In eras with a focus on private life support for the settlement practices of community building and social action declined, leading to a narrowed focus on recreational and categorical programs and more individualized interventions. But the history of financing for settlement houses demonstrates greater complexity than recurrent cycles of expansion and contraction. For example, the history of the settlement house demonstrates that at the beginning of conservative eras, such as the 1920s and 1950s, there is an initial contraction of both programs and funding because the settlements' mission and goals are increasingly seen as problematic. Funding is reduced, especially for social action and community building. As the historical period develops, however, funding becomes increasingly available again if the economy suffers no downturn. While there is no wholesale funding for all settlement programs, there is increased funding for educational and recreational services with continued restrictions on financial support for efforts at social reform. At all times, settlement houses and other voluntary organizations provide valuable services, most of which pose no threat to conservative funders and serve important functions for recipients. During periods of predicted contraction funding for nonthreatening programs can be equal to or greater than during periods of social investment, once the initial conservative reaction subsides. But it should be emphasized that as funding levels change, over time the settlement's programs and structure grows consistently more restrictive and formal. Studies of the history of settlement financing and administration reveal strong continuities as well as ebb and flow. Over time settlement houses have become increasingly centralized, publicly financed, bureaucratic, and reliant on formal structures. Their services are also more likely to be defined by categorical programs initiated by those outside the settlement house, whether by the local Community Chest (a predecessor of United Way) or public sector contractors.

These broad national patterns of finance and administration are congruent with the experience of New York City settlement houses. Throughout most of their history New York City settlement houses were funded largely through financial gifts from wealthy patrons. This occurred in an obscured private process built on relationships between settlement directors and board members, on the one hand, and between city elites and potential patrons, on the other. The quantity of funding and its allocation was up to many different decision makers, including head workers, board members, wealthy patrons, staff, and residents who used, developed, and sometimes paid for activities. But changes in the dominant political economy of an era impacted funding and programs. In general, in eras with greater concern for and fear of the urban poor, settlement houses in New York City received more attention and support. This funding tended to come with fewer strings attached; the relationships between settlements and donors engendered a significant autonomy for settlements regarding program offerings and practice interventions. In the early years financing and oversight structure were loose, spontaneous, and personal. Early settlement leaders believed that the very idea of an organized institution contradicted their goals of neighborly reciprocity and informality (Leiby 1978). The combination of informal structures and informal financing based on personal relationships enabled settlements to maintain a significant degree of independence. This independence, in turn, helped operationalize an autonomous, innovative, and flexible community-oriented practice.

As financing sources in particular and the not-for-profit world in general became more formalized and bureaucratic, funding continued to expand in public eras such as the 1960s but had more controls and requirements attached to its use. Over time the private funding of settlements waned as public-sector funding increased. Beginning in the mid-1960s, a new pattern of funding emerged for settlements, transforming both settlement financing and programs. Settlements in New York City during the years from 1886 to 1975 were transformed from relatively autonomous and informal agencies funded by contributions from the wealthy—that is, funded by private donations through a private process—into project-dependent and grant-oriented, publicly funded multiservice centers with much less program autonomy and control over funds. In this new context settlement houses have become ever more reliant on funding that comes from taxpayers through the public sector. The years 1886–1975 illustrate a complex process of both continuous as well as cyclical patterns of settlement house administration and financing.

Progressive Era

The settlement house idea originated in Great Britain but flourished in the United States (Reinders 1982; Skocpol 1992; Kendall 2000). The settlement movement began on this side of the Atlantic in New York City in 1886 with the founding of the Neighborhood Guild (later University Settlement) by Stanton Coit at 146 Forsyth Street on the lower East Side (Coit 1974). Three years later College Settlement at 95 Rivington Street and Hull-House in Chicago were established. In 1892 Lillian Wald helped create the Nurses

Settlement (later Henry Street Settlement) (Wald 1934, 1971). By 1910 there were as many as four hundred settlements nationwide. Nowhere was this expansion of settlement houses more evident than in New York City (Kraus 1980). New York City was the site of some of the most important social innovations of the era because it was at the confluence of the massive social challenges of the time—immigration, urbanization, and industrialization (Still 1974; Warner 1972). The 1880s and 1890s were marked by the business credos of social Darwinism and laissez-faire capitalism (Hofstadter 1944; Bannister 1979). It was also a time of crisis, as society seemed to be coming apart at its class and ethnic seams (Fisher 1994; Husock 1990; Kogut 1972). Settlement leader Vida Scudder saw the city at the turn of the century as a "cleavage of classes, cleavage of races, cleavage of faiths: an inextricable confusion" (cited in Shapiro 1978:215). In response, reformers, such as the founders of settlements, began to develop a communitarian counterideology and social movement that argued that society, not simply the individual, was responsible for social conditions and that the environment, not simply one's personal characteristics, strongly shaped life experience (Quandt 1970). As Robert Hunter, the author of the classic *Poverty* in 1904 put it: "Poverty was bred of miserable and unjust social conditions" (cited in Trattner 1999:101). The nation struggled to create a more inclusive sense of community before the conflicts of the late nineteenth century—the struggles between labor, farmers, and capital, immigrants and natives—tore it asunder (Hays 1957).

Settlements were clearly a special and unique response to the problems of the emerging urban-industrial order. They developed as a public response and public solution to what had been seen for decades as individual and private problems requiring only individual and private solutions. As Skocpol put it: "Social settlements in the United States remained for quite some time a prime outlet for the aspirations of idealistic, higher-educated young people who wished to find *public* solutions to the problems of urban, industrial capitalism" (Skocpol 1992:345, emphasis ours). Settlements differed from Charity Organization Societies, then the dominant approach to serving poor communities and individuals. The "scientific approach" of the COS sought to bring business principles of efficiency, management, and consolidation to the administration of charity. The structure of COS services rested firmly on the self-help ethos of the Gilded Age. It presumed that poverty and other social problems resulted from individual character defects and therefore should be resolved through individual improvement. "To begin with, charity workers emphasized the individual causes of poverty while settlement workers stressed the social and economic conditions that made people poor. . . . The settlement workers tried desperately to disassociate their movement from charity in the public mind" (Davis 1967:18–19). They were social reformers and social scientists, not charity workers (Crunden 1982; Deegan 1991).

Core Principles of Settlement Practice: Collaboration, Community Building, and Social Action

Settlement house workers came to understand that it was not possible to alter slum neighborhoods without transforming urban life as well. Settlement work generally included a dual focus on function and cause, that is, the workers delivered services to neighborhood residents *and* provided leadership in analyzing, easing, and eradicating the causes of suffering and oppression.[5]

Building on their sense of the interconnectedness between individual problems and social betterment, settlement workers' method was based on three core elements: (1) an integrated collaborative practice that intervened at the individual and the community level and sought to develop solidarity between settlement workers and neighborhood residents, (2) a sense of the essential importance of community and community building, and (3) a willingness to organize and advocate for social, political, and economic justice. In terms of collaborative practice, they integrated working with individuals with trying to change the larger social environment. Settlements emphasized both character building and community building. As Barbara Simon puts it, "The settlement house movement gave to . . . the emergent social work profession a core principle of practice, that of the indispensability of collaborative 'give and take' alliances between settlement workers and neighbors in the larger endeavor to build enduring communities" (Simon 1998:3). Regarding collaborative practice, Mary Simkhovitch, the head worker at Greenwich house, saw it as a process of "fruitful contact between the forces from without and the forces of the neighborhood" (Simkhovitch 1938:73). The settlement workers sought to develop "far deeper mutual understanding" between themselves and neighborhood residents and to work together to improve living conditions.

Certainly settlement leaders were not of the people, and they did much more *for* the people of the neighborhood than *with* them. Settlements were fraught with an upper- and middle-class bias of "bringing culture to the masses" (Gittell and Shtob 1980:570). Chambers and Hinding (1968) see this as a natural development of the period. "Those who lived in poverty around the turn of the century were unable to articulate their needs to the American public. . . . Others had to speak for the poor" (101). However, settlement workers were committed to a version of collaborative process that sought to build long-term relationships and trust by working and living together in the same neighborhood. They felt that "their neighbors were superior to them in knowledge of life and the living conditions in the neighborhood, whereas they were superior in training and understanding of the problems of social democracy" (Chambers and Hinding 1968:99). The goal of collaborative practice, grounded at it was in the concept of settlement worker *residency*, was certainly more democratic and egalitarian than previous charity approaches and most subsequent forms of professional social work, which focused on character building and encouraged a more consciously hierarchical relationship between social workers as professional experts and individuals as clients (McKnight 1995; Putnam 2000). Collaborative practice extended at some houses to relationships with philanthropic supporters as well. The "giving relationship" was seen as reciprocal, encouraging a dynamic relationship of responsibilities and benefits between funders and recipients (Pottick 1989).

The second core element of early settlement life and work was a communitarian vision emphasizing community-building practice. The settlement's communitarian vision rested on a conception of an inclusive organic community in which all residents and institutions were members. Simkhovitch said, "The aim of the settlement or neighborhood house is to bring about a new kind of community life" (cited in Kennedy, Farra et al. 1935:3). Division along class lines was perceived as a social construct and an opportunity for reform efforts. Settlement workers defined themselves as "interpreters," facilitating communication and interactions between those inside the neighborhood (the masses) and those outside the neighborhood (the classes). This vision of building community extended beyond the local neighborhood. Jane Addams had "this dream that men shall cease to waste strength in competition and shall come to pool their powers of production" (Addams [1910] 1999:103). This element of settlement practice stressed the interdependence of all social groups and the organic relationships within society as a whole (Melvin 1987; Miller 1981). Settlement leaders were among the first to underscore the importance of building "social capital," that is, increasing social cohesion and social solidarity (Simon 1994; Putnam 2000).

Many settlement leaders sought to involve people in public life, to enable people of the neighborhood to help themselves and their families while simultaneously working to improve social conditions, such as poverty, slum housing, health epidemics, and the scarcity of space. Jane Addams sought to "interpret democracy in social terms" (cited in Husock 1990:80). She wanted to develop among the working class "a code of social ethics" that would emphasize a worker's social as well as industrial value as a "conscious member of society" (Addams 1902:192). The essence of settlement work was to move people's problems out of the private into the public realm and help build a sense of public life, of inclusive community, in which people and civilization could flourish. As Simkhovitch (1938:301) summed up her settlement experience: "If I, too, have learned anything throughout these many years, it is surely this, that it is our common life that matters, and that to stay apart from it is the death of art, of politics and of religion." For most settlements the communitarian philosophy grew out of a hard and critical appraisal of the difficulties of urban life and the need for social supports and social solidarity. This was as true for settlement staff, who were almost always college-educated and mostly but not exclusively women, as it was for neighborhood residents. Almost all of the activities of the settlements—the basic social and health services, recreational activities, educational programs, and especially the club work, which was an essential feature of settlement life—were part of the process of community building. For example, as Simkhovitch (1938:168) noted, "The neighborhood festivals started by the House were the means of bringing together the various groups of the locality who hitherto had lived a somewhat self-enclosed life."

Third, because settlement leaders understood that the causes of most community problems lay outside the neighborhood, they promoted social action to tackle larger social problems and conditions. Leaders of the most progressive settlements saw themselves as organizers of the neighborhood and advocates for residents (Fisher 1994). They were appalled by the widespread economic, social, and political inequalities of the emerging urban-industrial order. As organizers, they sought to empower residents to enter public life and confront those with power (Simon 1994). They worked to convince the women in their neighborhoods that "running New York is just a big housekeeping job, just like your own home, only on a larger scale. Therefore you should be interested in citywide affairs" (Rothman 1978:117).

Jane Addams sought to "arouse" a neighborhood's "civic and moral energy" (cited in Holden 1922:77). Settlement houses fought to improve local health conditions, develop small parks and public recreation, reform municipal politics, upgrade public schools by promoting their extended use after school hours, and establish public nursing and school social worker systems in the public schools. Leaders lobbied for legislation, served on public boards, promoted political candidates, occasionally ran for office themselves, conducted social research, and participated in broad campaigns for tenement house reform, defense of labor unions, and the rights of workers, women, and children. In general, settlements fought to revitalize the local community by reforming the local political economy and providing social services (Lasch-Quinn 1993). The larger settlement houses, however, especially in New York, tended to be more involved in social action. While their daily program of day care, medical care, recreation, and education gave the settlements viability and permanence (Rothman 1973), it was the combination of collaborative practice, community building, and social action that gave their practice significance at the time and for later generations. Vida Scudder, one of the founders of the College Settlement in New York City, emphasized the importance of social action to settlement work: "Unless settlements continue to hold and foster this attitude of protest, their highest possibilities will be forfeited. Only as they sting to an impassioned, rational discontent with existing conditions, only as they resist the seductive encroachments of social fatalism and remain full of hope that never wavers, are they true to their initial impulse and to their best ideal" (cited in Pacey 1950:72).

Just as there were many strands of reform during the Progressive Era, from the "corporate liberal" agenda of the National Civic Federation to the more moderate progressivism of Theodore Roosevelt and Woodrow Wilson to the socialism of Eugene Debs, settlements also housed a range of political perspectives from "Americanizers," who used settlements to try to control the new immigrant groups and prevent social disorder, to the social feminism of Jane Addams and the socialism of Florence Kelley (Kalberg 1975; Shapiro 1978; Chambers 1986; Sklar 1995). The settlement movement was full of contradictions—compassion and protection, reform and coercion, noble goals, well-intentioned interventions, and lamentable failures—as was the larger Progressive movement (Crocker 1992). Not all settlement houses and settlement workers were involved with social action or seen as advocates of the working-class immigrants in the neighborhood.

Francis Hackett, a columnist, observed in 1915 that for many people the social settlement suggests images "of young ladies with weak eyes and young gentleman with weak chins fluttering confusedly among heterogeneous foreigners, offering cocoa and sponge cake as a sort of dessert for the factory system they deplore" (Rose 1994:4). Of course, conservative business values and interests influenced almost all Progressive Era reforms. But whatever the significant differences of motivation and politics were among reformers and settlement leaders of the Progressive Era, there was general agreement that in an urban-industrial context offering few services and allies for the immigrant poor, settlements met important needs and provided important programs. The attendance records bear this out. As Crocker (1992:224) put it,

> Thousands of people, young and old, black and white, Americans and immigrants, came to settlement classes, clubs, and socials, used settlement facilities, and attended settlement events. . . . People came to the settlement because they needed what it had to offer. For people who had no alternative, the weekly health clinic was an important resource. For children of the city, the settlement playground, with its grass and seesaws, was better than the streets. The settlement dance . . . has a middle-class aura that appealed to the upwardly mobile. For immigrants, the night schools, cultural programs, and English classes of the settlement could make the difference between a low-paying job . . . "cutting up cows" . . . and a chance at clean, higher status work.

The administrative and financial structure undergirding settlement work in this era made it possible to pursue the goals of collaborative practice, community building, and community organizing. This financing and oversight structure was often loose, spontaneous, and personal. Early settlement leaders believed that the very idea of an organized institution contradicted their goals of neighborly reciprocity and informality (Leiby 1978). The combination of informal structures and informal financing based on personal relationships enabled settlements to maintain a significant degree of independence. This independence in turn made possible an autonomous, innovative, and flexible community-oriented practice. While little has been written about the financial and administrative structure of early nonprofits, including settlements, such material is absolutely critical to understanding their work.[6]

Private Financing and Informal Administration in the Progressive Era

From the outset, financing the settlement house was a private matter. In the early years of the settlements money and funding sources were rarely discussed publicly. Even head workers did not seem to know the exact financial condition of their house; financial accounting was quite rudimentary with probably few or no financial audits or annual budgets prior to 1912 (Lohmann 1991). Funding is rarely mentioned in the writings of settlement leaders or historians.[7] Settlements grew and prospered, buildings and programs multiplied seemingly on their own. Based on his relationship with Mrs. Loeb, the wife of one of the partners of the investment house of Kuhn, Loeb, and Company, financier Jacob Schiff gave Lillian Wald the buildings at 265 and 267 Henry Street to stabilize her work (Hall 1971). Of course, as administrators of voluntary associations, they knew well the importance of money and fund-raising, even if informal accounting systems kept them unaware of their actual financial condition. As Helen Hall (1971:87) noted of her experience at Henry Street,

> I have sometimes noticed a tendency on the part of some social workers to feel that they should be above the battle when it comes to fund-raising. This, it seems to me, is wishful thinking and avoids the job of interpreting their work and the problems they are trying to meet. . . . The director of any voluntary agency must be at least a partner in the onerous job of getting the wherewithal to support the work that they, above all people, must believe in deeply.

Despite the reform fervor of the era, fund-raising was never easy. Settlements did not have the unlimited support of the economic elites of the day. Even at Hull-House, which experienced extraordinary growth prior to World War I and became not only the leading settlement and a center of national progressivism but *the* model for social service delivery, funding was precarious. As Jane Addams noted in discussing the erection of a new building,

> I do not wish to give a false impression, for we were often bitterly pressed for money and worried by the prospect of unpaid bills, and we

gave up one golden scheme after another because we could not afford it; we cooked the beans and kept the books and washed the windows without a thought of hardship if we thereby saved money for the consummation of some ardently desired undertaking.   (Adams 1910:89)

For its first seventy years, the Henry Street Settlement depended solely on private donations. The head worker and board members were actively involved in fund-raising, seeking private contributions, bequests, foundation support, and so forth.[8] Henry Street always needed funds. Lillian Wald, its renowned first head worker and Helen Hall's predecessor, was a most talented fundraiser. To raise money in 1913, Henry Street developed a twentieth-anniversary celebration endowment campaign. As one friend observed, "It costs five thousand dollars to sit next to her at dinner" (Wallach 1978:348). While the financial structure of settlements varied, most seemed akin to a "multifunded agency," with funding coming from donations, rents of rooms, royalties, revenues from things sold at the settlement house, interest on investment income, and so forth (Lohmann 1991).[9]

During the Progressive Era funding for settlements did expand quickly and dramatically. The budget of the University Settlement in New York City increased from $2,500 in 1889 to $29,687.47 in 1909. As settlements grew, they were forced to become more bureaucratic and formalized, and financing, at first rather informal and personal, became more bureaucratic. As budgets grew to cover growing expenditures for personnel, buildings, and programs, the roles of head workers were increasingly defined by administrative and fund-raising tasks, and they became less able to function as innovative and inspiring leaders (Kraus 1980). A study of New York City settlements concludes:

Not only was the search for money a continuing struggle, but the justification for funds too often was based on the quantitative measurement of how many baths were provided, how many books taken from the settlement library, how many clubs were meeting at any given time, or how many children were enrolled in the kindergarten. How many hours were spent in the accumulation of such data can never be estimated; how much dedication to settlement work found a frustrating end is impossible to determine.   (Kraus 1980:33)

The demands of bureaucratic, formalized organizations, such as increased paperwork and accountability for administrators and staff, while still modest, were evident even in the early history of the settlement house.

Nevertheless, private funding of settlements during this era underwrote the expansion of programs and supported the organizational autonomy necessary to engage in sometimes controversial work. Two generations of head workers later, Bertram Beck of the Henry Street Settlement thought the support for settlement work, even social action, was what distinguished the pioneering settlement houses from their counterparts in the 1970s. "The early settlement leaders were able to win continuous financial support from the rich despite their advancement of unpopular social causes" (Beck 1976:271). Carson (1990) disagrees. She thinks larger settlements like Henry Street were more successful in terms of fund-raising than smaller houses because they had "special, expensive programs," such as visiting nurses, summer camps, or a neighborhood playhouse. It was always harder to secure funding for the more traditional role of being good neighbors or social activists because, unlike the big-ticket programs, "the fruits of reform were often intangible" (185). Yet, in the early years of the settlement movement, when head workers were very well connected to funding sources and the settlement movement was in the vanguard of contemporary reform efforts, settlement leaders clearly knew that funding was available for good projects (Addams [1910] 1999; Wald 1971). As Addams ([1910] 1999:89) put it, "in spite of our financial stringency, I always believed that money would be given when we had once clearly reduced the Settlement ideal to the actual deed." This first generation of settlement leaders, especially at the most heralded settlements, was well connected. Funding was more a matter of building or sustaining private relationships with monied reform-minded people than the public process it has since become. Part of this private process included a tacit agreement that private funding for public purposes would remain a private matter.

Prior to the 1930s settlements avoided public subsidies. They depended on private funds, which was consistent, in theory at least, with the settlements' ideal of serving as a bridge between the rich and poor. Because the communities in which settlements resided were too poor to fund their own institutions, financing had to come from the "outside." One of the key ingredients in bringing "the classes" and "the masses" together was encouraging the former to help finance programs for the latter. Nevertheless, while it is clear that the settlements began as private-funded social organizations and remained so for decades, many settlement leaders at the time understood that public funding of community-based multiservice centers, such as the use of public schools after hours as social centers, could expand the settlements' practices and objectives (Mattson 1998; Fisher 1994).

Settlements in the Progressive Era were dynamic, innovative, pioneering social service organizations, central to the reform efforts of the time. The most progressive ones effectively combined service delivery, community building, and social action and did so with the support of progressive elites. When the context changed after World War I, so too did the nature and funding of the settlements. They were reduced to a much less significant role, primarily that of deliverer of recreational and educational services.

The Return to Normalcy, 1918–1929

The political economy of the 1920s dramatically altered the social settlements. It was not so much that settlements declined in numbers (though they did at first) as that they seemed to shrink in significance. They persisted in the 1920s, but not as vital institutions. A variety of pressures during these years helps explain the changes in the settlement houses. The newly emerging field of social work and the formation and consolidation of power in most cities of Community Chests had an especially profound impact on settlements. However, it was the conservative political economy—the "return to normalcy" and the rejection of the reform impulse—that gave these and other developments particular salience and legitimacy.

The twenties were an archetypal private era. With the end of World War I in 1918 right-wing repression against social activism, exemplified in the so-called Red Scare of 1919–1920, demonstrated the requisite delegitimization in private eras of prior victories. The antiradical Red Scare was followed by the business ethic of the 1920s, which replaced the social reform impulse of the Progressive Era. Heightened individualism prevailed over concerns about social cohesion. A resurfacing of laissez-faire ideology drove out analyses of structural causation of social problems. Society receded from a concern with social issues into more individualistic and materialist pursuits, including the purchase of new consumer durables, such as radios and cars. In order to increase demand for these new products businesses began to invest heavily in advertising, encouraging purchasing on credit, which had been taboo up to that point in American history. Right-wing social movements resurfaced as well, such as religious fundamentalism, the Ku Klux Klan, and other nativist organizations (Chambers 1963; Fisher 1994; Carter 1975).

World War I was a watershed in the history of settlements. Most settlement workers saw the war as an opportunity to increase social solidarity and complete the Progressive movement's agenda. Instead, the war delivered a traumatic shock to liberal and collective sensibilities. With the Red Scare and attacks on progressive reformers and immigrants, key aspects of settlement house practice were in retreat. In place of the core settlement elements of collaborative practice, community building, and social action, the 1920s institutionalized a much more restrictive and confined settlement practice. Jane Addams said that social work reflected the "symptoms of this panic and with a kind of protective instinct, carefully avoided any identification with the phraseology of social reform" (cited in Lundblad 1995:667). The entire atmosphere of social work changed in the 1920s (Lubove 1975). Leaders in the newly emerging profession of social work thought that it needed to reject the romantic "do-goodism" of the Progressive Era in order to gain credibility as a profession. Among social workers there was a new emphasis on being a disengaged, dispassionate, objective expert rather than a social reformer (Tobin 1988). Social work students in the 1920s were said to scoff at the very idea of community service.[10] Social work became preoccupied with professionalism, which included a focus on attaining acceptance, status, and power. The rise of professionalism in social work pushed settlement practices out of favor. The new mantra of social work in the 1920s directly critiqued settlement work. Social workers were to deliver a professional service, not be almsgivers, friends, or neighbors (Ehrenreich 1985). In the 1920s settlements were seen as unscientific, friendly visiting on a group scale. They faced a doubly negative opportunity structure: diminished ties to social work because they could not specifically define their "unique knowledge and skills" and diminished connection to reformist causes, which had receded from national consciousness (Wenocur and Reisch 1989:72). Consequently, the settlements found it more difficult to attract new, young, and committed workers. Additionally, funders felt less impelled to support settlements and were especially wary of social change work.

A critical element of the rejection of social change and settlements in the 1920s was the renewed emphasis on the individual. Part of the shift to individualism and personal issues in the 1920s resulted from a cultural rebellion against a world whose collective ventures appeared to have thrown people into arguably the most brutal and devastating of wars. In social work, the renewed emphasis on the individual led to casework becoming the dominant approach; Mary Richmond's *Social Diagnosis, the* textbook for social work in the era, rejected the social settlement's "moral certainty" and community-based approach and instead instructed social workers to focus through "rational inquiry" on the needs and problems of the individual (Franklin 1986). This reemphasis on the individual provided an opening for psychology to become a primary knowledge base of social work practice. The "science" of psychology, at least in American hands, located both problem and solution in individual characteristics, whether visible or not.[11] As Lasch-Quinn (1993:152–53) underscores, in the 1920s the very innovation of psychiatric social work "threatened to break apart the marriage between social service and reform, the union that distinguished the settlement. . . . [The] triumph of psychiatry stressed the individual's deviance from an imagined norm. It also emphasized individual health at the expense of the group and wrenched individual fulfillment out of context, thus denying the interdependence between group and individual well-being." While in practice most social workers followed more closely the ideas of Mary Richmond than those of Gordon Hamilton—that is, they focused more on social diagnosis than psychology—the dominant trend in the field was nevertheless to concentrate on psychological theory. This focus on individual deviation from the norm was clearly a return to the nineteenth-century charity practice settlements had sought to transform.

Social reform was also hurt in the 1920s by a social context that seemed highly prosperous and by the ideological framing of affluence as due to unbridled capitalism and unassisted individual initiative (Chambers 1963; Ehrenreich 1985; Trattner 1999). Concern about poverty and the poor diminished. In private eras with expansive economies the credo is that all boats will rise and that those who don't are defective crafts. The larger society, and social workers in particular, increasingly thought poverty would be eradicated by the new economy. So too did many donors, who relaxed their concern about social problems.

Settlement work did not change abruptly. Houses continued to focus on supplying recreational, educational, and social services to the community (Karger 1987b). The proliferation in the 1920s of other recreational services, such as neighborhood youth centers, YMCAs, night school programs, summer camps, and so forth, represented new competitors for the settlement house. But they also reflected an expanding demand and support for recreational services (Kennedy 1932). However, the raisons d'être of the settlement house—collaborative practice, community building, and social reform—seemed anachronisms throughout the decade. Of course, as Chambers (1963) emphasized, reform organizations did not evaporate in the face of Red Scare repression and an inhospitable social and political climate. "Voluntary associations, most of them born during the Progressive Era . . . remained faithful to the cause of reform throughout the 1920s" (87). But the social climate no longer supported or extended settlement efforts.

Some aspects of settlement life and practice were profoundly affected by the change in context. In the 1920s there was little settling—living at the house—by head workers. The new professionalization in social work encouraged dispassionate and objective experts, who maintained distance—emotional and physical—from the problems of their "clients" (Austin 1983). To be sure, the decline of settling began earlier, but it was the pressures of professionalization in the 1920s that provided a rationale for discontinuing the practice. Likewise, club work dramatically declined in the 1920s as educational and recreational service delivery, without an emphasis on community building, became an increasingly dominant feature of settlement practice. Certainly club work and programs designed to build social solidarity did not disappear entirely. New group solidarities were developed during the postwar years; those settlements that had been truly committed to community building prior to the war sustained aspects of that work. But the work was now situated in a different context, one that broke the connection between community building and social change, replacing it with an emphasis on individual enhancement, market-driven conceptions of change, the rise of casework in social work practice, and a faith that hard work could triumph over individual adversity (Lundblad 1995; Karger 1987b).

Increasingly Conservative and Bureaucratic Administration, 1918–1929

With the Red Scare, settlements declined not only in the popular but also in the philanthropic imagination. In the troubled postwar years, fundraising continued to be a perennial—or more accurately, annual—headache for head workers and their boards (Carson 1990). Funding not only determined whether settlements would exist at all but also shaped the nature of their programs. In response to the Red Scare, more conservative settlements attracted business support. As Crocker (1992) writes, after the First World War, as labor militancy seemed to threaten corporate hegemony, in Gary, Indiana, U.S. Steel invested in settlements in order to build goodwill in the community and to use expanded services to pacify discontent. In more progressive settlements, such as Hull-House and Henry Street, support declined. In 1918 Henry Street was so concerned about the impact of the war on funding, it became one of the first voluntary organizations to hire a public relations expert to promote the organization (Carson 1990).

Financial support also declined due to the politics of settlement leaders such as Jane Addams and Lillian Wald (Sullivan 1993). Many donors would no longer fund social change, especially if it seemed controversial or "un-American." From the beginning of the First World War through 1935, Romanofsky (1978a:353) writes, "the financial situation of Hull-House suffered as donors withdrew their support because of Miss Addams's controversial pacifism and opposition to the war. . . . Leading contributors of the early period were dying, and potential other supporters feared Hull-House's reputed radicalism." The same was true at Henry Street. Wald's settlement aims had generally been supported by her wealthy patrons, but they withdrew financing because of Wald's pacifism during and after the war (Wallach 1978:348). Wald scoffed at them. "Confidentially, my political attitude is making some of our generous friends uneasy and one of our largest givers—nearly $15,000 a year—has withdrawn because I am 'socialistically inclined.' Poor things; I am sorry for them—they are so scared. It is foolish since, after all, counting things in the large and wide, I am at least one insurance against unreasonable revolution in New York" (Chambers 1963:25).[12] Carson (1990:185) therefore notes that "In formulating their fund raising goals . . . the settlers were forced to reckon with their ultimate aims and whether these should change to fit an altered social context."

Once the Red Scare climate had subsided and the prosperity of certain sectors of the economy was renewed, aggregate funding improved for voluntary associations such as settlements. This is a significant pattern of private eras: initial retrenchment of programs and funding is followed by expanded support if economic growth occurs. Charitable giving, however, is more circumscribed than before, with allocations provided for services such as educational and recreational activities but not for social advocacy or activism. Toward the end of the decade most settlement houses did experience expanded and stable funding. In the larger society, rapid accumulation of wealth reinvigorated private giving. It was within this context that in 1928 United Neighborhood Houses (UNH), the association of New York City settlement houses, urged its member settlements to "ask for large gifts and expect large returns" (Herrick 1970:144).[13]

Many settlements in the 1920s became increasingly dependent on Community Chests. Business involvement in settlements accelerated during the First World War and became formalized in the 1920s with the establishment of Community Chests nationwide. Chests reduced the dependence of some settlement houses on religious institutions by offering a potentially steady stream of stable, alternate funding. Chest support, however, also required standardized operations. It transformed previously informal organizations into ones that had to move toward an effective and accountable administration. The early style of settlement voluntary work—autonomous, innovative, informal, passionate, and committed—became more administrative, businesslike, bureaucratic, and constricted (Trolander 1975).[14]

There was another price paid for Chest support. Community Chests were run by conservative business interests and social work agency executives strongly opposed to social action. Increasingly, for organizations interested in social reform and social action, the whole decade, as Grace Abbott remarked, was "a long hard struggle . . . uphill all the way" (Chambers 1992:492). Trolander (1975) argues this resulted primarily from Community Chests' concentration of power in regard to administration and funding. "For the most part, however, by the time of the New Deal the effectiveness of the settlement movement as a force in social reform had been curtailed; its demise paralleled by the rise of the Community Chest" (16).

Even in New York and Chicago, in the absence of Community Chest control, settlements found it increasingly difficult to focus on the poor and social change. Prior to the advent of the New Deal in the early 1930s, the effectiveness of most settlements as a force for social change had been curtailed dramatically. In New York and Chicago this shift could be traced to the general decline of support for the settlements' reform work. The reform work that had once seemed so vital and significant, a central purpose of the settlement houses, had to take a backseat in the 1920s as settlements devolved into more professionalized and conservative multiservice centers.[15] This trend would not become fully operational until later private eras, but the course was set in the 1920s.

Depression, New Deal, and War

The Depression and the vigorous public reaction to it, at both the grassroots level and in Washington, D.C., dramatically altered settlements yet again. When the social reform impulse resurfaced in the 1930s, settlements did not return to the central role they had held during the Progressive Era. The 1930s response to economic disaster and social need was much more centralized and national, the settlements too decentralized and local to be as important instruments of social change as they had been at the turn of the century.[16] But the settlements were an integral part of work toward social change in the 1930s. Settlement leaders played a major role in redirecting society toward a concern with social problems and social responsibilities. Harry Hopkins, Frances Perkins, Henry Morgenthau Jr., Herbert Lehman, and Gerard Swope, all of whom played important roles in the New Deal, were either former workers or former residents at settlements.[17] Helen Hall was frequently invited to Washington to testify on a wide variety of social issues researched by Henry Street and with which she was intimately familiar. Settlement issues such as poverty, delivering needed services to the poor, community building, organizing, and expanding public life and public sector responsibility became central once again. Perhaps most significant, as Mary Simkhovitch noted, "During the depression years the life of the region swung back to a reemphasis on the social significance of current events" (Simkhovitch 1938:233). As social problems and needs worsened in the 1930s, with all the attendant pain and human suffering, a sense for the importance of public life and the need for social change revived. Settlements, which had languished for more than a decade, drew upon their historic experiences and commitments to assist in that process of social change.

Putting the Social Back Into Settlement Work

Even before the stock market crash in 1929 and certainly through the early years of FDR's first administration, poverty and unemployment were pervasive. "All around the social workers of Hull-House," commentator Edmund Wilson wrote in 1932, "there today stretches a sea of misery more appalling even than that which discouraged Miss Addams in the nineties" (Davis and McCree 1969:177). Helen Hall underscored that "unemployment was the overpowering, ever-present concern against which everything else was insignificant" (Hall 1971:6). Simkhovitch (1938:284) added that since the beginning of the Great Depression, "food and shelter have become life-and-death matters. Economic concern has taken root." The massive problems of poverty and unemployment forced society and social workers to confront once again the social and structural dimensions of individual problems. Yet again they had to face the fact that poverty was principally bound to economic and social factors, not individual failings. "While your eyes were on the misery and the bit of immediate help you could give," Hall (1971:14) said, "you continually had to be working on the broader picture."

Other social workers argued that the recent emphasis on casework was inappropriate as it denied the relationship between social context and the problem of individuals. Harry Lurie, director of the Bureau of Jewish Social Research, criticized his fellow social workers for being as responsible for the Great Depression as were leaders in industry and politics, because social workers had turned away from the social dimensions of problems in the 1920s and had focused instead on issues of professionalism and technique. Grace Coyle, in a presidential address to the National Conference of Social Work emphasized that "there is no reasonable doubt that poverty itself is responsible for increased illness, that unemployment breeds unemployability, that crowded housing undermines family life" (Trattner 1999:297). For historian Walter Trattner (1999:297) "the message was clear: Social workers could best make their contributions by allying themselves with those groups in society working for political, social, and economic change. This, in turn, of course, tended to politicize social workers once again, a sharp contrast to their nonpartisanship of the prior decade."

Of course, the primary characteristics of social work in private eras—casework as the dominant method and level of intervention, psychology as the knowledge base, and the individual's character development as the primary focus—did not yield completely to concern for a more politicized version of social work practice focused on the structural dimensions of problems and solutions. Most charity work in the United States has always been too firmly rooted in conceptualizations and analyses of private causation and self-help to yield much ground even during highly public eras (Wagner 2000; Katz 1986, 1989). What happens in these periods, however, is that the broader, contextual dimension of problems and solutions becomes a more central, dominant factor in daily practice and discourse.

This change in emphasis away from the private and individual to the public and collective occurred slowly and reluctantly at the national level even in the depths of the Great Depression. Early in the depression, President Hoover was overwhelmed by the economic catastrophe and continued to propose voluntary private-sector solutions, avoid government intervention in the economy, and promise that "prosperity was just around the corner." FDR took office in 1933, but his reaction was little different at first as he also feared government intervention. What pushed Roosevelt toward the Left was the unwillingness of the corporate sector to work closely with him, advisers such as Frances Perkins who prior to 1935 had been drafting social legislation, *and* the emergence of local and national movements around issues of wealth distribution, hunger, housing, unemployment, social security, welfare, and industrial unions. In response to these developments and in preparation for an upcoming election, FDR proposed social initiatives for the elderly, unemployed, and others in need. The Social Security Act of 1935 was crafted during this period and became the foundation of the American welfare state. In response, groups continued to mobilize for greater equity and social initiatives. The dialectic of interaction between local initiatives and the national political economy was most evident during these promising and difficult years. Grassroots social action around such issues as unemployment and welfare benefits helped cause a shift in the national political economy (e.g., the passage of the Social Security Act of 1935), which in turn stimulated further social change (Leuchtenburg 1995; Polenberg 2000; Kennedy 1999).

Revived Social Action and Community Building in Settlement Houses

Accordingly, one of the major developments of the period for social settlements was the reemergence of social action as an essential part of their practice. They continued with the programs that characterized their work: social services, adult education, health care, and recreational programs (Hawkins 1937). But in the 1930s the social agenda of the National Federation of Settlements and the most progressive houses included, among others, the old-age pension movement, compulsory unemployment insurance, workers' education programs, nationwide minimum standards of relief, minimum health services (later national health insurance), workers' rights, and new industrial relations as they would be embodied in the Wagner Act of 1935 and the Fair Labor Standards Act of 1938. Most settlements were noticeably quiet on issues of race, which would continue to undermine their local work (Lasch-Quinn 1993; Karger 1986; Philpott 1978; Crocker 1992). But the period revived the central mission of the more progressive settlement houses, namely, "the pursuit of social and economic justice through social reform initiatives and social action" (Simon 1998:7). Social work leader Frank Bruno, writing at the end of this period, emphasized the importance of the social action principles of the pioneering settlements.

> A settlement is not only pageantry, classes, and clubhouses for those who can not afford them. It grows out of an attitude toward the gross and unjust differences in opportunity enjoyed by different portions of people making up our communities, and an irrepressible ethical drive on the part of the privileged to understand the under-privileged better and to attempt to do something about it.   (Bruno 1948:116)

New York City was a center of revived social action in the 1930s. Trolander (1975:115) asserts that social action characterized the New York and Chicago settlements but was "largely absent in settlements elsewhere." In cities with a Community Chest settlements were constrained by funding regulations (Karger 1987a; Crocker 1992). But settlements in non-Chest cities, such as New York and Chicago, were among the first in the 1930s to organize protests and demonstrations for adequate relief programs. While settlements in other cities must also have protested depression-era conditions, the New York settlements along with Hull-House in Chicago were clearly in the forefront of the movement in the 1930s.

While most of the social change policies of the 1930s were initiated at the federal level and through centralized bureaucratic government agencies, settlements maintained their focus on the core principles of local community building and social action. Settlements continued to attend to neighborhoods first. "Whatever happens in our neighborhood concerns us" (Simkhovitch 1938:279). The New Deal promoted a powerful vision of national community and social cohesion, of a federal government interested in and willing to act on behalf of the welfare of its citizens at multiple levels of intervention. There was a clear potential for tensions between settlement programs and the centralized public funding structure of the New Deal. Government programs were more bureaucratic and came with administrative requirements. Federally initiated, centralized programs build relationships and allegiances that have the potential to "destroy any . . . vestige of community feeling" (Kirschner 1986:187). While such pressures would be-

come critical for settlements after 1975 as the system of contracting expanded, in the 1930s these conflicts were less significant. For many settlement leaders, the expansive national agenda was calculated only on the basis
of present and projected benefit. Helen Hall testified in 1934 before the
House Committee on Ways and Means arguing that unemployment insurance could not be implemented state by state. "We need federal initiative
not only to get action but to make for unity" (Hall 1971:56). Poverty, settlement leaders argued, caused most social problems, and poor neighborhoods
required federal support and initiatives. National policy was also considered
an alternative to piecemeal interventions at the local level. Nevertheless,
new financial and administrative relationships with the federal government,
discussed in more detail below, did present both challenges and opportunities for settlement houses.

Ironically, the Great Depression led to some successes for social settlements, certainly when compared to their status in the 1920s. During the
1930s many of the causes for which settlement houses had fought were
won, including child labor laws, unemployment assistance, kindergartens,
support for workers to unionize, and social security (Carson 1990; Smith
1995). The labor movement's strength increased significantly. The whole
intellectual tone of, for instance, the Greenwich House neighborhood, as
Simkhovitch (1938) put it, benefited from the depression. And a wide array
of settlement activities, such as adult education classes and clubs, were
once again ascendant. Clubs had always been central to the project of
community building, though less so during the early 1920s. The study by
Kennedy, Farra, and others (1935) of eighty settlements in New York City
documents the renewed importance of clubs in settlement work. They note
that "If there is one activity which can be said to be more characteristic of
the settlement than another, the club holds that position" (9). But the
primary victory of the depression era, at least for Helen Hall, was the acceptance of federal responsibility for human welfare, which she called "a
monumental step forward" (Hall 1971:37). Such steps forward occurred,
however, in a context of deep economic despair and financial pressures for
settlement houses.

The Origins of Public Federal Support of Settlement Work

The early years of the Great Depression hit settlement financing hard.
United Neighborhood Houses almost went out of business in 1931. The

overall number of settlements declined significantly. In the 1930s a National
Federation of Settlements (NFS) study reported that approximately 230 settlement houses remained in the United States, which was just over half the
number of settlements operating in 1910 (Wenocur and Reisch 1989).[18]
Many settlements experienced budget cuts of up to 70 percent, which resulted in widespread reductions in programs and salaries. Henry Street cut
its budget significantly by reducing salaries and discontinuing entire programs in music, arts, and crafts (Simkhovitch 1938; Herrick 1970). Year after
year, as the depression deepened, settlements learned the limits of local
relief, Community Chests, and private philanthropy.

In response to the drastic need for additional support and to the emergence of federal social welfare programs under the New Deal, many settlements in the 1930s relaxed their resistance to public funding. Concrete
benefits were extended to the settlements through New Deal programs
such as the National Youth Administration (NYA) and the Works Progress
Administration (WPA). These initiatives expanded settlement programs
and volunteer resources. Federal support for settlement work was often
sudden and unexpected. Obviously the infusion of federal support helped
sustain settlement houses and assisted them in addressing the serious depression-era problems undermining their communities. Support from the
federal government, although a clear boon to the settlement houses' core
principles and programs, nevertheless presented significant financial and
administrative challenges. Settlements had always been susceptible to
changing political climates, but now, with the infusion of federal monies
and, shortly thereafter, their sudden withdrawal, the more centralized and
politicized funding process actually left the settlement houses with a less
stable and more externally directed programmatic and financial structure
(Lasch-Quinn 1993). Federal support fundamentally altered the settlements' funding patterns and relationships. Consequently, key administrative issues began to surface.

The sporadic influx of public employees rapidly changed the patterns
of settlement staffing. Kennedy, Farra, and others (1935) calculated that
seventy-four settlements in New York City had 1,524 volunteers. Many settlements increased their workforce tenfold with NYA and WPA assistance.
One settlement house, with a staff of eight received eighty-two WPA workers
(Trolander 1973, 1975). Hall recounts, "One day I was suddenly informed
that Henry Street had been assigned fifty white-collar workers at one fell
swoop" (Hall 1971:30). Clearly, both pluses and minuses were associated
with the influx of stipended volunteers. In interviews with settlement staff,

opinions ranged from "Volunteer help makes possible some budget saving; work can be carried on that otherwise would be financially impossible" to criticisms that "settlements have cheapened themselves by accepting all volunteers indiscriminately," "we feel volunteers are a necessary evil. We use them only where we have to," and "turnover among volunteers is high; provision of training is a real problem" (Kennedy, Farra et. al. 1935:503, 528). Settlements preferred paid staff to volunteers, even during the depression. They discovered afterward that the temporary influx of public-sector employees had squeezed out well-to-do volunteers, who did not return after WPA and NYA funding ceased.

Another administrative problem associated with the structures of depression-era public funding was that money could only be used for specific programs or needs, not for general purposes as determined by settlement staff. For example, even with the infusion of NYA and WPA support, practically all the settlements studied were seriously handicapped by the inadequate allocations for clerical help. Money went to staff volunteers, but few if any resources were expended on infrastructure needs. Forty-three houses with aggregate expenditures of a million and a half dollars and averaging $35,000 in expenses, employed at the time of the study fifty-two clerical workers. Of the forty-three houses studied, eleven had no clerical help, one relied on temporary clerical assistance, twenty-two houses employed only one clerical worker, and the remaining ten houses had two or more clerical workers. The ratio of the average number of clerical workers (slightly more than one) to the average number of professional staff (twenty-five) vividly highlights the scarcity of funding available for settlement support staff and infrastructure during the 1930s (Kennedy, Farra et al. 1935). Paradoxically, new forms of partnership with the federal bureaucracy demanded greater attention to administrative detail at the same time as federal aid limited funding for administration. This characteristic of public-sector funding was to seriously burden settlement houses and other nonprofits in the future.

Nevertheless, New York City settlements in this era did not capitulate to pressures from either funders or the social work profession to become "modern" welfare agencies, complete with more bureaucratic procedures and administrators burdened by "complex guidelines for accepting and dealing with clients" (Herrick 1970:154–55). While they adopted many techniques of professional social work, settlements retained an open, neighborhood-focused approach and resisted the program and project specialization that would later define their mode of service delivery. While public-sector funding in the 1930s did not transform settlement administration, neither did it resolve funding problems. Even with New Deal support, money remained scarce.

Economic hard times and consequent tight funding for settlement work during the depression prompted the development in Chicago in 1935 and New York City in 1939 of the "deficit fund system." In both cities settlements were wary of Community Chest control but slowly accepted the value of a privately raised, centralized fund other than a Community Chest to help with settlement expenses. In New York the independent board was called the Greater New York Fund. Like a Community Chest, it solicited money from corporations and employee groups. While such boards tended to be almost as conservative as Community Chests in other cities, under the deficit fund system there was greater individual autonomy. Individual settlements received only a small part of their budget from the fund, with a large part of the remainder coming from wealthy donors. "The main responsibility for raising money remained with the individual agencies" (Trolander 1975:57). Despite the growing gap between expenses and revenue, important segments of settlement leadership remained wary of the trade-offs that might be associated with accepting dollars from a Chest-style fund. Until her death in 1935, Jane Addams kept Hull-House out of the deficit fund system. She was an international figure and an excellent fund-raiser and during her lifetime "obtained from friends or gave from her own resources about $30,000 a year" (Trolander 1975:57).[19] After her death, in the midst of a financial crisis, Hull-House joined the system. Helen Harris, a member of the executive committee of the UNH, opposed the deficit system because centralized private boards in other cities had done little to fund "unmet" needs and had provided little support for long-term social welfare planning. Helen Hall's objections were more political. In New York City, she noted, there was no labor representation on the Community Chest's board. She and Stanley Issacs, the president of UNH, also feared the Greater New York Fund would be dominated by "Wall Street businessmen [seeking] to impose their will on the community" (cited in Herrick 1970:152). Wherever Community Chests financed settlements in other cities, Hall said, social action was under attack by these powerful interests that were essentially hostile to social reform. Nevertheless, UNH voted in 1938 to join the deficit-funding system, partly because settlement leaders—for example, Mary Simkhovitch—supported it but fundamentally because of what UNH treasurer John Bloodgood referred to as a "drying up" of voluntary individual contributions, the traditional basis of settlement financing (Herrick 1970:153). Settlements in New

York City preferred federal funding and control to that of a centralized private board, but in their practice sought a combination of federal public assistance and more traditional voluntary contributions. Lillian Wald, the founder of Henry Street, concluded that while a central lesson of the depression era was "that government must take more responsibility for social welfare," she also thought that private contributions were essential too. "It is impossible to wait upon government appropriations for all the emergencies that clamor at the door" (Wald 1934:128).

One of the key challenges posed by federal funding was that such assistance depended on national, not local, needs and initiatives. It could be withdrawn as quickly as it was allotted. When the nation entered into World War II, all national attention and energy focused on the conflict. Clearly, the war united the citizenry in a struggle against totalitarianism and oppression abroad. Many of the problems of the depression—poverty, unemployment, national purpose, and community building—were resolved or transcended by the war effort. The settlement houses went into a tailspin during World War II. While some settlements had increased staff nearly tenfold during the New Deal, by 1940 the number of government-paid staff diminished substantially, and by 1943 it was down to nothing (Bryan and Davis 1990). The quick and permanent withdrawal of public employees resulted in severe problems for settlements that had become highly dependent on such staffing.[20] World War II provided many opportunities for social workers to deliver services and promote social cohesion through their activities in United Service Organizations, emergency components of public welfare agencies, the Red Cross, military hospitals, welfare departments in defense factories, and programs under Community Chest and war fund auspices, such as canteens, child care centers, and outdoor recreation (Soule 1947). On the other hand, the settlements were reduced to mere skeletons of their prewar institutional selves. Most settlements survived the withdrawal of workers paid from public funds, but not without great sacrifices in terms of activities and staff. Furthermore, new programs during World War II—services for preschool children as well as those for soldiers and displaced people—imposed new burdens while funding and staffing remained in short supply. By 1943, for example, Hull-House seemed closer to demise than ever before (Davis and McCree 1969). Declining funds and the new pressures of the war were powerful crosscurrents that reduced settlements to their nadir during and just after World War II (Trattner 1999:307).

Cold War and the Fifties

The postwar era was a difficult time for settlements. Perhaps most important, settlements found it nearly impossible to sustain their core principles in a reactionary social and political climate. Once again, as during the Red Scare after the First World War, social change and democratic dissent were widely perceived as a threat to the nation. This was an era of highly conservative cold war politics, dominated by the fear of communism abroad and at home (Fried 1996; Pells 1994; Fisher 1994). Equally important, the architects of this conservative post–World War II political economy feared another economic depression. There was deep concern about the fragility of the American economy and of capitalism in general. Federal deficit spending for war and defense—what President Eisenhower later called the "military-industrial complex"—appeared to be the only answer to economic depressions. Insecure about American prospects at home and abroad, cold warriors in both political parties sought to silence those who raised concerns about the direction and priorities of postwar America (Kolko 1976). In such a context, quite similar to the one that prevailed directly after World War I and during the 1920s, issues of poverty, social problems, and urban slums were as absent from daily life as they had been omnipresent just a decade or so previously (Galbraith [1958] 1998; Harrington 1963).

Settlement houses interested in social reform were among those most silenced and marginalized. After World War II settlements initially sought to transfer the democratic impulses for which the war was fought to the home front. They hoped to build on the domestic social cohesiveness and progressive spirit that had characterized the war effort. After the war and on the heels of the victories of organized labor in 1946, the NFS as well as some key settlements, such as Henry Street and Hull-House, continued their social action efforts. In the late 1940s they advocated for public housing and citizen participation. In the early 1950s they engaged in social action to promote national health insurance and oppose cuts in public assistance, especially in 1950 and 1951 before the anticommunist fervor reached fever pitch. But their efforts were short lived. The political opportunism of Senator Joseph McCarthy and others in Washington, D.C., promoted a climate that labeled social reform as dangerous (Andrews and Reisch 1997). In the face of this danger, most settlements withdrew, not only from reform causes but also from public visibility. The NFS, for example, was silent on the issue of loyalty oaths and McCarthyism after 1951 (Romanofsky 1978b). UNH opposed loyalty oaths for public housing tenants in 1953 but feared working with other progressive groups to challenge them. All this was for naught, however; liberal leaders of the settlements were harassed anyway. Helen Hall was targeted for being in favor of rent control and milk cooperatives, which the House Un-American Activities Committee (HUAC) considered communist programs (Trolander 1987). After McCarthyism had subsided by middecade, a few settlements planted seeds for the kind of community-based activism that was to flourish in the 1960s. In 1957 Union Settlement's East Harlem Project experiment in community organization sought to identify indigenous leaders and work with city officials to improve local schools and housing opportunities (Schwartz 1983). In 1958 Philadelphia settlements hired twenty community organizers, who promoted social action in that city (Trolander 1982). Such initiatives, however, were the exception that proved the rule of declining social action and reform at settlements during this era.

Complicating matters further, the settlement house method of neighborhood work was in "disrepute" within the profession of social work (Bryan and Davis 1990:277). In the late 1940s and 1950s social work turned away once again from the interconnection between individual problems and the social conditions that produced them. It focused instead on individual maladjustment, the classic turn in private eras toward "character building" and away from "community building."[21] An argument increasingly persuasive in social work was that professions must be based on disciplined practice and knowledge, not on political passions or agendas. Consequently, in the 1950s social work turned to a narrower definition of professionalism, focusing more and more on casework as its method of choice and experimental psychology as its knowledge base (Tyson 1995; Austin 1986; Fisher 1999). Yet again social reform and settlements were seen as anachronisms, out of step with the profession of social work (Trattner 1999).

In addition to the challenges from the national political economy and from within the social work profession, in the 1950s settlement neighborhoods were changing from white, ethnic, working-class communities into black and Latino ones. They were challenged to effectively address the issues of race and racial exclusion within a context characterized by the growing pressure of intensifying mass migration of blacks from the rural South to cities, both in northern and southern states (Grossman 1991; Lemann 1991). New York City was again a major terminus for African-Americans who were fleeing the effects of the corporatization of agriculture in the South and drawn by the promise of less oppressive lives in northern cities. Concurrently, white, working-class ethnic populations began moving out of inner-city neighborhoods, first to outer-city neighborhoods and then to the sub-urbs. Increasingly, the communities in which some settlements had been located for more than two generations were racially transformed (Suarez 1999; Piven and Cloward 1971). These changes significantly challenged settlements that had, since their inception, focused almost exclusively on white, first- and second-generation immigrants from Europe and had essen-tially ignored the plight and needs of African-Americans.

To their credit it must be said that some of the leading settlements in New York City had begun to grapple with their history of racist exclusion as early as the 1930s. As one critic asserted then, "let's face the issue. What is the Settlement doing for the Negro who has settled on its doorsteps?" In most instances they had not "even scratched the surface of this problem" (Lindenberg and Zittel 1936:563). Partly in response to such charges, by the mid-1940s the National Federation of Settlements stepped up its efforts, urging local settlements to begin to fight for civil rights and to demonstrate a commitment to racial equality in settlement programs (Trolander 1987). However, progress was slow (Stuart 1992; Kennedy, Farra, et. al. 1935). On the eve of the Great Society programs and the War on Poverty in the mid-1960s, events that were to transform social settlements once again, they were still a primarily white organization burdened by a long history of racial seg-regation and disregard.

In response to the demographic transformation of the inner city and the centrifugal expansion and suburbanization of the postwar metropolis, many settlements decentralized and relocated their services to outer-city commu-nities (Tsanoff 1958). In part they were avoiding their new neighbors in the inner cities, and in part they were following their constituents and their funding base. They became known less as settlement houses and more as "neighborhood centers." The most dramatic example of this dispersion was Hull-House, which became the Hull-House Association. Over time the new, decentralized Hull-House Association even lost its original home. In 1949 the National Federation of Settlements changed its name to the National Federation of Settlements and Neighborhood Centers. "The necessity for relocation or expansion of services brings a special challenge to neighbor-hood centers today," an NFS report noted. In the past settlements had fo-cused on poor neighborhoods. In the 1950s they were in "neighborhoods of varying economic levels" (Hillman 1960:v). The growing detachment of the settlements from their original communities is illustrated in their discovery in the late 1950s that many people attending settlement functions were increasingly coming from farther and farther away. As late as the 1930s on average 57 percent of settlement house participants lived within one-quarter mile of the house, 79 percent within one-half mile. In some settlements, as many as 85 percent lived within one-quarter mile (Kennedy, Farra, et. al. 1935). While exactly comparable data is not available for the 1950s, by that time, especially at the bigger settlements that offered services and opportunities not available in all communities, NFS reported that people traveled from different parts of the city to use and receive services (Hillman 1960). The 1950 data of member dispersion, reflecting contemporary trends of centrifugal growth in most metropolitan areas, suggested the value of a decentralized network of neighborhood centers expanding to outer-city communities and suburbs (Tsanoff 1958; Warner 1972). This expansion, however, occurred at the cost of settlements maintaining their historic relationship to particular inner-city neighborhoods. By the late 1950s, according to Peterson (1965), houses had moved from being community-based social settlements to more generalized social agencies.

To their credit, it should be pointed out that settlements in the 1950s survived the reactionary onslaught of anticommunist and antiliberal fervor. Moreover, in the second half of the decade settlements developed innovative programs for the prevention of juvenile delinquency, began to address the needs of new constituents and a prior history of racism, and planted the seeds for more progressive work. More significant, however, the 1950s were an era in which the funding of settlements began to change to an increasing dependence on public-sector allocations for specific projects, a change that was to have profound implications.

Expanded Public Financing of Settlements in a Private Era

Throughout the postwar years and until the 1960s, lack of funds constrained settlement programs. The trend of defunding and eking out an existence during and directly after World War II continued through the mid-1950s. Once again, settlement funding in a private era followed the pattern of initial financial retrenchment, defunding of social action and social reform programs, and then, with the return of economic growth, increased funding for recreational, educational, and social services. Even more important, however, the 1950s represent a critical watershed for the transformation of settlements into bureaucratic, publicly financed social service agencies. The opening of Community Assistance or Lanham Act centers in 1943 offered direct federal subsidies for day care and a momentary glimmer of future fund-raising relationships. While WPA programs during the New Deal had provided direct relationships between federal and city governments, the Lanham Act, which ended abruptly in 1946, promoted a direct relationship between the federal government and private agencies (Trolander 1987).[22]

The lessons learned about the power and effectiveness of federal intervention during the New Deal and World War II created a basis for continued funding of specific social services. In 1953–54 the federal government allocated $124.1 million to such social welfare services as school lunches, vocational rehabilitation, institutional services, and child welfare. Moreover, state and local governments disbursed $605 million, most of it for public institutions such as schools for the developmentally disabled, hospitals for the mentally ill, and training programs for juvenile delinquents (Smith and Lipsky 1993). But rarely was any of the money channeled to nonprofits. Public funding for nonprofits in the 1950s was rare and generally limited to few claimant areas, most of which did not include settlements. One of them, however, did directly affect settlements: juvenile delinquency.

Juvenile delinquency was to the 1950s what poverty and race would become to the 1960s, the defining social issue of the decade. In keeping with the conservative context of the decade, prevention of delinquency emphasized traditional family values and law and order. Of particular importance to this book's broad purpose are the public contracts for juvenile delinquency prevention that began the modern trend of using federal government grants to private institutions to address specific social problems (Trattner 1999). Settlements had been engaged in working with youth for decades. They were well positioned to renew their efforts when delinquency became a "hot" social issue and funding was available for efforts to prevent delinquency. In the latter part of the 1950s, a grant proposal regarding juvenile delinquency had an excellent chance of being funded. For example, the Juvenile Delinquency and Youth Offenses Control Act was a source of substantial grants for experimental programs during the late 1950s (Trolander 1987). These grants, however, only foreshadowed a larger and more complex system of public contracting for nonprofit services that would begin with the Mobilization for Youth (MFY) and the Great Society programs of the 1960s. They antedate a broad infusion of public funds and something of a second heyday for settlements in the decade after 1965. While the 1950s ultimately served as a fertile seedbed for future changes in funding arrangements, organizing work, racial relations, and service emphasis, the decade was a relatively quiet and limited time for the settlement house.[23]

The Sixties: 1960–1975

Throughout the 1950s settlements developed into multiservice neighborhood centers increasingly distant from the principles of settlement founders. They did so partly because they were swimming against a tide of reaction. Executives and staff at the most progressive houses hoped to stay afloat long enough for another wave of social reform to sweep them into a new movement for social change (Trolander 1987). When another "urban crisis" occurred in the 1960s, as it had in the first decades of the twentieth century, however, the settlements were ill prepared. The decade was one of conflict, direct action, even revolutionary struggle. The civil rights protests, antiwar demonstrations, and urban rebellions were dramatic and divisive events. The settlements preferred a consensus-building, incremental approach. Margaret Berry, the director of NFS in the 1960s, opposed transforming the settlement house into a "protest agency for the poor," because she felt blacks could make significant gains by bridging rather than exacerbating class and race tensions (Lasch-Quinn 1993:161).[24] On the other hand, the dominant social and cultural movements of the era, such as the New Left and counterculture were marked by increased opposition to class privilege (Cohen and Hale 1966). They were opposed to elite domination and to racist oppression; they were not trying to build bridges between rich and poor. Settlements were used to being marginalized in private contexts, but were not prepared to be characterized as anachronisms in an era of social investment.

A host of critics on the left thought settlements were outdated at best, part of the problem at worst. For instance, community organizer Saul Alinsky, after working with the Hudson Guild in the Chelsea neighborhood of Manhattan, felt that the settlement house was too closely connected with mainstream social welfare agencies and too beholden to established and traditional channels to effectively organize for change (Horwitt 1990; Trolander 1982). Others, like sociologist Herbert Gans (1962 and 1964), criticized the settlements for being more committed to helping middle-class social work professionals than to poor people. He considered their concept of working with rather than for neighborhood residents just a concept. Alinsky, Gans, Richard Cloward, and others saw social settlements as elite organizations on the wrong side of the struggle (Horwitt 1990; Beck 1976; Cloward and Elman 1973; Cloward and Piven 1972). Throughout their history settlement houses had worked with those who came to the settlements rather than with those who needed settlement services the most. More to the point, they tended to work best with the more upwardly mobile members of their communities who sought out their services rather than with the more alienated and marginalized residents who had little interest in settlement programs. In contrast, social change efforts in the 1960s focused on those most in need, especially poor people of color. Settlements, however, still suffered from a long history of racial segregation and disregard (Lasch-Quinn 1993).

Nevertheless, settlements did play a role in the struggle for black equality. As noted earlier, in the 1940s and 1950s settlement houses affirmed their commitment to an integrated society. The racial composition of settlement program participants and staff slowly changed throughout the 1950s. During the 1960s, however, some houses evolved from a mild advocacy on issues of race to a willingness to engage in direct action protests and marches. In 1959 representatives from New York settlements participated in Washington, D.C., in a march for integrated schools that attracted 26,000 people. New York City settlements supported sit-ins at southern lunch counters during the early 1960s. More than a dozen New York settlements sent contingents to the 1963 March on Washington for Jobs and Freedom. These efforts culminated in an NFS proposal in 1967 that settlements should support and resort to militant direct action strategies if traditional means of communication with those in power were unsuccessful (Trolander 1987).

But for most activists these were the exceptions that proved the rule of the settlements' irrelevance in the struggle for racial equality. Especially at the start of the decade, prior to the Great Society programs, settlements generally seemed old-fashioned and out of touch with the pressing concerns of poor communities of color. How could neighborhood centers designed to work with and help the poor not be a major presence in black slums in the early 1960s? How could they not be doing more around the issue of poverty? Why did it take socialist Michael Harrington's *The Other America: Poverty in the United States*, first published in 1962, to alert leaders to the issue of poverty and class stratification, as Jacob Riis's *How the Other Half Lives* (1890) had done three generations before? Where were the settlements? They were at best just awakening and at worst indifferent to matters of race and class that were having an increasing effect on poor neighborhoods. In the early 1960s settlement practice was too often unresponsive to the changing needs of communities of color. As late as 1961 an appeal by groups in Harlem to UNH to establish a new settlement there so that they could be included in the Astor-funded juvenile delinquency project went unheeded. UNH responded that most settlements already served African-Americans. Accordingly, in the mid-1960s, when multimillion dollar funding came to Harlem for an antipoverty program, in the form of the Harlem Youth Opportunities Unlimited (HARYOU) project, the African-American leadership there excluded the settlements (Trolander 1987; Clark 1965). The characteristic timidity of the settlements in the post–World War II era, especially in terms of addressing issues of race and class, hurt them in the early 1960s.

As it turned out, however, all criticism notwithstanding, the settlements were extremely well positioned in the neighborhoods of the poor to contribute to the egalitarian and democratic goals of the decade. Their core principles of collaborative practice, community building, and social action were highly congruent with the decentralized, participatory, and direct action politics that were the hallmarks of dissent in the 1960s (Fisher 1994). Many of the sixties' social reforms, from Mobilization for Youth to Students for a Democratic Society (SDS) and Student Nonviolent Coordinating Committee (SNCC), unlike comparable efforts in the 1930s, were about community-based, participatory models of social change in poor neighborhoods (Evans 1979; Breines 1982; Carson 1982; Chafe 1980). Social worker George Brager, who headed MFY for a time, sought to create on the lower East Side "a well-integrated" participatory and politicized community of people who "identify with their neighborhood and share common values" (Santiago 1972; Brager 1999). The decentralized, social action movements of the 1960s and the War on Poverty incorporated community building and organizing into the equation of urban social change to an even greater extent than had been the case in the Progressive Era (Halpern 1995). It was within this context that the community-organizing and community-development initiatives of settlement houses grew.

The settlements were equally well positioned as liberal organizations to benefit from more radical alternatives and revolts that at the time appeared to threaten established systems of class and race domination. Liberal efforts such as the settlement house tend to fare well in public eras when radical activism makes them more attractive to funders, in part because such activism forces social issues into contemporary politics and discourse, and in part because funders seek more moderate alternatives to radical change.[25] In a conservative era social problems can be ignored by those in power or repressed as deemed necessary. In more public eras, however, economic and political elites have to be more attentive, preferring to support "the velvet glove of liberal reform" to the "iron fist of conservative repression" (Weinstein 1968; Fisher 1994). In such a political climate the social settlements functioned as safer alternatives to more radical options. Significantly, the shifting of the center of the American political economy and the changing role of voluntary and public-sector organizations help explain why the settlement method of neighborhood work, in disrepute in the 1950s both in society at large and in the social work profession, seemed "vindicated" in the 1960s (Bryan and Davis 1990:277).

The "Great Society" Institutionalizes Contracting

Specific changes associated with the sixties quickly transformed the settlement houses. In terms of practice and programs, the era reinfused settlements with a social reform and social action component—turning them into tarnished but resharpened spearheads for reform. In terms of administration and financing, government funding profoundly altered settlements structurally, a change that has persisted to the present.[26] Private funding to private institutions for public purposes had been the "settlement way" since the settlements' inception. With the 1960s and the institution of large-scale federal funding to nonprofits in the form of individual disbursements for such programs as Medicare and Medicaid and aggregate funding for contracted projects like Head Start, the system became one of public funding to private institutions for public purposes. Funding for settlements was now not only qualitatively but also quantitatively different.

Qualitatively, the War on Poverty of the mid-1960s "breathed new life" into the settlements (Trolander 1982:347). It gave extensive federal financial support to organizations working with the poor, addressing the "social" causes of poverty, and pursuing a decentralized strategy to tackle poverty at the neighborhood level (Marris and Rein 1967; Kramer 1969; Peterson and Greenstone 1977; Moynihan 1969). Of course, the settlements were not passive recipients in this process. Henry Street, for example, was an initiator of Mobilization for Youth, an experiment in community-based responses to poverty and powerlessness. Helen Hall and others first began work on the project in 1957; President Kennedy launched it officially in May 1962. In short order Henry Street lost control of MFY to activist academics at Columbia University's School of Social Work, among them Lloyd Ohlin, Richard Cloward, and George Brager (Brager 1999; Hall 1971).[27] But the initiative was Henry Street's, the prime beneficiary was the lower East Side neighborhood the settlement had served for decades, and in the waning days of MFY, when Bertram Beck, the last director of MFY, accepted the position of head worker at Henry Street in 1967, he headed both organizations simultaneously (Beck 1976, 1977).

Quantitatively, MFY represents an early benchmark in the developing relationship between federal grants and nonprofit social service agencies. By 1968 the federal government had invested over $30 million in services to residents of the lower East Side of New York City (Hall 1971). Limitations notwithstanding, from the mid-60s onward, the Great Society wrought profound changes and brought massive funding for neighborhood work and social change (Halpern 1995). Federal expenditures for social welfare services tripled in only five years, increasing from $812 million in 1965 to $2.2 billion in 1970. In contrast, local and state expenditures grew only by 50 percent over the same period. Most important for settlements, a large percentage of the public funding for social welfare services was now being spent through nonprofit agencies. The Office of Economic Opportunity, developed in 1964 to administer the War on Poverty, dramatically expanded the amount of money available for community-based nonprofit programs such as settlements (Kravitz 1969). Additionally, as popular pressure mounted for increased public support, Congress amended the Social Security Act in 1967 so that states could develop purchase-of-service contracts (POSC) with private agencies. This program guaranteed states federal support for up to three times (300 percent) the amount they could raise from private or other public sources.[28] Funding under this Title IV-A amendment jumped from $281 million in 1967 to $1.6 billion five years later (Smith and Lipsky 1993; Levitan 1969). These new financing arrangements created more opportunities to promote social change and develop community-based programs.

As noted earlier, in 1964 as part of the Great Society, the Johnson administration launched the Economic Opportunity Act. Programs under the new Office of Economic Opportunity included Operation Head Start, Job Corps, Neighborhood Youth Corps, Upward Bound, VISTA, and the Community Action Program, which established community action agencies throughout the nation (Marris and Rein 1967; Kramer 1969; Piven and Cloward 1971). Impoverishment was seen once again as a federal problem, not a social problem of local origin that could be handled at a neighborhood level. In 1965 Medicare and Medicaid were enacted as amendments, Title XVIII and Title XIX respectively, to the Social Security Act. New federal programs for health care for the elderly (Medicare) and for the poor (Medicaid) meant more money in the hands of neighborhood residents who needed to purchase health care services (Jansson 2000).[29] Settlements were directly involved in some of these developments and were indirect beneficiaries of others. For example, settlement leaders at the NFS helped develop the VISTA program. Many of the VISTA volunteers, required to work in impoverished communities, ended up at social settlements. This infusion of public volunteers expanded settlement staffs and programs, just as New Deal programs had done a generation earlier. The Community Action Program of the 1964 Economic Opportunity Act directed millions of dollars to poor neighborhoods. It sought to improve living standards and enable people in poor neighborhoods, through their neighborhood centers and community organizations, to effect social change. The Community Action Agencies (CAAs) legitimated and supported the core principles of settlement work: organize the neighborhood to help itself; get residents involved. Settlements were seen as very attractive funding sites for public leaders because of their location in poor neighborhoods and because of their interest in poverty-related problems (Fisher 1994). Throughout the nation settlements got support from varied OEO programs, grants to develop neighborhood health clinics, funds for Head Start programs, and day care funds subsidized through Title IV-A and Title XX. Head Start alone channeled millions of dollars into settlements for supplemental preschool education programs.[30] It was as though Lyndon Johnson and the United States Congress were trying to do for the settlements and poor urban neighborhoods what Jane Addams, Lillian Wald, Vida Scudder, and countless others had only dreamed of half a century earlier. Not only were they making neighborhood-based poverty work a concern of American social policy, they were funding it (Halpern 1995).

The National Federation of Settlements estimated in late 1965 that the OEO had distributed over $10 million in contracts to settlement houses (Trolander 1987).[31] The experience during these years of Hull-House, while not representative of all settlements, concretely illustrates the impact of public financing on settlement staffing and budget. From 1962 to 1969 the Hull-House staff expanded from about forty people to more than three hundred. In 1969 its budget doubled, increasing from under $1 million to $2 million (Romanofsky 1978a; Trolander 1987; Bryan and Davis 1990). Its contracted services included such War on Poverty programs as VISTA, Meals-on-Wheels, Head Start, and Neighborhood Youth Corp.

Increased federal support, channeled primarily through individual re-imbursements via Medicare and Medicaid as well as aggregate contracts for specific programs and projects, changed the composition and role of settlement houses. In the past, when settlements had been dependent on private donations, board members were drawn from the city elite. Securing support was an expected responsibility of board appointees. With the Great Society programs, however, there was an increased emphasis on the poor represent-ing themselves. This tendency was maximized as a matter of policy through "maximum feasible participation of the poor" (Moynihan 1969; Piven and Cloward 1971; Arnstein 1972). Pressures for participation and equal repre-sentation mounted throughout the public and nonprofit world. A 1936 study of settlements in New York reported that twenty-five of thirty-four settlements had no one from the neighborhood on their boards. By 1968 the NFS es-timated that 25 percent of settlement boards were comprised of neighbor-hood residents or their representatives. By 1970 the figure was 75 percent. Increasingly the board changed from being all white to including mostly people from ethnic minority groups. By 1975 more than half the directors of settlement houses were nonwhite (Beck 1977). Clearly, settlements were responding to pressures from the social movements of the 1960s for inclusion and democratic process. But public contracting also promoted diversifica-tion and democratization of settlement boards because settlement houses were no longer dependent on private funding.

As this book will document in subsequent chapters, public funding was fraught with challenges and dilemmas for settlements, ones that were ap-parent early on. Settlements clearly benefited from the expansion and di-versity of funding, but the money also exacted certain prices and trade-offs. Settlement leaders such as Helen Hall, who retired from Henry Street in 1967, saw advantages and drawbacks in federal funding (Andrews 1990). First, securing funding from the public sector was very difficult work, es-pecially for smaller agencies. "Just filling out the forms and questionnaires required to get public money is an exercise in perspicacity and endurance, aside from the real job of interesting the beleaguered public servant in even your most creative plans" (Hall 1971:87). Second, contracts were always a compromise between what the settlement wanted to do, or what the settlement really needed money for, and what the government wanted or was willing to fund. "Sometimes the combination is a reinforcement and improvement on the original [settlement] plan, and sometimes a distortion" (Hall 1971:87). Third, government funding often steered settlements toward subordinating their own and/or the community's needs in favor of federal priorities. Instead of identifying a community's needs and finding funds to develop a program to address them, there was an increasing tendency to launch programs simply because government money was available. Hall preferred funding for "basic on-going budgets," rather than the restrictive funding for specific projects. "I have often wished that more foundations would decide to give not only to new projects but to put aside a good percentage of their funds for the support of the basic on-going budgets of the kind of agencies in which they are interested, using the rest for the experiments of limited duration" (Hall 1971:88). Running programs demanded increased bureaucratization and formalization as well as ever increasing attention to the whims of policymakers in Washington or Albany. Moreover, government funding fluctuated. Program support, here today, could be gone tomorrow depending upon the action of Congress, the President, or a state legislature. Contracting also seemed to overextend programs, creating a need for additional monies not provided in the contracts. Despite its big budget in 1967, Hull-House had a $200,000 deficit, "and it was larger in each of the next two years" (Bryan and Davis 1990:279). While settlements benefited from Great Society programs in particular and public funding in general, Trolander (1987:187), wary of the relationship between settlements and government, concludes that "the net effect of the War on Poverty may well have been to contribute to the demise of the traditional settlement house movement."

Concurrently with the institutionalization of the new contracting relationship between nonprofits and the public sector, support for social action waned. By 1967 conservatives in Congress were undercutting the social action component of the War on Poverty (Fisher 1994; Piven and Cloward 1971). These legislators were reacting to the fact that federally funded community groups were challenging local authorities in countless towns, cities, and states across the nation. With the reaction against the War on Poverty and the decline of funding for social action, settlements had to reduce their more activist programs, for example, training projects in community organizing to develop neighborhood leaders. But the demise of the Great Society programs during President Nixon's administration from 1969 to 1973 created even greater financial strain for settlements. Regarding Hull-House, for example, by 1971 funding from the federal government had been cut by $700,000 from its 1968 level, forcing its head resident to resign (Romanofsky 1978a). Funding from the Office of Economic Opportunity at Hull-House was terminated in 1974; VISTA had been ended several years earlier (Bryan and Davis 1990). Cuts during the Nixon era were directed more at social change programs and projects than at overall funding.

Policies enacted during the late 1960s and early 1970s anticipated contemporary programmatic and funding relationships: public funding through contracts for restricted nonprofit categorical projects in a volatile context characterized by both infusions of public funding to nonprofits and by periodic funding decreases. The cuts during the Nixon era turned out to be only a temporary if difficult downturn for contracted funding to nonprofit service providers. For example, federal spending on OEO and ACTION programs increased from $51.7 million in 1965 to $2.3 billion in 1980. Likewise, spending at the federal level for community mental health centers expanded from $143 million in 1969 to $1.4 billion in 1979. With the passage of Titles IV and XX of the 1974 revision to the Social Security Act, which allows the federal government to purchase services from private agencies, public funding for community-based nonprofit work increased yet again. This was as true for settlements in New York as it was for Hull-House in Chicago. For its first seventy years Henry Street was heavily dependent on private funding. That changed dramatically in the 1960s. By 1975 funding from the federal government accounted for approximately two-thirds of Henry Street's $4.5 million annual budget. It had a staff of five hundred, most of whom were involved in government contract projects (Wallach 1978). What developed and was permanently established in the 1960s was a new funding relationship with federal, state, and local governments that transformed the settlement house into a different organization after 1975. Contracting in an era of privatization and economic globalization had begun.

2 Privatization, Contracting, and Nonprofits Since 1975

A study undertaken by the United Neighborhood Houses of New York (UNH) for the Ford Foundation in 1991 calculated that 80 percent of the funding for the thirty-eight member settlements in New York City came from public contracts. The settlement houses benefited from the public dollars. With public support they were able to help address the needs of poor children, their families, and their inner-city communities by providing a broad array of neighborhood-based social activities and human services. But they were burdened by the public contracts as well. They were overwhelmed, the executive director of United Neighborhood Houses stated, by "the administrative time and cost now spent in issuing and responding to multiple requests for proposals and in preparing and processing thousands of forms for auditing, monitoring, and reporting on programs" (Marks 1993:24). Equally significant, public funds were becoming more and more restrictive, their use allowed only for "single-problem categories" such as illiteracy, substance abuse, or child care. Funding was "too inflexible to permit appropriate responses" to the worsening and ever changing needs of the community (Marks 1993:24–25). This report antedated the public-sector cuts in social service funding produced nationwide by the United States Congress in its Contract with America and the draconian social service policies implemented in New York State and New York City under Governor Pataki and Mayor Giuliani respectively. These developments at the national and local level greatly affected both the settlement house and the system of contracting (Smith 1995; Gibelman and Demone 1998a, 1998b). Both have been dramatically restructured by the changes in the national and local context. The new context of voluntary-sector privatization under which settlements and nonprofits must operate, the system of contracting that reflects the demands and prerogatives of corporatization, and the barriers to nonprofit agencies posed by corporate globalization and the system of contracting are the subjects of this chapter.

Private New World

First, building on our analysis in chapter 1, we evaluate the contemporary context in which community-based social service agencies exist, a context that shapes the nature of service work and determines the varied constraints and hurdles agencies must contend with. In our historical model, the years since 1975 are a classic example of a more private-focused context. Regarding almost all the indicators—the turn to greater individualism, conservative politics, right-wing discourse, laissez-faire orientation, right-wing social movements, and corporate hegemony—these years exemplify the model. Numerous commentators have referred to the excessive individualism of the period (Bellah, Madsen, Sullivan, et al. 1985; Lasch 1978; Sennett 1990; Bookchin 1992; Putnam 1996). Robert Putnam's *Bowling Alone* claims not to be a study of the decline of civic interest and social capacity, but it does emphasize the recent decline of community, social cohesiveness, and public consciousness characteristic of private eras. Conservative critic Kevin Phillips (1990), stunned by the greed of the 1980s and using a cyclical historical model, characterizes the post-1975 context as akin to both the Gilded Age and the 1920s. For him, "the 1980s were a second Gilded Age, in which many Americans made and spent money abundantly." Moreover, "the Reagan administration, from the beginning, was openly committed to copying the economic style and incentives of the Calvin Coolidge years. Critically, Reagan's politics were more precarious and debt-dependent than [those of] the original era" (Phillips 1990:xviii, xxii). The Gilded Age, which experienced the urban-industrial transformation of the United States, was an extended private era. The twenties and fifties represent briefer private contexts. Like the Gilded Age, our contemporary era is significantly longer in number of years than its predecessors in the twentieth century and seems to be ushering in a new economic structure, as did the urban-industrial transformation of the late nineteenth century. Chapman (2000:4C) underscores this when he notes, "We are clearly in a new Gilded Age today. Disparities in wealth, the influence of money in politics, the decadence and self-segregation of the affluent classes, the colossal mergers of already behemoth corporations—these features of our time all mirror the era of [more than] 100 years ago."

Three trends consistent with private eras but unprecedented in their magnitude have facilitated the development of our contemporary private context. First, we increasingly live in a world that emphasizes a culture of private individualism rather than a sense of public good and public participation (Bellah, Madsen, Sullivan, et al. 1985; Putnam 1996, 2000; Sennett 1974, 1990; Lasch 1978; Specht and Courtney 1994). People focus even more than before on their own individual needs and growth and that of their family to the exclusion of concern about, much less participation in, public life (Ryan 1992; Habermas 1989; Bellah et al. 1991). Increasingly, this leads to a preoccupation with individual deficits as opposed to social problems and to a belief that if all problems are caused by the individual, then solutions also must come from within the person. The very sense of social problems and social solutions disappears as issues of poverty, violence, education, environmental pollution are redefined as individual problems with individual solutions (Fisher and Karger 2000, 1997; Schram 2000).

Second, private space is replacing public space. (Sorkin 1992; Blakely and Snyder 1997; McKenzie 1994; Davis 1992; Boyte 1992). The urban landscape is increasingly being restructured to remove people from public spaces (streets, parks, beaches, libraries, mass transit, dense city neighborhoods, downtown street shopping) and have them inhabit private ones (private homes and backyards, country clubs, private bookstores, private cars, fortified gated and suburban communities, and shopping malls). In such a world opportunities for building social solidarity with others, for knowing the existence, let alone the importance, of public life, are dramatically diminished (Suarez 1999; Eisenstein 1998; Sandel 1996; Putnam 1993a, b; Fisher and Karger 1997; Boyte 1989).

A third characteristic that the post-1975 context shares with its more private-focused predecessors is a penchant for private institutions, both as the engines of economic and technological progress and as primary instruments to address and resolve social problems. This tendency translates into a withdrawal from social problems that do not affect the business community and marginalization of those who try to address them as public issues. The efforts in the 1980s and 1990s to dismantle the welfare state of the 1930s and 1960s underscore the hostility of private eras toward the public policies and programs of prior public contexts. In our contemporary context—influenced heavily by a culture of individualism, a physical world of private spaces, and the domination of private institutions—policies and programs of the welfare state are being transformed. Instead of addressing contemporary inequities, the new welfare state exacerbates or ignores them (Greider 1992; Block, Cloward, Ehrenreich, and Piven 1987).

The Political-Economic Context: Unease and Inequality Since 1975

The years since 1975 have been a difficult time for agencies interested in addressing social problems and for individuals, families, and communities having to contend with contemporary social conditions. Clearly, since the mid-1970s we have been living in a time of dramatic and unpredictable change, a period quite harsh for many people. This is especially evident in the unpredictability and inequities of the American economy. Despite pundits and economic advisers who tout the strength of the economy, critical indicators over the past twenty-five years reflect an unrelenting economic crisis for many (Schor 1999; Phillips 1990; Greider 1992; Bluestone and Harrison 1982; Bowles, Gordon, and Weisskopf 1990; Boyte 1980; Alcaly and Mermelstein 1977).

We think the source of the crisis is obvious. Around 1975 a number of factors coalesced to give rise to the emerging global political economy. To begin with, the OPEC embargo stalled the American economy. Second, the end of the Vietnam war vividly underscored the long-term drain of military expenditures on productive investment. As a consequence, the U.S. abandoned the fixed exchange rate of the gold standard. These changes occurred in a context of rising global economic competition and rapidly precipitated a crisis in capitalism of global proportions. Economic growth rates, corporate profits, and manufacturing fell dramatically in almost every Western industrialized nation. To address this decline in profits, U.S. business leaders argued that a new political economy of unbridled capitalism should be introduced. Initiatives should be advanced that minimized government regulations and high social expenditures and negated a number of the compromises made with labor unions since the 1930s and with social action groups since the 1960s.[1] Business leaders proposed that the social welfare obligations of society should be curtailed to allow American businesses to compete more effectively worldwide (Fisher 1994). This strategy of privatization, also known as economic restructuring or globalization, would soon set the ground rules for sweeping changes (Fainstein and Fainstein 1974; Smith and Feagin 1987; Kling 1993; Sassen 1994; Bauman 1998; Brecher and Costello 1994).

This corporate strategy led to the undermining of labor unions, large-scale lay-offs of workers, scaling back of the social welfare state, dismantling of federal programs that did not assist corporate activity, and various other means of cost-cutting necessary to maximize profits in a new global economic order (Barnekov, Boyle, and Rich 1989; Fisher and Karger 1997; Brecher and Costello 1994; Barnet 1994). The economic bottom line became the basic measure of evaluation in the new corporatized, free-market world. In response, cities had to restructure as downtowns withered and factory towns collapsed due to deindustrialization (Bluestone and Harrison 1982; Logan and Swanstrom 1990; Alcaly and Mermelstein 1977). Businesses also had to restructure through "downsizing" their labor force. In turn, a nation, state, or city was increasingly measured not by the quality of life it afforded citizens or its commitments to promoting the social good, but by how costs could be cut or incentives created to attract economic investment (Blau 1999; Kuttner 1991, 1992, 1997).

Sandel argues that this restructuring strategy ignored the "corrosive" effects of global capitalism. Power rests in corporations increasingly unaccountable to society (cited in Lasch 1991). Unrestrained capital mobility both ignores social needs or problems and disrupts community. A sense of social cohesion, public life, and a public good wanes (Fisher and Karger 1997; Putnam 2000). Not only has capital become distanced from the social, it seeks to become unchained from government, even at the national level. The increased mobility of capital and the new types of international investment transcend the nation-state, seeking to erode the power of the public sector to control economic and social matters (Kuttner 1991, 1997; Eisenstein 1998; Ferguson 1995; Brecher, Childs, and Cutler 1993).

Ultimately, this leads to a nearly complete public distancing from social issues at the very moment when global corporations are responsible for profound social changes and damage worldwide. Of particular concern in this changing context are accelerated joblessness and declining tax bases (Bookchin 1992). As noted, this strategy increasingly demands the adoption of economic over social objectives and focuses on corporate over public needs. It ignores festering social and urban problems that now, like almost everything else, are left to the marketplace (Kuttner 1997; Blau 1999). Political opposition is muted by efforts to promote a corporate and right-wing agenda and, relatedly, to delegitimate and defund progressive social change and proponents of social welfare programs (Starr 1987; Amin 1990; Fisher and Kling 1991, 1993; Boggs 2000, 1986).

The 1980s

Many people benefited from the corporate policy of privatization. The economy expanded from 1983 through 1990, and price inflation fell from the double-digit highs of the late 1970s. Approximately 30 million people earned between $50,000 and $200,000 per year during the 1980s. Those at the top flourished (Phillips 1990; Greider 1992).[2] The goal of neoconservative economic policy was to unleash the creativity and daring of American entrepreneurs, whose success, wealth, and reinvestment would "trickle down" to all segments of society.

In fact, "the much vaunted economic recovery of the 1980s did little or nothing to pull the country out of the economic crisis that began in the late 1960s and deepened during the 1970s and early 1980s" (Bowles, Gordon, and Weisskopf 1990: 4–5). Throughout the decade the average weekly wage fell; by 1990 it had declined to $258, which wiped out about half the gains U.S. workers had made since World War II. The percentage of employees working full-time and earning a low wage—currently defined as less than $12,195—increased from 12 percent in 1979 to 18 percent in 1990. Significantly, low-wage work increased from 6.2 percent to 10.5 percent among college graduates (Kuttner 1992). More banks failed between 1989 and 1991 than in all the years from the end of the Great Depression until 1980 (Mead 1991). Relatedly, the savings and loan scandal and bailout cost the American people some $500 billion. Key economic indicators, such as output and productivity growth, investment and profit rates as well as real wage growth, all were well below the levels of the 1950s and 1960s. Home ownership declined precipitously. Overwhelming trade deficits turned the US from the largest creditor into the greatest debtor nation.

During Reagan's presidency the tax rate for those in the highest income group dropped from 70 percent to 28 percent in only seven years. The 1986 tax reform law, sponsored by both Republicans and Democrats, reduced the levy on the top income bracket from 38.5 percent to 28 percent, while those in the next lower income bracket paid a higher rate of 33 percent. Corporate and capital gains taxes were reduced. At a time when funds were increasingly needed to finance the social needs of a nation in dire economic straits, public policy was to *spend more* on the military-industrial complex and *collect less* from those who could afford it most. Numerous studies by authors on both the Right and Left document the extraordinary upward redistribution of income in the United States during the 1980s (see Phillips 1990; Greider 1992). The top 1 percent of income after taxes in 1990 almost equaled that of the bottom 40 percent; in 1980 the top 1 percent had only half the total income of the bottom 40 percent. Of the total income gain from 1977 to 1989, 70 percent went to the richest 1 percent of Americans (Kuttner 1992). The incidence of poverty, declining in the late 1960s and early 1970s, jumped during the next decade up to 1964 levels, hitting women, children, and people of color the hardest (Sidel 1986; Reed 1999).

In the 1980s cities were especially vulnerable to dislocations, social breakdown, and shrinking tax bases. The incidence of poverty for inner-city residents rose from 30 percent in 1968 to 43 percent in 1988. Federal spending on cities fell by more than 60 percent from 1981 to 1992; the federal share of city budgets plummeted from 18 percent in 1980 to 6.4 percent in 1990 (*New York Times*, editorial 1992; Tilly 1990). Crime rates, drug use, racial and ethnic conflict, gang violence, infant mortality, teen pregnancy, homelessness, inadequate health care, substandard housing, and AIDS—to name but a few of the most publicized problems of the decade—all increased in staggering and alarming proportions. Finally, urban infrastructures, even in major cities such as New York, eroded after years of neglect (Sites 1997; Judd and Parkinson 1990; Gottdiener 1986).

While settlement houses expanded during the 1960s and 1970s due to increased federal funding for social welfare programs, in the 1980s neighborhood centers experienced hardship. According to Rolland Smith (1995), executive director of the Greater Cleveland Neighborhood Centers Association, the combination of neoconservative social agendas, a more constrictive and volatile system of contracting, and declining private money despite increasing upper-class wealth led settlement houses "to use up fund balances, defer maintenance on buildings, pay salaries well below parity, scramble for funding, and often operate with a crisis mentality" (2132). Throughout the 1980s nonprofits like the settlement house faced increasingly restrictive, volatile, and expensive funding. This trend did not improve in the next decade.

The 1990s

The economic crisis and problems of the 1980s persisted, certainly at least until the mid-1990s. The recent economic recovery has helped ameliorate some aspects of the economic crisis of the prior two decades. The American economy has been characterized by sustained growth, low inflation, and increases in certain forms of investment as well as by real spending on producer durables. These economic advances are grounded in the rapid and dramatic technological innovation that characterizes our age and the draconian neoconservative business strategies that boost certain parts of the economy while ignoring others (Kuttner 1997; Eisenstein 1998; Bauman 1998). For example, the corporate pursuit of cost cutting—that is, achieving efficiencies through downsizing, hiring more contract workers, employing more part-time employees who receive fewer benefits, and so forth— when coupled with technological innovations has led to the recent increases in worker productivity and declines in unemployment (Roth 2000). But these increases in productivity often coexist with declines in individual purchasing power and job security (Blau 1999; Boggs 2000; Skocpol and Leone 2000).[3] Thus, wages and salaries for most Americans were either unaffected or hurt by economic developments in the 1990s. "Resources are allocated in a more marketlike manner, but overall performance is nonetheless mediocre and living standards are mostly stagnant" (Kuttner 1997:24). Economic inequality and the conditions of the poor in the 1990s in many respects are remarkably similar to those in the 1980s. The worsening of income inequality that began in the early 1970s and accelerated dramatically in the 1980s continued apace in the early 1990s and seems only to have slowed slightly in the past few years. While there is recent good news—infant mortality, elder poverty, high-school dropouts, births to teenage mothers, and unemployment are declining while real wages of those at the bottom are improving (Miringoff and Miringoff 1999; Roth 2000)—the persistence of poverty (especially among children and people of color), the number of Americans without health insurance, and the static median family income throughout the 1990s reflect a decade and a half of worsening conditions (Miringoff and Miringoff 1999; Wilson 1999).

Moreover, income and wealth inequality have continued to deepen. Between 1983 and 1995 the net worth of the top 1 percent swelled by 17 percent, that of the bottom 40 percent diminished by 80 percent, and those exactly in the middle fifth lost more than 11 percent. An economic boom "has been built on the sweat of the 30 percent of American workers who earn poverty or near poverty wages" (Schor 1999: 4). The booming stock market notwithstanding, the late 1990s actually saw an increase in the percentage of full-time workers earning incomes below the poverty line. Robert Reich, former secretary of labor under Clinton, puts the problem of increasing economic stratification in the 1990s bluntly: "Most workers in the bottom half continue to experience shrinking paychecks. The gap between the best paid ten percent of Americans and the lowest paid ten percent is wider than in any industrialized nation. *Every* rung on the economic ladder is growing wider apart " (Reich 1997:137–138, emphasis in original). As if such conditions did not pose sufficient challenges, the policy of privatization—a mechanistic free-market response to vast global changes—further exacerbates social problems and undermines attempts at meeting social needs.

The new privatized political economy of the 1990s provided certain opportunities for decentralized, voluntary-sector, community-based social service programs such as the settlement house. Growth of the voluntary sector was expected to fill some of the service gaps produced by a reduced public sector.[4] The settlement house persisted into the 1990s and even experienced a potential revival, thanks to a transformation of its programs and structures and the recreation of the welfare state. But in the new privatized welfare state, settlement houses, like most nonprofits, while enduring, are besieged by dual pressures from an intensified and corporatized contracting system and from growing and unmet chronic needs of their communities (Smith 1995; Gibelman and Demone 1998a, 1998b; Sclar 2000).

Privatization

These changes in the voluntary sector in general and in social settlements in particular are part of the most significant international development since 1980, the rise of privatization strategies in both economy and government. As a result of the pressures from profound economic and social changes that began in the early 1970s that were discussed above, the very idea of public social programs has been delegitimized. Particularly in the Reagan-Bush era, but continuing into the new millennium, "big government" has become *the* problem. Neoconservatives and neoliberals sought to dismantle as much of the welfare state as possible (Piven and Cloward 1982; Kuttner 1991, 1996; Starr 1987). Free-market economics is now a worldwide phenomenon that is transforming the globe (Blau 1999; Kuttner 1992, 1997; Bauman 1998).

Proponents of privatization suggested that in the new global economy nations cannot afford social programs. In large measure the intent of the policy of privatization is to dismantle the state as much as possible so as to reduce passing on "social costs" to the corporate sector and the affluent, those in theory responsible for stimulating the economy (Feagin 1988). If nations do not adopt such policies, if capitalism is not "unbridled," investments will go elsewhere. These are clear guidelines from the World Bank, the International Monetary Fund, and global corporate investors (Barnet 1994; Brecher and Costello 1994). Not only in the United States and Europe, but in Asia, Africa, and South America, the context of privatization forces almost all social and political agendas away from social welfare conceptualizations toward laissez-faire capitalist ones.

Privatization refers not only to transferring governmental operations and roles to business but also to the reorientation of political, economic, cultural, and social institutions, such as the settlement house, to corporate needs, values, goals, and leaders. Barnekov, Boyle, and Rich (1989:4) propose that privatization "reflects a general policy orientation rather than a finite set of policy alternatives."[5] This policy direction contains four key elements. First, priority is given to economic considerations in almost all aspects of domestic politics. Second, private markets are preferred over public policies in terms of allocative social choices. Third, if public intervention is deemed necessary, it must supplement private market processes and include maximum private-sector participation. Fourth, public programs are expected to be modeled on the methods of the private sector.

In such a framework government becomes the problem, and champions of social programs become the enemy. Why are the poor impoverished? Because government programs create dependency (Murray 1984). Why has the American economy been so plagued by crisis and volatility for most of the past twenty-five years? Because government taxation destroys entrepreneurial incentive and risk-taking (Gilder 1981). Why were key American corporations not more competitive in the global economy? Because government regulations imposed unrealistic and costly programs on businesses (Friedman 1962; Gilder 1981). Public schools, the U.S. Postal Service, and most public social services, especially those directed at providing income support for the poor, all are said to be not only ineffective but wrongheaded. The public sector and advocates of allocative programs are seen as doing more harm than good.

In fact, there is more than a grain of truth to some of these suppositions. Government defense expenditures in the 1980s did dramatically increase the federal debt. Bureaucracies are autocratic and inefficient. Small autonomous community organizations, such as the early settlement houses, address local needs more efficiently and effectively (Kramer 1981). But the argument for privatization conveniently forgets the different missions and roles of the public and corporate sectors (Smith and Stone 1988; Spann 1977). In liberal theory at least, the public sector serves the public good, the general welfare. This is why elected officials in the recent past were called public servants. The public sector is the primary sector of the polity that has sufficient resources to effect significant social change, and, at least in theory, it has the mission to do so. The business sector has a very different mission. It produces profits; it does not address social problems. Its responsibility is only to investors and stockholders, not to a broader citizenry. How can corporations be expected to address social problems in a highly competitive economy in which they are under severe economic pressure to restructure and downsize their operations? Social policy and programs are not the business of the private sector (Kuttner 1991, 1997; Blau 1999; Fisher and Karger 1997; Schram 2000).

Arguments for dismantling the public sector and turning social issues over to the private and voluntary sector prove problematic. For proponents and architects of the strategy, such as E. S. Savas (1982), former assistant secretary of housing and urban development in the Reagan years, "privatization is the key to both limited and better government: limited in its size, scope, and power relative to society's other institutions; and better in that society's needs are satisfied more efficiently, effectively, and equitably" (288). Sclar (2000:11) says that "depending on where one looks, virtually every public service is now considered a candidate for privatization, including public schools, public hospitals, social services, penal institutions, police and fire departments, and transit systems. All these initiatives are proposed or implemented in the name of managerial efficiency and effectiveness. The most vehement advocates of privatization believe that government should, indeed could, be all but put out of business." Privatization is fundamentally a political rationale for shedding governmental social responsibility, keeping social costs down, decreasing taxes on the wealthy and powerful, selling off valuable state-owned industries or land, and deregulating trade and investment (Barnekov, Boyle, and Rich 1989; Simonsen and Robbins 2000). Ultimately, such policies have a corrosive effect on public life and the very fabric of society. As noted earlier, social problems in the privatized context mount as they go unattended and unaddressed (Karger and Stoesz 1998; Fisher and Karger 1997; Feagin 1988; Warner 1968).[6]

In the new fee-for-service political economy those who have the money to pay for private services—whether private schools, private security systems, or private health care—are among the fortunate. People who must rely on public services are increasingly discouraged and turned away. Because the public sector was defunded and derided for two decades, it no longer has the resources or legitimacy to address many social problems (Murray 1984; Gilder 1981; Piven and Cloward 1982; Kuttner 1997). As a result, recipients of public services, including the middle class, receive less assistance. Most important, social needs and public life are not the real concerns of the corporate designers of the privatization strategy. In the short run this strategy makes for good business policy, i.e., cutting costs and regulations in order to maximize profits. In the long run, as social or public policy, it is highly problematic. Nevertheless, the arguments for the privatization of institutions have been very effective; they have taken on the status of global common sense despite their destructive implications (Kuttner 1997; Boggs 2000; Singer 1999; Blau 1999).

Privatization and the Welfare State

The lessons of welfare state formation run counter to free-market formulations. After the debacles of unregulated capitalism in the Gilded Age and the 1920s, the public sector expanded to address social problems, curb the excesses of capitalist profiteering, and relegitimize the system (Piven and Cloward 1982; Gough 1979; Fabricant and Burghardt 1992; Fisher 1994). Public-sector programs have always functioned as means of accumulation and legitimation in capitalist economies (O'Connor 1973). They help businesses accumulate capital in the form of government subsidies and supports, such as land grants, tax breaks, and defense contracts. They also legitimate the system, helping preserve order and harmony through education, social programs, and the like. More recent scholarship on the role of the state (Fabricant and Burghardt 1992; Gough 1979; Piven and Cloward 1982) argues that public programs are not simply handed down from above to pacify the masses and legitimate inequality. Social programs also demonstrate the victories of social movements and citizen resistance (Amin 1990; Fisher and Kling 1993). The Wagner Act of 1935 (which gave workers the right to collective bargaining) or the Voting Rights Act of 1965 (which outlawed barriers to participation in the electoral process) demonstrate not simply the legitimation function at work, but a public sector whose policies were shaped by the needs and demands of ordinary people, such as industrial workers and civil rights activists, organizing at the grassroots level. Thus, the development of social welfare policy reflects the level and nature of democratic social struggle.

Since the late nineteenth century, when either unbridled capital became excessively disruptive to society (e.g., controlling stock markets or the price of gold for the benefit of a few individuals) or when these excesses spawned mass disorder (e.g., conflicts with industrial workers), new and more social democratic public administrations came to power to address instability and rising social problems. The current proliferation and widespread acceptance of the privatization of government and institutions, which seeks to undo most of the progressive and hard-earned victories of the past two generations, illustrates not only the dominant position of conservative elites in the 1980s and early 1990s but also the weakened influence of opposition efforts. The affluent, powerful, and right-wing factions have been handily winning the social struggle of the past two decades. Nevertheless, the persistent need for legitimation and the potential of citizens to resist draconian attacks on their standard of living and hard-won social supports limits the ability of privatizers to dismantle the social welfare state. They have had to move very slowly, selectively, and carefully (Piven and Cloward 1982; Block, Cloward, Ehrenreich, and Piven 1987).[7]

Within the broad framework of privatization, the contracting system has been reshaped in the past two decades as an alternative form of social welfare funding and service delivery. It enables privatizers to dismantle public programs and legitimacy while continuing to meet many basic needs and demands of citizens through nonprofit social service providers like the settlement house. In the process, the settlement house has been transformed into a multiservice agency that functions as an administrator of public programs. Equally important, the settlement house is increasingly pressured to shed structural characteristics and core values that once made it a significant community institution.

Contracting and the Financing of Nonprofits Since 1975

In the past generation, contracting from the public sector to nonprofit human services organizations has altered the relationship between the voluntary sector and government. According to Wagner (2000:131) "contrary to the mythmaking of the 'independent sector' we now have a system in which large parts of the nonprofit world are not independent at all, but governmentally financed." To some (Wolch 1990; Goldstein 1993) these nonprofits have become "agents of the state." Milward (1994:76) argues that contracting demonstrates a "hollowing out of the state," that is, a weakening of its capacity and responsibilities. Clearly the relationship between the public and voluntary sectors is characterized by greater complexity than any single analysis can capture (Gibelman and Demone 1998b; Salamon 1987a, b; Salamon, Musselwhite Jr., and de Vita 1986; Salamon and Abramson 1982). Settlement houses hardly seem agents of the state, though they too have been profoundly altered and shaped by the requirements and limits of public-sector funding in a privatized context.

Since the 1960s settlement houses have become heavily dependent on government contracts, which constitute on average from 50 to 85 percent of total settlement funding (Kraus and Chaudry 1995; Beck 1977; Smith 1995).[8] As Hasenfeld (1992) underscores in his analysis of government contracting, dependence on such external funding significantly increases its influence. Or as Loavenbruck and Keys (1987: 561) in a telling understatement describe the issue for the settlement house: "changes have been determined in part by the agencies that fund the centers and by the amount of money that is provided to them. That is, governmental agencies and the United Way have specific priorities for the use of funds that may or may not be consistent with the needs of a particular neighborhood."

In the past the influence of public-sector contracting was not as powerful or politicized as currently. Contracting has been reframed as a tool of privatization, corporatization, and the dismantling of public-sector funding and responsibility (Milward 1994). Purchase-of-Service Contracts (POSC) have been dramatically transformed since the 1960s (Gibelman 1998b). In the 1960s and early 1970s, the intentions of the framers of contracting were mixed and contradictory, achieving public purposes as well as cutting public costs. The market model had not yet come to dominate (Reichert 1977). According to Gibelman (1995:1999), they sought to "provide an alternative means of delivering services that would better achieve public purposes." A number of policymakers in the War on Poverty hoped that contracting out services to nonprofits would avoid expanding government efforts such as job programs or income transfers (Wagner 2000). Other motives included developing new innovative programs and solutions to contemporary problems, limiting the public payroll, avoiding government controls of hiring, decreasing red tape, and channeling dissent (Kettner and Martin 1986, 1993a). These diverse and contradictory motives differ from the narrower and more uniform goals of contracting proponents after 1980, which are discussed below.

Public-sector contracting with not-for-profit social service agencies expanded substantially in the 1970s (Sharkansky 1980). As noted earlier, in 1969 almost all restrictive language pertaining to POSC was removed from regulations. Amendments to the Social Security Act and social service legislation contributed to an expanded use of contracting (Gibelman 1995). A 1971 study of state spending for social services concluded that 25 percent of the allocations were dedicated to purchased services. By 1976 the proportion was up to 49 percent. Twenty-five states spent more than half their social service allocation on contracted services. This data does not include federal investment in a vast array of categorical programs in the early 1970s—such as Head Start, community mental health centers, community action agencies, Title XX, etc.—that grew dramatically throughout this period. For community mental health centers alone, federal funding increased from $143 million in 1969 to $1.4 billion in 1979 (Smith and Lipsky 1993). Between 1971 and 1978 the proportion of federal social service funding dedicated to contracting under the Social Security Act increased from 25 percent to 54 percent (Wolch 1990). Between 1975 and 1980 state spending for both public and private social service agencies nearly doubled, jumping from $2.6 billion to $4.8 billion (Smith and Lipsky 1993). The National Federation of Settlements reported in 1975 that at least 50 percent of the settlements' total services were financed with public funding, approximately $84 million that year (Beck 1977). Just prior to the Reagan-Bush years, government funding of settlement programs amounted to between 50 and 70 percent of total budgets (Trolander 1987). After the twelve years of the Reagan-Bush administrations, 85 percent of funding came from public sources (Kraus and Chaudry 1995).

The Reagan-Bush administrations accelerated trends dating from the mid-1970s to transfer costs to the states, expand contracting, and cut support for social action efforts (Kramer 1985, 1994). As early as 1982, the nonprofit sector was providing 56 percent of government-financed human services (Wolch 1990). During the Reagan-Bush years federal expenditures for the Social Service Block Grant program decreased in real-dollar terms from $4.4 billion in 1980 to $2.6 billion in 1991, while state and local expenditures for social services rose from $4.8 billion in 1980 to $7.3 billion in 1988. A 1991 survey of more than 350 Massachusetts social service agencies concluded that 52 percent of the agencies' income came from state contracts, 17 percent from federal contract funding such as Medicaid and SSI, and only four percent from United Way. "Government purchase of service contracting with nonprofit service agencies in Massachusetts rose from $25 million in 1971 to $850 million in 1988" (Smith and Lipsky 1993:6). Total public funding for human services increased in the 1980s, but the federal portion shrank from 64.6 percent to 52.4 percent.[9] Public responsibility and the costs for social service delivery increasingly devolved on the states (Wieman and Dorwart 1998).

Equally significant, this period was distinguished by selective cuts that disproportionately affected programs for the poor and discretionary human services. Between 1982 and 1985 the government cut $57 billion from programs earmarked for the poor. Between 1982 and 1986 social service, community development, and housing programs were reduced by 35 percent (Wolch and Akita 1989). In addition, advocacy groups experienced deep declines in their contract revenues from the federal government (Piven and Cloward 1982; Kramer 1985). Nevertheless, these targeted areas of rollback did not alter the broad expansion of government service contracts for mainstream nonprofits. In the early 1990s providers continued to depend heavily on public-sector contracts, despite policy changes in the share of federal and state financing and despite the fact that for many programs the amount of funding available, especially for social change efforts, had declined since the days of the Great Society (Gibelman and Demone 1998a, b; Smith and Lipsky 1993).

Although contract funding continued to increase, a dramatic shift occurred during the Reagan-Bush era regarding the nature and goal of such financing. As Kettner and Martin (1993a) suggest, essential differences exist between early POSC efforts and those since 1980. In the former the private sector was not seen as inherently superior to the public sector, and POSC was seen as essentially an administrative tool, not an ideological one" (92). In the 1960s and early 1970s, federal social policies, such as contracting, were intended to overcome the limits of private charity and local and state governments. Privatization efforts during the Reagan-Bush years, on the other hand, sought to achieve different objectives. They also wanted to improve the public sector's efficiency, but more important, Reagan-Bush policies sought to end social welfare expansion, reduce the role of the federal government, unburden the federal government of more expensive civil service employees and unionized workers. These policies were developed to shift funding responsibility from the federal government to the states (Peat and Costley 2000).[10] In theory at least, Reagan and Bush preferred that the private sector, rather than the states, independently pick up the costs and the burden of responsibility for social service provision. They hoped that charity and altruism—Bush's "1,000 Points of Light" strategy—would replace government as the primary source of funding for social services.[11] Paradoxically, while private-sector charities were being asked to pick up the slack, they were simultaneously becoming ever more dependent on public-sector funding (Wolpert 1993; Wolch 1990; Salamon 1987a, b).

The privatization of social services is thus not so much about government declines in funding, but more about the transfer of responsibility and resources from the federal government to nonprofits via state-funded and locally funded POSCs (Gibelman and Demone 1998a, b). In 1993 the thirty-eight member houses of UNH had a total budget of $180 million, 80 percent of which came from public contracts, but 65 percent of the public contracts were provided by the City of New York (Marks 1993). "In this respect, POS [purchase of service] and privatization have been viewed as ideologically compatible, with POS representing one means to accomplish public divestiture. It represents a midpoint between predominantly government provision and total privatization" (Gibelman 1995:1999). Contracting has become a compromise structure for privatizers. It removes the federal public sector from its former service delivery function and enables privatizers to create a political climate hostile to public ownership of and responsibility for social service programming. This, in turn, delegitimizes both current and future claims for the responsibility of the public sector (Gibelman 1995). The success of the nonprofit world actually helps to discredit the public sector at the very moment nonprofits become more a part of government.[12] As Offe (1981) argues, given the structure of the current system of contracting, it is logical to identify government as the primary determinant in the transformation of the welfare state and the voluntary sector. But our analysis emphasizes how the contemporary context of economic globalization alters the prerogatives and power of government, so much so that the system of contracting refashions both government and the nonprofit sector as extensions of corporate structures and processes.

A Reinvented Public Sector

Because of this complex interconnection between public, private, and voluntary sectors, wholesale attempts at dismantling the federal public sector turned out to be unsuccessful, certainly when compared to the rhetoric and intent of Reagan-Bush era policies. Organized resistance to cuts for middle-class programs, such as Medicare and Social Security, the popularity of and demand for social service programs, and the significant entrenchment of the voluntary sector, due in no small part to prior contracted funding, slowed down federal efforts to dismantle public social services (Wolch 1990; Piven and Cloward 1982). Nevertheless, a dramatic policy shift has taken place. Purchased service contracts are being used as a tool for privatization initiatives. Through contracting privatizers have been able to realize public purposes without expanding the public sector or the number of public employees. Overt government intervention has been kept to a minimum as nonprofit agencies, contracting with the public sector, accomplish the tasks and deliver the services. As a result, citizen support for and confidence in government institutions have been undermined (Simonsen and Robbins 2000). According to Smith and Lipsky (1993), contracting has actually allowed a growth in public services because contracting agencies can hire employees at cheaper rates and with fewer public-sector requirements. If the hires had been public employees, an antigovernment response would have been likely. But as employees of contracted agencies, they are private-sector workers, albeit those who deliver and implement public policy. Contracting hides growth in the public sector. This is especially ironic as a policy designed to reduce government evidently has the opposite effect. In this way, as Wolch (1990:218) argued, "Far from orchestrating a neoconservative rollback of the welfare state, current policies intensify the grip of the state."

While some might misunderstand and evaluate contracting as a value-free, practical technology for social service administration and intervention, it must be seen as a political strategy and ideological choice (Kettner and Martin 1990). According to Gibelman and Demone (1989:28), "a number of features of the Reagan domestic agenda tended to favor the use of pur-

chase of service. . . . When viewed collectively, these approaches to the financing and delivering of social services overwhelmingly point to purchase
of service as a logical, practical, and proven method of furthering political
goals and priorities." Curiously, as Wagner (2000:131) notes, "although par-
tisan debates have occurred over privatization, little public dispute has occurred over contracting out large segments of public work to nonprofits."
While contracting has remained outside the realm of public discourse since
the inception of POSCs, academic discourse has not ignored the phenomenon. Much of the academic literature, especially earlier work, has been
quite skeptical and critical (Manser 1974; Reichert 1977; Abramovitz 1986;
Gronbjerg 1990; Hardina 1991; Netting and McMurtry 1994). More recently the growing literature on contracting in human services, while not
uncritical, has tended to accept the basic premises of such initiatives while
exploring specific features and impacts of these financing arrangements
(Peat and Costley 2000; Gibelman and Demone 1998a, b).

Nonprofits Under Contracting

Purchase-of-service contracting continues to be the dominant method for
financing and delivering social services, despite growing constraints and
funding volatility (Kettner and Martin 1996a; Gibelman 1998b). Any funding arrangement so widely accepted and widespread must have some merit
(Richter and Ozawa 1983; Kramer 1994; Gibelman 1998a). Kramer (1994)
argues that POSCs enable nonprofits to maintain, expand, and diversify
social services in ways not possible without public-sector funding. This is
especially the case for newer and smaller community organizations that developed out of social movements of the past generation. Certainly the demands of contracting weigh disproportionately on these smaller community
organizations, but for many, proponents argue, government funding is the
primary, often the only, source of financing (Kramer and Grossman 1987).
For larger organizations, even with the attendant pressures and constraints,
government contracts provide an opportunity to expand services in a context
of social service downsizing (Peat and Costley 2000; Kramer 1994). This is
critical in a period of federal cutbacks, state and local attacks on government
expenditures, and stagnant charitable contributions by corporations since
the mid-1980s (Karger 1994; Karger and Stoesz 1998). As Kettner and Martin
(1996a:23) argue, "the ability of nonprofit agencies to refuse to enter into

contractual relationships with the state is reduced by agencies' increased financial vulnerability and dependence." The general benefit of money for nonprofits should not be underestimated. It expands the range of services, salaries, and employment opportunities. Moreover, organizations that secure contracts often have enhanced visibility and prestige in their communities, which can be traced to both their increased service delivery and new connection to public-sector decision making (Kramer 1989). Lester Salamon and others suggest that contracting forces nonprofits to serve the poor and oppressed, requiring them to address the issues and needs of the most disadvantaged (Wagner 2000).

However, contracting also comes with high costs. At the very least nonprofits become more constrained under contracting, more corporate in their modus operandi and objectives, and more concerned with resources than with their neighbors (Smith and Lipsky 1993). While privatization intensified under the Reagan-Bush administrations, it has also continued throughout the Clinton years. Although politicians of all persuasions seem to support it, occasionally some openly worry about the contracting system. For instance, Leon Panetta, former budget director to Clinton, feared that POSCs were neither cost-effective nor justifiable (Gibelman 1995).[13] The discussion that follows analyzes some of the major concerns with contracting: how it alters power relations, makes heavy accountability demands, changes the practices of the social service workplace, increases the costs of nonprofits, displaces goals, obscures political processes, and diminishes social action and community building.

Altered Power Relations

The contracting system alters power relations between the state and nonprofits. Goldstein (1993), Wolch (1990), and Manser (1974) emphasize the threat government contracting poses to voluntary-sector agencies.[14] As the percentage of total agency financing that stems from contracting increases, nonprofits find themselves increasingly dependent on the government for resources (Gibelman 1995). Wolch (1990:xvi) underscores and expands the point when she suggests that a voluntary-sector *shadow state* has developed: "a para-state apparatus comprised of multiple voluntary-sector organizations administered outside of traditional democratic politics and charged with major collective service responsibilities previously shouldered by the public

sector, yet remaining within the purview of state control."[15] Nonprofits become government-controlled substitutes for public services and distance
themselves from their traditional role as voluntary-sector alternatives, com-
plements, or supplements to public-sector programs (Kramer 1994; Richter
and Ozawa 1983; Manser 1974; Reichert 1977). This shift in power relations,
this alteration in the very nature and autonomy of nonprofit organizations,
is the basis of most subsequent concerns in this book.

Accountability Demands

Under contracting, large agencies find themselves challenged by the demands of regulations and red tape, on the one hand, and funding volatility,
on the other. Perhaps the heaviest burden, especially on smaller nonprofits,
is the increased demand for agency accountability—all the restrictions, requirements, and bureaucratic paperwork that accompany government contracts (Kettner and Martin 1998, 1996b, 1993b). The executive director of
United Neighborhood Houses of New York relates how "one settlement,
which has Head Start and day care contracts totaling approximately $1.7
million and provides services to 190 children, is required to submit 500
reports a year just for the fiscal side of the program" (Marks 1993:25). Of
course, the problem is not simply government bureaucracy. Even those nonprofits without public-sector funding are increasingly overwhelmed by accountability demands from funders. Increased accountability demands reflect new developments in the American welfare state and the voluntary
sector. In the past two decades government has been forced to follow the
prerogatives, modes of operation, and goals of the corporate world. Moreover, the privatized context seeks to hold the voluntary sector accountable
to corporate bottom-line goals of cost savings, efficiency, and output (Kettner
and Martin 1998).

Accountability requirements dramatically alter the organizational form
and culture of nonprofits, forcing them to develop greater internal organizational formalization which distances them further from the communities
they serve. As a result of the demands of contracting, organizations have to
devote more resources and personnel to meet both fiscal and programmatic
accountability requirements. For example, they must develop an ever more
sophisticated capacity to write contracts and negotiate. Additionally, contracting increasingly comes with complex demands in terms of fiscal man-

agement, with various financial monitoring procedures and multiple reporting sources. Finally, measurement of program success makes greater claims on limited agency resources. Such regulations were less evident in the 1960s and 1970s, in part because contracting was a relatively new development with room for nonprofits to maneuver as government consolidated the system (Wedel 1974). Over time, however, the system has been characterized by more and more regulation, as officials hoping to cut costs developed new expectations of accountability in exchange for public expenditures (Smith and Lipsky 1993). Bertram Beck of Henry Street Settlement saw all of this as early as 1977. "There is increasing concern with overlapping, duplicative, and inefficient service delivery. . . . This concern gives rise to fresh demands for accountability by sources of finance, and new levels of managers are formed to render the service-giving organization accountable. In this way the federal, state, city, and neighborhood bureaucracy has become increasingly complex" (Beck 1977:1266).

The intensifying demands by the state for accountability directly impact nonprofit administrators and staff. Accountability requirements increase the amount of time agency administrators and staff must devote to paperwork (Gibelman 1995). Such requirements also increase the number of people employed by the agency to address accountability matters, including professional managers and administrative personnel with business and technical skills, rather than backgrounds in social service delivery (Wedel and Chess 1989; Jansson 1989; Kettner and Martin 1985). Furthermore, structural changes may be subtly forced on agencies. For example, with the new emphasis on the executive director, primary power may shift away from the board of directors (Smith and Lipsky 1993). This can occur in response to the greater range of demands on the organizations that requires a highly knowledgeable leadership. Moreover, as Karger (1988) and Fabricant and Burghardt (1992) emphasize, the increasing pressures of accountability can promote an almost assembly-line atmosphere for social service line workers, who now must emphasize more uniform responses to different needs. Relatedly, their loss of autonomy and heavier caseloads make it ever more difficult to effectively meet the diverse needs of clients and communities. The settlement house once had the distinction of being an innovative, autonomous, flexible agency embedded in community life. But the bureaucratization and formalization that accompanies contemporary contracting promotes other forms of organizational development (Powell and Friedkin 1987; Rudney 1987).

Altered Workplace, Services, and Roles

Voluntary organizations that contract substantially with the public sector are not only required to be more formalized and corporate in their financing, accounting, and evaluation, but also in the structuring of their services, clientele, and workplace. The staff of nonprofits must increasingly contend with heightened tensions between a corporatized funding process, the needs of the workplace, and the circumstances of the people who come to them for services. These tensions influence client selection, the composition of the workforce (volunteers v. paid staff, levels of education, etc.), the time available to meet with clients, and, perhaps most fundamental, the nature of the service exchange. Under contracting considerations of cost-effectiveness dominate decision making. In the past, certainly prior to Community Chest/United Way or public-sector funding requirements, such considerations were secondary to those of meeting human needs and addressing neighborhood concerns (Beck 1977; Hall 1971; Gibelman 1998b).

At the same time, contracting produces greater uniformity within types of services—limiting what workers can actually do in terms of service delivery—while simultaneously creating increased pressures for organizational diversification in an agency's programs. Uniformity drives service practice toward conventional and prescribed methods and away from innovative and/ or adversarial approaches (Kramer 1981). Increasingly, voluntary organizations alter their perspective on what constitutes good practice and adopt government norms (Smith and Lipsky 1993).

Moreover, according to many commentators, extensive contracting dramatically impacts agency staff by significantly increasing their workload. For Karger and Stoesz (1998:206) standardization "induces human-service organizations to accept an industrial mode of production in which the accepted measure of success is not necessarily the quality of service rendered but the number of people processed. Organizational surplus . . . tends to be derived from increasing the intensity of production and lowering labor costs." As Kettner and Martin (1996a:30) conclude "Clearly, this is an environment in which morale would likely be very low and could easily affect the quality of services provided to clients." Fabricant and Burghardt (1992) and Karger (1981) see both increased workloads and declining morale of service workers as parts of a broad trend of proletarianization in social service agencies in both the public and the voluntary sector.

Contracting also increases pressure to reduce payroll costs. Social service labor is cheaper in the nonprofit than in the public sector because of greater insulation from civil service requirements and union-negotiated pay scales. Kettner and Martin (1996c) found that 69 percent of state administrators thought POSC reduced the number of public employees. Faced with conflicts between community and government standards of care, service workloads, and reduced levels of financing, agencies turn to contracting to deprofessionalize and use volunteers in order to reduce costs (Smith and Lipsky 1993). Clearly there are costs to clients in the reduced quality of service frequently accompanying deprofessionalization (Fabricant and Burghardt 1992; Fisher and Karger 1997). Of course, volunteers have always been essential to the voluntary sector and especially to settlement houses, but demands under contemporary contracting alter traditional relations with volunteers while at the same time jeopardizing the status of paid professionals. Increasingly, the social service private sector costs less because it treats its workers worse, both in terms of pay and worker power (Smith and Lipsky 1993; Karger and Stoesz 1998).[16]

Central to contracting are higher administrative costs resulting from public-sector monitoring (Wedel and Chess 1989). Moreover, contracts often demand that facilities meet specific standards, both in terms of quality and quantity. Despite these often challenging demands, contracts do not adequately finance the maintenance of physical and personnel infrastructure. As Husock (1992:68) writes, settlements increasingly have difficulty attracting funds "for what they call 'core support'—financial support for their central administration and non-categorical activities." Although new contracts may offer some "overhead," they are often unable to address many infrastructure needs of the past, let alone the present. The agency expands when contracts are increased, but even with overall budget growth, the agency may simultaneously experience infrastructural decay. Without adequate infrastructure, organizations cannot satisfactorily perform many of their tasks, and over time pressures mount for administrators and staff (Ghere 1981). This puts the organization in a downward spiral. The catch-up strategy of seeking fresh revenue streams often ends up making ever greater claims on the agency and is more likely, given the constraints and demands of the contracting system, to contribute to the continued decline rather than the strengthening of an agency's infrastructure (Smith and Lipsky 1993). As Sclar (2000:116–17) puts it, "one of the main characteristics of undercapitalization is the tendency of such firms to have chronic cash flow problems. They eagerly seek new business to mitigate this cash crisis. The problem of taking on more business than the organization can realistically absorb becomes manifest in poor service."

A major motive for government contracting is cost cutting, that is, lessening both the costs of government and those of social service delivery. One of nonprofit agencies' primary incentives for contracting is anticipated fiscal stabilization. Much of the literature, however, describes an erosion of agencies' financial solvency due to contracting structures and constraints. According to Kettner and Martin (1996a) 80 percent of respondents at contracting agencies reported that contracts do not cover the full costs of service provision. Despite this tendency toward financial instability, agencies continue to accept contracts in the hope of providing better services, meeting community needs, and reaching more clients. Revenue shortfalls occur frequently, causing serious service disruptions and reductions in service to clients. Gibelman (1995) concludes that the "transactional costs" built into the contracting process and forced upon agencies cancel the cost savings to funders that result from the standardization of contract financing. Of course, as with most aspects of contracting, insufficient funding hits small agencies the hardest. A study of nonprofit agencies in New York City concluded that smaller agencies, as compared to midsized and large agencies, spent a higher percentage of their own funds to support contracted government programs (Kramer 1981). In a case study of programs for the mentally retarded in Massachusetts, Regan (1998) comes to the related but much more devastating conclusion that contracting can result in nonprofit agencies experiencing bankruptcy and organizational failure.

Displaced Goals

Agencies seek opportunities for program expansion and financial stability, often ignoring, at their own peril, the contradictions associated with contracting revenue. For instance, embedded in the contracting relationship between government and nonprofits are conflicts over the goals of the funder and the goals of the service provider (Hardina 1991). While most organizations would deny it, service expansion is driven by contracting opportunities rather than by the agency's program development priorities or community needs (Gibelman 1995). According to Goss (1993), what once seemed like a high-minded and innovative voluntary sector now increasingly looks like grant-hungry agencies often out of touch with their constituencies and their own ideals.[17] More to the point, seizing opportunities available through contracts is not always consistent with an organization's mission or goals. Ultimately, contracts can undermine, and certainly alter, an agency's mission and goals. In Massachusetts, as Smith and Lipsky (1993) report, the Department of Pubic Health requirements for a modest program from the Center for Disease Control to sixteen rape crisis centers included hotlines, short-term counseling, preventative education, case management, information and referral, and interagency coordination with criminal, medical, and law enforcement communities. These programmatic demands pushed agencies into a formal care system and away from their original intention to be informal rape crisis centers. Such goal displacement is especially relevant to settlement houses. As noted in chapter 1, settlements increasingly function as multiservice centers delivering contracted programs. Consequently, they have less contact with specific neighborhoods and are more and more removed from their original ideals and practices of community building or community organizing.

Finally, programmatic demands emphasizing government requirements over community norms also promote goal displacement (McGovern 1989). Voluntary agencies increasingly become outer-directed, handling a myriad of programmatic opportunities and meeting service needs, but these programs and services do not necessarily evolve from the agency's own initiative or goals. Settlements may manage dozens of programs and contracts, none of which grounds them better in the community or helps build community cohesiveness. Given excessive accountability requirements, contracting imposes demands that can undermine the agency and its relationship to service users and community. For example, in a New York City settlement, separate funding streams for Head Start and day care "created a programmatic nightmare. Settlements operating both programs must have two kitchens, two cooks, two different food services and menus, two bookkeepers, two curricula, and two groups of teachers with different salaries and benefits, all to deliver services to children who are very similar in age, education, and family needs" (Marks 1993:25). Under such fiscal and administrative pressures, contracted voluntary agencies lose "their uniqueness" due to tensions over goals. Kramer (1985:378) proposes that "many voluntary agencies face an identity crisis as they and their counterparts have become more bureaucratic, professional, political, and entrepreneurial."

Obscured and Incorporated Political Processes

Contracting obscures the public sector's accountability in particular and undermines the public sector in general at the same time as it incorporates nonprofits into a highly political public-sector process. It undermines public accountability and responsibility by passing services from the public to the nonprofit sector and "trusting businesspeople, highly paid executives, and boards of directors to do what is best for all citizens" (Wagner 2000:134). The relationship between the public sector and service provision is also obscured. Private service provision establishes a buffer between citizens and the public sector, and despite the goodwill that often develops between service providers and clients, contracted social services with nonprofits do little to foster popular support for government services. The delivered services may be effective and competent, but citizens' experience does not translate into goodwill toward the public sector that financed them. Therefore, when government seeks public support for social services, the public may be indifferent at best, hostile at worst. In this way the obscured relationship between the public and private sectors, the buffered relationship that contracting establishes between citizen and state, reinforces the goals of privatizing and corporatizing public institutions and undermines the legitimacy of the public sector. As Simonsen and Robbins (2000:119) put it:

> The promoters of privatization, entrepreneurial government, and "downsizing" of services that touch large numbers of people, regardless of motive, may be eroding the financial support that makes the broadest functions of government possible. . . . As the types of services from which citizens can see results made manifest in their daily lives begin to be delivered privately, the functions that remain with government may be those that are the most difficult to explain and justify. Furthermore, moving individual services out of the government sphere might have real impacts on the ability of governments to pay for the collective services that remain . . . as general support for taxes may also erode

Paradoxically, although contracting undermines the public sector's legitimacy and significance, it simultaneously demands that nonprofits be active participants in the public-sector political process. Social service agencies seeking contracts must build relationships with public-sector officials. They become ever more enmeshed in a political system that, ironically, is prone to lobbying, pressure, waste, and fraud. New York City, for example, distributes almost 50 percent of its $5 billion in government contracts without a process of competitive bidding. Increasingly, as relationships develop between voluntary agencies and public-sector officials, contracts are susceptible to the same political pressures, inefficiencies, and excesses that public social services have been charged with (Gibelman 1995:2004). As Sclar (2000:69) notes, "most public contracting takes place in markets that range from no competition (monopoly) to minimal competition among very few firms (oligopoly)." Relatedly, political incorporation entails a shift in the role of the agency's administrator from day-to-day administration of the agency and contact with service delivery staff to increased involvement in public-sector affairs (Richter and Ozawa 1983).[18]

This increased political involvement, however, should not be confused with the social reform and social action efforts of the settlement house and other voluntary-sector social service agencies in prior eras. On the contrary, one of the central tenets of the neoconservative privatization strategy has been to undermine social action oppositional elements, both through delegitimation and defunding. The political incorporation of service agencies in the contracting system differs dramatically from the kind of advocacy and social action that once defined the settlement house. Political incorporation strengthens the clout of the organization, but it also restricts its broader advocacy (Manser 1974). Neoconservatives attacked service allocations in the past two decades not only to save costs and improve government efficiency but also to undermine social reform. The dismantling of Legal Aid, Community Action, and Aid to Families with Dependent Children not only cut public-sector costs but eliminated programs that supported activist groups or programs through which recipients were organizing opposition and making claims (Kramer 1985, Piven and Cloward 1971, 1977). Manser (1974:426–427) proposes his own "law" on the relationship between contracting and social action: "An agency's freedom and effectiveness in social action or advocacy are in inverse proportion to the amount of public money it receives. Some local agencies have admitted that they could not publicly expose the effects of a regressive public welfare policy because 80 percent of the budget comes from the county." Mollenkopf (1992) similarly reports that in New York City agencies have become more conservative under contracting. They are increasingly fearful of losing funding by simply associating with efforts that might challenge political incumbents. Political activity is likely to be more about agency survival, as a part of the funding process, than about fighting for the clients' benefit or struggling to advance a larger, more collective social action initiative.

Diminished Social Action and Community Building

The shift under contracting away from social action is especially troubling. Increasingly, contracting forces nonprofits into circumscribed, uniform approaches that undermine their role, or their potential role, as community-based social action organizations. Kramer (1985) argues that the essence of the nonprofit voluntary sector is its ability to engage in independent and militant voluntarism. For the settlement houses, contracting undermines their heritage of social activism and significantly weakens the "call to social action" in their contemporary work (Beck 1977; Hirota and Ferroussier-Davis 1998).

Contracting also undermines community-building practice. Community building, whether through clubs, recreational services, or communitywide events, has always been an essential component of settlement work. Settlements sought from the outset to build a sense of neighborhood identity and cohesiveness. Their view of society as an organic whole required the elements—inside and outside the neighborhood—to work together (Melvin 1987). They strove for "community embeddedness" (Hirota and Ferroussier-Davis 1998). Increasingly, however, under contracting the local focus of settlement houses has been reconfigured. Contracts are defined more frequently by categorical service programs such as Head Start or day care, not by neighborhood needs or community initiatives. Consequently, service delivery is more likely to extend beyond a specific neighborhood. Of course, reaching other citizens in need who live outside the neighborhood is a positive element. To the new approach's credit, under contracting locality is defined more inclusively, and services are delivered to a broader constituency. Conversely, however, contracting often undermines the very ties of the settlement house to a geographic place; their very identity as neighborhood institutions may therefore crumble. It is within this context that contracting pulls nonprofits away from an emphasis on community building. In this regard, Emily Marks, executive director of United Neighborhood Houses, comments that "In order to secure government and foundation support over the last 40 years, however, settlements have had to adjust to an increasingly fragmented and categorical funding environment. Aimed at ameliorating deficits, the structure of both public and private funding has limited opportunities to develop community-building approaches." (1998:i) Geographic community and even cultural community are assigned less importance within a fiscal environment that emphasizes a variety of categorical programs and a wide range of multiple service contracts. As a result, contracting undermines the ability of nonprofits, such as settlements, to build local social solidarity and to enhance a sense of community.

The Settlement House Under Contracting

The trends resulting from contracting that generally affect not-for-profit social services have also specifically impacted social settlements. This section shifts the focus of analysis from nonprofit social service agencies generally to community-based settlement houses in particular.

While some may consider the settlement house an artifact, the current thirty-seven houses in New York City deliver an impressive array of services to nearly 200,000 people annually. These services, as with the nonprofit sector in general, are heavily influenced by government funding. As Kraus and Chaudry (1995:34) put it: "Eighty-five percent of the funding for these activities comes from government. In too many instances, settlements have grown to resemble their funders—with specialized staff, organized by categorical programs, who often answer more to the rules and regulations of their funding agencies than to changing neighborhood conditions." Bertram Beck, head worker at Henry Street, saw these trends developing as early as 1975, when he wrote that settlement work today "is only a dim reflection of the social activism of the past" (1977:1265).

Themes developed earlier in this chapter for nonprofits are identified by Hirota and Ferroussier-Davis (1998:1) as applicable to the more specific experience of settlement houses. They note that:

A range of current social, political, and economic pressures have often undermined the connections between settlements and their neighborhoods, weakening the call to social action. . . . Perhaps most critical, settlements have become increasingly dependent on funding from public social service agencies, each with its own particular mandate. In order to survive economically, settlements have had to shift their

focus from the community to discrete groups of need residents, bu-
reaucratically defined.

In her earlier work Trolander (1987) concurs. She emphasizes the expanding availability of government contracts for direct service activities, such
as day care, but not for community organization or social action. Trolander
notes that when the Reagan-era programs were implemented, settlements,
which by that time depended on government programs for between 50 and
70 percent of their funding, experienced "devastating" cutbacks (Trolander
1987:230). The settlements that best survived the cuts were those that
adopted more mainstream social service programs and turned away from
social action and community building. They emerged as "individualized
agencies that are difficult to distinguish from a host of other varied agencies
that have no common settlement heritage" (241).

Loavenbruck and Keys (1987) also emphasize that Reagan-era rearrange-
ments in the voluntary sector were especially damaging to those settlements
committed to social action and community building. The contracting system
hurt small and midsize settlements interested in social action and community building more than it did the large ones like Henry Street and Hull-
House with annual budgets of over $7 million. As Loavenbruck and Keys
(1987:555) remark, resources shifted away "from neighborhood-development
social action programs toward such services as Head Start, the prevention of
adolescent pregnancy, job development for young adults, and services to the
elderly." Increasingly, funding tended "to follow the categories that receive
priority for governmental funding and to concentrate on services to specific
age groups: children, youths, adults, and the elderly. . . . Social action [is]
supported less now than in the 1960s and 1970s" (558).

More recently Smith (1995) reports a continuation of all these trends. By
1995 the successful settlements had become "large agencies run by professional staff and funded primarily though government grants . . . [which] provide an array of specialized services to clients who are identified by their
deficiencies: fragile elderly people, substance abusers, unruly youths, dys-
functional families, and mentally ill people" (2131). Today, he continues,
many settlements have become large multiservice nonprofits with multiple
contracts. "Their financial reports, audited annually, may exhibit up to 30
accounts related to separate sources that fund separate programs that require
separate reports" (2132). For example, a settlement may offer an array of
services under its contract programming umbrella, perhaps including a

Head Start program contract, food programs funded by the Department of Agriculture, a housing program financed by a New York City Community Development Block Grant, employment training underwritten by the Job Training and Partnership Act, services for the elderly supported by Title III of the Older Americans Act, gang prevention through New York City's Police Department, residential services funded by a county mental health program, and so forth (2132). This plethora of programs and directions makes contemporary settlements less able to address the needs of their communities and residents. Current categorical funding programs not only determine the settlements' direction, they also orient agencies to focus on individuals, families, and neighborhoods based on their deficiencies and service needs rather than on the basis of their capacities and need to organize. This is the antithesis of contemporary notions of community-building institutions.

Neoconservative developments in the 1990s pushed settlement houses and nonprofit social service agencies in general to a new contract relationship with national, state, and local government. With the Contract with America produced by the 1994 Congress the federal government symbolically emphasized the ongoing importance of contracting. Not only would nonprofit agencies contract with the public sector, but now the public sector would contract with citizens nationwide. Predictably, in the new privatized economy the Contract with America sought tax and social service cuts and the general dismantling of social welfare programs (Arenson 1995; Gimpel 1995). The "contract context" changed the world of POSCs as well. Under the older contracting system, nonprofits and settlement houses traded off professional autonomy and organizational independence for a degree of financial stability in an ever more fiscally unstable political and economic context (Dailey 1974). Under the new contract, engineered by House Republicans such as Newt Gingrich at the national level and Governor George Pataki and Mayor Rudolph Giuliani in New York, pressure on the nonprofit social service sector intensified (Gimpel 1995; Kiely 1995; *Business Week* editorial 1995; Smith 1998; Sites 1997; Tusiani 1995). Increasingly they were forced to sacrifice not only professional autonomy, but with the fiscal cutbacks and intensified economic pressures they were expected to endure less financial stability and greater demands for accountability.

These conditions were not unprecedented in the history of social settlements and nonprofits. The settlement house persisted in earlier historical periods when both independence declined and funding was volatile and

uncertain. Since the late 1960s the system of contracting has been characterized more by economic unpredictability than stability. But the draconian
cuts of the mid-1990s seemed even more threatening due to the fierce rhetoric for privatization and against social welfare services. This fiscal and political climate made it far more difficult for settlement houses to meet the
demands of funders, clients, and communities. These conditions also weakened community-building and community-organizing efforts at the same
time that the context of economic globalization and neoconservative policies
demonstrated the importance of such work for poor and decaying neighborhoods (Fisher 1994, Smith and Feagin 1987; Sandel 1988; Brecher and
Costello 1994).

Putnam (2000) underscores the importance of latent community-building
organizations like the settlement house as a political counterweight to the
contemporary decline of civil life and social cohesiveness.[19] What he fails
to realize, however, is the impact of the contracting and privatizing trends
on the organizational culture of settlements. To serve as counterweights settlements at the very least must have the space to innovate, attend to relationship building, and address collective as well as individual needs. Increasingly, however, agencies have been robbed by the contracting structure, the
resulting instability, and the uncertain levels of funding of any such
possibility.

In the 1980s and 1990s due to the heightened pressures of contracting
and the highly private nature of the larger context, community building and
organizing were not on the agenda for most settlement houses. Such policies
were simply outside the discourse and funding streams of the period. The
settlement houses that sustained a commitment to community building and
organizing encountered a very difficult environment in which to apply or
develop such work. By the mid-1990s, however, the pressures of providing
social services in poor communities in a privatized context pushed the more
progressive settlement houses in New York City to an increasingly vocal and
sharp critique of contracting (Marks 1998). Furthermore, the settlement
houses began to reconsider the importance and need for expanded community building and social action in their neighborhoods (Hirota, Brown,
Mollard, and Richman 1997; Hirota, Brown, and Martin 1998; Hirota and
Ferroussier-Davis 1998; Marks 1998). They began to respond to two decades
of being under siege.

The following five chapters (chapter 3 through 7) explore the conditions
and prospects of contemporary settlement work through the eyes and voices

of settlement staff. These qualitative findings offer a complex and often rich insight into settlement life. The workers provide a particularly compelling view of the intersection between contracting, the state of settlement services, and the project of community building. The systematic development of such a perspective helps to fill a critical void in the literature on contracting and social services. The pressures and challenges that will be identified as intrinsic to settlement life are increasingly familiar to most contemporary institutions. Finally, chapter 8, with an eye to the interconnection between the contemporary political economy and the importance of agency-based community building, outlines an alternative course for the settlement house and other community-based institutions.

Part 2

Contracting and Corporatized Social
Services: Voices from the Field

3   Fiscal Instability: Rewriting the Contract

The recent fiscal and political climate is experienced by settlement workers as increasingly volatile and hostile. Critical aspects of agency life have been affected by changes in the dollar value and structure of contracted social services. The reinvented and/or volatile fiscal relationship between the government and settlement house can have unanticipated outcomes that are not easily contained. Once unleashed, such changes can affect vital underpinnings of social services, including the relationship of the settlement workers to the delivery of service and that of the agency to the community. For settlement workers, the changing fortunes of their programs are not idiosyncratic or momentary but rather part of an extended and intensifying process of budget instability.

> We've had cuts all the time in day care. It's just a lot worse now than before, and I don't think the teachers realize the impact. Since I've been in day care, I think there was just one period of time about five years ago where we never worried about cuts or changes or anything else. (A8)[1]

> We've been experiencing cuts since 1979. The first cut was from NEH which is a part of NEA, the National Ethnic Heritage. They reduced our budget for the research and exhibit on the history of Latin music in NYC since the 1930s. In the 1980s we got cut when Reagan was

in office. His cuts were across the board and it dwindled down to the state and city level. And of course the beat goes on.   (G10)

This is the worst it has been in terms of economics impacting on social service delivery. . . . I lived through the cuts of the 70s and 80s but that was nothing compared to what we're looking at now. . . . We often say that we've been through a couple of world wars and the depression, we'll get through this. But there's a legitimate concern about our future, our ability to provide services.   (F7)

Environmental change can be a critically important trigger for the reinvention and strengthening of an organization. Whether in the marketplace or the not-for-profit sector, environmental turbulence can provoke changes that are perhaps initially wrenching, but will over time improve the work processes and products of the organization. Change can be a stimulant for innovation and growth. Such an outcome, however, is not assured. Environmental instability can also promote changes that harm organizations and their constituent groups. The abstraction of change may be neutral, but the intention of those unleashing it often is not. The second point is especially germane to this discussion.

The budget cuts were not generally perceived as a politically benign policy initiative. Instead, many respondents linked recent changes in the political climate to the public sector's disengagement from social services. It was repeatedly suggested that an increasingly conservative electorate, both less patient with and more hostile toward recipients of various government programs, elected many more representatives in the 1990s who reflected this mood. These elected officials initiated policies often described as part of a general political attack on the "poor and social services." Change then was at least initially characterized as part of a larger political agenda. The intent and implication of this most recent wave of change are described below:

You can throw your hands up and give up on all of it, or you can say there's a new reality, and this is what we're dealing with and we'll do the best we can within it. But the other piece of this is recognizing, and I think increasingly staff is recognizing, everybody is recognizing, that what we're dealing with is a totally changed political environment, and what are we doing about that is up for grabs.   (G2)

That's where we are politically right now. Politically, it seems to be the war on poverty has now changed to the war on the poor. So, you can eliminate poverty by getting to it at its source — just rid yourself of poor people. Maybe if you cut services enough, you can just rid yourself of poor people. They'll move to Connecticut or elsewhere. So, each state is competing to basically make life as difficult as they can for poor people with the hope that the problem will just go away. The problem is not going to go away, but it requires us on an agency level to realistically look at the political atmosphere we're in and to not bemoan our fate and just sit on our hands.   (D5)

Embedded in the volatility of agency contracts is a profound shift in commitment to a larger social contract. More to the point, the reconfiguration of contracts at the agency level reflects a wider discontent with social commitments financed by the state. For example, the understanding of social obligations regarding seniors, recent immigrants, the disabled, the homeless, and the ill is being redefined. Settlement workers repeatedly noted that the volatility inherent in agency contracts has critical consequences. As an agency's responsibilities are redefined, its capacity to meet historic contractual obligations is diminished. As a result, respondents suggested, specific members of the community become more vulnerable.

People are heartsick who have been doing this stuff for 30 and 40 years. Everything that's been built, and all the kids you've gotten to finish high school, and all of the kids maybe that you've kept out of real trouble, and sort of the fringes of trouble, what's going to happen to them now?   (E8)

It's the shift in social responsibility. It translates into cuts, dollars, saving money but how do you propose to not provide assistance to needy people or if someone on welfare has another child not providing additional funding. What are you saying about that child? Who takes care of those people being written off. . . . There has to be some sense of social responsibility, some compassion to help people who are less fortunate. . . . Will we abandon these people?   (F7)

We are seeing more and more difficulty here and I think in the whole country . . . taking someone for employment training who is not legal and documented. More restrictions, less services unless you have all proof of income and residence. Even for legal immigrants, more difficulty. Seems as though the public is less willing to help immigrants.

(A5)

The next sections of this chapter describes the unstable structure, process, and funding level(s) of contracted services. The present consequences and future threats of this unpredictable funding environment are also broadly considered.

The Volatile Agency Contract

The revision of agency contracts is a complex phenomenon. It is often most concretely experienced on the basis of the disruption it provokes. Such rupture represents both the unraveling of historic understandings between not-for-profit agencies and the state and the consequent discomfort of workers as they struggle to realign their practice with the stipulations of the new contract. At times, budget cuts have functioned as a powerful lever for contractual destabilization. Settlement houses in New York City have not been spared budget reductions during the last decade. They have experienced cuts, both modest and deep ones, in a variety of programs. Budget allocations have been affected both directly and indirectly. For instance, the state has directly reduced the dollars available to programs by changing grant amounts contractually allocated. At the same time, new forms of contracting, such as managed care, are indirectly altering funding allocations by intensifying competition between agencies for clients, reworking reimbursement schedules, and redefining eligibility as well as services. Although the level of funding is only one dimension of contractual volatility, it has a particularly powerful and unsettling impact on agency operations.

Funding equals service. If you don't have the money to provide services to the kids, then it all falls apart. If you don't have the money to implement, then the services can no longer be provided. So, it's been a 50 percent cut and then another 45 percent cut. We're talking about a survival budget at this point. (E6)

Before January we had these two cuts, about 2 percent across the board. . . . We were basically able to absorb that without having to lay off anyone. We just retracted certain other expenses like supplies and equipment and things . . . so it wasn't as devastating.   (B2)

We lost most of our tax levy money for the mental health program to be replaced by Medicaid patients. But we know because of the managed care scramble we are losing clients, we're getting less referrals, and we know there is going to be a dollar impact on our mental health programs.   (E7)

In the senior program we've taken it in the OTPS area, so we tried to cut back on the amount of food we give to the seniors.   (D4)

I know in the senior center, because they have a separate budget and for various reasons they were hit very hard, they went down a lot. Senior services, the largest budget around, maybe went down 10 percent or something. I'm not sure, but the senior center had a lot of big cuts so that their whole recreation program is gone.   (C6)

The arts and education program was severely affected. They did receive about a 35 percent cut. That money was from the city. The city wanted to cut the whole budget, but wasn't able to.   (I5)

The hours of home attendants are being reduced. At the same time we're seeing that the overall budget of our home attendants program is being reduced dramatically. We had a nine-million-dollar budget a year ago. This past year, it was closer to eight million, and it was based on fewer hours being approved for the clients to have home attendant services.   (J3)

Social service programs in settlement houses have not experienced uniform budget cuts. A substantial number of respondents indicated that their funding levels remained fixed. Funds allocated to such programs were either modestly raised for cost-of-living increases or remained stagnant. Yet, standstill budgets were consistently described as producing losses. The cost of phones, rent, fuel, and food are not fixed but subject to increases. Clearly, vendors will not hold their prices constant on the basis of state policy. Viewed from the outside, fixed budgets suggest stability, but in actuality they represent another source of fiscal strain. This incongruity was remarked upon by settlement administrators:

INTERVIEWER: Can you give me an example of how, when the budget is not increased, you lose?

RESPONDENT: They put the same amount of money in my OTPS, personnel and facility costs. Of course, when you get the same money, you get less. The prices for many things are a little bit increased, and so you have to buy less or raise dollars elsewhere. It just puts more pressure on the program.   (A3)

With the senior center, I wouldn't say we've experienced cuts, but our budget hasn't gone up either. No one seems to consider what costs we have to contend with. We have increased costs of food and household supplies. That has had an impact upon us. What we may have been able to do before with $9,000–$10,000, now may take $11,000. You can't get as much now for your money.   (B4)

At the other end of the spectrum were programs able to implement ambitious plans for expansion. In general, these agency initiatives were underwritten by a reallocation rather than expansion of public resources. For instance, one settlement house was able to significantly expand its homeless services unit by accepting contractual responsibility for a men's shelter that had previously been run by the city's homeless services agency. In another instance, responsibility for a program was shifted from one agency to another because of the failure of the initial provider to meet its contractual obligations. Reallocation of funding for social services rather than increases in the larger funding pie generally provided the basis for budget expansion.

Last year the day care programs all went up for bid. While we were bidding for our contract, we bid on the Morningside facility as well. We won that, which has been a major undertaking. That's a 160-children day care service on 120th street that had been basically unloved for a long time and nearly run down to nothing.   (D10)

There was a day care program on site here that was run by another
not-for-profit. We decided when the lease was up that we were going
to sponsor it ourselves. So, we got the contract with ACD which added
$577,000—it's a new contract. Then we successfully competed for the
contract to run the Park Avenue Armory for homeless women. That's
a big contract that's going to be a $2.1 million contract. So by adding
these two programs we've expanded our budget substantially.   (E1)

Program expansions underwritten by increased public dollars, although
scarce, also occurred. For instance, a recently completed supportive housing
project expanded service options for the chronically mentally ill.

Well, in the mental health area it's kind of crazy. At the same time
you're talking about all of this hardship and have to plan to balance
the budget, we're also in the middle of expansion. We just started a
supportive housing program for chronic mental illness. It's the first
project of its kind I think on the East Coast for Asians.   (A1)

In general, the funding of settlement programs is seen as at risk. As contracts are rewritten, the public sector, although not abandoning social services, is more restrictive in its financing. These changes have taken a variety
of forms. As noted earlier, entitlement programs, such as Medicaid, have
spending caps and stricter eligibility requirements. These new conditions
for financing have substantial implications. Historic levels of funding are no
longer assured. Additionally, as the reimbursement schedule for Medicaid
changes, so too does the agency's capacity to provide its historic level and
type of service. Program grant contracting between the state and not-for-
profits is also being reconfigured. Government program grants obligate agencies to provide specific services to, for example, homeless people, seniors,
or the mentally ill, but increasingly definitions of eligibility, funding levels
for discrete units of service, timetables for initiation and conclusion of service
cycles, and the type of service covered by such agreements are more limited.
Narrowed definitions of service can contribute to a diminished funding base.
It is important to note that such budget reductions are not a consequence
of direct cuts to programs or agencies. Rather, new contract structures may
simply make it increasingly difficult to sustain historic levels of funding by
reducing the revenue-producing capacity of specific services and clients. The
indirect cuts associated with contract restructuring, however, have indepen-

dently and subtly contributed to the destabilization of specific programs. The rapidity and intensity of this change has left a variety of programs facing budget deficits.

It was also unclear with certain changes how you get reimbursed for senior services that you do not provide directly. These services are called holds. . . . Part of what's happening as a result is we're running at a budget deficit. (J3)

Because of the change in the way ACD [Agency for Child Development] is doing its contracts and vouchers and is just focusing on preschool services, I am looking at a very serious reinventing of the services for the fall. . . . I don't know what the shortfall will be, but I suspect it will be over $500,000. (C1)

This year, we are looking at a net deficit. The state reduced our contract because they said we could make it up with Medicaid dollars. These cuts occurred two years ago. At that time, managed care was just coming onto the scene. . . . It seemed with our case load we could make up the deficit with Medicaid patients. But now, two years later, Medicaid patients are the crème de la crème of private hospitals who in the past never wanted to deal with these patients. Now, they want to hang on to them as long as they can. . . . But this whole thing with contract changes is a very serious question. Right now we're $250,000 short. There's a point where you become totally dysfunctional. So it's serious. (H8)

Clearly one factor promoting organizational instability is the contraction of service funding. The fault lines of agency instability, however, are complex and not simply caused by the aftershocks of a diminished budget. More important, once dollars are allocated and a budget is calculated, there may not be sufficient assurance that the numbers are stable. If understanding is constantly fluid and subject to ongoing renegotiation, the reverberation in programs can be substantial. Patterns of staffing, job protection, and continuity of service are but a few of the aspects of agency operation that may be placed in constant jeopardy. Vulnerability to changes in operating budgets creates strains of instability regardless of the direction of the reworked allocation. For instance, cuts may be enacted and the dollars may later be restored; yet, the program will be affected by this often abrupt recycling of allocation. The most striking examples of cuts, restoration, and subsequent unpredictability of programs occurred in the area of youth services.

> For some staff these shifts are taking place constantly. One day they think they've lost their jobs or they're being reduced, and the next day they're restored or we've shifted them to a mixture of different jobs. Later though the money is restored, restored in the greater mix. . . . It's hard. If I were a youth worker, I would want to cry. For a kid experiencing the paper-clip, scotch-tape nature of things, desperately in need of a steady staff and a feeling that somewhere in their lives there is a safe solid place, it's got to be awful.   (G3)

> Last year, they cut it, then put it back, took some money out then put it back.   (I2)

> They said we were going to get a 100 percent cut . . . then they said we were going to get an 80 percent restoration. . . . Then they said a 70 percent restoration . . . then they said we're waiting for the letter . . . we're waiting for the letter . . . and who's got the letter. . . . And when is it coming?   (D2)

Critical to the stability of programs is the opportunity to plan for change. Short notice regarding contract changes can also have a disruptive effect on agency operations. Rapid unanticipated shifts in a budget, although rare, can produce a frenzied planning environment that is intensely focused on the crisis of a critical gap between revenue and expenses. This is draining and distracting. Unanticipated budget crises further erode confidence in the predictability of the contracting environment.

> I've said several times that one of the hardest things about the cuts was the way they came down. If they had said phase out your programs over the next three months completely, in a way, that would have been easier to process. There's this feeling that they are going to slam us again.   (C8)

> Last December they came down with a midyear budget modification, that for us was the most severe because we were not prepared. We had

no advance time to think about how we would handle losing basically half our funds because we were halfway through the year and basically lost half of what was left for the rest of the year. And so, we faced immediate closure of programs and a layoff of an enormous number of staff. We put a plan together very quickly. Our operating philosophy, however, was to keep as many programs open albeit in a skeletal fashion, because we hoped we would be able to build these programs back again at some point.   (E5)

We got a small contract, about $15,000, to do housing counseling and landlord rental assistance—which is actually our only public money for that . . . it's hard, tenant organizing. We also got a letter that our funds were being cut by $10,000 the next day.   (C12)

The rhythm of resource disbursement by the state also affects the equilibrium of a program. Settlement workers reported that state contractors often fail to disburse dollars in a timely manner. Consequently, the cash flow of programs is disrupted, and the capacity to meet payroll and pay vendors is jeopardized. Over time, delay in payment has a ripple effect. It undermines the legitimacy of an agency by destabilizing its relationships with key stakeholders. Equally important, agencies may be forced to borrow dollars from one program to stabilize another while waiting for funds. One contradictory consequence of such borrowing is that it stabilizes specific programs while spreading financial exposure or risk across the agency as a whole. Like the service user, the agency is more frequently placed in the situation of having to make short-range planning decisions that may erode long-term solvency.

We've had situations of cash-flow breakdowns because of late reimbursement. It's been serious, I mean very bad. It's the worst I've experienced, and I've been here since 1978. I've had to juggle the budget for months. This has not let up since December. Increasingly you are losing a quarter of the year and there is no way to make up for those dollars.   (C1)

Cash flow has been very difficult to deal with. For every one of our city contracts, they are still paying us for our last one. So what happens is the administrative staff on several occasions has had to wait for checks until Monday, payroll is on Thursday. This is not great for people's morale.   (D1)

The issue is the state puts a hold on our money and it just sits there. We're supposed to get a check every month but they hold it 21–25 days before they release it. When I don't get the cash in here, and then I have to borrow, and maybe day care will get their check but I won't get mine. And we have to borrow from each other until we meet payroll. All of this borrowing can get a bit dicey.   (B4)

Reimbursement from the state and city has gotten worse and worse. There have been times where, because we are a small agency, we have to borrow to meet payroll. Eventually we get the money, but a lot of the time, eventually is just not good enough.   (J3)

During a period of rapid change in public contracting, to whom can social service agency personnel turn for clarification of new rules or for help with disrupted funding? The answer to this question may be especially elusive in a context of reconstituted funding agencies, contracting rules, and funding streams. Yet often various kinds of information must be obtained before an agency can understand the reason for or develop a response to a funding disruption. The experience of trying to understand the decision making of contracting agencies can be especially daunting. Such difficulties were most frequently cited by respondents working with managed care companies and the New York City Agency for Child Development.

INTERVIEWER: So how are you notified about changes?
RESPONDENT: We are not! I find out people are gone when I call for something. That's when I learn she is no longer there. So I ask who is taking her place? No memos are sent. I get things from other sources but nothing from 30 Main Street. Nothing from them, other than the specific forms they need filled out.   (I7)

If you were having a problem you could always say why you're not doing A, B, C—you had an explanation and the funding source evaluated the situation and if necessary got you some kind of help. Now, the role of OMH [Office of Mental Health] and the city is diminished, and the managed care companies and their insurance companies control more and more of the funding. Right now, it's not always clear who we can turn to for help in those companies when things are unclear or break down.   (F7)

This destabilization and/or reduction of public contracts clearly says to agencies that revenue stability can only be achieved if they locate alternate sources of funding. Historically, a principal source of revenue for settlements has been private patronage and gifts from foundations. Although such revenue continues to support specific activities of the settlements, proportionately it represents less and less of an agency's total budget. For instance, of the ten settlements participating in this study, nine reported that 75 percent or more of their total budget was derived from public-sector contracts. The degree of reliance on government dollars highlights the movement of settlement houses away from their original fiscal dependence on private funding. Currently, the shifting political and fiscal environment is an incentive for settlements to aggressively seek ways to redress their public and private revenue imbalance. However, settlement program administrators and executive directors indicate that private dollars, although increasingly critical to agency operations, are unlikely to be dramatically increased. This perspective is more fully elaborated below:

> So often you hear that as government funds are cut, the private sector should pick it up. Well, it doesn't work that way. The private sector is not a bottomless pit and you get increased competition between not-for-profits with diminished resources.   (F8)

> INTERVIEWER: So you lost about a half a million dollars from DYS [State-Division for Youth Services] and city money? How much additional money were you able to raise from private sources?
> RESPONDENT: Maybe half of that. It is not covering the gap created by that loss.   (B5)

Despite the changes in the funding pattern, many respondents suggested that their worst fears had not come to pass. The threat of draconian cuts to social service programs created expectations of immediate disaster. During the course of the public battles over social services, settlement administrators were subject to media and private reports that deep cuts would be made to service programs as disparate as mental health, substance abuse, homelessness, and youth services. Republicans in Washington, D.C., attempted to implement the Contract with America, which promised to dismantle large parts of the welfare state. Additionally, the mayor of New York City, Rudy Giuliani, offered proposals that threatened the funding base of youth services and questioned the rationale for services to the homeless. The heated rhetoric of budget cuts was part of the ongoing drama of negotiation between political adversaries. The scope of the threat was almost without exception substantially moderated during extended political bartering. However, the specter of dramatic program rollbacks gave rise to an anxiety that turned to relief when modest reductions or standstill budgets were announced. In some sense, the sting of incremental yet intensifying funding difficulty was readily accepted as a modest inconvenience when contrasted with what might have been. The political climate and its anticipated impact was a powerful agent in accustoming settlement workers to the increasingly tenuous state of contracted services.

> I think we were a little nervous about our mental health contracts and luckily that played out O.K. and we were not hit with any reductions. . . . I think it was more the tone of uncertainty that prevailed. . . . Our after-school program did suffer a 3 percent cut. The big thing though was the uncertainty. The funding agency just could not tell us anything. They had no idea how it was going to play out and that was the scariest thing. It was not like there was a set policy on how it was going to happen. It was week-to-week and day-to-day. You would call up the agencies and ask where it's going to be cut, how it's going to be cut, is it going to be across the board or targeted to specific agencies and get little information. So, it was hard to know. But, for now we're O.K. It wasn't as bad as it might have been.   (A6)

> We were threatened with not only cuts but a total elimination of the program this spring. But thank God, Congress did not vote for that!
>
> (D2)

The Uncertainty of Future Funding

The reprieve is perceived as momentary. The threat to agency funding is consistently described in both present and future tense. However, it is the future that seems most uncertain and often occupies so much of the emotional attention of respondents. For many there is a clear sense that the worst has not yet come to pass. The public and political debate about the future of social services continues. This future uncertainty has powerful implications for the present lived experience of workers. Workers are not only required to engage the present but also a potentially unstable future in organizing and handling their daily work. The backdrop of political hostility to social services and the channeling of such sentiment into proposals that restrict funding create, to some extent, an organizational culture of diminished expectations.

In the recent past, when the federal government planned specific budget reductions, the state and city were often prepared to absorb some part of the shortfall. The local political culture in New York City and New York State was more favorably disposed to social services and consequently provided a modest buffer against federal policy. These levels of government helped to stabilize the flow of specific revenues and the integrity of a contract. Currently, the fiscal threat is not restricted to one level of government. Instead, settlement workers suggest that proposals for future cutbacks are surfacing at every level of government. Consequently, the prospect of respite in the near future appears unlikely. This deepening threat to future services is described in the following passages.

> We've managed to maintain the outlook, the commitment. The agency has been here a hundred years. It is my guess, it will ride through it, but it will be very difficult. In the past a place like this could weather the storm because it had many different programs. If child care was down, mental health was up. Now though everything seems to be hit. And not only that, if the federal government was down, the state or city was up. Now you have the rare uniformity and absence of commitment. We're being hit by Gingrich, Pataki, and Giuliani. So it's pervasive. (G10)

> I think it's this sort of depressing feeling. Most of the people I know feel this way. The idea is it is going to get worse. You don't think it's going to get better. What we're imagining is that there's going to be an across-the-board decrease in services across the board for all sorts of people and all sorts of problems. (G7)

It's like when it hits, I'll deal with it. But you know it's out there, the new cuts, and it affects the way we work. Right now, though, I have to struggle to just deal with day-to-day survival for some of my programs. I can't help it. I'm saying hello, hello, do you see the brush fire here? There's an unreal quality and I know it . . . but until the other cuts are in my face, I'm not going to get ready. Yet it's always back there, in my mind. If I think about it too much, it could create hysteria. At times I can't believe it, I can't believe it. This is serious.   (F2)

Anticipated funding difficulties are not simply understood as a hostile ideological response to social services. They were also linked to changes in how the state pays for social services. For instance, respondents described managed care companies as real and prospective brokers in the areas of health, mental health, and foster care services. These for-profit companies were perceived as planning a substantial restructuring of the conditions and rates of reimbursement for services. This reworking of contracts was expected to have a substantial impact on the practices and revenue of many programs.

Moreover, the federal government's devolution of fiscal responsibility for various categories of social services to the states through block grants is proving, in the opinion of those interviewed, a threat to many programs. Respondents anticipated that the allocation of all federal social service dollars through block grants would result in a more highly politicized process. Monies previously restricted to social services become, at least hypothetically, available for other forms of state and municipal services, such as fire fighting and police. The temptation to fill local budget gaps and fund more popular services with these federal dollars is, at the very least, a source of concern.

Various entitlement programs, such as Medicaid, that provided part of the bedrock of settlement funding are also being restructured. Some of these changes interact dynamically with the ascent of managed care companies. Some respondents suggested, for instance, that Medicaid clients could be expected to locate a managed care umbrella company in order to access services. Consequently, historic relationships between clients and agency would at the very least be less stable. Based on current policy discussions, many respondents also feared that the financing of Medicaid would be capped. Such caps might reduce either the rate of reimbursement or simply limit specific programs' capacity to bill for services once the national cap was exceeded. In either case, the flow of dollars would be threatened.

At the local and state levels, policy discussions are also underway to re-structure various service contracts. For instance, the City of New York is increasingly intent upon imposing ever more restrictive eligibility require-ments for sheltering the homeless. New standards of service provision for employment training and developmental disability programs are also being discussed. This public policy discussion seemed to encircle settlements and offered few prospects in the near future for stable or sufficient funding. Respondents suspected that the tightening vise of proposed changes might squeeze and eventually break many settlement programs.

> I think the prevailing attitude in the agency is to wait for the shoe to drop and to try to improve the internal operations as much as possible. Most of our work is going to come down to marketing our services to HMOs and things of that sort. We're really trying to figure out what we're going to do with Block grants, welfare reform and managed care.
> (G4)

> Managed care is moving more and more into health care. Arguably, they're going to take a lot of our clientele away from us. We will be forced to downsize and reduce staff. Clients will continue to go else-where. By the time things settle out, we may be hanging by a slender thread. (G6)

> So what's the scenario? A widespread rate reduction in Medicare would be catastrophic, and that's what I think they're talking about doing. It's really the only way you could do it, the state's proposal is not to have a rate reduction but a block grant, here they would supply the city with 25 percent less money. . . . You can't say that we will serve x number of people and no more, because then a person who becomes ill wouldn't have any access. Likely the way they'll do it is to pay less per person and hope that stretches out. If they impose that kind of 25 percent reduction it's doomsday. (D2)

> I think, in the long run block grants will be a disaster. Maybe not in the long run, maybe even sooner in the short run, because if the money goes to the localities, you're going to get local pressures as to

how to divvy up the money. I can envision the Giuliani administration taking the money to balance the budget and cut services.   (F7)

The contracts with the state and city are also changing. You know, employ so many people or we'll cut your funding. It is, of course, one thing to teach students to get them ready for employment. It's another thing to tie the contract to employment rates. It's one thing to try, it's another to be held accountable to actually get people jobs. We know we're supposed to get students jobs and we try, but it's hard out there. They haven't said yet what they'll do to us if we don't place them. But they are saying, if you accept these students you are expected to find them employment.   (C6)

Based on my meeting today, to maintain our present funding level a lot of overall improvement will be needed. DFTA [Department for the Aged] is changing their assessment tool, and it's going to be on a point system and standard compliance will need to be met to trigger funding. So we'll see how it works out.   (A6)

As fee-for-service structures are being reinvented, especially in health care, there is both the expectation and reality of heightened competition for clients. They are viewed as a precious and scarce commodity. For instance, the Medicaid-eligible poor are increasingly considered attractive to out-patient mental health clinics in hospitals because of changes in the land-scape of funding. Insured clients at the very least provide a relatively stable source of income. On the other hand, program grants/contracts are both less stable and less available.

Settlements, however, are likely to be increasingly dependent on HMOs for referrals. These companies are selecting clients into programs on the basis of a number of criteria, perhaps the most critical of which is relative cost. Smaller agencies may be less able to compete with larger, established hospitals and other clinics for such clients because of economies of scale. Agencies may also experience reduced caseloads and/or referrals because they do not have the political capacity to influence the HMOs' decision making. No matter what the explanation is, the suggested outcome is clear: low referral rates will translate into reduced caseloads and revenues. Increasingly, agencies find themselves in the position of having to ratchet up the intensity of competition for insured, revenue-producing clients. Conversely, uninsured clients are less and less attractive to agencies and programs. Settlement programs, however, may become a refuge of last resort for the uninsured. To maintain the historic commitment to this population clearly will further strain already overtaxed resources.

> At our last meeting they told us our bottom line was the same, but they were reducing our city contract by $325,000. So now all we have on our city mental health contract is $425,000. All the rest has to be generated. Some of the bigger houses might say what's the big deal. They would say we've been generating 90 percent of our mental health budget from income. But they have a different population. Their population is heavily Medicaid, ours isn't. What are we going to do? I don't know. How do we continue to provide services to people in need in this community when we are going to be so strapped? (A10)

> More and more Medicaid patients are the crème de la crème of private hospitals who never wanted to deal with these patients and are now holding on to them.   (H8)

> Other agencies are hungry for the same number of patients too. Everybody is signing on to the managed care bandwagon, everybody wants Medicaid patients, so it becomes a scavenger hunt.   (E1)

> Well, I think the whole issue is really a kind of life-and-death issue. A lot of people are not sure that community mental health clinics will have any part to play in this thing. We're signing up with some of the big providers, but it's not clear whether even when we sign up, that they're going to send us any referrals. A lot of us are feeling that, in the coming years, places like this clinic may just go out of business.   (I7)

Fiscal Instability as a Defining Feature of the Settlement Experience

For many, the present round of cuts represents a stage in a continuous and deepening disinvestment in social services. Those respondents whose experience goes back the farthest in history recounted episodic periods of substantial cuts over approximately the last twenty-five years. The impact of these cuts was softened for some programs as parts of the excised budget were restored or replaced. However, what remained constant was the sense that fiscal threat and budget instability were chronic and intensifying features of social service programs. Despite partial replacement and restoration of funding, the long-term trend was perceived as posing a growing challenge to the fiscal stability and viability of many programs. This is a critical point. The present instability of social service programs cannot be simply or entirely ascribed to the most recent political or policy changes. If that were the case, such changes might be interpreted as anomalous and unlikely to deeply penetrate the culture of the settlement house. They would emerge and pass as discontinuous fragments that do not have a cumulative, historic impact on the work of settlement houses. What respondents consistently noted, however, was that the present threat, although perhaps more dramatic than earlier ones, was historically consistent. The volatility of social service financing is embedded not in any single moment of policy decision making but rather in a historic web of intensifying constraint and instability. For some, past efforts to protect and stabilize programs have been depleting, and consequently the agencies' capacity to respond to present threats is diminished.

We're really creative in responding to funding changes in our housing department. I've been here nine years or since I was an intern, and I have to say we started to get hit with cuts from the very beginning. So from the very beginning when I walked in here I was used to this kind of environment and not having stable funding. It's getting harder and harder to keep things going though. You go back, move things around, and try to maintain service. And keep a vision of why certain positions and services are important.   (C12)

So far we've been doing OK with the most recent cuts, but as I say to people, we've been reeling since the fiscal crisis of 76. We've been reeling from it ever since, reeling. It's hard to function. . . . We're always skating right on the edge.   (G4)

I think it's the awareness, the awareness that these are more serious times. I have been in the field of aging for more than a decade, and I know that I've seen cuts in my previous jobs at two other settlements. There has always been a time in my experience that people had to organize, take an active role because senior centers were in some kind of danger. That hasn't changed, it's been accentuated. For those of us that are service providers—we know that it is a reality at all levels.   (G9)

The energized advocacy I felt in the 70s and 80s when we were threatened with cuts, I guess I don't feel as intensely anymore. I'm trying to pull it up but it does get harder and harder. I've asked myself, I've asked others what is the difference? Maybe it's simply because we were all younger. I've been around a long time and I'm getting a little tired.
                                                                          (J1)

Over time, the workers in settlement houses become accustomed to fiscal instability as a defining feature of social service work. Consequently, they are forced to invent practices that are increasingly predicated on both the reality and threat of various kinds of funding ruptures. The workers are expected to sustain services, to hold the pieces together, as the fiscal underpinnings of program are loosened. Many respondents feared that at some point this continuous, intensifying upheaval will reach the point of threatening the very legitimacy and future of social service work.

All of these cutbacks, changes are not good for growing things, growing children. It's like tearing up the streets. You can get groups to go out and watch as they tear up those streets. But what about rebuilding the streets, paving them, making them more useful after they've been torn up? Here it seems year after year we are tearing down programs but with no idea, or maybe it's interest, in rebuilding. It feels at times like a psycho ward, out of control with no direction. Yet we're supposed to hold it together keep the services in place. I don't know if we're prepared to handle the magnitude of the changes that are coming at us. But after a while you are not surprised by anything. In the meantime we just do the best we can with these kids.   (D9)

Every year it gets a little worse. We're faced with the threat of senior citizen centers being closed down but we survive and have to make do with a little less. But it creates a disagreeable work situation. We try to continue to provide services as we have in the past, but it just isn't possible. Plus our particular project and the building is a little older than most, but we can't get it rehabilitated.. . .After a while you have to ask why would a senior citizen want to come down here and spend the day here.   (D4)

4 Infrastructural Decline

    The delivery of social services is often influenced by factors that largely stand outside the human dynamics of such encounters. An array of basic organizational supports, such as secretaries, physical space, and technical equipment, directly and indirectly influence the quality of the exchange between worker and service user. Yet these supports, though vital to the creation of robust social services, are often overlooked or devalued because of the difficulty in teasing out their specific contribution to those who are delivering or receiving services. In addition, because such support is at least one step removed from the front line of service delivery, it is less obviously connected to the day-to-day work of creating and providing social services.

    In general, the strength of an organization's infrastructure will either inhibit or expedite the work of its personnel. For instance, the availability of computers, secretaries, and photocopying machines can affect both the development and timely completion of a proposal for funding. Moreover, continuity of supervision is likely to impact the staff's relationship to the authority structure of the organization. Over time, the strength of an organization's infrastructure may affect not only the volume and quality of work but also the staff's assessment of the agency's legitimacy. To the extent that the organization is unable to provide key supports, the relationship between staff and agency may be weakened. The greater difficulties in completing tasks and achieving specific objectives because of breakdowns in the infrastructure are often concretely understood as failures of the organization. For settlements, funding instability and reduction has had an especially powerful impact on the kind of infrastructural support they can lend to staff. This chapter will explore the consequences of present patterns of infrastructural financing on administrative, program, and physical plant supports often essential to the delivery of social services.

Infrastructural Financing of Settlements

For social service agencies infrastructural supports are financed through specific budget items such as administrative overhead and the "other than personnel services" category more generally known as OTPS. The level of financing for OTPS costs varies. According to respondents, the percentage of contract costs that could be charged to OTPS differed by program type and auspice of financing (federal, local, etc.). Charges ranged from 8 percent to 17 percent of the total contract. Administrative overhead was pegged at about 10 percent of the contract. However, the ripple effect of budget cuts on infrastructural capacity remained constant.

The overhead costs built into service contracts continue to finance critical operations of both the central office of an agency and the particular program. As budget cuts were absorbed, however, there was a dual impact on the infrastructure of agencies and programs. The reduction of program budgets created a potential downward spiral in the relationship between program and agency. The agency became increasingly vulnerable to the perception that it was less and less capable of meeting specific program needs while it continued to absorb a substantial share of its overhead budget.

> Each department supports the underbelly of the settlement. If I lose $350,000, the administrative services that support this agency are going to lose $100,000. That's bodies, personnel that service the settlement. It will eventually hit everybody, my program, other people's programs, and the central office.   (H8)

> I'm fed up. The contributions of the central office to our program are minimal. Of the 8 to 9 million dollars we get for our substance abuse programs about 800,000 dollars goes to the House for overhead. If we get another cut, that would be a good place to pass it on to. At this point we're getting less and less return on our money.   (G5)

The impact of budget cuts on agencies' infrastructure was compounded by an often powerful pull to preserve personnel to deliver direct services. Administrative decision making regarding distribution of scarce resources consistently emphasized direct services at the expense of infrastructural support. Consequently, the portion of the reduced resource pie that was allocated to infrastructure became smaller and smaller. The results and implications of such trade-offs are described in the following passages.

> Government contracts, of course, have the expectation that we're just going to be able to do more and more with less and less. We had always accommodated that sort of perception by stripping OTPs items from our budgets as we were faced with cuts. We kept everything in personnel so that running the quality program was, you know, paramount. What effect that had, of course, is that we are really running those good programs off of the backs of staff people who don't have the tools or support they need. The tools and resources of OTPS just weren't there.   (A1)

> The cuts have really affected us. In order to protect at least the basic salary and service staff, we have lost almost all of the OTPs.   (H6)

> With the cuts if anything goes, it will be administrative overhead costs. . . . If you have to make choices, the last choice will be to fire the line staff because in essence, they generate billable business, we can at least recoup part of the costs. It's easier to fire a supervisor than a line worker.   (G5)

The strain on infrastructure, however, is not simply a consequence of recent budget cuts and resulting trade-offs. Budget cuts have simply exacerbated a long-standing problem. For many agencies and programs the percentage of a contract allocated to infrastructural functions has simply been insufficient. To contain costs social service contracts systematically fail to acknowledge and to pay adequately for the array of supports necessary to provide services. In a sense, part of the cost of doing business with the government is the deficit structured into each service contract. The agency then has to make a choice between locating additional resources to subsidize a specific contract and reducing the array of supports available to a program.

The quandary for the agency is that each contract thus may contribute to a spiral of decline in services and increased demands for fund-raising.

> Well, we're going to have to increase our private giving. We're going to need to find ways to generate additional revenue. What a number of settlements have done over the years to remain solvent is to try to get large contracts with 8 percent to 8.5 percent overhead built in, which by the way is down from 10.5 percent. It's getting more difficult to meet overhead with those percentages, but it was never easy. Clearly with that overhead, for instance, on a 2.3 million contract you can meet a large part of central office expenses. But it never meets the full cost of running a program. So that's why we have to find other funding, private funding, to support parts of the cost of providing services.   (E1)

> We're talking about my budget needing more of an overhead percentage to have this building, to do the maintenance, utilities, and so on. But I can't get what I need on my contracts. For instance, in our contracts we get 10 percent for administration. Well, that just doesn't cover it. You're supposed to include accounting, fiscal—10 percent just isn't that much. The city says we can't go over 25 percent between administration and OTPs, but the costs put us over 30 percent.   (I2)

> We're always trying to fill the gaps on our contracts. And you kind of know that's exactly what the city wants you to do. It's sort of like they say you can do it with less because you care about the people. But there's a responsibility.   (A6)

Contraction of Administrative Support

At least part of the squeeze on overhead costs has been absorbed by administrators. As was suggested, personnel delivering direct services were spared cutbacks whenever possible during budget decision making. Middle management, however, was particularly vulnerable in programs that provide mental health services because it does not directly contribute to billable hours or revenue. Equally important, administrators are considered a relatively expensive cadre of workers. In a period of diminished resources and harder choices, the relative value of workers is weighed on the basis of concrete criteria associated with the agency's and the program's immediate bottom line. Consequently, administrative functions and personnel become relatively expendable. The choice to downsize the administrative workforce of settlements primarily targeted program rather than central office managers.

Moreover, many respondents consider administrative salaries insufficient or noncompetitive. Consequently, agencies and programs find they have to hire personnel who may be less able to meet specific job demands. In sum, the administrative support role is compromised by the loss of line positions and skill. The erosion of administrative oversight is illustrated in the following passages.

It has affected us in terms of the fact that in 1994 we had a full-time manager and assistant manager. In 1995, after our assistant manager resigned, we never filled the slot for two reasons. We did not have sufficient income to pay the salary, and two, people who were applying for the job, the ones that were qualified, were looking for very large salaries in comparison to what we could afford.   (C7)

Basically, they've been cutting middle management. Basically they had bigger salaries, and we're easier to let go.   (F9)

Youth services hasn't had a youth director in two years.   (A2)

My program, which was community services, was stripped down. The whole middle management throughout the agency that was here was encouraged to leave. Some people were promoted but others were asked to leave as programs were consolidated and middle management was reduced.   (D9)

Even when we hire new administrators, it's for less money, and we're not getting the kinds of commitment or skill that we've gotten in the past. We tend to hire people who are not up to speed on some things, and it is a growing problem. We just lost our MIS person, we are mourning his loss. The problem is we have new demands and have to update our clinical management system, which may have been state-of-the-art twenty years ago but is antiquated now. But unless we can attract someone at least as competent, which I doubt, it's just not going to happen.   (G4)

Programs in day care, youth services, homelessness, and mental health were described as less and less able to provide the kinds of administrative support that help direct delivery of services. The expertise, validation, and critique of supervision, which in the past was central to the development of line workers and to social services as a whole, is less and less evident in the day-to-day operations of many programs. The gaps in and increased demands on administrative support have eroded such relationships.

Because I'm overextended, I don't feel I can support them in the way I would like to or have in the past. I don't have the time to tend to their needs. Psychologically, they have so many needs, but I just can't take the time to provide ongoing support.   (H2)

We've lost supervision time, which is staff development time, so you lose staff development. So not only is there a quantity drop-off in what we can provide, there is a quality drop-off.   (D2)

The resentment is directed at administration for the most part because we're supposed to take care of staff, and I guess they feel we've betrayed their trust. It's kind of like we're not taking care of them. We just don't have the time to provide the supports that we have in the past.   (A1)

The expansion and transformation of settlements into midsized bureaucracies has fed the growing distance and fragmentation between the service parts of agencies. This has been a by-product of the historic evolution of settlements in financially good as well as bad times. However, a number of respondents ascribed some part of the widening gulf between program and agency to recent changes in funding patterns and the consequent shifting claims upon administrative time.

They have said at the agency that they will look into certain problems. What has happened over the years is that we have tried to integrate the pieces of the agency. But with managed care and mental health being highly regulated and having to meet its own quotas, things are changing. Everyone does their own thing. We're not as tied in with other departments, and in a sense more removed from the central office. This has been a problem as long as I've been here, but it is getting worse. Now is a wonderful opportunity to try to figure out how to change the service delivery patterns.   (H8)

The administrative support apparatus of settlement houses is also being tested by the increasing complexity and welter of government contracts. As contractual monitoring and billing demands have grown, the staffing of fiscal departments to fulfill such functions has not kept pace. Paradoxically, as administrative functions are underfinanced, agencies may be less and less able to meet the array of demands, both internal and external, to keep the dollars flowing. Such breakdown has immediate consequences because it creates an ever more tenuous relationship between the agency and at least two of its most critical stakeholders, staff and funding sources.

What we have you can describe on two levels. I can tell you in the fiscal office, spreading salaries and expenses over twenty different funding sources is an exercise in creative accounting. It is absolutely crazy. The shifts in money up and down take place constantly, and modifications are necessary. You have to figure out who's going to pay whom and do it in a way that is professionally sound without sufficient staff. But it's impossible, just impossible, and I am always a bit concerned that it will all fall apart and we will pay a price with our funding sources.   (G3)

We're bringing on three new programs without additional manpower for support. So everyone is just scratching their heads, we need to hire a new accountant and senior bookkeeper. How can we possibly expect the fiscal people to simply take all this on in addition to what they are carrying? It's just not possible and something has got to give.   (E3)

Within the program there used to be a lot of discussions around certain kinds of expenditure. I used to have my own lines and my own budget. I did my own purchasing. Now to save money it's central purchasing in a lot of things. There is some frustration in getting your needs met. It's not about any specific cut but general cost-cutting measures.   (C6)

In some settlement programs efforts are underway to offset recent losses in administration support and intraagency communication with enhanced forms of technology. The most popular response has been to introduce both the hardware and software of computerization to expedite communication between settlement houses, across programs, and within programs. Computerization, although not imagined as a panacea, is often described in terms that extend beyond its immediate capacity. The sense of excitement associated with such initiatives can in some part be attributed to their symbolic meaning. In stark contrast to recent trends, computerization represents a forward movement in upgrading agencies' infrastructure and offers at least a measure of hope that over time their work can be strengthened.

They seem so excited about computerizing the system. I don't know, maybe it's the novelty, maybe it's just the sense of finally doing something positive and not just responding to the cuts. Whatever the reason, the staff is very excited. . . . We're using the $50,000 to develop a computer client information system for my department so we can do ongoing needs assessments and identify service gaps in terms of presenting problems of our clients. We hope this will give us the data we need to get additional funding and to justify the services we provide. Unless we computerize, we just don't have the staff to gather the different kinds of information we need.   (H2)

We're trying to put together a wide-area network with five different houses. . . . So these five houses will be connected to a relay that will connect to the Internet, so that all of us will be connected together, and hopefully we can get different applications for programs and share.(C9)

Heightened Scarcity and the Decline of Program Infrastructure

Social service programs require an array of human and material supports to perform their various functions. These supports are as different as photocopying machines, supplies, secretaries, substitute staff when permanent personnel are on vacation or sick, and training. Over time, such support has been less and less available. The kind of scarcity experienced by programs varies, however. For instance, the loss of supplies is particularly acute in youth and child care programs. What pertains in general across all types of settlement programs, though, is a growing expectation that social service staff will perform their jobs with fewer supports than have historically been available.

As infrastructural support for programs evaporates, staff are faced with a number of hard choices. They must first determine how to create services that are increasingly isolated from infrastructural support. The services as a result become ever more dependent on the single resource of staffing. The line worker and program administrator must develop a calculus of trade-offs associated with specific supports. For example, does the program ration supplies to preserve a warranty on equipment or lay off a remaining secretary to replace an antiquated but essential piece of equipment?

At times staff also must determine whether they are prepared to pay for certain supports out of their own pocket to make up for the reduction in public support. The choice to privatize responsibility for elements of a program's infrastructure emerges most frequently in regard to supplies. Supplies for programs are subject to ever more austere rationing, and staff consequently must either adjust to intensifying scarcity or accept personal responsibility to fill the gap.

> Okay, what I've done actually, you know is lay out of my own pocket money for the supplies. Otherwise, the program would just be at a standstill. It's not something honestly that you would want to do on a long-term basis but otherwise the program would not function. You can't operate a program on matchsticks. You need to have, you know, materials, so the program has a chance for success because people aren't going to come unless the program offers something.   (A3)

> We have almost no money for materials. We used to have books for students, now the students have to buy the books because we cannot provide books. At this point we've generally exhausted our supply budget. We go through it within the first two months of the year. The whole year is exhausted because there's no money for it, for supplies.
>
>   (E10)

Even last year, usually I have a full supply closet for them to pick out of in the beginning of the year, it's empty now, we're running out of stuff, which we never used to. I know that the teachers have bought stuff on their own during this year and last year. Now how much can they continue to do that, I don't know.   (A7)

There's a teacher coming back and she feels all of her supplies are a problem. I told her she couldn't get new stuff because I don't have the money—it's that type of thing. Even if things have been worn out they will have to continue to use them, even with splinters on the blocks. We tried to replace the blocks every couple of years because the children would get splinters, but we can't do that anymore. We'll have to figure out something else—they'll use less blocks or sand them down.
                                                                            (A7)

Many programs are also affected by an inability to replace antiquated equipment or upgrade equipment such as computers. The breakdown of equipment can have a powerful impact on a program. Old photocopy machines with increased downtime contribute to the diminished productivity of staff; flyers, reports, interoffice memos, and announcements are less likely to be distributed in a timely manner. For senior centers, the timeliness and quality of food preparation can define the reputation of the program among the elderly. Therefore, dishwashers, ovens, warmers, and dryers are an essential part of the infrastructural stock of the program. The difficulty associated with replacing, sustaining or expanding a program's equipment is described in the following quotes.

I think equipment-wise we're back in the 1940s or 50s. The equipment we have here was donated when I got here. I would like to enhance the equipment we're using here at the [senior] center, but it's not possible. Therefore, we're limited because we don't have enhanced computers, we're limited because we have very old stoves and warmers. The lack of enhanced equipment just hamstrings. We can't move as fast as we'd like or do as much.   (H6)

Things get eaten away at through our OTPs. We just have so little for equipment. It's very difficult to operate with such teeny, tiny budgets particularly if you need equipment and early child equipment is very expensive.   (H3)

Clerical supports have also become increasingly scarce. The secretary/receptionist who typed forms, arranged specific referrals, billed public agencies for services, answered calls, or lent a more personal touch to greeting the public in face-to-face encounters is rapidly becoming an endangered species of personnel. As a result, the countless details of running a social service program are becoming less and less manageable. The greater difficulty in promptly attending to the many accountability and other demands associated with administering a social service program can in part be traced to the thinned ranks of support personnel.

> I can't do anything, but sit here and do paperwork because I do need at least someone who can take care of some of this clerical business for me. If I go on a trip, if I'm on a vacation, if I'm out sick, nothing clerical is done at all, and anything that I've tried to set up just falls through. I need someone who can help me comply with all the things that the funding sources want, and I don't have that someone.   (D6)

> If you want things, you have to do it yourself. It is a very tricky situation. Okay, you don't have a secretary, do it yourself. So the time you are supposed to be putting together a proposal, you are using to type a form that should be typed by someone else. So money-wise it doesn't make any sense, if you're making $20 an hour for you to be typing forms or dumping garbage makes no sense. It's getting more and more difficult to get to the things that have to be done to keep this program going.   (C10)

> In my program they are absolutely livid with our having to lay off the receptionist, but there isn't enough money. It's beginning to feel as we become more modern and expect our phones to greet people and have no one to say hi at the door, we're losing that feeling of family that I know my staff misses.   (E7)

> We had to cut the secretarial staff. When one of our two secretaries is out, we have problems. The one person who's answering the phones

upstairs is also supposed to be doing all the charting. So while she is upstairs, no charting is done. The other person does all the billing, all the verification and referrals to managed care facilities and that's not getting done. So there's a point when you're trying to save $21,000 dollars plus fringes and you're losing a lot of money because you can't bill or follow up.   (I5)

Other program support staff has also been sharply reduced. For instance, maintenance staff is being downsized. The increased pressure on program administrators to personally fill some of the gaps in coverage created by the receding presence of janitorial staff is evident in the following passages.

One of the considerations was cutting back the janitors' hours, which means from 12–3 every day we have no custodian here. Sometimes I have to pull out a mop to stop flooding or other major problems. It's not in my job description.   (B6)

We don't have somebody to take out the garbage so it becomes our job to take it out. So the time you're supposed to be spending running a program you're basically using part of that time to dump the garbage or get others to take on the responsibility.   (C9)

We trimmed the maintenance department, we eliminated a position, and then when somebody left, we only filled with a half-time person.
(D2)

Finally, social service programs in the past have offered specific opportunities for staff to upgrade skills through both formal training and supervision. Presently, however, the priority of the increasingly scarce supervisory sessions is likely to be not skill development but rather completion of tasks that directly or indirectly contribute to revenue. The program administrators' diminished capacity to develop a more skilled workforce is not offset through the expansion of other training opportunities. On the contrary, access to training has been compromised by other demands on staff time. For staff to attend training sessions other personnel have to be redeployed and assume a double workload to assure that services are not disrupted. This new demand must be considered in connection with the already greater demands being placed on staff time.

In this context, training is seen as yet another demand that programs are increasingly unable to bear. In a situation where short-term decision making exerts an ever greater pull and no powerful constituency is advancing a training agenda, staff development is likely to be given a lower priority. The long-term contradiction, however, is that lack of investment in a dwindling staff may over time have consequences for programs. Maintaining and developing professional skills is at the very least part of the ethos of an educated staff and the hallmark of a quality program. Reduced investment in supports such as supervision or training may therefore have a profound impact as it strikes at the heart of what it means to be a professional and to develop social service programs. Access barriers and costs, however, create powerful disincentives for programs to consistently invest in staff training.

It's difficult to free staff up for training. They're always in the classroom with the children, and we don't have substitutes. To go off-site, I mean every once in a while we can schedule it, but not very often. The travel time alone is more than we can give. It's just very difficult.   (H3)

I can't do a lot of the things I need to do because we just don't have the type of staffing we would like to have here. I can't have these people sub for me as much as I would like. There are trainings sponsored by the city I would like to attend that I should attend but can't because there is no one to sub for me. We have a limited amount of staff and that means that no one can replace me while I go out for training. I have to be here. It's mandated that someone from DFTA [Department for the Aged, funding agency] be here each day.   (B8)

Lack of Fit Between Physical Infrastructure and Service Needs

Another dimension of settlements' infrastructure is the physical space of programs. The size, attractiveness, state of repair, and stability of program sites represent only a partial listing of ingredients that influence the texture of a social service experience.

The visual or spatial impression clients get upon entering a program site is elemental to early experiences of engagement or disengagement. For instance, dirty, poorly lit buildings painted in flat institutional colors of green and white will affect the quality of the initial encounter between service providers and users. The relationship between program space and the quality of the service encounter likely also has a temporal dimension. For instance, unattractive facilities by definition do not convey an invitation to the community nor do they impel service users to return to the program. On the contrary, in the absence of other draws toward a service, the physical decay of a work site is likely to deflect in the short and the long run.

The quality of service space can also represent respite for community residents from environments and circumstances that often are in decay. The program facility or physical plant can have a meaning that extends well beyond the superficial because it can offer an alternative message regarding worth and hope. The decline of the infrastructure of programs has affected the capacity of settlements to create inviting, attractive spaces. The acquisition, construction, and maintenance of minimally adequate space has become a frequent pressing concern for administrators of settlement programs. The difficulty of maintaining basic standards in regard to space is increasingly evident in some programs.

> Very few of us in community-based organizations have the luxury of having a nice space for classes. These buildings are not built to be schools. We have an auditorium where you cannot hear very well. There is no money for the space we need. Because this is public housing, it's all very uncomfortable, very difficult.   (A2)

> I'll be subject to inspections from the New York City Department of Health and, of course, we're going to show deficit because of the situation. We're in the basement, we have a lot of pest problems, roaches, we're just not well situated here. It affects the amount of dirt we have to handle, no matter how much we clean, it looks bad, and it smells bad.   (G9)

> We have a lot of problems here, fixing things, it takes so long to fix anything. Sometimes I have ten items to be fixed, and it takes so long. And you feel you are not accomplishing a lot because when people come to see the program and they say well, the tiles are falling, the pipes are still leaking, it's not me, but it's there, and the report looks bad for the three centers.   (H6)

Perhaps the most pressing concern of settlement administrators, however, is the discrepancy between the size of the physical plant and present and anticipated demand for services. Respondents noted that their present space was increasingly unable to accommodate the need for privacy and confidentiality. In a sense, programs were outgrowing their space but often had no other option than remaining in overcrowded or cramped facilities. Future expansion was often contingent upon the acquisition of additional space; yet, because of uncertain financing such space was generally beyond the reach of programs. This set of circumstances ensnared many programs in a double bind that promised a trajectory of intensifying demand on ever more limited service space.

Space is an issue. I don't know if you realize when you came in here, all this is not parents it's staff, all crammed into this place. Seven people in a room this size is ridiculous. We do not have any space for confidentiality. When parents come in and they're interviewed, they're sitting on top of each other, giving personal information and identifying personal problems. That's not right. And both floors are just that way, we're crammed together. The rentals in these areas are ridiculous. So, that's a big issue, and you can't expand if you don't have space.   (B5)

Certainly, the nurse who is examining the people needs a private room, and there is none. And in the meantime I'm supposed to keep up the number of units of education recreation program when we don't have the money to rent the space we need.   (C7)

So my social worker supervisor lost her office on the third floor. So a decision had to be made as to where we could put her. She got into a space that was originally designated a family room. So now we have nine workstations down to six.   (H2)

The compression of space is also a product of the greater difficulty in meeting rents. As rents for space increase, programs are finding it more difficult to retain facilities. The consequent dislocation promotes movement to sites that offer programs smaller spaces for similar levels of work and staffing. The tensions associated with sustaining services as critical work space is withdrawn are illustrated below.

The Parks Department decided they could no longer allow people to use these rooms for free anymore because of their own budget cuts. And so they decided to charge us the going rate or 2–3 thousand dollars a year. We had no place in the budget where we could get that. In the meantime we have no access to that part of the second floor and some of the programs up there have been discontinued.   (C7)

With these cuts that are being projected and downsizing issues, what we're thinking of doing is maybe combining the 10th floor with alcohol because the lease runs out on the 30th of this year. Up until now we were able to get landlords to agree to an escape clause if we got defunded or couldn't meet present rents. Landlords are not stupid and are increasingly resistant to the clause because they realize the situation many programs are in. Also the rental market in the city is rebounding, so we are really caught between the rock and the hard place.   (G6)

The unit was evicted mainly because they were unable to meet the rent. So the unit has nowhere to go and can't afford to pay for new rent elsewhere. It looks like they will have to move into X House. Maybe come and share space or double up. I offered to chop the space in half. In good times we wouldn't have to do it, but this is hard times.
          (E1)

In at least some instances the hunt for new space has enhanced programs, and administrators were able to locate the necessary dollars to acquire and rehabilitate space. The new space created a better fit between the physical plant and service needs. Although illustrations of such initiatives were not abundant, respondents who were in the midst of upgrading their physical infrastructure conveyed a lively understanding of how space can enrich programs.

We finally found new space. We're always going crazy looking for space. Well, we found the right space, and what people are doing is incredible. They've taken classrooms and broken down walls. Now we have classes that will be able to work as learning environments. We don't have to sit on top of each other. Students won't be distracted by the conversations of other people. Our teachers can break up the bigger class into smaller groups. We're also adding bathrooms everywhere so kids don't have to line up and wait, which can be so disruptive. We're being creative and saying we'll get this done in a way that it can work.   (F9)

5 The Pressures and Fissures of Social Service Work

The most recent round of budget uncertainty in the 1990s did not produce the depth of cuts anticipated by many in social services. Some programs, such as those in youth services and in the arts, did suffer substantial cutbacks, but others serving the elderly and mentally ill experienced more modest, if any, reductions. The immediate and long-term impact of budget cuts in causing a rollback of social services must not be underestimated. However, the relationship between resource constraints and the changing content of social services is not limited to the relatively visible politics and consequences of cutbacks. A number of other, subtler factors have also contributed to the shrinking budgets of settlements. As was suggested in chapter 3, even if allocations remain constant, many costs continue to rise, and consequently the program is hard pressed to meet these new fiscal demands. In addition, as the structure of contracts changes, for instance, in the various forms of managed care, funding may remain constant or even increase, but the volume of the work demanded of agencies may be increased substantially. In this context, stable budgets may mask investment declines per service user. In the areas of health and mental health services demands for increased output are especially evident. These pressures, when combined with contracts that more restrictively define categories of reimbursable mental illness, affect the kind of services the worker can provide. For a variety of programs, as noted in chapter 4, contractual investment in infrastructural supports is often inadequate. Yet, as services are squeezed financially, programs are increasingly prepared to further strip their infrastructure by investing their limited funds in direct services. Finally, the threat of cutbacks also affects the way settlement programs do business. The constancy of such threats can contribute to an extended sense of crisis that influences the timing of hiring and the staffing of programs and has implications for the long-term relationship between worker and agency.

The threat to and disruption of social services cannot be effectively understood on the basis of the most recent dramatic events or visible policies. Instead, the changes must be considered on the basis of long-term trends that have gradually and subtly chipped away at both the content and fiscal underpinnings of social services. As one executive director noted, agencies can paradoxically grow in this environment and still become less and less healthy.

> As I said there is a paradox in some of this stuff. With all of the cutbacks, we've still found ways of doing more and even at times growing. It doesn't mean we're necessarily healthier. The problem is that even as some of us grow in size, we are not given the resources to make us healthier, often quite the opposite. A good example of that is the city capping fringes at 26 percent but in many of our programs fringes are at 30 percent. There is a paradox. (I1)

The experience of intensifying constraints and pressures is a defining feature of almost every aspect of agency life. What needs to be noted is that these tendencies, although not especially different from the situation in other areas of American work life, have particular significance for social services. The relational nature of social services makes them particularly sensitive to factors that put pressures and constraints on encounters between workers and clients. Equally important, adding restrictions and more demands to encounters between consumers and staff may transform the service. For instance, the meaning, commitment, and history people bring to such encounters are not peripheral but central to both the content and the possibility of the service. The above-named changes, although at first introduced gradually, beyond a certain point can have a cumulative and significant influence. It is within this context that the very relationship between worker and consumer and the meaning of the service itself are altered.

This chapter considers how social workers' full-time, professional, and salaried status is increasingly being supplanted by part-time staff, interns, and volunteers. The connection between the cheapening of social service labor and heightened demands for productivity is also examined. Finally, the consequent pressures and tolls on settlement staff and services are described.

Service Workers as an Increasingly Scarce Resource

The staffing patterns of agencies represent a mixture of full-time and part-time workers. This is not particularly surprising. Historically, not-for-profit agencies have employed part-time workers to meet very specific and discrete needs. For instance, after-school programs require teachers and counselors to work with children from the late afternoon to the early evening. Additionally, evening educational programs import teachers to instruct community residents on specific matters for relatively brief periods. Finally, summer camps employ staff for a period of approximately two months. These cohorts of part-time workers may return year after year, but their relationship to the agency is limited by the hours they work in any given week for a program or by their seasonal relationship to the agency. However, the numbers of part-time workers employed by settlements and the ratio of part-timers to full-timers are striking. The proportion of part-time workers employed by the ten settlements included in this study ranged from 33 percent to 80 percent.

> RESPONDENT: We have a total of about 30 full-time staff.
> INTERVIEWER: How many part-time staff do you have?
> RESPONDENT: A whole lot, anywhere from 30 to 75 to 100 depending
> on the season. (B3)

> In the whole settlement house about 150 people work here. It's somewhere between 80 and 100 who are full-time. (C12)

> Recently we did a count of our staff. We employ about 300 people full- and part-time. About 100 of those people are employed full-time. (D10)

For a number of programs full-time staff were especially scarce.

> We're all part-timers. John works 12 hours, he's the outreach supervisor. Darlene works 12, Ed works 6, and Mike works 6. If you add it all up together, we don't get a full-time worker. (C5)

INTERVIEWER: You said you use part-time staff?
RESPONDENT: Most of my staff for the senior center are part-time, in
   fact all of them. I'm the only full-time person.   (D8)

It's a housing service. To provide these services we have a social work
supervisor, an MSW, and 2 BA-level social workers. Even the supervisor is not full-time.   (C3)

Look I'm here 16 hours, and we have one other part-time staff person,
that's it. Between us we're one full-time worker, and we're dealing with
as I said about 850 to 1,000 young people.   (D7)

In a variety of programs, respondents reported a greater reliance on part-
time workers. Some suggested that increased use of part-time staff could be
directly traced to reduced budgets that needed to be stretched. Consequently,
workers were hired to fill roles limited in terms of time and budget. In some
programs, the often unstated hope was that staff would invest time beyond the
compensated hours. Personal commitment and staff volunteerism were, if not
expected, at least imagined as a stopgap measure to sustain programs. Moreover, budget savings accrue to agencies because benefit packages are often
either unavailable or lower for part-time workers. The pressure to reduce costs
existed in every program; however, youth and home care services for the
elderly were more likely to reduce staff hours to extract savings.

Workers, they go out into the field and talk to teenagers about drug
problems or any problem they have at home. Ms. Minetta, she was
the director of that. She was putting in thirty-five hours a week, and
her hours were cut down to fourteen or fifteen hours a week. She had
so many kids she dealt with. Some of the kids had real problems. She
feels real bad, sometimes she does it on her own.   (C5)

I don't think by and large we're talking about a huge staff turnover.
But you gotta understand even those who started out working thirty-
five hours with so-called benefit packages, they don't have that anymore, and they are still working with us. I don't know what we can
attribute it to, but they do remain.   (J3)

In the past year I've had a couple of people leave because they just
couldn't deal with the reduced work hours.   (I3)

Look, it's been very stressful. Some staff are looking for other jobs. But most of the jobs are for part-time people because they have already laid off the full-timers while cutting down administrative costs. (H6)

Part-time workers have also been affected by recent budget cuts. As programs shrink or are forced to redesign themselves, part-time staff are also increasingly vulnerable to a reduction of hours or layoff. The latter outcome is critical, because as staff identified with a program are laid off, its relationship to the community may become confused or limited. Service users may continue to bond with the staff of a program even when hours are reduced as long as there is a continuity of persons. However, as specific staff persons are laid off, an already tenuous relationship may lead to deeper estrangement between service users and program.

He wasn't the only person laid off at Christmas. About twenty-six part-time staff were let go. And in terms of the effect it has had, well, the relationships we've built up with community people to some extent also go with some of those staff.   (C6)

INTERVIEWER: How many part-time staff do you have?
RESPONDENT: Part-timers, let's see, five. I had twelve. All those individuals you see up on the board are volunteers and senior companions.   (D8)

I lost . . . part-time workers who do outreach that helps kids find the right direction. People who these kids came to trust. Now they're gone, and we're supposed to start all over again in trying to build up trust with them. They may not come back. I hope they make the right choices.   (I3)

I can tell you that since the beginning of the fiscal year, we've laid off part-time . . . workers. We've got caseloads and certain kinds of clinical work that are in process; I don't know who is going to pick up the cases. And, of course, every time we go through this, we disrupt relationships for people who come here very often suspicious and somewhat distanced. I hope we can help them to hang in with us.   (J5)

Staving off layoffs of full-time staff is a priority in every one of the settlement houses. Administrators consider such layoffs as a last resort, and they realize that as full-time staff is lost, the agency may begin to lose ground on a number of fronts. As noted, an overarching concern is that the agencies' relationship with staff and the community is likely to erode. Most community residents first encounter and later experience agencies and programs through available line staff. As these historic and present personal connections are severed or more limited, some part of the service user's relationship to the settlement program is washed away. Clearly, the durability and complexity of such connections extends beyond any single relationship. The standing of an agency is not so fragile that as a particular staff person or even cohorts of staff leave it will necessarily suffer dramatic declines in its legitimacy. Rather, the concern is that if staff turnover and consequent scarcity is chronic, the underpinnings of both services and relationships will be impaired. The subtle balance between staff availability and service possibility is likely disrupted as personnel becomes more and more scarce.

Many programs experienced cuts that resulted in the loss of full-time staff lines. As noted earlier, administrators were reluctant to reduce often already thin full-time program staffing. However, other options were increasingly unavailable as other avenues for budget savings were exhausted and the magnitude of cuts demanded reduction of the largest part of a program's budget, staff salaries.

Administrators maintained a commitment to softening the blow of such cuts by first attempting to reduce program and agency budgets through attrition, thus avoiding the necessity of firing people. Necessary savings were to be extracted from the natural turnover of staff. As personnel left the agency, positions remained unfilled for varying periods. This administrative practice was the least harsh method of resolving the conflict between fiscal responsibility and protecting the jobs of current staff.

We haven't had to lay off anyone. We've been lucky up to this point. We haven't had to let anyone go. Right now we have two vacant lines that we aren't filling.   (I2)

I decided that I didn't want to fire staff. So we're trying to find other ways. We're just not filling positions.   (G7)

But this whole thing calls up a much more serious question. I haven't fired anyone, but, we've left a program coordinator's job vacant. She got a new job in September, and we have not filled the position. A social work supervisor left in September, and we didn't fill that position either. We have a position for a psychological counselor, which is vacant. I could go on.   (H8)

Attrition was often not able to absorb the full weight of budget cuts. Consequently, despite the value conflicts associated with firing staff, administrators were at times left with no alternatives. The pressing need to balance the agency's budget was paramount. Plans were developed in a few agencies that restored the fiscal solvency of the program at the direct expense of members of the agency's present workforce. The firing of staff, however, has substantial significance. It may be experienced and interpreted as both a rupture and betrayal of relationships between specific administrators and service staff. At the very least, layoffs will promote a sense of economic insecurity among staff who are let go and those who remain. The emotional ripple of layoffs within an agency, although of concern to administrators, is generally of secondary importance. The more pressing concern is the impact of such layoffs on services. Due to their timing, especially if they are implemented rapidly, or due to their magnitude, layoffs may have significant implications for the functioning of a program.

We had to lay off almost all the staff, so now all we have is the program director. We're trying to get him to reorganize his focus and bring in other community resources. We're trying to rebuild this program without staff or dollars. It won't be the same thing. . . . It's real skimpy right now, but there is a potential for working this thing.   (C1)

Look, it doesn't matter if you serve seventy-five or forty. If you don't have the basic foundation in place, you can't serve anybody very well. So with all the cuts from the day program we've lost four staff who had to be laid off. You can't do it.   (I2)

Our street outreach program, which is a program I work directly with, had to lay off half of its staff. Now that is a very vulnerable group of people. But what are we supposed to do? The money wasn't there.
                                                                    (C7)

There wasn't any other answer that I know of other than cutting full-time people, because the fiscal director does her best to stretch the money in terms of overhead, and you know there really wasn't anywhere else to go. There was a sort of reserve of money that was gone through, and so after that was gone, there was no other choice.

(B2)

As full-time and part-time workers leave and are not replaced, the ability of programs to respond to service needs with their present complement of staff is compromised. The increased scarcity of staff resources has a powerful multiplier effect. The capacity of remaining staff to provide the scope or kind of services that was available in the past is gradually, and in some instances rapidly, eroded. Partly due to their reduced numbers, staff increasingly can provide only the most basic kinds of services and often to fewer clients than before. This in turn contributes to a new set of expectations for community residents of reduced access to and availability of services.

We haven't filled two slots for a number of reasons. What's important though is it has affected the way we do business. It has affected the quality of service that we can provide at the credit union, and of course it also affects the amount of work being done by others. My guess is we're also processing fewer people. (H5)

We worked very hard before we got cut. We've been cut back in the number of housekeepers we can hire. We can't do much about it. Now they're putting more clients into home attendants initially rather than later. There was supposed to be a continuum of care. Now that seems to be out the window. There is much less continuity of care or skill development. We really tried to make that happen before the cuts. Now it just seems to be stopgap. It's the clients though who are being shortchanged. (J3)

We have no new funding We had a staff person who was full-time and had to be laid off. This is a guy who created a whole field hockey league on his own with minimal supervision. Kids helped to structure the league. They had a newspaper they put together with league statistics, league highlights. It was like the back page of the *New York Post*. Most of it was due to the guy who created the league. Seventy percent of the kids were new to the program. Great, he was fired the 30th of June. The program was dormant for a period. The service was lost. Later we hired someone else who doesn't even show up on time. So these kids are coming to a program that they're used to having

somebody who's there like clockwork. First day they show up nobody
shows up. So what does this say to these kids?   (C5)

Some settlement houses and programs reported little turnover or retrenchment for full-time staff. The volatility and change in the larger environment was described in some instances as directly contributing to greater
stability in staffing or less turnover. The diminished availability of alternative
jobs left program staff with fewer options in the labor market. Consequently,
some staff remained for longer periods in one job. Part of this stability was
also attributed to the makeup of the people hired by the agency. Staff working in settlements are perceived by some as bringing a certain depth of
commitment to the work and, therefore, as prepared to struggle over the
long term with the current difficulties. The present workforce stability was
often compared to both past experience and future expectations, and the
current situation of equilibrium was perceived as a respite from prior losses
and anticipated future staff reductions.

I don't see our program as being influenced right now by the market.
So we don't have a big turnover and we aren't losing staff. But, on and
off we have always had this problem. Right now, this is a more stable
time because less people are quitting their jobs.   (C10)

There is a spirit among staff in this agency, a level of commitment.
It's already here. People come to this work with a lot of commitment,
and I think to some extent our agency inspires it. People don't leave.
(C1)

No, No. We are unique maybe, no real layoffs or much turnover to
our full-time staff. We do have access to philanthropy. The reductions
we've incurred have been to part-time and session workers. Thus far
we've been able to mitigate the more negative consequences of cuts.
(D1)

Lessening the Cost of and Heightening the Demand on the Social Service Worker

The history of settlement houses and social services is intertwined with
the development of volunteerism. Involving more affluent members of the

community to serve on a board may produce new resources both through direct giving and the creation of an expanded network. Moreover, volunteers allow programs to provide services that would be unavailable if they relied on paid staff only. Finally, volunteerism can vitalize relationships between settlement houses and the surrounding neighborhood.

As individuals and groups expand their involvement with a settlement house, they may develop a sense of personal investment or ownership. Such partnerships can promote alliances between programs and their clientele. There is no guarantee, however, that the volunteer work of neighborhood residents will lead to an expanded sense of ownership. Such affiliation needs to be nurtured. If volunteers are simply plugged into circumscribed functions with little autonomy or support, their relationship with a settlement house is unlikely to deepen. Volunteerism is a necessary but not sufficient basis for bringing the neighborhood into the life of the settlement house. In the past, such relationship building was a basic feature of settlement house work. Clubs, political groups, and services were organized to provide a social living room for segments of the surrounding community. For many houses, service as a gesture of solidarity was embedded in the culture and structure of the agency. The settlement struggled to join service, volunteerism, and the creation of a communal bond. Although volunteerism as an instrument of community building may now be less central to the work of settlements, it remains a critical support in the delivery of social services. The work of volunteers continues to be an enormous asset to specific settlement programs.

We have a music director, a dance director, visual arts director, arts and education director, and drama director. I would say we probably utilize ten to fifteen volunteers a year we are very understaffed. We have a long history here of people being committed to voluntarily providing services in the arts to community-based organizations. (I1)

We've been very fortunate in continuing to attract volunteers. This Christmas we opened up to serve the homebound, and we had forty volunteers; they came from all over the city that day to help us out. We've continued to be fortunate with volunteers. (B4)

We have a lot of volunteers in terms of fund-raising. We have very few public dollars in a number of programs. So the agency has events every year. For instance, we have a celebrity teddy bear auction. This year we had it at Sotheby's. Susan Sarandon and Kevin Spacey were the

hosts, and whatever we raised was really a result of the volunteers who
worked on the auction.   (H1)

We have a number of volunteers who have stayed with us in our adult
basic ed program. We, of course, have volunteers in our athletic program, and they come in the form of coaches. These are usually older
teens, alumni, and parents that come and help us during the summer
by taking over a team and coaching it.   (I3)

Many settlement administrators also see volunteerism as an opportunity.
Community residents are considered increasingly dependent on the services
provided by staff and are described as consumers of and not participants in
the service experience. A dynamic is created that promotes less and less
involvement of nonstaff stakeholders in the problems, development, and
daily activity of the program. To some extent, this is a natural by-product of
the settlements' historic shift to ever greater reliance on professional staff
and state contracts.

On the other hand, at the turn of the century, individuals gravitated to
settlement house work out of political and religious commitment and often
survived on stipends provided by private patrons. Additionally, the line between community people and staff was blurred. The choice to work in settlement houses frequently required that staff become residents of the house
and the community. Especially critical to this discussion is that the distinc-
tions between volunteers and paid staff were less clear. For many staff the
only form of compensation was room and board. Staff was often recruited
with the understanding that at best they would receive a modest stipend and
at worst no monetary forms of compensation.

The present squeeze on the settlements' resources has provided at least
part of the motivation for settlement administrators to reconsider community volunteer resources as not simply an adjunct to but rather a critical
element of their programs. The intention is to use present constraints as
an opportunity to return to a root commitment of settlement work. More
specifically, administrators are paying increased attention to expanding the
involvement of community residents in the work and life of the settlement
house.

Because they come in here for a service doesn't mean that they
wouldn't be interested in helping us out. That's the way it's going to

have to go because of the budget problems. For now, it's a positive way of looking at our problems. It's not as though we expect one or two people from the community to carry this burden, but if everybody participated, you wouldn't be counting so much on dollars but rather resources in the community. That could have many benefits even in the midst of all these financial problems.   (E3)

We're trying to increase volunteerism. It gives the seniors more of a sense of independence or a handle on the program. They're a generation that was brought up on morals and values and standards that had to do with work and the work ethic. So in the past few months we've been involving them more in the program activities, and that seems to be working. Many seniors are now a part of the steering committee, for instance. They are so much more a part of the program.   (A6)

Even some of the parents are volunteering, since you don't have this staff person now, they'll help out with specific classes. Mothers and fathers are participating. The kids are also selling candy, T-shirts, and Snapples to raise money. We usually give the T-shirts away each year, but since we have this crisis, we're selling them now. So every parent who comes here is buying T-shirts from the kids to help out. The community is really beginning to come to bat for the community house.   (C2)

Although volunteerism has clear benefits, it is not without cost. Increasingly, as paid positions dwindle, agencies are attempting to sustain historic levels of service, or at least approximate them, through the increased use of volunteers. This choice ultimately contributes to the cheapening of social service work.

As volunteers and interns step into roles previously performed by paid professional staff, salaries associated with specific functions experience a steep decline. Maintaining programs with such staffing has economic and labor market implications. For settlement houses, this strategy further erodes the already low wage level of staff. Furthermore, the downward pressure on wages in other sectors of the economy is increasingly enforced in settlements, not by directly slashing salaries, but rather through the more indirect method of replacing paid labor with free labor. The historic contribution and future benefit of volunteerism is thus combined with its more subtle and perhaps latent function of enforcing a wage decline. At this historic moment, the intimate relationship between social services and volunteerism provides a basis for reconstituting the composition and wage structure of the social service labor force. This is a critical point. Although the hidden benefit of such changes may be a closer relationship between community and agency, the detrimental cost of wage decline must also be recognized.

Community resident volunteers are most likely to perform highly circumscribed program functions that could no longer be performed by staff. Competing demands of family and paid work lead to a very focused relationship to volunteerism.

> Well, we've lost the . . . after-school program. I've lost all kinds of lines in my after-school program and teen evening program, and I lost Friday night recreation. We're reinstating some of these programs with neighborhood volunteers that can be here during very specific times.
> (B5)

> Basically, if you don't have a teacher, the students don't have anywhere to go. Now we are using community volunteers. Volunteers commit for certain time slots for about six months at a time.   (H7)

> A majority of my seniors are very old and some are very frail. I have had to rely on them more and more as we've lost staff. For instance, if we're having a party they'll come in and make sandwiches and do a lot of other things. They may clean up the bathroom or sweep the floor.   (D8)

> We have less staff and less ability to provide clinical services. We are getting volunteers from the area though to support some of our work, one of the volunteers even has her MSW. We're sort of making do with volunteers but that has its limitations.   (B2)

Student interns are able to devote more substantial blocks of time to the delivery of social services than community residents. They are also being formally educated to perform relatively sophisticated staff functions. For both of these reasons, student interns have become an increasingly prized volunteer resource.

Ten years ago we had four staff in that homelessness unit. Today we have two staff people. Thank goodness we have a social work student. That saves us because that's the equivalent to a part-time person who can really concentrate on organizing activities. That way the staff person can concentrate on what the contract expects. We move the student into the work where we need more flexibility.   (E3)

The social work interns are in all of our programs and the thing about the cuts is that we were really able to provide families services in spite of the cuts because we have increased our number of interns. This year we have eleven interns working in all of our programs, and so where one of the contracts upped the number of cases we're supposed to see, we upped the number of interns.   (B6)

One of the things we've had to do, and I guess this is where the impact of the budget cuts has gone, we've had to put more interns into our community centers. We've had to reshuffle the way we look at servicing the interns. Traditionally centers survive on six interns, we now have eight and we will be requesting nine or ten for this year. It's a catch-22 situation. Even though my centers are suffering because of budget cuts, my interns are getting much more out of it because they have more work to do and it is more interesting. Of course, the time to supervise that many interns is a problem.   (I7)

Although it is clear that both volunteers and interns have helped to shore up social service programs in settlement houses, it is equally apparent that these forms of substitute staffing represent an erosion of capacity. Volunteers and interns simply cannot replace the experience, availability, and skills of full-time staff. As dependence on volunteers grows, the reliability or continuity of services may undergo a corresponding decline. Yet, increasingly, settlements are forced to rely upon such staffing, not as supplement but as replacement of full-time as well as part-time workers.

Interns, although a growing cohort of part-time workers, have a time-limited obligation to the settlement. An intern remains at an agency for eight months to a year. Built into the reliance on interns is a constant turnover of personnel. Equally important, the apprenticeship status of interns means they are learners. Yet, increasingly, interns are expected to function not as apprentices/learners but as autonomous and responsible part-time workers.

The recent sweeping federal reform of welfare has accelerated the movement of recipients into work programs sited at social service agencies. At the time this study was conducted, only a relatively small fraction of New York City's welfare recipients were being channeled into the Work Employment Program (WEP). Some of the work assignments were located in settlements. The WEP workers were assigned to both clerical and, in some instances, paraprofessional work. Their labor, however, was strictly monitored according to city regulations. For instance, unwillingness to accept an assignment or repeated failure to appear at an assigned work site automatically resulted in the termination of welfare benefits.

The stated intention of the WEP is to accustom welfare recipients to the world of work. However, the supports necessary to systematically develop such a socialization experience are increasingly compromised. Consequently, disoriented, underskilled, and, at times, resistant WEP workers are inadequately prepared for their work roles. For settlements, increased reliance on WEP workers without adequate training or socialization can in turn affect both the quality and nature of support available to line workers.

Clearly, the settlements' often necessary choice to rely on a spectrum of cheapened forms of social service labor does not come without its costs. This point is more fully illustrated in the passages below.

Look, interns are a wash. We try training them on the thirty-one different entitlements. But it takes between a year and a year and a half to get someone up to speed, and we just don't have them nearly that long. So you don't really get any clean services out of it. It really is a strain. Right now we only have two people to supervise an intern, the supervisor and myself.   (E9)

Yes, we're using more and more interns as we lose staff. But it's a Band-Aid in my opinion. It helps, but they don't have the experience or skill.   (B5)

The idea is, if you don't have staff, get volunteers. But it's very difficult to get volunteers more than once a week. If volunteers work, they often miss classes. You just can't get them in here eight hours a week for four classes from six months to a year.   (H7)

We're finding that we're getting a lot of assigned assistance through the welfare department, the WEP program. We had so many people assigned to us, they were tripping over each other. Their program was meant to supplement help at the center, but they really replaced what should have been paid workers. They don't have the skills, and we can't provide the proper support. Often getting people referred to us to fill these basic functions can be more work than it's worth. I'm just pulled in so many directions I don't have the time for that kind of supervision or training.   (J5)

In some programs volunteers and interns are provided with stipends. A number of respondents reported that even these modest payments were re-duced or eliminated, and as a consequence the commitment and continuity of volunteers was affected.

We had volunteers—we had up to twelve volunteers here at one time. They were receiving a stipend of up to twenty-five to thirty dollars a month, and that was taken away. The role of volunteerism means vol-unteerism where there's nothing given for services. But giving nothing back is a bad situation. They don't see any kind of benefit, any type of voucher, any type of carfare money, to motivate them to want to volunteer and remain volunteers. So, now all of my volunteers have dissolved away.   (D8)

The cheapening of the social service labor force is multifaceted. One axis of this decline is the substitution of interns, volunteers, and enforced volunteer labor (WEP) for paid staff. Another axis, however, is the decline of the base wage of employed social service staff. The salaries of settlement workers and not-for-profit social service staff in general are often lower than those of their public-sector counterparts. The lack of a unionized work-force, constraints in passing on increased costs to funding sources, and historic assumptions regarding the worth of social service work have com-bined to create a relatively low-wage professional labor force. The lid on social service wages has, however, been tightened recently. Increasingly, even cost-of-living increases are not built into new contracts. Consequently, salaries of settlement staff are essentially at a standstill. As in the case of the settlement houses, standstill incomes represent a loss in purchasing power. The expenses of housing, food, and transportation, for example, continue to rise for settlement staff while their incomes are essentially held constant.

The situation of settlement workers is not unlike that of the larger American labor force. For most Americans, the recent economic expansion has not translated into comparable wage increases. On the contrary, until very recently the labor force for the most part experienced a decline in real wages. Numerous settlement workers described both the extended duration and consequences of living on an essentially fixed income.

> The agency has instituted a wage freeze and needless to say, that has been a morale problem.   (G4)

> We have not gotten wage increases at this agency for years, and that's something that is very very difficult to live with from the top down. The cost of living has increased. If your salary is not commensurate with that, then you really begin to struggle. In my situation that has caused me to take on another job. . . . I needed to get additional income to help me to survive out there. I love doing what I'm doing and the work has been rewarding, but it's also been more and more stress.   (D9)

> We haven't seen an increase in the base salary for some time. We were able to generate enough money last year to give staff a bonus last year, so they got a little bit more money. But their salary hasn't gone up in a couple of years maybe, a few years.   (H8)

Traditionally, settlements have been able to compensate for relatively low salaries with generous benefit packages. Vacation time, health coverage, sick days, and job security represented at least part of the economic trade-off workers made in choosing to work in settlement houses. Currently, the scope and concrete entitlements of these benefit packages are at risk. A number of executive directors warned that current allowances could not be sustained.

> In the past you know you walk into this place and after three months, you're eligible for five weeks of vacation and eighteen sick days and

holidays. I think that we, and others, are going to have to look at that in a very, very competitive environment. . . . A gap in funding will do that, will particularly do it, and that's the way I think it's all going.

(G3)

The benefits are higher than in the private sector because we pay much lower salaries. The health care costs are fixed, so the lower the salary the higher the proportionate costs of the fringe benefits. We're in a sense getting double penalties. We don't get enough money to pay decent salaries, and because we don't, the fringe rate is proportionately high. Now they're saying you can't pay more than 26 percent on fringes, which is going to make us look at both our pension and health care benefits very closely and maybe change them.   (I1)

In a number of settlements, the pressure to restructure benefit packages has moved from the investigation to the implementation phase. Administrators acknowledged that they were simply unable to maintain present levels of health care benefits. The combination of diminished contractual obligations to overhead costs and rising health care premiums have forced settlements to roll back coverage. Two distinct cost containment approaches have emerged. A greater proportion of health care costs may be passed directly to staff through higher deductibles or increased premium contributions. A second option promotes a search for cheaper vendors and benefit packages. No matter which strategy is selected, the outcome remains that health care and in turn staff costs have been reduced.

Well, one of the things the new executive director brought to the management of the agency was the fact that we could no longer sustain providing health care benefits of 100 percent for all family members. For new people, she's raising the deductible and instituting contributions. Most everyone is doing that because they cannot pay for full benefits.   (E2)

The benefits are the medical benefits. We used to have a better company. Better care, easier to get to a doctor, and quicker reimbursement. Now it can take months sometimes to get reimbursed. And, it's just been a lot of aggravation for some of the people. But, at least a benefit is still there.   (G6)

The agency was facing a deficit this year and they modified our benefit package. What they did was they raised the rate of the deductible amount out of the service, and they raised the copayment by $15 and and added some minor benefit changes. That's problematic for some of the lower paid employees, but it's a fairly modest change. It beats the alternative, which is poorer health care at higher cost or helping to pay the premium, which we have not had to do here. (G5)

Increasing the Pressure and Expectations

The work of social service staff in settlements is increasingly pressured. The mounting demands generally evolve out of staff's commitment to preserving certain baselines in the delivery of social services in the face of multiplying tasks and diminished resources. More specifically, these pressures are a consequence of both heightened external demands as well as the staff's internalized expectations that the basic service needs of clients must be met. The push-pull between the external pressures to economize and the interior pressure to hold the line on service components that are perceived as essential has had a powerful influence in defining both the content and experience of settlement work.

This increased demand has expressed itself in may ways. For instance, administrators, line workers, and clerical staff are more frequently expected to wear several hats. Job descriptions are increasingly fluid. Program directors are more and more likely to be called on to fill direct line service and administrative functions. Line staff are expected to perform various service, administrative, and clerical functions.

Clearly, social service work in settlement houses has always demanded a certain flexibility in job definitions and staff roles. What is changing, however, is the number and extent of these shifting functions. Settlement workers are effectively being asked to pick up more and more of the slack created by economizing measures while maintaining their prior work role. The role strain of the proliferating functional "hats" worn by staff is depleting and frustrating. Yet, staff see little choice but to accept their new responsibilities.

I may have to help out with the lunch program, or I may have to drive a van to take the seniors some place. . . . Things like that. . . . And I may be neglecting other things because I'm doing these nitty-gritty things. I shouldn't have to do them, but they won't be done otherwise. (A4)

A number of the cuts forced us to cut part of the arts program. Teachers had to be laid off. The cuts had to be picked up by the remaining staff members. We all teach now, myself included. I teach some classes during the week. The other program directors also teach some classes during the week to help make up for it.   (F4)

The staff, I think, is excellent in terms of their commitment and ability to engage young people. To reduce our staff as much as it has been means that everybody is wearing nine hats, and it's very difficult to maintain the program and keep its level of activity up. It's just about impossible.   (F8)

I've lost staff and it just makes the job so much more difficult. Each of the homes have to be visited seven times a year. When we go there we have to check on the children and talk to the providers to see if they are having problems with the children or parents. We get a lot of the kids from the shelters in the area and a lot of young kids who have children and don't really know how to parent. The kids may be dirty, unbathed, and wearing dirty clothes. Then I have to call the social worker at the shelter. That's when I wish I still had my social worker. I just can't do everything. There aren't enough hours in the day. Sometimes I'm here from seven to nine.   (F5)

You have to look at it as a constant juggling act. I've gotten good at keeping six balls in the air, but I can't expect my staff to do that. Two, three maybe. I have some staff who are pretty good at it, others who are poor at it. And there's no sense of job security at all. In the 70s and 80s there was more job security. It all wears on you.   (H1)

The increase in work requirements is driven to some extent by funding sources. Workers are expected by contracts to squeeze ever greater efficiencies from their limited time. Although the specific demands of the contracting agency may vary, the message of greater output is consistent. For instance, some contracting agencies may explicitly demand that caseloads be increased while others may more subtly ratchet it up by adding service requirements, such as follow-up work or home visits with no additional resources. These increased formal demands of funding sources contribute to the accelerated pace and increased pressures of the workday.

People used to see sixty or seventy as a high caseload. Now the highest is 100, and even 119, and there are caseloads that are uncovered. We have a backlog. We have a contractual obligation, and if we don't keep up, we're in trouble. We have to keep our noses to the grindstone.

(D3)

RESPONDENT: It's a lot to see five disturbed kids in counseling sessions in one day.

INTERVIEWER: So, he has a heavier load? Has this always been the case?

RESPONDENT: No, they've upped the ante in about the last eight months in terms of how many kids. (G8)

INTERVIEWER: Does it increase the day care teachers' workload because they now have to do home visits?

RESPONDENT: Yes, we have to squeeze it in, in the morning, lunchtime, or after work, or somebody else has to cover the classroom while the teacher does the visits. It's more difficult and adds to the stress of the day, but it's not impossible. (A7)

They've upped the amount of work they expect. Now we have to do 3 visits and a treatment summary on top of all the paperwork with five clinical staff. Something's got to give. (I7)

Workloads have also increased as a result of service commitments sustained by staff in the face of reduced agency and community resources. For many programs there is rarely direct correspondence between decreasing resources and a scaling back of programs. Parts of the program structure that are no longer specified as necessary in the contract but are perceived by staff as essential services are often continued in a modified form.

Furthermore, in many programs clients were described as having more serious and persistent problems. These more complex client profiles, though not fully engaged, are not ignored by staff. Efforts are made to secure the necessary resources and services to address growing as well as more intractable client needs. The maintenance of key service components and engagement with ever more difficult clients is not without cost. With ever greater frequency, sustaining such personal commitment means that workers have to absorb a greater workload.

We've seen a tremendous increase in the number of people who need assistance or who recognize us as the answer to providing assistance with entitlements, the HEAP application, tax forms. . . . They used to be able to get by on food stamps, but not now. The caseload demand has increased tremendously. (J5)

We're feeling it more than ever just in services. Not only are our services being cut back, but our services are more needed because of cuts elsewhere. We have a tiny group of incredibly dedicated and talented people who try to keep up with the change in entitlements and the increased needs. (C13)

Yet, we've been cut in our budget. People also live longer, and now we have all these people in their eighties who have absolutely no one and who are physically and emotionally a problem. Now, they can't come here, we have to go to them, and that takes more time. Coming up with that time gets harder and harder. (G9)

The staff have been told that if they want to continue to work here, the function and role that they were hired to do will continue, but they will be asked to do other things that are not in their job descriptions. Some people are going to be asked to cover the rec. room. The nurse has been asked to do the mobile crisis unit. Before, we would call on the mobile crisis unit, but they have been cut. So, we have to do our own outreach. The nurse will be doing that plus the medical and the psychiatric, administering the medications, and the health history. The demands on some workers is growing almost explosively. (I7)

The population has changed. The kind of families we're getting are more trouble. So, in that sense, workers feel they are doing more. (I5)

The strain on settlement house staff can also be traced to the increasing amounts of time that are devoted to filling out forms. Proliferating paperwork demands are driven by a number of bureaucratic tendencies. Increasingly, settlement programs depend upon an ever larger number of smaller contracts. Each contract has specific reporting requirements. In a sense, differ-

ent reports with similar information have to be developed to satisfy the paperwork requirements of each contracting agency.

In addition, the paperwork demands of funding agencies have increased.
Layers of reporting are often added to already existing accountability demands. As forms are modified, the tendency is to expand, not diminish,
paperwork. The funding agencies' appetite for data is in part fed by the
need to justify itself in a political environment that is increasingly hostile to
government-financed social services.

Accountability measures are necessary to determine both the effectiveness
and efficiency of public investment. However, the often unchecked expan-
siveness of reporting requirements can undermine the potential impact of
services. As the worker spends more and more time on paperwork, she or
he is less available for direct work with service users. There is a trade-off
between compliance reporting and engaging community residents. However, workers often have little choice but to prioritize reporting because it is
a trigger for present and future funding. Such a choice is especially frustrating to workers because at a time of substantial resource constraint and
growing need it offers little direct payoff to clients.

> The mental health clinic gets money from OASIS, so we are required
> to do both paperwork for Medicaid and OASIS. We have double pa-
> perwork, which is awesome, and then we also have to do quarterly
> reports to the foster care agencies.   (H2)

> We get forms saying check this or check that. Every year we do more.
> Now we're asked to check on them at home. I don't know what they do
> at home—maybe we have to go to the home to check how they look,
> how they cook, I don't know. What I do know is the demands are worse
> and the money is less, and it is very hard to be in this situation.   (A8)

> We're feeling so pressured just in terms of paperwork and account-
> ability. We have so little time as it is, and we're pulled more and more
> away from clients and to the desk to fill out forms. It's crazy!   (G6)

The various strains pressing in upon settlement staff have had a diluting
effect. Although the workday is stretched to absorb new responsibilities, the
sheer weight of multiplying tasks and increased demands causes workers to
spread themselves ever thinner. The worker is less and less able to ade-

quately juggle her responsibilities. At times, job demands require staff to be present in two places at the same time. At other times, workers question their capacity to stay on top of the mushrooming day-to-day details of the work. Some respondents suggested that the impossibility of managing their enlarged job without adequate support poses a serious long-term threat. They indicated that at least one trade-off is between the breadth of program coverage and the capacity to enforce or monitor the many specific details of contract compliance. As workers are spread so thin that they knowingly and unknowingly violate elements of their contract, the most salient question is whether they will be caught.

It's more frustrating. I feel sometimes I don't know what I'm doing. I have all of these papers on my desk, and I realize I can't do it. And then the phones start ringing and someone says I need help down here, and I'm stuck and I'm a little lost. I can't meet all of the contract demands because I have so much on my plate.   (C9)

Obviously, one of the difficulties is that you have to be running two programs that's not a great thing because either of the programs could conceivably be a full-time job. You find yourself trying to cut yourself in as many pieces as possible to get the job done.   (B3)

She knows a little arts and crafts, so when she's there, she moves around the program. But that's the only extra position I have. But what am I going to do if the lady is absent? I can't keep taking a person from the other center and move them over here, that would not be kosher as far as our contract. At times, though, we've been forced to do just that because I'm not willing to do all the running and the jumping.   (D4)

There have been times when I picked up supplies, picked up the lunch, transported a senior somewhere. But at the same time that is in violation of what DFTA is asking for because there is not another DFTA staff person in my absence. But what am I supposed to do, the job has to get done. So I violate the regulations by relying on volunteers to stay here and hold down the fort in my absence.   (D4)

We're trying to be everywhere at once. It's just too much. Something's got to give, and it usually does.   (H3)

In the face of these increased pressures, staff struggle to preserve the settlement mission and quality in their day-to-day work. Some respondents noted that the reduction of resources and supports has forced a healthy reconsideration of the kinds of services being delivered and the responsibilities of workers.

The struggle to preserve social services demands at times substantial sacrifice on the part of staff. The push-pull between commitment to preserve programs and the destabilization of funding often is resolved by staff drawing ever more deeply from their well of dedication to clients and service. Settlement workers may delay or simply not take accrued vacation time. Moreover, accumulated compensation time for working extra hours may have more symbolic than real value as workers refuse to leave the program understaffed for any time, however brief. Relatedly, workers in a number of programs often choose to volunteer their time to programs that might otherwise be unable to survive. Time and again respondents told stories about line staff and program directors who through sheer will and sacrifice helped to navigate their programs through difficult times.

> Some people I actually haven't seen take a vacation. If you look at some of the staff, they have red-eye and are waiting, hoping things will turn themselves around, so we can hire some of the people back. People like myself, I have six weeks of vacation time that I haven't taken yet. You just can't take all of your vacation time and expect that the agency can carry on. (C4)

> The amount of harm that's been done to programs, it'll probably take two to three years to get back to where we were five years ago. So that means long hours with no pay, but that's all right as long as I'm able to make headway on projects. (G11)

> I've been really working hard. Sometimes I work here until nine or ten o'clock at night because I really hate to disappoint a child. They don't know about budget cuts. I'm here for the kids, so whatever I can do. (D10)

> The impact on my program is that when someone goes on vacation, I have no backup. . . . It has impacted in the sense that all of us who work here have a lot of accumulated vacation time, but we can't take it and keep the programming going at the same time. (J5)

Many respondents wondered how much longer the heightened investment on the part of staff for the sake of maintaining the programs could be sustained. The commitment of staff was not questioned but rather the tenuousness of program underpinnings that are ever more dependent on repeated and intensifying sacrifices.

INTERVIEWER: How long can people continue to do more and more?
RESPONDENT: I don't know. At some point it's all going to break down. It has to. They just aren't going to be able to keep it up. I know I go out of my way to let my staff know how appreciative I am. What else can I do? We can't give them a fucking raise. I can remind them of how much I appreciate what they are doing and how heroic I think they are, but besides that there is little else I can do.   (A2)

INTERVIEWER: Has the work of the staff held up in the face of all these difficulties?
RESPONDENT: You have to figure that you can bend only so far before you break. At some point the staff is just going to break down. This can't go on forever.   (H2)

Patching Together and Breaking Down Social Service Staffing

As the funding of settlement programs becomes increasingly tenuous, administrators are expected to be especially nimble in both locating new funding and stretching old dollars. The funding base of programs is fluid and complex. Increasingly, a patchwork of funding sources has to be woven together into a coherent pattern of service. Funding sources may disappear and others may emerge. However, it is the administrators' responsibility to bind new funding sources to the historic functions of the program and to meet new contractual demands.

The increasingly fragmented and patchwork-like structure of funding has metaphoric power and analogs. Like a poor delivery man in desperate need of keeping a vehicle with balding tires on the road, agency leadership must remain ever alert to impending blowouts and be prepared to patch new holes. Program administrators are spending more and more of their time plugging leaks in the funding from one source with money from another. The juggling of multiple funding sources to maintain the forward movement of programs is illustrated below.

DYS [Division of Youth Services] cut back our funding and later restored it. But in the interim, we had to locate new funding. Instead of letting our evening recreational program die, we moved around some of our private funding. Of course, that affected other parts of our program.   (B3)

Our funding has really been disjointed. For instance, two years ago we received city funding through the emergency shelter grant. That eventually dissolved, and in place of that we have new state funding. The area of concern for us is that some of the areas funded under these grants are very different, and yet we are going to have to finesse it to keep essential services going.   (E3)

I feel like a marionette, always jumping and trying to fill holes with new dollars.   (H6)

The patching together of funding can cause a substantial undertow of additional demands on the program. To begin with, reporting requirements for administrators are likely to multiply. The relationship between specific funding and particular agency work may become increasingly confusing. As workers' salaries are drawn from not one but a number of contracts, the administrator must attach whole workers to fragments of both funding and output. The ongoing process of disassembling workers to allocate them to specific contracts and reassembling a coherent role can be time-consuming and frustrating. Additionally, workers may be pulled in many different directions to satisfy the disparate demands of the contracts that cover their salary. These contractual pulls represent, at the very least, a strain for the line worker.

We spend a lot of time trying to sort out where the money's coming from and going! I'll have one person doing five tasks. Many of these tasks may be funded from different contracts. So that's caused a lot of frustration for the people administering the program.   (I5)

When you find that you're trying to spread your staff to do all of the things required by all of the contracts, something may slip through the cracks. So in a funny way you may end up not doing a piece of a project, which happened to us and then discover there was money there to do it.   (H2)

For the staff, these changes are taking place constantly. One day, they are 50 percent in this program only to learn later that their time distribution across programs has changed yet again. We shift them constantly to a different mixture of jobs so that we can cover salaries. If I were a worker in that situation, I would want to cry.   (G3)

Ultimately, the fragmentation of funding and staffing assignments can have an especially detrimental effect on settlement services. Even enhanced funding can undermine the health of programs. For instance, worker roles may have to be cobbled together in ways that create less synergy within and across social settlement programs. The pieces of a job may not add up. Such job incoherence is likely to be passed along to the service users in the form of increasingly frustrated and less focused workers. Moreover, new patches of funding may create service quilts that are only loosely tied to what have historically been the core elements of the programs. Patching together of staff funding may therefore contribute to breakdowns in the historic underpinnings, continuity, and coherence of services.

We eventually pieced the funding together into something that translated into a full-time job. But the jobs were quite different. The job combined family counseling around drug abuse and working in our intergenerational project. But it didn't have the synergy. The pieces really didn't work well together.   (G5)

We replaced funding of our youth program recently. But the new funding really didn't replace our core. I liken it to having your hand with a palm and five fingers stretching out, and suddenly the palm is lopped off, now you've got five fingers sitting out there with no lifeblood. The new sources of funding were absolutely uninterested in picking up the cost of those core services. So now we've gotten money to expand something that really doesn't exist.   (B5)

The Toll

The wear and tear on workers in the more pressured and insecure work environments of settlements has been substantial and has taken its toll. For some, the constant threat to job security is a source of substantial worry. This tension tends to prey on staff both on the job and in their private life. Job security is a frequent topic of discussion in staff meetings and informal gatherings. The constant sense of threat is also transported into service encounters. Over time, the tenuousness of job security proves emotionally destabilizing.

The stress of social service work is also a product of increased workloads. The demand that present staff fill the breach of reduced staffing, diminished infrastructural support, and increased reliance on volunteers is wearing.

> It's not the most productive work environment to always have an axe over your head. People are stressed all the time about their jobs. The staff is worried about the future. We are especially vulnerable in the arts because we don't have solid base of funding; we don't have eight different revenue streams where we can jump from one to the other.
> (G10)

> You better be doing something else because you never know when it's going to end. You need a backup plan like teaching, consulting, or private practice. You have to have something else going, otherwise you could lose your sanity because the job is so uncertain.   (D12)

> There has just been so much more stress as the work around here has been increasing.   (C8)

> INTERVIEWER: It's very stressful?
> RESPONDENT: Stressful, you hear the stress in me! The work just keeps growing and growing. And part of the problem is that mental health in a settlement is not even a primary service.   (I7)

Equally important, even when staff shoulders greater responsibility this does not necessarily lead to added fiscal benefits for the program. For most settlement programs, contract grants are fixed and not responsive to the increased caseloads of individual staff. The return on increased investment on the part of staff in such cases is not additional revenue but the retarded erosion of the content and quality of social services. The lack of correspondence between ever greater levels of work demands and fiscal relief is yet another source of strain. The Sisyphean experience of more and more work to be done and unremitting instability can be especially frustrating.

You're tired. You always want to feel as though you are accomplishing something. We don't make a lot of money, lord knows. One of the primary benefits is a sense of satisfaction you're accomplishing something. If you're not seeing the results you saw before, even though you are putting in more effort, well it's frustrating, and it eats at you.

(A9)

INTERVIEWER: Has the present climate in the agency affected you?
RESPONDENT: Oh my goodness, has it affected me! It's incredibly stressful in a settlement house. I direct the program, I provide services, and I could go on and on. I've been having to do it all; as a result I'm stressed out, and I'm tired. I put in long hours. The bigger problem is that even as my work grows, very little changes for the program. Our funding is shaky and our services are of lesser quality. I think that is the shame of it and that really hurts.   (B7)

Many respondents distinguished between the anxiety, fatigue, and stress associated with settlement house work and general morale. Although it was felt that stress levels had increased, some disagreement existed regarding the impact on morale. In many programs the commitment of staff to clients was perceived as retarding the general corrosive impact of growing work demands and job insecurity. The staff was able to contain the emotional fallout associated with ever more stressful work environments by remaining focused on the larger purpose of providing services. Service to others in a sense functioned as a focusing device and shield.

However, there was also another strand of response. Staff were described by some as increasingly unable to compartmentalize the experience of more pressured and unstable work environments. Working conditions were perceived as affecting morale and staff engagement with the demands of service delivery.

I think that, overall, the impact of the work situation has been an emotional one, and it has affected morale. My feeling is that the people who work in programs need to be motivated, committed, and creative to make things work. But right now, morale is way down, and it is impacting the quality of service.   (C15)

The morale of staff has remained OK. The work situation has raised anxiety and stress. But, thank God, I have good morale with staff. They remain committed to doing the best possible job for the client. But there is always the potential that if things keep getting worse, the situation will be viewed as hopeless, and the staff will start to give up. (E6)

I would say that staff morale is down. Maybe at an all time low. People don't really feel as though they can do the treatment. So it's almost like I'm here because I need my job, but I'm not going to impact on the clients. Some people have kind of given up. (F7)

My daily morale is fine. I mean I love what I do and stay connected to my clients. So on a day-to-day basis it's fine. But when I think about the future, well, I try not to go there. (C11)

Although many workers struggle to preserve their connection to the work and the service user, the accumulation of demands and tensions nonetheless takes an emotional toll. The emotional drain for some was relatively slight; for others, however, it was more profound. Some respondents reported a near exhaustion of their emotional resources, consequent demoralization, and burnout.

I came into social work because it's fun. That's why most people choose this field. But when the fun is taken away, there isn't a lot left. The recent climate has taken the fun away. It's hard to keep reaching down deeper and deeper when you're really tired and depressed and to recapture the feeling of loving it. (H2)

INTERVIEWER: What has been the emotional consequence of all these pressures?
RESPONDENT: Well, clearly anxiety. But that's not it entirely. You know people working in mental health programs in the community have a commitment to serving low-income people. Day by day that is just being scooped out of us. You begin to ask why am I continuing to do this work? (A1)

INTERVIEWER: What has been the effect on staff?
RESPONDENT: Oh, there's burnout. The energy, sense of possibility, is just fading. We try to hold onto it, but there's less and less of it to hold onto. (G4)

The mounting pressure and emotional toll of settlement work can lead to a rethinking of career aspirations. The increasingly steep personal costs of providing social services may at a certain point be viewed as untenable. The resulting turnover can destabilize the makeup of settlement staffing. The settlement labor force is buffeted, on the one hand, by resource contraction and, on the other, by the attrition of overworked staff.

Clearly, some part of the decision to leave is affected by the availability of other jobs. For many staff, the concurrent downsizing of other social service agencies or a tight labor market in general often temper such impulses. Rates of turnover in settlement staffing are clearly affected by both working conditions and alternative job opportunities. During the period of this inquiry, the incidence of turnover slowed because of the relatively bleak job prospects for social service personnel in the larger economy. Despite these marketplace conditions, job change remained both a fantasy and reality for settlement workers. On occasion, the interest was not to replace one form of social service work with another but rather to find employment in another field.

> I would say that we lose our staff in the mildly chronic way, to use a clinical term. It's not that people find a new job and go within a couple of weeks or something like that. We lose them gradually. They gradually learn this is a stressful job and also from experience, they don't expect to get a large pay increase or cost of living adjustment. They also know that somewhere down the line they will have to learn to live with uncertainty, budget cuts, and so on. This is a part of the job, a chronic part of the job. And so the wish to leave is chronic, so we lose our staff that way. It is increasingly a dead end. They look for jobs often in the for-profit field or try to go into private practice.   (A2)

> I think that there is much less turnover because there is less in the papers. People are looking, but often they are afraid of being mobile because over time it may turn out that the new job offers even fewer benefits and less security. There are no guarantees even if you find another social service job. It's just getting rougher and rougher throughout the field.   (C2)

6 Scarce Resources: Rationing, Narrowing, and Redefining the Content of Social Services

A critical dilemma for settlements is how to redefine services in an environment in which both workers and settlement often feel besieged by the uncertainty of funding and the often growing needs of people seeking services. As noted in the preceding chapter, one potential response is for workers to dig ever deeper into their personal resources to hold the line on services. Essentially, they are expected to do more and more in an environment that offers less and less support. Relying exclusively on this approach is ultimately not tenable. Individual workers and settlements, no matter what the level of added investment, are unable to keep pace as their energy flags while fiscal destabilization and client demands grow unabated. Eventually other strategies must be introduced.

As the demands on workers and settlements intensify, the content of social services is gradually narrowed and redefined. Such incremental changes can have substantial reverberation. As services are narrowed, their content is altered. For example, pressured, overworked staff are less able to take the time to listen to the stories of community residents or to reflect on the kinds of services that might best meet specific individuals' or groups' needs. Yet, the capacity to listen and reflect on practice choices is a critical ingredient in the development of effective social services. What providers may be left with is less and less of the substance of social services and more and more just its shell. Although some aspects of services are retained, the very process of narrowing constricts the providers' capacity to establish durable and meaningful relationships with individual residents and the larger community. In a sense, such narrowing puts at risk those elements of social services most critical to their success. The Faustian bargain may, therefore, be that to preserve the enterprise of social services, both the quality of what is offered in the short term to people in need must be diminished and over the long term some part of its essential relationship-building character must be sacrificed.

This chapter will explore the character of specific rationing approaches and their influence on the content of social services. The subtle relationship between the intensifying demands of settlement work and the quality as well as meaning of social services will also be examined. A primary theme that runs through this discussion is that the palette of choices and the overall prospect of social services are being narrowed and redefined.

Rationing Social Services

Settlements narrow the availability of social services through the enforcement of rationing. The intention is to heighten the costs of accessing services. From the service users' point of view, a variety of obstacles make it ever more difficult to gain entry into or sustain involvement with a program. These obstacles grow organically out of the accommodations programs make to deal with shifting finances and a decreased workforce.

> The budget cut hurt our four centers. We had to cut back services. We would have seven or eight bus trips and we had to cut that back to four or five.   (D8)

> Some people come in here because they see our name under child care in the yellow pages. They don't want to wait anymore for services. We can help them fill out forms, but in the end, we have to turn them away. We have nothing for them.   (J5)

> We're being expected under managed care to ration the number of visits per client. It used to be we could see Medicaid patients forty times a year now we're restricted to twenty visits.   (G4)

> The after-school program is now 75 kids, it used to be 180. If I got the right funding from the city, the right monies, I could easily open an-

other four or five centers. That's how much demand there is out there for these programs. (B5)

As the following anecdotes illustrate, young adults, children, the unemployed, the homebound elderly, and teenage unwed mothers are all vulnerable to the reduction or rationing of available social services.

The office of unemployment continuously sends us people who have lost their jobs, low-level jobs in factories that are closed. They send them to us because they have to be doing a search to receive their unemployment money but also because they need more support to find another job. We serve not only the new immigrants but also the recently unemployed. These people are flooding our services, and we have to choose who we can serve. We can't serve them all. (H7)

Well, for a lot of people who have just had babies, it takes a long time to get into the program because there just is no room. In the past, the system made it easier for the parent to get some kind of even interim service, but that part of the program is just completely gone. (J5)

Of course, there are cracks in the program. There are youngsters with needs we're just not getting to at all, or even when they are served, we can't provide adequate follow-through. Kids who live in the community, but we just don't have the space in the program to include them or fully include them. (E8)

We cannot give the service to some of the elderly that are in real need of home care and are just waiting and waiting. They've yet to receive the service. (J3)

Controlling the Demand for Social Services

One of the ways for an agency to control its service is to indirectly or directly influence user demand. By raising the costs of accessing the program, the provider can soften the demand for social services. There is a discrepancy between the necessary investment to pursue services and the often modest resources of already beleaguered citizens. This calculus of return on investment and available resources influences the service users' decision to sustain, soften, or abandon their demand for social services.

Over time, the raised access costs are likely to fatigue and frustrate even the most resilient and resourceful community residents. The demand for social services is depleted not by one but rather by a number of barriers. Successful negotiation of these barriers demands financial resources and patience, two commodities that are often in short supply for community residents in need of settlement services.

An increasingly popular rationing strategy is charging a fee for service. Clients' access to the program is predicated on their bearing an ever greater share of the costs of the service. In effect, a larger proportion of the costs of the program are privatized. This is an especially daunting barrier and a powerful drag on the resources of the poorest consumers.

> When the cuts came in December we instituted the most modest fee. It was $95 for the rest of the year, it came to about 50 cents an hour. We still lost 20% of our families. They couldn't afford the 50 cents an hour.   (C15)

> Our clients have been affected basically because we've had to raise our fees over the past fifteen years. The program started off with children and adults paying $3 a week for a private music lesson. So, now for the private lesson it's $18 per week for the child and $21 for an adult. We had to raise the dance and theater fees as well. Fees have increased tremendously, but they are modest compared to what the outside world charges. For this community, the fees are high. Every time we raise the fees, certain people drop out. They just can't afford it anymore.   (F4)

> We have to serve either insured or fee-paying clients. It's getting more and more difficult to serve people who are uninsured and can't afford our fees. Substance abusers with HIV, for instance, often fit into this group.   (I7)

A number of after-school services have also increased the reporting and documentation requirements for the parents of potentially eligible children. As the following comment indicates, these requirements have tempered some of the demand for program services.

We've upped the ante on documentation. This last summer, we made sure that parents bring in tax returns. It's amazing the amount of scholarships we've cut back on just because of this new requirement. A lot of parents are paying more and continuing to use the program. The other side of the coin though is that some parents aren't willing or able to fill out the forms or bring in their tax returns. But the problem is that some of these parents also don't feel they can afford the full cost of the service. Bottom line, we've also lost some of our kids.   (B8)

Demand for a service can also be influenced by access to technology. For many service users, telephones are an essential conduit for initial and ongoing contact with a program. However, changes in the infrastructure of an agency can undermine the clients' ease of telephone access. The absence of staff to assure consistent taking down of messages, systems that require various steps to reach needed personnel, and voice messages that do not indicate future availability of workers are but a few of the ways that phones can fail to facilitate ease of connection and instead thwart community residents' attempts to access services quickly. Repeated phone calls that are unanswered or new systems that remain confusing and impersonal may over time cause clients to stop their pursuit of services because of the heightened time investment and, in some instances, significant frustration.

For other clients, such as seniors, the program's provision of consistent transportation to and from a service center literally assures the clients' physical access to a program. Consequently, the reduction of transportation services deflects relatively frail or vulnerable elderly people from programs that they otherwise would have used. Over time, more erratic provision of transportation can substantially alter the size and composition of a service population.

Clearly, various forms of technology such as phones and vehicles influence service users' capacity to initiate or sustain requests for services. As access to technology is altered, both modest and substantial declines in levels of consumer demand are the consequence. These channels of access are often narrowed in direct and indirect response to resource scarcity.

It's like now we're a business. When you call up, you're going to have to punch in the program you're in. We have fewer receptionists and secretaries so now the system has to make the connection. At times though, the technology is scary. It can drive people away who don't know initially how to use it. I think more important though, people needing counseling or other services used to get a human voice right away. Now the clients aren't getting that. I think there is a cost. The initial connection is just not being made in the same way.   (F1)

The seniors who come here need our services; the alternative is to stay home. Too often as they stay home, they get more and more sick and depressed. But it's getting more difficult to get some of the seniors here. We need money for the transportation. Years ago it used to be one of the services we could readily access, not only in the winter but throughout the year. But getting that transportation service from the city is not as easy as it's been in the past.   (I4)

People call and no one is here to answer the phones. People are put on hold and don't know what's going on. It looks bad for the agency. If there is no set person answering the phone or directing the infor- mation, then the client can get disgruntled. The client just begins to feel they can't get what they need. Some just give up.   (D3)

Settlement programs can also influence demand for services by in- vesting or disinvesting in outreach work. As the demand for services out- strips supply, settlement administrators may decide to lower the profile of particular services by spending less on advertising or by pulling back on activities that heighten the visibility of a program's services. Door-to- door canvassing to remind residents of services, flyers intended to attract potential consumers, and announcements at local organizations or net- works regarding program activities may become less and less part of the work of line staff.

Increasingly, the program may withdraw from contact with the larger community and simply serve those who are actively pursuing services. At least one consequence of this is that better informed and assertive residents are more and more likely to be served. Conversely, residents with fewer of the internal or external resources necessary to learn about or pursue services may be ignored. Moreover, a program's decision to lower its visibility can fracture relationships with the wider community. The program may come to be perceived as isolated and unresponsive. Long-term communal rela- tionships and the needs of relatively hidden consumers are more frequently subordinated to the immediate and pressing demands of day-to-day work.

The decision to reduce outreach work and soften demand for services is described below.

> Services that are available will become harder to find because we stopped advertising.   (C6)

> I put an advertisement in the paper about an available service, and we got a tremendous response. But there was a lot of community anger because the service was gobbled up so fast that if they didn't call in the first day, they were out of luck. We won't be so aggressive again in announcing these services.   (A9)

> We needed to hold the line so that prevented us from reaching out and serving additional youth. We know the need is out there. Many kids could benefit greatly from some of the services we provide. But we have to keep things low-key because we just don't have the money for it.   (B7)

Controlling demand for a service only makes sense when there is an essentially fixed or declining revenue base and a growing clientele. This is the case for many settlement programs. However, a countertendency exists for settlement programs that have an elastic revenue base keyed to the size of their clientele or the volume of service. For instance, a growing proportion of the program budget for mental health services is dependent on Medicaid or managed care reimbursement. Consequently, increases in client contact hours translate into more income for the program. This set of contract conditions when combined with an environment of heightened competition for revenue-producing clients has prompted a number of programs to step up their outreach efforts.

> I think HIP (Health Insurance Program) reimburses at about $40 or $50 dollars a visit. That means our revenue is going to decrease because we used to get more. So we are going to have to beat the bushes to find more clients to just keep our budget even.   (I7)

> Right now Medicaid clients are the crème de la crème for private hospitals. So, we find ourselves competing more and more for Medicaid-eligible clients. It's like a scavenger hunt.   (H8)

Reducing the Supply of Services

At least one consequence of scarce or destabilized financing is a corresponding decline in the supply of social services. The amount of social services can be reduced in a number of ways. However, whether the program outlines a particular strategy for rationing or not is, in a sense, immaterial to such an outcome. Program personnel can be deliberate or idiosyncratic, open or closed, in their decision making, but ultimately they are forced to ration a commodity that has become scarce.

A relatively sweeping strategy is to reduce the time a program is operational. The increased reliance on part-time workers and volunteers in youth programs, for instance, has caused some programs to reduce their daily or weekly work schedule. Other programs have decided to shut down services for relatively extended, predetermined periods to preserve scarce resources. Respondents implied that the burden of such rollbacks was equitably distributed across consumers who had a history of relationships with the program. The general intention was to offer fewer services to the same cohort of community residents.

We lost many hours of individual and group counseling possibilities. We had a weekend program we had to close down for a period of time, and we had to reduce the number of hours in our teen center substantially. We're trying to get to the same kids but in fewer hours and of course with less to offer. In the process we lost some of the kids. (C13)

The hours had to be cut back. We lost one of our evenings and some of our early morning work. Services had to be cut back radically. Home care and walk-in services were affected. We try to make up in other ways. But we have a membership of 3,000 seniors and 300 show up on any given day. Without the hours these services just can't be provided in the same way to our membership. We can't give them as much as we did in the past. (H6)

At the last minute, we put together a summer for these homeless children. We tried to maintain the services we provided in the past, but because of the cut backs we had to restructure. We had a shorter season. (C12)

Service shrinkage can be implemented without disrupting the schedule of a program. For example, a program for people with AIDS may sustain its scheduled hours of nine to five, Monday through Friday, yet curtail what it can provide daily or weekly. Targeted reduction and consequent rationing of specific social services are common in numerous settlement programs.

> In the day program that existed we used to serve about 100 teens over the course of two years. This is a very service-intensive program and each of those teens required many, many interventions, so we can't do what we used to do. A smaller number of people are going to be served in a less intensive way.   (B6)

> RESPONDENT: There will be four workshops that will be offered for employment training.
> INTERVIEWER: Rather than six?
> RESPONDENT: Rather than six.   (C6)

> The pool of money is decreasing, so we can provide only drugs that directly treat HIV-related infections. We can't provide vitamins anymore.   (H8)

> INTERVIEWER: What has been the affect on the level of your service?
> RESPONDENT: I have lost one ESL class and one GED class.   (H7)

> RESPONDENT: We provide meals on-site to hungry kids.
> INTERVIEWER: How many meals is that going to mean are no longer served?
> RESPONDENT: Between 5,000 and 10,000 meals a day will not be served.

> Little by little what we can offer is reduced. The number of hours of housekeeping services, and the number of meals for seniors for instance are less now than a few years ago.   (D4)

Specific rationing approach enables settlement administrators to stretch reduced services and resources. For instance, the number of people in adult classes are often increased to offset losses in faculty lines and sections. Additionally, a client's length of stay in a program may be restricted to permit a greater number of people to be served. The benefits and stresses of such approach are described in the following passages.

> The number of faculty lines has fallen. As a result we've eliminated some of our classes and increased the size of others. A number of our classes have increased in size by about 50 percent.   (H7)

> It's like a shell game. We just keep moving them in and out. They don't keep a job after they are placed. They are told your time is over, we have another group of people coming in, move on. I guess you could say we just keep rotating our clients.   (D5)

For a number of youth programs, the final step in the reduction of service supply was the end of rationing and shutdown of operations. At times the services were abruptly terminated.

> We tried to keep the program going. We got both public and foundation money. The program worked on pregnancy prevention and sexuality. We had as many as ten full-time people. We couldn't handle the fund-raising demands and costs, and eventually we had to close it. Just as an example, if a youngster didn't have medical coverage, we had to provide the service. In the abstract, that is wonderful, but we didn't have the funding to continue that kind of service.   (I3)

> Yeah, they shut some of these programs down very quickly. For example, we had to close five of our after-school programs, oh, about three weeks after the date we were notified of budget reductions.
>   (C14)

> This September will be the first in my memory without the WIN For Kids program. It was instrumental in assisting parents to register their kids for school, arranging for special ed evaluations, helping families obtain day care, moving their records from the sending schools when they relocate to the shelters as well as escorting them to services. None of that is available any longer.   (C12)

Impacts of Internal Rationing

The pressure of the disequilibrium between social service supply and demand is generally resolved at the expense of the service user. In a sense, some part of the pressure and cost of destabilized funding is passed directly from the settlement program to the community resident.

Waiting Lists

Increasingly, the transition from the status of applicant to that of service recipient takes extra time. The apportioning of a reduced supply of services creates client waiting lists. The community resident who does not have immediate access to a program must wait until either current recipients drop out or a new cycle of service provision is initiated.

The waiting lists concretely sustain the promise of service for those who remain outside the program. As programs expand or have to fill recently empty slots, community residents are moved from the waiting lists into the program. However, often the waiting list is more a symbol than a real possibility of a future relationship with a settlement program. The waiting list may not offer actual opportunities in the long or short term for transition into a program. The dropout rates of current consumers may be very low and the prospect of a future expansion of programs may be equally dim. Many consumers therefore experience relegation to a waiting list as a dead end.

> Our day care program has an immense waiting list. Our after-school and senior programs also have very long waiting lists. Getting into these programs is presently very difficult. We're talking very, very long waits for people.   (J4)

INTERVIEWER: How do you bring new clients into the program, first come, first served?

RESPONDENT: Yes, in the beginning it is first come, first served, then I make a waiting list. So, if I find a certain number of kids are dropping out of the program, I can bring in kids on the waiting list.

INTERVIEWER: Has any one dropped out yet?

RESPONDENT: After about three months none of the kids has dropped out yet. So our waiting list numbers are the same. Although sometimes we have kids dropping off the waiting list because they just grow impatient.   (C9)

We have waiting lists for the people on public assistance. We just don't have the employment training classes to meet their needs.   (H7)

We served 75 clients in internships last year, we had about 50 people returning for a second year. So I had about 25 positions to offer as open slots. We received about 125 applications for those 25 positions. Some of them are very qualified, and many were put on a waiting list. They remained on that waiting list the entire year because our turnover in the program has been very low since then.   (D3)

Waiting lists are not always easy to enforce. Community residents with a prior program history may be forced onto such list because of budget exigencies. However, for line workers and administrators such rational explanations do not necessarily ease the value conflicts inherent in the decision to deny service. The sense of ongoing need and the desire to serve are in conflict with the countervailing push to withdraw program resources. Such conflicts are often resolved by following the agency's protocol and disengaging from specific clients' needs. At times, however, this tension may promote modest responses to the needs of clients on the waiting lists who are known to the program.

There is this sense of frustration when we put people we know in the waiting list box instead of being able to serve them. What we've tried to do in the past is at least package something for people on the waiting list. Maybe line a teen up and get those meals served five times a week or maybe heavy laundry. We try to do something.   (C6)

Sure, there is a value tension for us. You meet a person that you've been dealing with for two or three years, and they ask can't you just squeeze so and so in. How do you say no especially when you know the person needs the service. But more and more we do have to say no to people we know. It's like saying Molly needs the service but I can't help her anymore. That's just really difficult.   (D9)

Privatization of Service Support

As settlements allocate available services more restrictively, community residents are implicitly expected to fend for themselves. The withdrawal of services such as senior support, child care, teen counseling, after-school tutorials, and adult education promotes the development of private makeshift arrangements. Working parents, for instance, may continue to require some form of child care when they are shut out of settlement services, and after-school supports for teens may remain a pressing concern for families that are intent on minimizing the influences of the street.

In the absence of alternative sources of formal social services, families are increasingly placed in the position of having to further strain their private networks for such support or expend more of their personal resources in the marketplace. The greater reliance on such resources is a concrete expression of the larger social tendency to redefine collective needs as the problem and responsibility of the individual. In effect, fiscal responsibility for these shared, social needs is being devolved from the state to the individual and is thus being privatized.

> We just don't have the child care space. A lot of times, the child is so much better off here than with an already overwhelmed parent. But the way it stands now, these kids are back with the family, and they have to come up with some other kind of arrangement, often with a grandparent or a friend. It's not the same. This was a haven for a whole bunch of kids, and it just isn't as available to them.   (C15)

> The after-school program is so diminished. Parents can't use it in the same way. Some who can't get their kids in here are going to have to find neighbors or friends to help out. Other parents who do get in are going to have to be able to afford part-time baby-sitters to use it. You've literally got to hire people to get younger kids here and bring them home if the parent is working, which is often the case.   (C9)

> I would say that the families of the frail elderly are going to have to do more. The services just aren't there anymore. They will need to step into the breach with money or time or their parents just won't make it. (E6)

Neglect of Community Residents

As resources are rationed, the needs of many community residents are increasingly underaddressed or unaddressed. For some preschool youngsters, alternative arrangements often represent a stopgap measure. For instance, exhausted and emotionally depleted family members are less likely to be able to provide the continuity or quality of care available through a formal child care program. For other families, a private network as an alternative to formal child care may not even be available. A number of respondents noted that teenagers unable to enroll in after-school recreational programs are increasingly vulnerable to various kinds of trouble. Elderly people with less and less access to critical services will likely suffer a decline in physical health. Finally, for community residents struggling to enter the labor market critical high school equivalency courses are less available. The neglect of these needs and groups of citizens may have profound consequences over time.

When you begin reducing child care, you are often putting more pressure on already depressed and overwhelmed parents. For some, that may be a recipe for abuse. (C15)

After we reduced the hours, we saw a real increase in the drug taking and drinking of some of the kids. After talking to them, it became clear that these kids began getting into substances more and more when the activities here were less and less available to them. (B5)

INTERVIEWER: Where did you send the kids when they couldn't get in here?

RESPONDENT: Other programs are out there but they were affected too. Most of the kids during the summer stayed on the street. But those streets aren't like the ones you or I grew up with. Some of them got into trouble. Now, during the school year they just go home. My guess is they're home watching TV. In a sense they're latchkey kids. (D10)

INTERVIEWER: What has happened to the frail elderly as you've had to cut back on hours?

RESPONDENT: We're seeing more bouncing around from hospitals

> back to their homes and for some placement into nursing homes.
> It's not cost-effective. And more important, all of this takes its toll
> on people who are already teeter-tottering. (G9)

The rationing of social services has created anxiety and anger about "making it," not in regard to an abstract future but rather to the present moment. The settlement consumers' social and economic margin is often very narrow. The rationing of settlement services creates ever greater doubt about the capacity of dwindling resources to meet even basic needs.

> You get a lot of anger because the system just isn't working for them.
> People are feeling as though they are at the very edge, another little
> push and they will be over it. (C11)

> The whole community is concerned about the loss of services. We hear
> the concern from seniors, parents, and children. People are feeling des-
> perate, and more and more don't really know where to turn. (C1)

Rationing of Services External to the Agency

It is relevant to this discussion that consumers' experience with rationing extends well beyond settlements. Income supports and social services are being rolled back in many, if not most, public and private not-for-profit agencies. This creates a twofold problem for settlement workers. On the one hand, they have an often diminished amount of social services to offer, and on the other, the rationing of settlement house services is compounded by the greater scarcity of services in the wider community. The pressures on the workers cannot be relieved by quickly referring consumers elsewhere. In a landscape of retrenched social services, referral demands a greater allocation of already scarce time to advocacy. Equally important, such investment may produce few if any payoffs.

> We have long waiting lists, and the population that we serve is mostly
> chronic and very needy. We don't have access to resources elsewhere.
> No matter what we do, the resources just aren't as available in the
> community, and so the options for our clients are fewer. (B3)

There just aren't services available elsewhere. We make the effort, but the places we might have referred to in the past just aren't taking. (G8)

The small stand alone. What can I say, it feels like we have fewer and fewer places we can refer our clients to. The resources are just drying up. I guess you could say we feel more isolated too.   (D10)

As more and more agencies are cut back, we have fewer and fewer places to go with our referrals. We can't handle cases in the same way and neither can they. New agencies aren't starting up to pick up the slack. More and more it feels like we're alone out here trying to hold on with fewer and fewer places to turn to for support.   (B1)

Perhaps most distressing to respondents is the greater difficulty of accessing an array of basic income and support services. Such services are perceived as a lifeline for many community residents. But as, for instance, Medicaid is altered under managed care and as welfare devolves to the states, these services are undergoing intensified rationing.

Critically, face-to-face encounters with welfare workers at intake provides less and less assurance that those referred will be found eligible. Equally important, more and more welfare recipients are finding it increasingly difficult to stay eligible. New eligibility and work requirements have made the recipients' relationship to welfare less stable. The welfare rolls in New York City have dropped by more than 50 percent in the 1990s. Consequently, settlement workers experience welfare as a less reliable source of income for both potential and current recipients.

In New York City the intensified rationing concerning basic needs such as health care and income has also been extended to shelters for homeless families. Many respondents remarked that referrals to family shelters impose more and more demands on both the consumer and the worker. To begin with, the waiting periods are longer at intake because the number of access points in the city have been reduced from three to one. Second, some respondents suggested that the definitions of homelessness are more restrictive and that documentation requirements necessary to establish eligibility have increased. As a result, entry into the shelters is both less predictable and more time-consuming. With consumers waiting for longer periods of time in often makeshift, substandard, or dangerous housing situations until their eligibility is determined, there is a growing sense of reduced options for some of the most desperate community residents.

As new rationing standards are applied to health care, income support, and sheltering resources, settlement referrals are likely to generate less for consumers yet paradoxically demand greater investment on the part of the workers. The growing confusion and difficulty in navigating these mazes of critical community resources is illustrated below.

I'd say that we're spending more and more time trying to get people on Medicaid. It is very time-consuming and interferes with our ability to help those clients who are not trying to get on Medicaid. Even after they are on Medicaid and having to do the recertifications, it mounts up.   (E5)

Vision, ears, speech, and language in the past with Medicaid they could go to any provider. Now, though, this is not considered important, and so they can't get a referral. Now they tell us they are no longer on Medicaid, but this or that HMO service. There are about twenty of them competing with each other in the Bronx. Lo and behold, we sent them to try and get the evaluation services, and they were rejected. The rules, what is available to these clients is all changing.   (D9)

We used to be able to send families to the EAU [intake agency for homeless families in the New York City Emergency Assistance Unit], and it went pretty smoothly. People got into the shelters. Now though it is so much more difficult to prove they are homeless. Even if they are living in a trebled-up situation with an abusive person, which in the past was never questioned, now they may not get in on their first or second try at intake.   (F8)

If they need medication, the Health and Hospital Corporation, which used to give it out, charged $1 for it. Now that's gone. So, people can't afford to pay for psychotropic drugs. So, when someone calls we have to ask, do you have insurance? Do you have the money to pay for it? Some of the medication costs $100 dollars a week. More and more, really desperately needy people are not getting what they need in medication. And we can't solve the problem, we're not a dispensing agency, we're not a place that can give out medication.   (I7)

For people on welfare, it is getting harder and harder to get people on and keep them on. For those clients it means that we have to work harder and harder just to keep them even. If they are threatened with eviction and need extras, well, you have to dance even faster, and even then you don't know if you will get what in the past was always there.   (C2)

Income support grants lag behind cost-of-living increases. This gap has significant implication. For settlement workers, the consequence is that even as such dollars are accessed or sustained, the payoffs are more and more limited. Some respondents remarked that the payment schedules are placing the most vulnerable clients in ever greater jeopardy.

Sometimes, I think that welfare is kind of not real. Even when you get people on the grant, it is less and less able to keep people going. People with great needs are more and more at risk. The teen mom with nowhere to turn and no skills is in a situation where the housing costs and size of the welfare check make it very difficult for her to break into the housing market. The single guy on SSDI, what can he afford without some kind of housing break. But the breaks, like Section 8, that may have been there in the past just aren't there now.
(A1)

For our seniors, the value of whatever they get from Social Security and SSI is getting smaller and smaller. Even as they get a little more, their rents are automatically adjusted upward. It adds very little to their disposable income. They're having to do more with less. They keep stretching. What they worry about and what concerns us is when they are no longer able to make ends meet.   (D8)

The rationing of services external to settlements extends well beyond shelter, income, and health care needs. Grassroots agencies and schools with whom settlements have often partnered in providing, for example, food, counseling, and remedial education have also had to ration their scarce supply of program services. Clearly, the calculus of rationing varies. A point of agreement among respondents, however, was that previously accessible community programs have become less able to quickly process and accept referrals.

> We used to have more agencies in East Harlem we could refer our clients to for counseling, day care, recreation, or a bag of food. Now there are fewer of these programs with less money. People are having a harder and harder time accessing services. Our referrals mean less and less.   (H8)

> When we couldn't provide the needed housekeeping services, we could depend on the visiting nurses. They have nurses who have worked in the community for a number of years. But it's getting more and more difficult. The manpower is just not there in the same way. They don't have the personnel anymore to take care of the people we refer.   (I4)

> The students don't know where to go. Throughout the community and city, bilingual programs are being cut back. Few of us are keeping these programs alive. Where do you send these people, it's a critical need, but those agencies that are providing the service have long waiting lists.   (H7)

> Look, there are fewer places to send these kids for after-school recreational programs. Even the board of education's programs have been reduced. We wait longer, and for some kids the connection is just never made.   (J4)

> More and more we don't know whether the hospitals are going to be there. A kid that needs a psych evaluation has more and more difficulty getting it. These are things you need right away, you can't schedule it for three months from now. We really need the services to be there. We all know when you put things off, it just becomes more costly.   (J2)

Redefining the Quality of Social Services

Social services are being redefined along two axes. Along one dimension the quantity of services is being reduced; these changes are generally measurable and visible. Palpable drops in service supply are more immediately experienced by service users, settlement workers, and the larger community. Often conversation regarding service changes focuses exclusively on scarcity and restricted access. Such a narrow quantitative perspective on current changes often reinforces a mechanistic understanding of social services. The aspects of services that are highlighted are those that lend themselves to relatively easy measurement. Too often, the full experience of service is reduced to discrete items such as outcome or output. What is lost or gained during moments of change may only be understood in terms of such indices.

The second axis of social services is directly concerned with matters of quality. The reconstitution of social services in settlements extends beyond supply and quantitative product to the quality and content of what is being offered by providers. This point is generally illustrated in the comments below.

> Even though money is key, money is essential, even though money is what keeps things open, the quality of the service is not the same. Quality has been suffering even when the program has been generally on an even keel, but when you get cuts, it gets even worse.   (C9)

> Look, quality of services especially in mental health is really seriously threatened. I think in the future mental health services will be like a pharmacy, just a series of quick fixes.   (F3)

> So you try to keep the core services and trim the other kinds of things. The problem is as you trim, you keep carving away a lot of what added quality to your overall program.   (E3)

Reduced Relationship to Consumer and Community

A robust service experience can often be traced in part to the relational connections between line staff and community residents. The technical skill of staff or inventiveness of the program structure are necessary ingredients in the mix of effective social services. However, these technical and structural dimensions of effective service must be linked to the work of relationship building.

Many respondents remarked that the scope of social service relationships is being narrowed. For some programs increased internal demands on the workers have translated into more restricted encounters and conversations with community residents. For others, heightened external demands on clients from income support programs, such as welfare, have reduced their capacity to more fully engage with settlement workers and services. Across a broad range of programs, the pressures of time and demand are creating decreasing and narrower opportunities for building service relationships.

> The effect on our services is qualitative. We have less time to see people. The people doing the serving are more anxious and angry and probably less motivated because of the pressure to keep up their counts. If I were getting services, I would probably feel shortchanged.
> (H8)

> There has been a huge downside of the restructuring. The plan moved really fast, and somehow the personal touch that we were able to give, more of the hand-holding, taking more time to listen to people has been lost. We had to do it because we are just so overworked, we just don't have the time for that anymore.   (E8)

> Our clients are more subject to the demands of WEP. The whole idea of teaching and learning is more and more subject to the disruptions of WEP. Students are pulled away from class because of their work schedules. We are a second priority. Teachers have less time to build relationships with the students or get the material to them. Every day is more difficult.   (H7)

> The quality of the relationships that we can establish with the kids has changed. We have less time to to work with them on their problems, to make sure that they are guided. We just can't help them as much as we did in the past to develop the kinds of experiences necessary to lead productive lives.   (I3)

> The whole notion of dealing with self-esteem or interpersonal issues has changed. It's much less of a priority. Now it's just getting people to function in a very quick way and getting them back to school or work.   (G5)

The quality of a service relationship is the product of the richness of encounter both in a single moment in time and over time. If the ongoing relationships with a service provider or program are disrupted or ended, the consequences can be significant. Breakdowns in service continuity can unravel ties that bind community residents to a specific program or provider. Service disruptions are often remedied without regard to repairing the consumers' quality of relationship and engagement with staff.

> The process just gets worse and worse. You have all of these kids you lose in between because there is no continuity of service. You may never see them again. You may get one or two shots at a certain population, and after that they are done with you. They may smile at you as they walk past you, but after that they are done with you. They won't really deal with you again in the same way.   (C5)

> People who have a relationship with the home attendant for a number of years went through the turmoil of having to see that relationship end because home attendants were no longer able to maintain the jobs they had. Some actually quit because they did not want to go from one client to another in the same building or in the community. It seriously affected the lives of many seniors who had established relationships with housekeepers.   (I4)

> You can't have real quality of relationship without continuity of personnel. But without stable funding you can't have continuity of personnel.   (J4)

The quality of a service can also be traced to the breadth of relationship. For instance, the capacity to work between programs and provide more wholistic or integrated services for consumers represents at least one benefit of interdepartmental cooperation. Such ease of movement and development of a joint plan, however, is less and less possible as each unit is pressed to simply provide the basics. The complex needs of the individual consumer are less likely to be systematically explored, coordinated, or addressed through a variety of settlement programs as resource constraints worsen.

> We've always talked about more holistic services within the agency. We talked about integrating services. It's clear with budget cuts, that is becoming more and more difficult.   (I2)

This is a place where services have been connected to each other. Teens used to come here for employment counseling. That was a way we were able to get parents in an ESL program or grandparents in our senior center. Now though with less time and attention to the whole family, we are losing that connection.   (C13)

Sometimes the children in our day care program have emotional problems. We depended on our mental health units here to give us some priority. We've always used our people, some of them right here in the building. In that way the child could come right out of our program and go to a play therapist. We just don't have that as much now, since they cut back.   (A7)

We had kids who would come here twelve hours a week on an intergenerational grant providing some of the services to the seniors. It was good for the elderly people here and the kids. They learned about each other. The work became a learning experience for the teens and not only provided concrete help for the seniors like escort and shopping assistance, it also put them in contact with young people, which for some was a source of energy they fed off of. What happened though was they cut the stipend, and it's become more difficult finding kids.   (B4)

The relationship of the settlement houses to the larger community has also narrowed. Contact with community residents not presently receiving services to identify their needs or strengthen services is less and less frequent. Specific prevention services have also been rolled back. Developing relationships with the underserved to extend services, prevent problems, or deepen ties to the broader community is less and less a priority in the qualitative work of social services.

We had an alcohol and substance abuse program that was lost. Our work on the streets to prevent youth crime was also affected by budget cuts. These programs got us into the community and allowed us to do prevention work. It gave us a different kind of connection to the neighborhood. To some extent it got us out of the agency. But now that's all been cut back.   (G2)

We used to go into the community and find out what the young people were interested in and develop a program around their interests. Out of that would come a trust with the kids because we were out there touching base, listening, and trying to create programs that were responsive. It helped to bring kids in here who otherwise might have gotten into trouble. Now though, we can't be out there like that, and I know it affects our relationship with the kids in the neighborhood.

(C5)

We go into the community and try to help them get stabilized, so they won't become homeless again. This money is more and more restricted, and we've taken some hits. The unfortunate part of this is that people sometimes become homeless because the services are not in the community to prevent it. We need to provide more supports not less. (I5)

The families or friends of the homeless clients knew we were not shelter employees and they could come and talk to us rather than the caseworkers who they often feared would be punitive. We were a buffer between the shelter and family or friends outside of the shelter. We helped prevent some things from building up and blowing up. But now with the restructuring we can't do as much of that kind of work anymore.   (C12)

The Narrowing of Service Relationships and Income Generation

For mental health services the relationship between consumers and providers is being rewritten by managed care companies. Financial incentives have been developed that join the maximization of program revenue with briefer forms of intervention and more circumscribed problem definitions. On this basis the definitions of eligibility criteria and services have become narrower and narrower.

More restrictive matching of needs to program responses, although promoting certain efficiencies, simultaneously shoehorns consumers into service categories that may be inappropriate to their circumstance. For such consumers the quality, if not the very legitimacy, of the service experience will be tainted. These intensifying limits on interventive choices and service relationships are especially critical for populations with chronic or complex mental health problems.

> We have to learn short-term techniques, which to me is contradictory to whatever we have been taught. This is especially true for chronically ill patients. You cannot use short-term techniques for very chronically ill and socially disadvantaged or multiproblem families and individuals. (E1)

> You've got to do it if you're going to survive. You've got to move people through the program in briefer periods of time. There is always the balancing act between the dollar side of it and the quality of the service. I think most of our senior staff think that dollars are driving it, not best service. . . . I think they may be right. (G7)

Increased emphasis on the revenue-producing capacity of consumers results in a more commodified service relationship. The connection between provider and user is experienced less as a complex caregiving relationship and more as a fiscally driven marketplace exchange. This shift restricts and redefines the way in which providers imagine and structure the service relationship.

The consumer's claim on the provider as a result of specific needs or prior history with the program is diminished. The new imperative of the service encounter requires that staff spend more of their time and imagination on assessing the financial benefit the consumer brings to the program. Calculations regarding benefit are more quantitative and financial and are assessed from the point of view of the program. What is gradually lost are the qualitative, relational benefits the program can offer to the consumer. It is important to reiterate that this is not a zero-sum game but rather part of an ongoing push-pull that gradually redefines and narrows parameters of the qualitative relational aspects of service provision.

> I think that is the struggle, that you want to offer quality services to people, and at the same time you have to worry about where you are going to get the money. I think that we are paying more and more attention to the eligibility and revenue issues and less and less to the simple need for service. That changes things for us. It's sad that you have to look at people as dollar bills instead of people in need. (A3)

We're are losing the freedom and the real humaneness in treating someone who is ill. More and more we have to look to the billing, it's inhuman especially in mental health.   (B3)

Redefining the Concrete Dimensions of Social Services

The quality of social services is also associated with the range of choices available to recipients. After-school youth programs that include tutorial, recreational, counseling, mentoring and leadership services are qualitatively different from those focusing exclusively on sports. In addition, within each of these areas of program service, choices are made about the kinds of activities to be promoted. For instance, recreational services may include indoor and outdoor sports as well as trips outside the community. The dimensions of services are therefore constituted on two levels: programatically and within the specific modules of service activity.

The dimensions of services are subject to flux. For example, as more and more demands for productivity are imposed on workers, specific kinds of service activities may be emphasized as others are deemphasized or eliminated. Ultimately, the composition of services is not static. Often these changes can occur gradually; over time, however, the quality and kind of services offered may be substantially altered.

It is important to note that the content of services has been analytically bundled with matters of quality. This merging is consistent with respondents' understanding of service. For instance, the elimination of counseling in a youth program is experienced as not only redefining the nature of the service but also undercutting its quality. Social services were implicitly described as a kind of commodity that tightly intertwines matters of quality and content.

In many programs the concrete activities associated with the service were narrowed. A large part of this change was experienced as a peeling away of options or choices associated with specific services.

So, there are service cracks that occur. There are young people who are leaving, and we're not following up. We can't anymore. We want to but can't. We have one social worker for 1,000 sometimes 2,000 kids who have crises. We're trying, but we just can't follow up in ways that we might have in the past.   (I3)

Part of what we were doing was exposing youngsters to computers and technologies to develop them as leaders. We can't do that anymore. We are cutting basic components of the program. It changes what we can do.   (D5)

We lost a pre-GED service that combined high school equivalency preparation with basic English literacy skills. Many people in the neighborhood needed it, recent immigrants and even people native to the country. It really limits what our program can do for a group of people who have a real need for our services.   (H7)

So, the staff is left with almost double their caseload, and that, of course, impacts on treatment. The workers are not going to be able to provide the kinds of services that they always have. They're just not going to be able to provide concrete and advocacy services. Also, advocacy with the schools for the children will at least be cut back. This was an important part of our mix of services. What we're doing is changing the quality of what we offer.   (I2)

What they used to do was they could go to the home, they would take the kids to the park, they would provide meals, everything. Now that doesn't happen.   (J5)

For some programs, part of the struggle is to preserve not simply quality but core services.

In redefining our services we're trying to figure out what hurts the least, what will hurt the program the least. So, you try to keep core services and trim the other kinds of things you felt were adding a lot of quality to the program.   (D11)

Restructuring has at times forced a rollback in essential or core services. As these basic elements disappear, the very legitimacy of a service may be called into question. A threshold in the basic makeup of a service may ultimately be crossed, and then intensifying dissonance may occur between present and past understanding regarding the components and, perhaps more fundamentally, the meaning of a specific service. The shedding of basic or core elements of a service promotes a critical trade-off. The shell or name of a service may be preserved while the most elemental aspects of the identity and experience of what is provided are sacrificed. Such changes were especially evident in the area of youth services.

> Do I still provide the same type of service as before? No. In fact we've had to give up such basic parts of the vocational service I don't know if we really can call ourselves a vocational service any longer.   (E8)

> I think, you know, we are trying to preserve what we have as much as we can, but there's a lot missing. Basic stuff now is missing. The gym alone in terms of a sports program was an enormous draw. To tell a kid that it's no longer available is hard. All they want to do is play ball. The gym is there collecting dust. We can't open it because we had to make choices. No staff, too much in terms of liability costs. So I have basketballs, a gym, and no after-school sports program. That's basic and we can't provide it.   (D10)

> The core program now doesn't exist, the trips, the recreational kinds of things, the arts. We don't have the resources for them. But increased funding for the counseling and prevention is there. I try to stay with a plan and say we are providing a comprehensive network of services for youth, but it doesn't wash anymore because the things that get them through the door are missing.   (E8)

The Tension Between Increased Paperwork and the Quality of Services

The amount of paperwork associated with government contracts is perceived as growing. The burden of these paperwork requirements has implications for the content and quality of social services. As line workers and administrators spend more time filling out forms, certain aspects of service provision are neglected or rushed. The direct trade-off in time investment between paperwork and the quality of a social service is illustrated in the comments below.

> We're always under the gun for reports, paperwork handed in on a timely basis. You can't have that kind of pressure and still try to provide

a quality service. Something has to give, and almost always it's the
service.   (F6)

Every year we have to add one more item to the reports. The report
used to be one report twice a year, now we have to report every month,
and every month has a deadline, and we know if we miss the deadline,
we may lose funding. Everything is reprioritized. The time we spend
with students has to be decreased because without getting all this paperwork done, we don't get paid.   (H7)

The demands of paperwork, however, extend beyond time spent filling
out forms. The most recent generation of forms promote a more restricted
and, at times, punitive service role for providers. Increased emphasis on
quantifiable measures of worker productivity legitimates or delegitimates the
provision of specific services. In this way, paperwork has made it more difficult to preserve specific qualitative aspects of service provision. Moreover,
new eligibility demands imposed on consumers require that the social workers monitor compliance or noncompliance. The workers are expected to
enforce or police the heightened eligibility requirements set by the state.
These policing functions influence the concrete content of service as well
as the relationship between consumer and program personnel.

Our teacher likes to teach for the sake of teaching, and we think that
students should study for the sake of studying. Now we are like a
policeman, we have to make sure that a person stays at least a certain
amount of time. We also have to report if the person doesn't come. I
have to tell our funding agencies that attendance is not satisfactory,
but then you know she's going to lose living expenses; how is she going
to live. They relate to us differently as a result, and we relate to them
differently.   (H7)

The paperwork changes everything. Everything is based on productivity. What we do must fit into the boxes on the forms. We had evolved
into a program providing different services in drug and alcohol treatment. So much of what we provided though was outside the boxes.
So, really we can't do it and expect to be funded. Also, because everything about the forms is about efficiency and productivity, the way we
do things is changing. For instance, to make intake quicker; we'll do

it over the phone. Is the assessment the same as when we do a face-to-face? Of course not, but it is quicker.   (G7)

The forms restrict the services we can provide. They put the money in a particular category, and then whatever services are provided have to be match the category. I cannot spend over here and must spend over there. And if I have to spend over there, I have to fill out a special requisition form, which is discouraging. These categories are more and more restrictive and tie our hands on the kinds of service we can provide. At times there are ways around it, but it's cumbersome and time-consuming.   (A3)

7 Navigating the Current Fiscal Turbulence While Struggling to Chart a Social Services Future

The destabilization of settlement house funding and the aftershocks to its infrastructure, workforce, and services represents a fault line in the experience of social work practice. Settlement house administrators are struggling to preserve some part of their program structure while simultaneously using the current difficulties as an impetus to develop innovative ways to deliver social services. This tension between the immediate, often constraining, consequences of fiscal instability and the strategic effort to sustain and reconceptualize social services is perhaps the most defining feature of settlement life.

The proactive response developed by settlements has been multipronged. One feature is the systematic attempt to develop fresh revenue streams. Although new sources of funding are necessary to recreate fiscal equilibrium, such resources do not assure innovation. On the contrary, fund-raising is often intended only to preserve or expand existing services. Financing, though necessary, is not sufficient to promote innovation. The latter often emerges from a complex mix of an agency's history, leadership, and commitments.

Finally, settlements cannot unilaterally impose a particular imprint on present or future programs. As the preceding chapters have indicated, shifts in the larger political environment have affected settlement life. Consequently, respondents suggested that agencies must make more of a commitment to political advocacy and organizing if they intend to open up new lines of funding or debate on social services.

Almost without exception, interviews with settlement administrators focused on present instability and perceived possibilities. Although conditions were described as increasingly difficult, constrained, and unpredictable, there was little, if any, sense of surrender. Time and again respondents returned in their discussions to new or proposed services that offered some hope for expanding the shrinking boundaries of their practice. The content of these initiatives varied by agency and program; however, the intention to hold the line and, over time, to create approaches that provided greater benefits to community residents remained constant. The struggle to maintain fiscal viability while reimagining the settlements' community-building role continues to be a defining feature of settlement life.

Managing Fiscal Change

Trawling for Dollars

The broad destabilization of government contracts has encouraged more entrepreneurial approaches to fund-raising. Increased attention is focused on replacing uncertain or shrinking public dollars with private revenues. There are many sources of private funds; for instance, foundations, individual patrons, and fund-raising events, such as cookie sales or auctions, are distinctive pathways to private resources. Each of these approaches requires different kinds of skills and networks. A basketball fund-raiser likely will draw on community residents to sell tickets, locate teams, organize a concession stand, and secure a facility. Alternatively, foundation fund-raising requires a polished proposal, an articulate presentation of program ideas, and contacts capable of assuring an initial audience with key decision makers.

Such fundraising is not new. Settlements have traditionally developed private fundraising initiatives. There is a growing realization, however, that the balance between private and public dollars must be altered.

> The public money is just running out. We're all looking more and more to find private contributors to fill the gaps in our funding. More and more of what we do will depend on raising private funds.   (B2)

> There is a constant need to find resources. It is especially difficult now because of the uncertainty of government funding. So we have proposals for foundations slated for an expansion.   (H8)

There's always the feeling of the unknown on government funding. That's the primary reason why the development director has been charged with finding alternative revenue streams so that we're not as dependent on government funding.   (E10)

We're doing quite a bit more private fund-raising. We have a theater fund-raiser in the fall. We're doing some things in East Hampton in the summer. Two of our dance companies go out there and perform.
(F14)

Private fundraising is up this year, we're making a concentrated effort. It relates specifically to foundations, individual contributions, board giving, and the antique show, all of which have gone up significantly this year.   (A1)

Agency assets that have not yet yielded maximum return on their value are another source of private revenue. Space previously given away was more likely to be rented out. Revenue-producing programs, such as fitness centers, were enhanced and the price of membership increased to correspond to market value. Increasingly, sliding-scale fees were charged for certain program services. Finally, board members were expected to take on a growing fund-raising role. In a sense, the resources of the settlement were increasingly commodified and evaluated on the basis of their income potential.

We're reconstituting our board. We're taking on new people. We're looking to take on people who are networked at higher levels of business. Others may be successful professionals and have money. We need board members who have money themselves or access to money.   (H1)

One of our main goals is to increase private revenue by renting our facilities. We have gotten more birthday parties here. We've rented the pool. At times we've inadvertently rented out the space on program time, and they can't run their program. We're trying to minimize those conflicts. But we desperately need the private revenue, it's a catch-22. Bottom line, we hope to generate $35,000 to $40,000 dollars a year in renting out space.   (E4)

We need to shore up and charge more for our revenue-producing programs, like our fitness center.   (E5)

The minimum that we were charging for therapy was $7 on a regular visit and the maximum was $40. We have increased that to a minimum of $20 and a maximum of $50. One or two patients said, I was wondering why you didn't charge more. Staff is uncomfortable with it and I understand, but the thing is you can't charge that little anymore.   (A10)

The increased emphasis on private fundraising is not without its limitations. A number of respondents remarked that the competition for private dollars has intensified, and once secured, private funding produces only time-limited support for a program.

A lot of us are trying to raise private dollars. The problem is a lot of people are often fighting for the same money. The competition is intense.   (F16)

The experience I have is that when you connect with one of these organizations or individuals, they'll support you for a period of time, then from their perspective, they want to share the wealth and switch to another organization. I can understand it from their perspective, but it hurts everyone.   (G11)

The settlement houses' stepped up fund-raising is not limited to private dollars. Administrators have also cast their gaze on funds previously dedicated to running public programs. As public services are privatized and put out to bid, settlements have had the opportunity to compete for these contracts. However, the scaling back of public services has provided benefits to only a modest number of settlements. Moreover, the benefits of such privatization were neither equally shared across settlements nor were they limitless. On the contrary, often the larger settlement houses were better prepared to capitalize on such opportunities. Finally, public-sector sheltering services in New York City were especially vulnerable to privatization during the period of the study.

We're taking over the armory for homeless women. If someone is going to run a program for homeless women in the neighborhood, it really should be us. The city shelter system, much of it is being privatized. They're currently in the process of turning seven shelters over to not-for-profits. That is a direct result of cuts in the DHS [Department of Homeless Services] budget. Not-for-profits do it cheaper.   (E3)

> We are in the process of taking over the Third Street prenatal shelter.
> It went up for bid. The city ran a shelter for homeless pregnant women
> for many years, and it was put up for bid and we won the RFP.   (I1)

The search for new dollars extends to public contracts that have been
terminated. In a highly competitive funding environment, there generally
is no shortage of applicants for dollars that have to be reallocated because
an agency is assessed unfit to continue providing a specific service. In this
zero-sum game of mobile service dollars the misfortune of one agency may
advantage another.

> They call me and say we have a program that hasn't worked out at
> another agency can you guys take it. That's how our midnight program
> started.   (D2)

> There's a day care program, which Bethlehem used to run out of here,
> out of our building. They were a tenant of ours for thirty or forty years,
> and we just felt very strongly we could do a better job. The city recently
> gave us the contract.   (E4)

Finally, the pursuit of public dollars demands ever more intense scrutiny
of RFP (Request for Proposal) listings at all levels of government. The general intention is to capture dollars to support existing services. At times,
however, the public sector's expectation is to start up new services and projects. This funding stream available for more experimental uses, although
limited, offers modest opportunities for settlements to reinvent services.

Public funds, however, are difficult to access because of the growing
competition for scarce resources and complex proposal development requirements. Larger settlements enjoy a distinct advantage in this competitive
process because they more often have development offices. The fund-raising
professionals working with these offices have the expertise and time (often
unavailable in smaller and even midsized settlements) necessary to complete
the daunting requirements of a public sector proposal. Housing creation for
specific populations, crime prevention, and the development of for-profit
work programs were most often cited by settlement administrators as recently
funded or subjects of proposals in progress. Interestingly, public funding of
for-profit companies, brick-and-mortar projects, and crime reduction initiatives, although having certain merits, is in harmony with a more constricted,
politically conservative understanding of social services.

The New York City Housing Authority in conjunction with the Department of Health has given us $200,000 to reach out to young people who are involved in drugs, using them, or selling them in the projects of East Harlem. We've been in this for over a year in a not very effective program that could be a bit of an embarrassment. Yet, they've got lots of money and are talking about adding another $100,000 to the mix.   (H1)

We developed a proposal for the federal government's Job Program. I was working as the program director and at the same time trying to get letters of support, writing parts of the proposal, and so on. I can wind up doing this kind of thing five or six times a year; it takes a lot of time, which I really don't have.   (C11)

We just started the supportive housing, which is a new program. It is housing for chronically mentally ill Asians. It's the first program of its kind, I believe, on the East Coast.   (A5)

We decided about a year ago to develop a consumer-run business. It's a wonderful idea that also has a funding source attached to it. So we're talking about developing a messenger service that is a business rather than a part of the rehabilitation program.   (E4)

The biggest thing is the AIDS housing. It was conceptualized seven years ago as a three-generation model to ensure the survival of kids. It was the first model in New York that was developed to assure the survival of the kids. It was designed with suite apartments so that the grandparents could move in and support the parents. The grandparent allowed the parent to stay home and provide more consistent support. They are only hospitalized when their condition is acute.   (I7)

Focusing on the Bottom Line

The settlement and its workforce are coping with the current turbulence by hunkering down and attempting to assure perhaps the most primal form of bottom line, survival. A basic touchstone question that is asked again and again in this process is "how do we remake ourselves to assure survival?" Old methods may have to be melded with or give way entirely to new approaches. This reorientation requires not simply supplementing or replacing one set of techniques with another but also the acceptance, if not internalization, of a shifting conception of social services. These accommodations, as noted in the previous chapter, often place greater emphasis on easily quantifiable, short-term, and restricted interventions.

> We are going to have to change the way we do things. We have to sort of go along, if we intend to be around in the future. The people who manage mental health services think anything can be quantified, rationalized, and shortened. We will continue to try to do our job in more creative and effective ways, but we have to go along with the general philosophy and retrain ourselves as well as retool our services.
> (A2)

> Our program has to pull back. We have to rethink what we are doing and how we are doing it if we want to survive. That's always on our minds. (D12)

> We have to think about doing things in a different way. Less of a mom-and-pop store. Survival will be based on doing things in a different way. We need to get our staff into courses at schools like NYU that gives them a new way of doing the work. (G11)

Surviving fiscal turbulence or uncertainty requires that greater attention is paid to developing ever leaner, more efficient budgets. Fiscal equilibrium is a top priority for administrators. The concrete concern is that the program not fall into a deficit situation. No matter what the trade-off to services, the program must above all remain fiscally viable or solvent. This bottom-line principle is rarely violated.

> No matter what, the budget has to add up. What we are spending has to be covered by the dollars that are coming in. If this doesn't happen, nothing else is possible. If we project a deficit, then we have to take steps to reduce our costs. That's very basic. Otherwise we may not be around next year. It gets tougher and tougher to make it all add up. At times we have to really dilute what we are offering. (C1)

> Everything's up for grabs. We're talking about restructuring all the programs. We knew we were going to have to stretch the budget to

make it all work. Departments had to meet separately and submit 4 percent to 5 percent cuts. In areas where the cuts didn't come through, it made us more cost effective.   (G1)

The staff has a terrible problem dealing with the changed environ-ment, the fact that we are no longer a charity and we have to break even. Mental health has screamed for years about not wanting to be a Medicaid mill, and they have run a very high quality program. Yet the pressure for productivity, to see more people, to make sure we survive, has been difficult. It's also difficult in day care.   (H1)

As the agencies' work is focused on tending to the bottom line, the lan-guage and orientation of administrators become more businesslike. The bot-tom line, it is suggested, requires that settlements adopt a more corporate or businesslike approach to their work. The culture of settlements, which often ascribes greater importance to needs than to costs, is perceived by such respondents as increasingly out of sync with the new demands of service delivery.

You may have an idea of what a settlement is, but I've given up on that idea. You have to have a good business if you want to survive and help poor people.   (G5)

For funders, it's more and more the bottom line or results. The current atmosphere has forced us to think more and more like business people even though we are not trained to think that way.   (F13)

We need to be more corporate. Just because you're a not-for-profit, there is no reason not to run this place more like a business. It is a business. We need to think more like businessmen if we're going to survive.
                                                              (G11)

It's been difficult to move into the new mind-set of social services. Mak-ing sure we have the enrollment and attendance to gather our maximum number of dollars. To be as efficient and businesslike as we can. To be tough and aggressive in making the thing work. I think we in the not-for-profit field are terrible in thinking this way. It's been a struggle to move into a more realistic mind-set.   (H1)

With the rise of managed care, there has been intensified competition among not-for-profits for clients. Moreover, as resources have diminished in areas such as youth services, programs have attempted to position themselves in the competition for remaining dollars. This heightened competition in combination with the more businesslike practices of settlements has led to social services being marketed. The intention is to more effectively reach critical stakeholders, sell the advantages of a program, and ultimately maximize revenues.

> We're just trying to market ourselves so that we offer something that other programs don't. We know managed care is here, and we have to learn how to work within it.   (F7)

> To be managed-care ready, you really have to look at your own system and gear up to market yourself. We have to keep up with what other agencies are offering but at the going rate to be able to compete. We have to ask "what do we offer that is unique and could attract clients?" It's a money game not a quality game.   (C2)

> The way youth service RFP's are set up, and with less money to go around, there's a constant battle in this community between agencies. Part of our job to remain competitive has been to figure out a special role for ourselves and market it with funders.   (E2)

A final step in any transition to a business orientation is the incorporation of profit making in the design of a service. A few settlement administrators noted that they were actively exploring the possibility of developing for-profit enterprises. Profit-making activity, though still only in the exploratory stage, was perceived as an essentially untapped and critical new source of revenue. A concern, however, was that competitors in the private sector might object to not-for-profits encroaching upon their markets and lobby to limit, if not eliminate, such initiatives.

> One of the things that has been percolating for a while is developing a for-profit business. We need to be more entrepreneurial, develop new ways of thinking, of adding to the budget of the agency. We're thinking of starting a gardening room business. We've had discussions with people in Riverdale, and they've told us there is a need. So now we're setting up a meeting with a foundation to see if we can get it off the ground.   (D1)

The museums have done for-profit work very effectively over the past twenty years or so. Now we're thinking of moving in this direction. What we need though is an education effort as to what the breadth of our activity could be. A lot of agencies are frightened that business-people will react, and they're not sure what is allowed under the not-for-profit umbrella. We need to be educated about how we can do this kind of work legally and not cross wires with the business people or the government. (G10)

We're thinking of starting up a for-profit messenger service. I'm not saying for-profit business is the future of settlements, but we do need to think about ways of creating programs that serve people's needs and at the same time can bring extra dollars into the agency. It makes sense financially and in the way we present ourselves. These kinds of jobs get people ready for the real-world demands of for profit work. (I1)

The narrow focus on bottom-line business approaches in organizing and delivering social services, as one respondent notes, is potentially hazardous, and may put vital parts of the mission or purpose of the settlement at risk.

The new orientation is about efficiency. But, of course, when it cuts to the bone, it affects your mission. We had an expressed interest in improving the quality of life. Now we are being asked to change to survive. Are we going to be the same organization or something else? How do you make the decisions to create these new services? There are technical models, but we're not General Motors. We're not talking about a company that says if the Opel doesn't work, let's come out with another model. We may survive but as what? (G11)

Political and Social Action in Defense of Social Services

The settlement movement is no stranger to the political arena. Histori-cally, settlements have been among the most politically active social service agencies. Such work was most frequently organized as an offensive and de-signed to extend the network of available services. More recently, the po-litical agenda of settlements has been structured to defend the perimeter of their programs. It is focused on averting or deflecting changes perceived as damaging.

Political organizing in the defense of settlements in particular and social services in general did not originate over the past decade.[1] Several respondents, however, suggested that organizing is increasingly recognized as the most critical tool and best hope of preserving at-risk programming. Its primary intention is to activate the natural constituent groups of settlements. Perhaps the most dormant yet potentially powerful ally of settlement programs are service users. The success of a political strategy is therefore contingent upon how well it engages and involves consumers. This point is underscored in the comments below.

> In some ways the clients have been affected positively by the cuts. As they have become more aware of what was happening, they have become more involved in the political process. We've worked to make that happen, and it's been empowering for us and the clients.   (B3)

> I think it's made it easier to say to staff, if you don't get parents involved even at the very lowest level, you may not have a job down the line. Our work has been successful because we do have parents involved and we have a presence when we go places. It gives us more legitimacy, more power.   (D1)

> We have to bring more people on to this leaky boat, our constituents, our clients, our consumers. We can't simply pray that things will change for the better, we're going to have to be more political. (H1)

Many settlements are trying to enlist service users to exercise their most basic political right to vote. A first step in this process is to get eligible citizens registered to vote. Fuller participation in the electoral process is perceived as critical because of low voter turnout in poor communities. The indifferent response of elected officials to the needs and interests of poor communities can be traced in part to the lack of a voting block that enforces shared interests. Voter registration is described as having a potential extending beyond short-term defensive maneuvering. Over time, a greater turnout by poor people at the polls is considered essential to creating a political environment more inclined to respond to the shifting and growing needs of economically marginalized communities.

> Communities such as this one get overlooked and suffer because the politicians are politicians, and they see the bottom line, how many

people voted. We've gotten more and more involved in campaigns to vote to get our issues to matter. We're trying to get people to understand that if you vote, just vote, you're going to be taken into consideration more during budget time, especially if they're looking to take something away. Now we're looking further into getting people to vote, not just register but actually getting people to vote.   (I7)

We're still fighting to protect summer youth employment services. There are going to be 2,000 youngsters going after 600 jobs. We're going back to voter registration. Getting people to vote their interests. It's part of both a local and national campaign.   (I3)

Promoting contact between elected officials and consumers is an especially important means of protesting budget cuts. Less direct contact, that is, without face-to-face encounters, has been organized through letter-writing campaigns and petitions. The intention is to press legislators with a volume of concerned responses and force them to reconsider a particular policy. The breadth of letter writing across service areas and issues is illustrated in the following passages.

Our seniors have written letters to protest budget cuts. My suggestion is that letters mean more than petitions. I can't tell them what to do. I say, if you feel like writing, these are the people to write to.   (A4)

We had a letter-writing campaign earlier this year. Some of the letters were published in the local newspapers. It served a lot of purposes. It can empower people by allowing them to address issues affecting their lives. They come to see they don't have to sit back and accept the cuts. It makes people more aware of the political process. It makes the politicians hopefully a little more aware, that these are people who eventually will be voters once they get an apartment.   (C12)

On a program level, we've done petitioning and had youngsters writing letters. At an agency level we've had board people writing letters. (J5)

Our parents are always writing letters. Last spring, we had one parent, she got out 2,000 letters by herself. She worked the entire agency, went to all the programs, and had the parents write the letters, got them signed, and got them mailed.   (B8)

> We had a broad letter-writing campaign that solicited a lot of letters from different programs. It included our senior center, our homeless services, and our family department.   (E2)

Contact between decision makers and consumers is in part intended to personalize the impacts of proposed changes to programs. The stories of service users who have been or are likely to be affected are solicited. Often the full impact of such a story is most directly and viscerally felt as consumers bear witness to their own personal experience. The raw power of these stories can move an often narrow policy discussion to another plane of understanding and to a point of emotional connection.

Equally important, frontline advocacy as contrasted with letter-writing campaigns more fully involves consumers in the political process. Though requiring preparatory training and face-to-face contact, the possibilities and difficulties of political change are more directly evident here. Such encounters also provide consumers with the opportunity to experience the potential power of their voice and actions.

> People went to speak with officials at city hall and in Albany. Did we have massive numbers of people? No, we didn't. Did we have some people who for the first time in their lives advocated for themselves and services? Were they scared and in the end moved by the experience? Yes! I think one of the things that happens when people come and advocate from the community and talk about their own difficulties with what is coming down from the city or Albany, is it helps them to mobilize as a group, and it also helps individuals to feel they have some power.   (B6)

> We've had the kids testify at the hearings. It has at times really moved some of the legislators. They're kind of insulated from the consequences of their decisions. This helps to break some of that down. Whatever will work.   (C9)

> I said, if I go in there, I am seen as just another executive director who is giving very good testimony. But it is heard in another way when a mother says, "I've been putting myself through school one class at a time for the past eighteen years, and now you are going to take away the one thing that allows me to do it, and you are saying that this makes sense."   (D1)

Settlement administrators noted that political advocacy cannot be effectively waged by individual houses. In order to be heard, each house and service program must make common cause with other groups similarly threatened by proposed and implemented changes. Joining in coalition relationship with consumer groups, professional organizations, and other agencies has shaped a part of the local political organizing work of settlements.

The concentric circles of coalition work are not limited to the locality. Some part of local political work is also attuned to regional and national motors. Consequently, houses and programs have joined and helped to create state and national coalitions. However tight or loosely formed, coalitions are perceived as an essential tool in the fight to minimize the damaging impacts of present social policy.

> RESPONDENT: A lot of the changes in day care and mental health are a result of federal policy. We can't change things by simply advocating at city hall or Albany.
> INTERVIEWER: It's a national problem, so what is the implication for the agency?
> RESPONDENT: Well, we have had to get more involved and try to find ways to support national groups like the Coalition of Mental Health Agencies. They're getting involved, they are much more active.   (F2)

> Well, we dodged a major bullet from the city and state. We did a lot of political organizing, buttonholed councilmen, people in the assembly and state senate and our congressman. We did letter writing and exerted a lot of political pressure with other organizations. We worked as part of a coalition. It seems to have had an impact. They did preserve preventive services.   (B3)

> The New York State Adult Day Services Association has been very good over the past eight to ten years in educating people, getting legislative support for services. We've worked with them through the Greater New York Association and Queens Association. Now with all the threats to medical services, things have gotten worse, and the feeling is we need this association even more. They're going to have to work even harder on more and more desperate need.   (C7)

I've been involved in the Summer Youth Employment Coalition and it's partly because of the work of the coalition that we still have programming. We're still fighting. We're now joining state and national coalitions.   (I3)

Settlements have also employed activist, outsider tactics of protest. A majority of houses indicated involvement in rallies and demonstrations to protest current policies. Staff and users of programs serving seniors, youth, and the homeless were initiators as well as participants in local actions. A number of settlements also participated in national and state demonstrations. These events were coordinated by coalitions of agencies, community groups, and unions.

Rallies are perceived as offering potential short-term and long-term benefits. To begin with, they provide a forum more amenable than, for instance, legislative hearings, to expressions of anger. In addition, the rally can offer opportunities for participation as simple as a chant or as complex as the preparation and delivery of a speech. The full range of emotion and participation associated with such an event can promote a deeper understanding of social solidarity.

We've done a good job along with other settlements in terms of getting the steam rolling and getting the participants and members to turn out at the rallies. We had hundreds of people show up. We're really trying to get more involvement. These events can get parents to see the connection, feel the connection, between them and others and how they are being hurt as a group by what's going on. Getting them involved to take ownership, it's hard but it's necessary.   (E2)

One of the positive things about the cuts is it's gotten people together—united some in a common cause. At one of our rallies, we were able to bring together youth, parents and seniors. Getting people to come together, help organize others, and speak up at the rally and talk about what it has meant to them, at times it's been powerful. I've seen some people who have connected with others and have a different sense of commitment to turning it around. For that reason alone, the event was effective.   (B5)

We are very close to the unions and have worked with some of the them on demonstrations to keep funding alive.   (F1)

The agency is very activist. We've helped to support rallies in D.C. to protest cuts. The agency chartered a bus and allowed some of the staff to go. We've brought young people to be speakers at rallies in New York City and Albany to protest cuts.   (C9)

The activist impulses of a number of settlements, however, have been dampened by recent federal legislation. In general, the law stipulates a reduced political participation for nonprofits receiving public funding. The penalty for violating the law is intensified scrutiny of an agency's operations and its defunding. Concomitantly, the climate locally is perceived as predisposed to identifying and punishing agencies involved in visible protest.

Although most settlements continue to promote political responses to present threats, they are more cautious in their actions. Recent restrictions have narrowed both the amount of time and form of political participation that is permitted. In a sense, just as the prospects for social service provision have been narrowed, so the settlements' tactics of political defense were curtailed through legal stipulations.

The new restrictions have helped us to be sharper and use times other than work hours for our political work. We have our lunch hours, evenings, and weekends. So, if we send clients to a rally or hearing, we send staff, but only on their lunch hour.   (I5)

Because we have government contracts, we can't make phone calls to legislators. People are entitled to participate in rallies, but only during their off hours.   (I4)

The 60s style of organizing is disappearing. A much more subtle approach is needed because you have to protect yourself to some extent. The mayor [Rudy Giuliani] isn't the type of guy who takes criticism of any kind. He makes his hit list and checks it twice, and if you're on it, you're gone.   (H3)

Congressional bills are calling into question our mission. Settlements have always been involved in organizing and tried to have political influence. Now though, if you get one federal dollar, your first amendment rights are taken away. The bills take away our political rights. If we challenge these laws, we risk not only our funding but our tax-exempt status.   (G12)

Mounting a political defense of settlement services thus represents more and more of a challenge for organizers and advocates. A primary constituent group for settlement programs are consumers. Yet, service users have competing demands on their time that create a powerful counterpull to more fully involving themselves in the politics of social services. The difficulties of a program may often seem less immediately pressing than family or employment obligations.

Furthermore, individuals and groups that have traditionally defended social services are now more often described as exhausted, their resources depleted. The ongoing effort to defend entitlements and services has worn out and thinned the ranks of advocates. The paradox is that as the perceived threat mounts, the potential for a vigorous effective defense, at least in the short run, may have been diminished.

> INTERVIEWER: Are there objective differences between the responses to the crisis of social services in the 70s and now?
> RESPONDENT: You bet. Then you had people waiting for us to sit and plan. People were much more prepared to get involved, to fight politically. Now I don't know, it seems that fewer and fewer people are participating. Some are scared and others are burnt out. In the past, there was more of an energy, a spirit, a fight. Now it's just not the same.   (G1)

Even in our families, our after-school programs, child care programs, we have difficulty getting parents to stay and learn more about the cuts. Their own mission is sort of, I've got to get my kid, I've got to get home. They are in a rush to cook, make sure the homework gets done, and make sure they get the child back to school fresh in the morning. But there is no question we are working to push for more involvement.   (E2)

Inventing a Future for Social Services

One of the questions currently being raised by settlement administrators is how to develop more effective programs in an environment that is less than hospitable to social services. The intention is to develop a conversation among agencies and actions that extend beyond defensive maneuvers. To be sure, some part of this conversation must deal with present fiscal and structural realities. However, the focus shifts, as administrators and workers struggle to discover and actualize new opportunities.

For many settlements, such discussion is modest. Others have promoted a substantial dialogue but are still struggling to implement salient ideas. A few settlements, however, have begun to translate such discussions into new programs and services. These initiatives are often fragile, limited, and tentative. This early stage of discussion and experimentation, however, represents at the very least a basis for discerning potential new directions for settlement programs. Where community-building practices are being explored and seriously tested, it has required the commitment of a visionary agency leadership willing to take risks for change and resist the present trend. A subgroup of leaders in this study are testing the boundaries of present contract policy and developing a preliminary range of alternate practices. They are central to the struggle of developing agency practices that are better aligned with community needs. What the following findings reenforce is that constrained visionary leadership is an essential stimulant to the rebuilding of an agency's life and practices.

A recurrent theme is that settlements must nurture more collaboration and team building between service stakeholders. It is suggested, for instance, that partnerships with other agencies can create economies of scale that attract public funding. Alternatively, more fully involving staff, consumers, and the surrounding neighborhood in specific decision making is expected to promote trust and heighten investment in the program service as well as in the agency. Perhaps most important, unions between the settlement and its constituent groups are seen as having the potential to strengthen political muscle.

Forging partnerships with other agencies and with service users is complex and poses a number of risks. With partnership comes at least a modest reconfiguration of historic lines of authority and centers of power. This is but one of the dilemmas of collaborative social service work. Yet, greater risk taking is likely necessary if settlement leadership is to reinvent present conceptions of organizing and social service delivery. A number of administrators reinforced this point when they remarked that new forms of social service better able to meet the community's needs and respond to the larger political threats will not be created in isolation but only in ongoing collaborative relationships.

Involving Stakeholders in Planning for Change

Efforts are underway in many settlement houses to plan for present and anticipated changes. The planning processes are both short-term and adaptive to immediate shifts as well as more long-term and strategic. The latter meetings are intended to promote new ways of thinking about the delivery of services that are consonant with the mission of settlements. The planning process is not experienced uniformly in all settlement houses. For some settlements the process has been relatively smooth. Meetings have been convened in a timely manner, and the tone has been generally harmonious. Other houses indicated that although planning efforts were underway, the rhythm of the process was often out of sync with the intensifying demands of recent change. Furthermore, meetings between key administrators were described as tense and too often driven by conflict. These difficulties were attributed to a lack of leadership. Although the rhythm and leadership of settlement planning processes varied, the increasing importance of such tools in adapting to present change and creating a proactive service agenda was uniformly understood by key decision makers.

> Our strategic plan is more important than ever. We have continued certain program directions irrespective of shifts in the field. We have a game plan, and we are going to try to march to that game plan as long as our circumstances permit.   (A1)

> For the past year, we have been developing a strategic plan for our youth department. Actually in a time of cutbacks, it ended up being a fairly optimistic plan in terms of not calling for great reductions of services and trying to focus more sharply on the needs of the department. Service needs, training needs, technology needs are all included in the plan. Now of course, the challenge is to put the plan into action.   (I1)

> Ever since our new ED came on, there has been a change in focus here. Less on just working from day to day and maintaining what we've got and more toward planning for what we want to provide in the future. In the past, it was, oh here is an opportunity for funding, so let's do it. Everything was short run. Now we're going through a process that looks toward the future. We're trying to figure out what we want to provide first. The assumption is that at some point we'll figure out

how to fund those things that need to be done and that some of them won't happen now because of the political climate.   (E3)

We definitely see the importance of the planning process, especially now. The execution and leadership, though, is flawed. There are about three or four of us who have meetings regularly but it is often difficult to get agreement. The common vocabulary is not there yet, I think we're getting there though.   (G5)

Efforts are underway at some settlements to engage staff in the planning process. Initial attention is focussed on keeping personnel abreast of recent funding and other developments. In a number of houses staff participates more actively in planning decision making. Personnel have been invited to plan for change across a relatively narrow range of often pressing concerns. In a few instances, service workers have also been asked to attend meetings to offer more general input on future directions for a program or the agency.

Whatever the level of involvement, the tendency is to promote more staff participation in the agency's planning process in order to, among other things, blunt the often fragmenting, isolating, and distancing consequences of recent program changes.

There is frequent communication about the threat to our programs. Morale is low and we're trying to involve staff in more of the planning to dig out. Staff have come up with lots of suggestions. We have regularly planned meetings and often deal with what people suggest. People recognize they have a vested interest in survival, and we're trying to pull together. There's often a very thin margin which determines survival or nonsurvival, so we're working pretty hard and making suggestions. (H8)

Our executive director has attempted to involve staff in agency planning. We have task force meetings and agency-wide community meetings. She takes these meetings very seriously and acts on suggestions that come from them. The discussion can focus on the details of agency operations, like use of space, or look at larger service issues, like how can we make more of a difference with the community. We're trying to get staff feeling like more of a partner in this process. This is especially important now when things are a little bleak and staff become like moles just digging in.   (H2)

You need to have everyone feel ownership in running programs. You need this, especially now. If staff feel uninvolved in decision making or planning, you have a bad climate. The important issue even with budget cuts is that you need to have everyone informed of it and involved in addressing it. The effects are felt at every level and if people aren't involved, they will feel isolated and may give up.   (D5)

Subtle tensions often exist in promoting such involvement. A number of respondents remarked that staff do not have the final say in decision making; this prerogative is usually reserved for key administrators. A concern is to make sure that staff do not feel betrayed because suggestions made are not acted upon. Key decision makers therefore walk a thin line between soliciting participation and promising that recommendations will be followed. Additionally, staff may not feel comfortable voicing complaints or offering suggestions in forums that include administrators to whom they are directly or indirectly accountable. Consequently, safeguards have been instituted in some settlements to protect staff from the perceived threat of reprisal and assure a fuller, more candid participation in planning meetings. The conflicts and tensions associated with such planning processes are illustrated in the following passages.

I think there is a fine line that if you begin to cross it, you are in trouble. We need to involve people in decision making in trying to help us figure out what we're going to do. People feel if they offer what they think needs to be done and you don't follow it, they've been fucked. Yet if you do listen to everything that is offered, you may be fucking the program because they don't have as much of a sense of all the things that are being juggled. They don't sit where we do. In some sense, it may be a no-win situation. But it is our responsibility to be up-front and talk about the limits of their power. We need to include staff though, it really wouldn't be fair to exclude them.   (B6)

We have a staff advisory task force, which consists of line staff from departments across the agency. None of the program directors are there. The executive director and associate directors attend. So it's a direct line to our top administrators. We don't hear what they're saying, and it really allows them to talk more freely than if supervisors were in attendance.   (E3)

The planning process has also been opened to community residents. The perspective of consumers is solicited through regularly scheduled advisory group meetings and survey research. The influence of such input on subsequent decision making remains uncertain. It is clear, however, that fiscal instability has led some administrators to rethink the role of consumers in planning programs. One administrator remarked that increased participation of the community in program/agency planning represents a return to the settlement's historic mission.

> I think one of the things that we're most excited about is developing a planning process that tries to get the community involved. We're pushing families to get more involved agency-wide in planning and implementing programming. In the past, settlements were a model of community participation. It was our mission, and we got away from it. The problems with funding have just pointed out to us that if we can't do this as a staff, we have to do this as a community. The community has to begin to recognize how these cuts are impacting us and them, because in the end we're just a vehicle for the community.   (E5)

> The clients haven't been involved before, but they have been in the last year. We sent out a questionnaire to users of the program and community leaders. The survey helped us evaluate about seven of our programs. (D2)

> What we saw coming down the road a few years ago indicated that we needed to get the community more involved in the center. We knew if we just waited until the time where we really needed such involvement, it would already be too late. We began to develop advisory committees about three years ago. I meet with an advisory committee from every program. Each committee has two community members. We want them to help us with program development, help us to think through how we can get the neighborhood more involved, and work with us on improving our programming.   (B3)

Settlement Services, Stakeholders, and the Building of Community Solidarity

Settlement programs are increasingly perceived as promoting limited and fragile relationships between administrators, staff, and community residents. As the earlier chapters indicate, fiscal instability and contractually driven reconfiguration of services contribute to a restricted exchange between worker and consumer.

Yet, as a cross section of respondents noted, the very essence of social services is embedded in the development of a fuller relationship. The social service relationship has increasingly focused on highly individualized forms of exchange. For instance, service recipients often remain in highly circumscribed roles as consumers of material and other services, such as counseling, tutoring, or recreation. Historically, however, the relationship between settlement house and community resident often extended beyond individualized services. The agency was frequently experienced as a communal living room. Various political activity and service clubs were organized to facilitate a fuller and more communal relationship between the house and neighborhood residents.

Paradoxically, the present push for ever narrower and contractually prefabricated forms of service relationships has led in some settlements to a reconsideration of this historic community-building mission. Only a small minority of respondents specifically articulated community building as a future or present objective of settlements. Many more described building team spirit, partnership, or ownership among the primary stakeholders of settlements as priorities. In general, these differences in language are less important than the overarching desire to create greater solidarity between line staff, administration, and community residents.

Perhaps most important, this part of the analysis draws on the work and thinking of only a small fraction of the study sample. In general, program and agency administrators were stymied when queried about future directions for settlement services. Their vision did not extend beyond short-term adaptation to present changes and threats. The respondents cited in this section of the analysis might be characterized as a more visionary leadership engaged in trying to reinvent some part of the fundamental mission and purpose of settlements. This discussion is therefore based on the preliminary thinking and initiatives of a select subset of agency administrators.

The meaning of community building, though often vague, is tied to the belief that settlements must do more than simply provide individualized, categoric services. The larger historic mission of settlements to empower communities, respondents noted, must be more fully woven into agency work. The future of settlement work, it is reasoned, requires new and more participatory forms of relationships. Specifically, the agencies' monopoly on service provision is perceived as simply not sustainable. Some part of the load must be shared by the community.

The impetus for community-building initiatives is complex in as much as it represents a renewed embrace of the settlements' historic mission and resistance to a confluence of contemporary political and social forces that define their work more restrictively. This complexity starkly contrasts with respondents' preliminary and general impressions of what constitutes a community-building praxis. This work must begin, it is suggested, with not-for-profit, community-based social service agencies creating new forms of partnership with staff. Line staff are the primary connection between agency and community. The logic offered suggests that the relationships staff facilitate with consumers mirror the relationships they experience within the agency. More to the point, hierarchical, distanced relationships between staff and administrators will be reflected in the service exchanges between workers and service users. Alternatively, new forms of partnership forged between administrators and staff will help to shape more collaborative relationships with community residents. Staff, it is suggested, can model to consumers only what they experience as workers. This point is more fully described in the following passages.

> We are moving toward a community-based model, and I think that's good. But I still think that unless the administration does a better job of creating community within the agency, their attempts to build community outside are going to only have limited success. Our workers have to experience it inside before they can take it outside. That will be tricky. But we're working on it.   (B3)

> I'm positive community building is the way to go. But I don't know how we're going to have staff do this when they already feel overwhelmed. How can they be given the support to see the people they are serving as participants and getting people to see they have a stake in what's going on here? If they get involved, they may be able to keep a service going, but if they don't get involved, they may not have a service.   (C14)

Such participation, although essential, is often viewed as hollow if staff are not first engaged in activities intended to build a sense of camaraderie and trust. The most popular means for this engagement work with staff are training events and staff development retreats. Although these initiatives are relatively modest, they do represent a time investment on the part of the agency and a starting point for promoting a new orientation to settlement work.

We did an agency-wide staff development day. That was a first for us. We closed the place down. Every staff member who works in the place attended. The workshops were internally staffed. It was very successful. There was a strong sense of community that came out of it. They liked the idea of coming together to talk about how this place works and how to build a sense of team here. We plan to follow up with trainings in the next month or two.   (F1)

One of the things we're actively working on is building a sense of team. Our director is committed to this. She wants to create a cohesive group of staff that has greater commitment to the agency and departments. So the whole idea of team building is to work within the department first to create a sense of team and then do some things across departments. Workshops are being planned.   (E7)

We're trying to foster a sense of people thinking of themselves not as individuals but as part of a community. Staff are being encouraged to develop a sense of ownership in the programs and agency. We listen to their ideas and also have trainings on how to build a sense of team and try to model the kind of team we want to build in those sessions. Part of what we need to do is convey a sense of respect and dignity to staff.   (C12)

The effort to get staff to identify more fully with the programs and agencies is both complex and multifaceted. Training events and staff development, although a necessary part of such a process, are not sufficient. The day-to-day practices of the agency, respondents noted, must reflect new and less distanced ways of working with staff. One suggestion was that staff and consumer contributions to settlement life should be more systematically acknowledged. Moreover, respondents recommended more consistently celebrating special events.

Events of celebration were considered an especially important type of affirmation or acknowledgment. Celebration was perceived as a counterpoint to the more usual activity that defines settlement life. It offers staff and service recipients a venue to gather, not to solve pressing problems, but to remember special moments in people's lives. The acknowledgment and celebration ceremony stood as a counterpoint to the often grim work of providing social services. The relaxation and joy associated with such moments can contribute to a deeper connection between honorees, organizers, and participants. Equally important, such events, if widely attended and ritualized, can foster a broadened identification with programs and agencies. Affirmation was perceived as instrumental to the development of a more personal and, eventually, a more communal relationship between agency stakeholders. Targeting community-building initiatives at staff as well as at service recipients represents an important change in the practice of agency administrators.

> Look, we try to acknowledge achievements of our homeless residents. We have an award night for them when they graduate to apartments, complete programs, and so on. It is important, first of all because many of our residents have gotten so little of that kind of thing. It also helps us to create bonds with people; they are so appreciative when we take the time to award them for an achievement or remember something as simple as a birthday.   (C12)

> I came into social work because it is rewarding and fun. Some part of that though is being taken away. It's up to us though to give it to each other, to remember each other. You have to show your staff appreciation and help to give their successes back. We're trying to do this on a day in, day out basis. But we're also trying to have more parties and staff recognition nights. It's important because of what it gives to staff, it builds togetherness. We feel like more of a family.   (H1)

> More and more we try very hard to let staff know that they're ours, we value them and wherever we can, we try to show them that. We thank them through staff recognition, little parties for a staff birthday, someone having a baby. We're in this together, and we need to appreciate each other. They are small things, but it helps us feel like we're a part of each other. We also do small things for clients so that they know they're part of us. Little things again like a gift or organizing a party. They are little things, but they can build into feeling part of something larger, more whole like a community.   (I6)

Perhaps at the core of developing more communal relationships is the question of power. Some part of the movement to identification with the agency and ownership of programs must include shifts in power relationships. The reconfiguration of power arrangements is perhaps the thorniest issue in any internal or external process of community building. It has been suggested that the critical lubricant for social relationships, trust, is associated with the development of more equitable and reciprocal exchanges. Who controls specific areas of programming, how power is exercised, and the roles of stakeholders are issues highly intertwined with the culture of an organization. Community-building processes must address these core issues of an agency's culture and power distribution if they are to be perceived as authentic.

It is therefore essential that more decentralized power arrangements not be merely token concessions but substantive. Earlier, the participation of staff and community residents in planning program changes was described. These initiatives represent an effort to include key stakeholders in episodic activity to rethink present programs. In general, the process was future oriented and insulated from the day-to-day operations of the program. A deeper level of inclusion, however, would involve stakeholders in the everyday details of present programs and in an agency's decision making. Such participation promotes an enhanced and daily sense of lived partnership.

A number of administrators remarked that they are actively attempting to stimulate a dialogue or conversation with staff about program operations. These exchanges are the primary venue for leveling the playing field between staff and administration. The effort to promote staff ownership of programs through genuine dialogue on matters of immediate concern is illustrated in the following passages.

It's a lot less of what is right or wrong, a lot more of let's try it, what works, what doesn't work, and what did we learn from it. People are encouraged to develop a sense of ownership in the programs, what are your ideas about how to fix what isn't working, what do you think, what should we do? (C12)

This staff know most of the membership. They are key in knowing what's happening out there and how budget cuts, for instance, are affecting the membership. Any decision being made in the program, regarding fees, interest rates, whatever, it's discussed with staff first because they are in contact with members on a daily basis. (H5)

You need to have everyone feel ownership. If you are up here and staff is down there, it's a problem. That's important in running a program. It's especially important now because of the bad climate. You have to get staff involved with administration in working out solutions to problems. That's an important issue. It can't be any longer I'm up here running this alone. We're in this together, and staff involvement and ownership is key.   (D5)

Community residents' relationship to the settlement house is also perceived as needing to be reworked. The simple equation of a relationship driven by service provision is viewed as less and less viable. The intention is to develop a fuller range of participation. Input on decision making, volunteering in programs, creation of family rooms, which invite residents to mix informally with each other and staff, as well as political action are described as potential ways in which such relationships can be fostered. Respondents envision residents as experiencing the house as a hub of communal activity.

An implicit by-product of such activity is a sharing of responsibility. Often less clear, however, are the ways in which consumers can be invited and engaged into this more participatory form of relationship given competing demands on their time. Moreover, how such participation would affect the present disequilibrium of power between staff and service users is rarely considered. Power distribution and engagement are subordinated in practice conversations to the need for greater participation. In a few instances, respondents indicated that participation could be stimulated through more channels of open communication on issues of pressing concern to the program. These venues mirror what is available to staff. In general, however, administrators are wary of promoting anything more than an advisory planning or political mobilization role for residents. The struggle to promote greater participation and give service users a voice in the daily work of settlement programs is described in the following passages.

So we are trying to get more involvement from our participants. We would like to get people to the point where they can actually offer something to other participants, be it through volunteering or by becoming a staff person. We're looking inward and trying to perfect that in our day-to-day work. We used to call people patients or clients and we sort of moved away from that usage. Now we're talking about participants because that is what we're trying to accomplish.   (D9)

The interest of tenants wanes, they did come to one of our planning meetings. When we are at a point in our plan where tenant input is essential, they will be more fully involved not only in the development of the program but concrete changes that need to take place as it is underway. They have a big say in what happens, and the staff up there are tuned in to that.   (E3)

The community has to get a lot more involved. A lot more. We have to open up more avenues for that to happen. There is a need to bring staff together to look into more fully involving parents and grandparents. Not only just in the specific political process of budget cutting but generally to formulate a community agenda. We're putting into place now advisory committees, parent action groups, and family rooms, which will be a key.   (C14)

Even though this has always been a part of our mission, it seems we're just beginning to get around to it now in a serious way. Creating a true partnership with clients. Where it's clear that it isn't just staff providing a service but getting people more involved as leaders and participants. Getting through their participation, leadership, and organizing skills.   (C13)

I hope that we never feel like we have all the answers for the community we are serving. We need to hear what the community desires and involve them in defining the programs. More and more we are moving to try to empower the community, clients, by involving them in our program planning. It is also especially important now, given the cuts, that we involve clients politically. There has to be a sharing, but I think it has to be limited to those areas, it will never be fifty-fifty.   (E2)

Collaborative relationships are also traced to efforts to identify and respond to the larger community's needs. Clearly, the neighborhoods in which settlements are located have an array of concrete needs that are persistent and in some instances growing. The houses' efforts to respond to such needs with programs were described earlier in this chapter. However, when discussing how programs could promote a greater sense of solidarity with the neighborhood, discussion shifted to the role of the agency as an employer and a mechanism for leadership development. Although "growing their own" employees and developing indigenous leadership were described by some administrators as representing a bedrock commitment, they were less clear about how such initiatives could be systematically incorporated into the work of the agency. Clearly a philosophical priority for some administrators, particularly against the backdrop of budget cuts, yet such initiatives appeared more a product of idiosyncratic hiring patterns or sporadic events than a planned strategy with deep organizational roots. Nevertheless, the following responses underscore the perceived intersection of mission, solidarity with the surrounding community, and the settlement's needs to promote the leadership and employment potential of residents.

> We have to develop the capacity of the people in the community to lead. I mean if I say to a family, are you happy with the education that your child is getting in the public schools? Do you feel comfortable with them walking around the streets at 5:00 after dinner? The next question is how do you get them past the point of feeling like "well, there is really nothing I can do about it." We have to go back to our roots and give people a sense that they can lead change for the better in the community. We've done a little of that at rallies. How do we make it more a part of what we do every day, now that is the question.
> (D1)

> There has not been enough work developing, educating our constituencies in the community. The settlement house movement hasn't done enough of that, and in that sense we've neglected our heritage. It's especially important to get back to that now. I think people are taking this change in climate seriously, and it can't be completely business as usual.   (I1)

> RESPONDENT: To some extent you are simply bending to the reality of where you are located. Where we can, we hire people from the neighborhood.
> INTERVIEWER: How much of the commitment is philosophical and has to do with agency mission?

RESPONDENT: Probably more philosophical at times than pragmatic. After all, our hiring is more often driven by who is available and what we need.   (D1)

INTERVIEWER: What you are describing sounds like "grow your own."

RESPONDENT: Yeah, it's saying let's keep our eyes open, identify parents who might fill a position. I mean, maybe we're talking about eight, ten, or twelve jobs. But if we can hire ten people from the community for jobs that pay $20,000, that's positive. It puts out a message about our commitment. Also as you hire people, I think, maybe where the community begins and we end and vica versa is blurred. Who knows, maybe it will grow bigger than that, that's the hope anyway.   (B5)

In a few settlements efforts are underway to develop a proactive collaborative agenda with other agencies. In at least one instance, such activity was intended to organize the community around broad economic needs. The settlement joined with religious organizations and the IAF (Industrial Areas Foundation) to establish both an agenda and the community base to claim new resources. This broader attempt at political solidarity was unique, and at least in its earliest stages this initiative did not attract many community agencies or other settlements. Other more popular forms of interagency collaboration were achieved through coalitions and consortia to attract public money to new projects. These more pragmatic and less political interagency ventures were, at least in part, motivated by the public sector's new emphasis on the "efficiencies" of collaboration.

Two years ago we got involved with a lot of churches and such in organizing the East Harlem Partnership for Change and hiring an IAF organizer to come on. It is the joy of my life, there is something we can do about that very political part of our mission, which in recent years is not much honored. I think we're the only nonreligious group that is part of it. The other settlement houses didn't get into it, numbers of other groups in the neighborhood didn't get into it.   (H1)

We've been awarded a grant which supports our efforts to create a community network of homeless providers. The HUD grant emphasizes making maximum use of community resources. It's designed to really pull together all the resources for homeless people, making maximum use of what we have and closing the gaps. Between the three agencies we've been given $500,000 to do this work, it's a drop in the bucket really.   (E3)

We helped put together a consortium of agencies for a federal proposal. It brought in 17 million over five years. It's geared to emotionally disturbed children and trying to fill the gap in services.   (A1)

Collaboration is the trend of funding sources. They like agencies that are established and can put together a continuum of services. They want to use the strengths of the different agencies to collaborate on specific programs so the money can go to better use. It's not a bad idea. The trend is more toward augmenting programs through this money. (D5)

Dilemmas

Any effort to create collaborative or more communal relationships demands time. Staff and residents must be engaged in the dialogue necessary to foster trust and new kinds of relationships. The ongoing difficulty for the settlements, however, is how to promote such processes when the demands and pressures of the work are intensifying. The choice is often between working in a more collaborative, less immediately efficient manner and finding the quickest route to fulfill the myriad and often mushrooming responsibilities of staff. How collaborative dialogue is shortchanged in the rush to complete tasks is described in the following responses.

Even our meetings have to be short because we can't spend too much time away from our regular duties. We need to take the time to listen to each other to talk and share, but it's harder to do it now because it is much more necessary to do the work now.   (J5)

There isn't enough listening, everything is rush, rush, rush. Everything is done, but there's no time to hear each other.   (B2)

What we find is that in this program, if we have a formal meeting, we will be taking hours away from the client. Since we're a performance-based program every hour is a unit of service and impacts on the service. The clients are assigned twelve hours, eight hours, four hours, and three hours. If they are assigned twelve and we can only give them nine, we will hear about it. For us to take the worker away for a meeting or meetings certainly impacts the service. Yes, we have to break it down to hours because it's like piecework, make ten sleeves a day.   (J3)

To some extent the effort to create more collaborative or communal relationships rests on commitment and faith. The doubts about how and whether such relationships can be created or sustained in the present environment are persistent. Critically, though, a segment of settlement leadership, despite doubt, pressing immediate concerns, and fatigue, continues to struggle to discover how the agencies' historic community-building mission can be aligned with present circumstance. Although the effort may be incremental, limited, and ultimately insufficient, the work of inventing a more collaborative or community-building future for settlement services continues.

We can't create the services of the 1890s or the 1960s. We have to develop more community-building approaches, but they can't simply duplicate what existed earlier. The supports, some of the community strengths even from thirty years ago are just not here in the same way. We have to start from a different point. We've got to find another way. What it is I'm not sure. Can we build a stronger community through what we do? I'm not sure, but I suspect we can. We will have to change in basic ways. We will have to become something that right now we aren't. What do we have to change? How do we get there? That's part of what we will have to figure out, it will take time and support and that's part of what we are going to have to create for ourselves.   (E3)

Part 3

From Corporatized Contracting
to Community Building

8 From Corporatized Contracting to Community Building

Settlement houses and nonprofit social service agencies in general have undergone a sea change over the past two decades in their contractual relationships with the state. This shift has not been restricted to a single unit of government. Settlement houses in New York City experienced altered contracting arrangements with local, state, and federal agencies.[1] These changes were evident in reconfigured levels of funding, the rhythm of disbursing promised dollars to agencies, eligibility requirements, and the criteria for reimbursable services. Recent changes in contracting affected both the stability and structure of funding. Smith and Lipsky succinctly underscore the dynamic between the restructuring of contracts and the growing difficulties of not-for-profit agencies.

> We write in a period of severely diminished revenues for many of the social services. Not-for-profit agencies are being asked to, and their own inclinations toward altruism dictate, that they cushion local, state and federal fiscal crises by treating more and more clients and more difficult clients without compensating reimbursement. The saints of the nonprofit world must be admired for their selflessness in the face of severe budget reductions, but asking providers to do more with less and seeing many service providers sink under budget reductions does not bode well for public policy in the long run.
>
> (Smith and Lipsky 1993:224)

Moreover, change in the contracting environment is not restricted to policies that reduce funding. Although such reductions are visible and dramatic, they often mask other currents in contracting decision making. As noted in chapter 3, the rhythm of reimbursement has been slowed in some programs. Additionally, a number of programs experienced cycles of budget cuts, retrenchment, and restoration of original allocations. These tendencies contributed to an instability in continuity of service and composition of the workforce. As reimbursement was slowed or cuts were temporarily exacted, the agency had to find new ways to balance the scope of its services with its workforce. Conversely, the unpredictability of these dollars paved the way for a cautious reintroduction of services and staff. The cautiousness of administrators in returning to historic levels of service and funding was a pragmatic decision to hold money in reserve for the next round of uncertainty. Complicating matters, managed care has imposed additional demands on agencies. New guidelines have reduced levels of reimbursement for specific units of service and restricted access to programs. Managed care financing requires agencies to work harder to generate revenue. Further, the public contribution to building maintenance, supervisory support, purchases or replacement of equipment, and secretarial staff has often been reduced. The rollback of such infrastructural support has added yet more strain for remaining service staff and administrators expected to manage with depleted agency resources. Finally, budgets that remain constant or grow only modestly leave little, if any, room for salary increases. A stable contract may offer workers little more than declines in their standard of living. Therefore the stress for workers and administrators in dealing with public contracts cannot simply be traced to the diminished size of the total allocation. On the contrary, often hidden in the structure of stable allocations are unpredictable disbursement patterns, new demands, reduced supports, and the diminished real-dollar value of salaries. It is precisely these contracting trends that caused a director of a New York settlement to remark, "It is kind of strange. I've seen the budgets of many of our programs increase in recent years. But, at the same time, the contracts that we are forced to work with have made each of these programs weaker." Chapters 4 through 7 documented the impact of these contracting trends on the agencies' life.

As in academic settings, where Stefano Harney and Frederick Moten describe faculty and staff as having to "put up with crowded offices and broken copier machines," social service workers experienced intensifying infrastructural decline (Harney and Moten 1998). They were often frustrated by the scarcity of supplies critical to the direct or indirect provision of services. Many workers chose to privatize the cost of necessary program materials by purchasing the supplies rather than risking delay or the clients' disappointment. Essential elements of the physical plant were often undependable, unavailable, or in decline. Machinery that couldn't be repaired or replaced was more likely to break down and create disruption. Space was increasingly scarce. Reduced office space in turn led to fewer private conversations between staff and service users. Peeling paint, crumbling foundations, and leaking pipes promoted a sense of physical decay at some settlement houses. Finally, there simply was not sufficient time for administrators to address the pressing demands of day-to-day service provision, contract compliance, and the learning needs of staff. Administrative supervision, which could have prompted practice growth, became less structured and less available to social service line staff. Supervisory sessions increasingly emphasized the compliance of individual staff members with the quota or productivity requirements of specific contracts. Under contract policy the physical and relational supports available to line staff and administrators were permitted to decay, and this conveyed a daily message of the low worth assigned to social services. Both the experience and message eroded the capacity of service personnel to engage others.

Not-for-profit social service agencies, such as settlements, are contractually required to do more with fewer resources. These conditions have substantial implications. Diminished resources demand that agencies find cheaper ways of providing services. For instance, programs are expected to reduce the costs of staffing. The reduction of labor costs is most often achieved by some combination of reduced benefit packages, increased reliance on lower paid, less trained workers, recruiting volunteers/interns to fill functions previously met by salaried staff, and waiting before filling vacant positions. Social service contracts also demand increased productivity from programs and workers. As a result, caseloads have generally been ratcheted up. The number of people processed through agencies and the volume of documentation are increasingly emphasized as measures of success. Shorter, more focused, and frequently superficial encounters and higher caseloads are characteristic of the new service work (Fabricant and Burghardt 1992). For line staff and administrators, increased work demands accelerated the rhythm of a workday, contributed to a sense of being overwhelmed, and depleted energy. Service staff experience fatigue if not burnout. The interplay between increased productivity demands and the lowering of labor costs has been particularly demoralizing. These pressures also have an impact on workers' capacity to build relationships. As the demands of a workday grow, workers are less able to invest the time, consistent attention, imagination, and emotional resources required for building relationships with service users and colleagues. Clearly, the structure of contracting has penetrated deeply into the experience of social service work and agency life. Not only have contemporary contracts altered the workday, but they have also redefined the meaning of social services and the agencies' culture.

As emphasized in chapters 2 and 6, explicit and implicit contract demands of increased caseloads, paperwork, and job functions when combined with intensifying accountability requirements are contributing to an increased proletarianization of social service work.[2] It is within this context that staff come to rely less and less on their training or skills and increasingly respond in ever more prescribed ways to complex individual and community problems. The strictures of this contracting environment over time contribute to a deprofessionalization of the social service workforce (Fabricant and Burghardt 1992; Fabricant 1985). Equally important, contract reimbursement is generally keyed to individual, not community or group, outcomes. These tendencies are especially salient to not-for-profit agencies struggling to rebuild very poor communities. Community building requires that at least equal attention be paid to individual and community outcomes. Perhaps most important, the development of such approaches is dependent upon a willingness to risk innovation in social services. New forms of community-building practice are unlikely to be nurtured in environments that restrict the workers' autonomy, flexibility, judgment, and, perhaps most important, their imagination. The tension between the proletarianizing consequences of contracting and social service community-building initiatives will be further explored later in this chapter.

Chapter 6 makes clear that as services become less available or diminished in scope their meaning shifts. Less accessible, flexible, or responsive programs may be viewed as remote islands, untethered from the community's or the individual's needs. Interpretations of what a service means may also be influenced by the intensifying constraints reimbursement procedures impose on service encounters. The more rapid, circumscribed, and often discontinuous contacts that characterize the service experience tend to commodify it. The more clients are processed, the more revenue is generated. Increased emphasis on contractually defined quantitative definitions of output as synonymous with service has subtly and gradually rewritten the underlying conception of the social service exchange. The relationship between the client and service worker has always been a dynamic, dialectic, and tension-laden one, but never before has it been so circumscribed and undermined. As noted earlier, what has changed for workers is both the opportunity to respond to needs not neatly prespecified and to engage in a process of gradual discovery regarding circumstances and the most appropriate service responses. Instead, the worker and service are often straitjacketed into a predetermined contract structure. Consequently, clients often experience the service as unresponsive and mechanistic.

The process and qualitative dimensions of the social service experience are traded off in favor of quantitative indices of output or outcome. The new contractually defined structure of services offers less space and time and fewer rewards to accomplish what is most basic to the provision of services, the building of relationships. The industrialized model of efficient, productive service delivery creates the basis for producing measurable output that is paradoxically divorced from the core meaning of service provision. Ultimately, the contract may produce more and more output while simultaneously eroding the conditions necessary for trust, reciprocity, empathic connection, and relational continuity. Service contracts' neglect of infrastructure, contribution to more "productive," pressured workdays, and predetermined quantitative understandings of service problems and responses combine to narrow encounters between clients and staff. In the emotional and substantive compression of this service exchange, a large part of the relational possibility of social services is lost.

The tension described in chapter 7 between predetermined, private-sector interpretations of social services and the more open-ended, discovery-driven intention to build community and social solidarity offers a glimpse of future possibilities and constraints for settlement work. The emphasis on marketplace principles and values in settlement houses threatens to corporatize the culture of social services. The language and practice of the market (bottom lines, efficiencies, and profits) redefines the settlement houses and not-for-profit social services in general. As Robert Kuttner remarks, "there are dangers of the absolutization of markets. . . . The . . . danger is that market norms drive out nonmarket norms . . . the person who helps a stranger . . . , who agrees to work for a modest wage out of a commitment to the public good . . . begins to feel like a sucker" (Kuttner 1997:62). Such an environment endangers the norms essential to the development of a social service ethic and social solidarity. Nonmarket organizations that support "employee participation, civic education, or community service projects nourish solidarity values as a counterweight to market values" (Kuttner 1997:64). More important, a social service ethic and an intention of building social solidarity are the very essence of settlement house practice.

The logic and experience of the marketplace is being imposed on a growing number of nonmarket institutions. These conditions are increasingly evident not only in social services but also in higher education and in the health care industry (Readings 1996; Aronowitz and DiFazio 1994; Aronowitz 2000). Taylorization or scientific management has been a particularly powerful tool in subtly introducing and enforcing market values in the daily practices of nonmarket employees. Christopher Newfield remarks that when documenting the recent experience of the university, "Retaining scientific management's emphasis on external supervision, finance resists being contextualized as one of a number of considerations in an intricate corporate culture. . . . Financial culture tends to view labor as a cost, as a site of potential savings. From this perspective, better means cheaper, growth means restriction, productivity means discipline and knowledge means regulation" (Newfield 1998:81). The penetration of organizational culture through financial mechanisms and scientific management logic is part of a broad attempt to recast nonmarket institutions in the image of the for-profit corporation. As Peter Drucker suggests, however, the intention to reinvent nonmarket institutions may paradoxically threaten the underpinnings of the larger economy:

> Above all, we are learning very fast that the free market is all it takes to have a functioning society—or even a functioning economy—is pure delusion. . . . For any time period longer than five years a functioning civil society . . . is needed too for the market to function in its economic role.   (Newfield 1998:83)

Daniel Walkowitz notes that Taylorization is not new to social services. To the contrary, early evidence of the introduction of Taylorist principles in social work practice can be traced back to 1923 (Walkowitz 1999). What is new, however, is the intensifying penetration of such approaches. There is less of a counterbalance to the drive to Taylorize the practice of social services. Consequently, the basis for developing or producing a collective good is being lost. This "good" is not easily measured or nurtured and has little if any corollary in the marketplace. However, nonmarket organizational practices contributing to the creation of the collective good, no matter how difficult to monitor and at times ineffective, are essential to the development of a civil society. To be certain, as Lipsky and others suggest, in a democracy, such organizations must be held accountable if they receive public money (Lipsky 1980). However, if these standards of accountability do not incorporate an understanding of the organizations' critical nonmarket mission, then they will fail to meet the larger public need to build civil and communal relationships.

Never has it been more critical to find new ways to strengthen community and civic society than now. The internationalization and growing mobility of capital has created greater and greater strain and ever more profound dislocations for local communities. The movement of jobs and tax bases to other parts of the world and rapid changes in the technological engine of the labor market have had an especially unsettling impact on very poor communities. It is within this context that Fisher and Karger remark:

> Increasing globalization requires the building and rebuilding of communities to provide a basis of stability and identity in a global context that challenges both. Without such community building, we will find ourselves without any form of political community that expresses our shared identity, and knits us together in the families, schools and neighborhoods that democracy requires. . . . Community provides a base to stabilize and organize public life, to give people training in citizenship and public responsibility. Because global capitalism generally ignores its impact on community life and is fundamentally unaccountable, unrestrained and corrosive to the traditional stability of the community . . . grassroots organizing and *community-building practices* becomes a means for dealing with the antisocial aspects of global privatization.   (Fisher and Karger 1997:60, emphasis added)

Yet, at precisely the moment when nonmarket institutions are critically needed to engage in the work of community building, the cultural dominance and intrusion of marketplace values threatens their very capacity to promote such processes or outcomes. As has been noted throughout this book, the structure of state contracts has made it especially difficult for voluntary social service agencies and, more specifically, contemporary settlement houses to promote social solidarity and thereby help address the crisis of the community. Robert Kuttner warns that a fundamental conflict may exist between contract logic and the dynamics of building social relationships.

Deborah A. Mott, a law professor at Duke, warns that reducing all relations to short-term calculation can witlessly provide the mechanics to undermine the normative core of many relationships. Her illustration is the fiduciary relationship, a legal concept of special confidence and trust. . . . To reduce relations to nothing more than ordinary, breachable contracts is to destroy their special nature.   (Kuttner 1997:65)

Conservative political arguments have recently suggested that not-for-profit agencies are a critical locus for the building of community. The public sector has been characterized as bloated, overly bureaucratic, and removed from the needs and experience of local neighborhoods. Because not-for-profit agencies are often situated in poor neighborhoods and of modest size relative to units of government, they are described as more responsive and better able to meet community needs. Not-for-profit social service agencies are therefore promoted by conservatives as an alternative to public-sector intervention, particularly if the objective is the strengthening of local communities without further expense to the public or private sector. Recently, communitarian liberals, such as Robert Putnam, Amitai Etzioni, and others, have also suggested that not-for-profit agencies are a particularly critical locus for community building. "Mr. Putnam sees his own efforts and those of others engaged in community organization as the beginning of a revival of the old connectedness in new ways not yet evident" (Uchitelle 2000:11, *New York Times*, B section). The paradox, however, as chapters 2 through 7 underscore, is that ever more constricted structures of accountability and reduced levels of funding imposed through contracting make it increasingly difficult for not-for-profits to promote such connectedness.

The traditional liberal Left often misses the point regarding social capital. Its policy initiatives too often presume that the problems of poor people need only be addressed through entitlement programs or by putting more dollars into the hands of individuals. Clearly, income support is necessary to any strategy intended to assist or support the poor, but it simply is not sufficient. Proposals that focus only on the individual and quantitative and economic aspects overlook the collective, qualitative, social needs of low-income neighborhoods. In this way the Left may unwittingly reinforce present trends that emphasize the individualization and privatization of social problems and policy responses.

Both the Left and the Right have been unable in their policy initiatives to develop strategies that effectively address the compelling communal needs of low-income neighborhoods. Critical to such initiatives is the capacity of not-for-profit agencies to participate in a process of building partnerships with community residents. Presently, the contracting culture of not-for-profits minimizes the possibility of such collaboration. Future policy agendas must focus on how contracting can be used to promote new forms of organizational or agency culture. The next generation of policies must join the mechanism of social service contracting to the mission of building community. Clearly, such a project will be fraught with conflicts and contradictions, not the least of which is the present drive to corporatize social service agencies and individualize social problems. It will be the purpose of the next section of this chapter to explore the possibility of such policies by first describing some part of the context and circumstances of low-income neighborhoods. This discussion provides a rationale for investing in community building. Subsequently, a preliminary framework intended to inform and stimulate the development of community-building practices for social service agencies will be outlined.

The Decline of Community

Historically, the work of settlement houses varied by region, organizational culture, and leadership. Despite these differences, many settlement leaders shared a common intention to embed their agency in the life of the surrounding community. Encouraging staff to live in the houses where they worked, using groups or clubs to structure services as a collective experience, and organizing members of the neighborhood to address broader concerns, such as sanitation and housing, were but a few of the ways in which settlements promoted relationships between the house and the neighborhood. Clearly, the work of the settlements was often compromised by uncertainty, dilemmas, and definitions of community that at times restricted participation on the basis of race and class or imposed hegemonic understandings of culture (Lasch-Quinn 1993; Fisher 1994). Despite its limitations, the settlement house remains a historic experiment in the use of social services as instruments to build community and social solidarity.[3] Such initiatives, however, are increasingly scarce in contemporary settlements and in not-for-profit social service agencies in general.

I had occasion recently to spend considerable time with the local branch of a famous social service organization, committed in its public pronouncements to serve its clients humanely. I have reason to believe that the agency uses its funds carefully and provides services dutifully. But the rich opportunities it has to provide an experience of community with clients who desperately need that experience are squandered. It is a station for the delivery of social services, but one might find more sense of community among the patrons of the nearest motel.

(Gardner 1992:26)

The settlement houses that nurtured sewing clubs and civic activism a century ago, embodying community as much as charity, are now mostly derelict.   (Putnam 1993b:40)

Paradoxically, the need to build social networks has never been greater. Robert Putnam suggests that declines in attendance at town meetings, Sunday church services, and PTA meetings represent at least partial evidence of weakened associational relationships (Putnam 2000). These trends have significant communal implications as "members of associations are much more likely than nonmembers to participate in politics, to spend time with neighbors, to express social trust, and so on" (Putnam 1995:29). Fisher and Karger describe a major shift in the past two decades toward an increasingly private world focused on private individuals, private spaces, and private institutions. They argue that these intensifying forms of privatization have led to dramatic declines in public life, social cohesion, and an inclusive conception of a public good (Fisher and Karger 1997).

The decay of local institutions has had an especially profound impact on the very poor. Wilson notes that recent out-migration of residents has depleted poor neighborhoods of political and financial resources as well as key leadership participation in churches, schools, and other local institutions (Wilson 1987, 1991). Lasch argues that this out-migration of resources is compounded by suburbanites' withdrawal from public life. The tendency is to promote more privatized, or narrowed, forms of relationship. From gated communities to increased reliance on private schooling, suburbanites, he suggests, are withdrawing into a more secluded culture of contentment (Lasch 1997). Consequently, "families in low-income urban neighborhoods are increasingly disconnected from the power and money they need to rebuild and maintain their communities" (Cortes 1997:2).

It would be a mistake in the midst of this trend to ignore the many strengths and the potential of poor neighborhoods (Guttierez and Lewis 1997; Putnam 1993a, b; Kretzman and McKnight 1993; Delgado 1994). Extended family, church and fraternal associations continue to play a critical role in maintaining and revitalizing social life in poor communities. However, increasingly, these institutions are being asked to shoulder more responsibility with diminished monetary, human, and other resources. These strengths, although substantial, exist in an environment of diminished support and increased isolation. This dynamic results in the ongoing depletion of finite and critical communal resources.

Both James Coleman and Robert Putnam have helped to link the concept of social capital to the project of building community. Social networks, they suggest, are critical to building new opportunities, resources, and communities (Coleman 1990; Stone 1995; Putnam 2000, 1993a). Neighbors may join together to create better schools, share child care responsibilities, or establish a community garden. Such relationships create a kind of wealth or social capital for the neighborhood. Mark Stern notes that "'social' refers to the features of social organization—like trust, norms and networks—which improve the ability of individuals to coordinate social actions" (Stern 1998). More important, social capital can over time be transformed into political capital and social solidarity. Isolated individuals and communities do not have the political strength to promote access to social services or affect the distribution of resources for their communities. A community comprised of strong and extended social networks is more likely to be able to develop the stock of political capital necessary to leverage resources (Mediratta 1995). Putnam suggests that social capital is perhaps the single most important ingredient in building strong communities because it is an essential underpinning for the development of a stable and effective political as well as economic project (Putnam 2000).

Civic capacity refers to the ability of citizens to utilize existing resources and create new ones to strengthen their communities. However, Stern, Mediratta, Boyte, and others note that while civic capacity denotes the ability to bring about change, it does not indicate who has control of the process or how it is exercised (Mediratta 1995; Stern 1998; Boyte and Kari 1996) The importance of democratic processes in fostering an engaged citizenry and in turn civic capacity too often receives only scant attention (Cohen and Rogers 1995). The discussion on capacity building in, for instance, the communitarian literature almost exclusively emphasizes common social values as a basis for regenerating poor communities. The filtering differences of race, culture, class, and political economy are too often ignored in this discussion (Breton 1989; Fabricant and Burghardt 1998; Mediratta 1995; Stern 1998). It is not the purpose of this chapter to analyze these conflicts, questions, and omissions. It is important at this juncture, however, to acknowledge the critical connection between democratic participation, appreciation for differences, and the building of social as well as political capital. By neglecting this dynamic, those involved in community building may unwittingly promote not the enfranchisement of community residents but rather only further estrangement.

The impacts of strong and extended social networks on the well-being of communities and individuals are well documented. Some of these outcomes include: (a) the creation of opportunity structures (Naperstack and Dooley 1998), (b) maintaining health (Bloomberg, Meyers, and Braverman 1994; Cohen and Syme 1985; Potts, 1998), (c) educational attainment (Coleman and Hoffer 1987; De Souza Briggs et al. 1997), local economic development (Putnam 1993b), and individual mental health (Minkler 1997).

Historically, settlements understood the importance of building social solidarity through the provision of services. Some part of their work linked services and activities in ways that concretely addressed the needs of individuals while amplifying neighborhood residents' voices in the house, the community, and larger political arena (Mulroy and Cragin 1994). Efforts to promote social solidarity and networks have both historic antecedents as well as contemporary significance for the work of social service agencies (Landers 1998; Berman 1991). Although in the social service literature the terms for this objective may have shifted from "social solidarity" to "collective empowerment" to "social capital formation" or "community building," the underlying intention has remained constant. The objective of agencies engaged in such work is to promote deepened and extended forms of affiliation among service users. Over time, these networks are expected to coalesce into social and political activity that will benefit the larger community while simultaneously reinforcing and institutionalizing the benefits of service provision.

Building networks or social capital through planned intervention, however, is difficult. Exemplary Community Development Corporations (CDC), for instance, have created both jobs and housing while having little if any impact on the social embeddedness or networks of neighbor-

hood residents (De Souza Briggs et al. 1997). New Community Corporation, a program rightly extolled by Senator Bill Bradley for its record of
economic accomplishment, was far less successful in promoting social relationships among tenants (Bradley 1995). A recent survey suggests that 55
percent of its tenants had no close friends in the neighborhood. A majority
of tenants also agreed with the statement "I have no influence on what this
neighborhood is like" (De Souza Briggs et al. 1997:202). The difficulties
associated with building social capital extend beyond CDCs to social service agencies. A variety of barriers can thwart efforts to build social capital
through formal and informal organizations. These obstacles include a
dominant culture of privatism, matters of trust, high neighborhood crime
rates, which impede residents' attendance at meetings especially in the
evenings, and the transience of residents (Fabricant and Burghardt 1992;
Dachler and Wilpert 1978; Comer 1980; Berman-Rossi and Cohen 1988).
However, these inhibitors of social capital formation, although influential,
are not necessarily definitive. It is also true that neighbors may be important
without being "close" and that social solidarity can exist outside one's
neighborhood (Delgado 1994; De Souza Briggs et al. 1997:203; Fisher and
Kling 1993). Without discounting the complexity and dispersion of social
relationships, it is reasonable to suggest that community will continue to
be built in large part on a foundation of extended and deepened relationships within the locality or neighborhood. This is especially the case in
poorer communities where residents are less mobile.

This discussion is intended to link a reexamination of the mission and
practice of not-for-profit social services with the project of rebuilding public
life and social solidarity. Dating back to more than a hundred years ago, the
settlement houses, the precursors of the modern not-for-profit social service
organization, struggled to build communal relationships both inside and
outside of the agency. There is a compelling need to return to this historic
purpose while simultaneously illuminating present community-building
practices. More systematic attention must be paid to projects presently attempting to create social capital (Aspen Institute 1997). A central project of
this book is to begin to understand how to deliver social services in a context
of contemporary capitalist practices that undermines the social fabric essential to effective service delivery, citizen development, and community building. Not-for-profit service agencies are in a unique position to contribute to
the rebuilding of poor communities. Direct service provision offers a basis

for establishing the relationships and trust necessary to build both extended social networks and political capital. Equally important, community building strengthens the impact of direct service provision. More to the point, people are able to more effectively utilize formal services because of a greater stock of communal supports and more robust relationships with line staff and agencies. In earlier historic periods settlements understood the reciprocal relationship between service provision and community building. Clearly, any contemporary experiment to link social service delivery to community-building practices will be difficult and fraught with dilemmas, but it is possible. Only in this way can the potential contribution of social service agencies to the welfare of individuals and communities be maximized. The following sections of this chapter will outline a framework that links service provision with norms, processes, and strategic interventions that foster social and political capital. More generally, it represents a preliminary effort to illuminate the special promise of not-for-profit social service agencies as effective and innovative practitioners of community building.

Social Capital Formation: Place and Auspice

It is in the connection between residents and neighborhood institutions, whether informal associations (family, fraternal) or formal organizations (not-for-profit or public agencies), that neighborhood embeddedness develops (Naperstack and Dooley 1998; Minkler 1997). Cohen and Rogers address the potentially powerful role informal associations can play in reinvigorating democracy and stimulating a deepened sense of identification with neighbors and neighborhood (Cohen and Rogers 1995). They find the centrality of informal associations in building and sustaining neighborhood relationships indisputable. This discussion, however, will highlight formal organizations rather than informal associations as an instrument for building community relationships. The reason for this is that formal organizations, such as social service agencies and public schools, have a primary if not exclusive responsibility to tend to the social needs of neighborhoods and their residents. Equally important, the recent historic role of public agencies in delivering social services is being curtailed as the scope of responsibility of not-for-profits is expanded correspondingly. This discussion will therefore primarily focus on community-building work by not-for-profit social service agencies and local public schools (Weil 1996).

The type of organization likely to promote communal relationships is not easily defined or distinguished; yet, a number of basic characteristics can be identified (Handler 1996; Cortes 1997; Chapin Hall Center for Children 1995; Drucker 1994; Weil 1996; Jason 1997; Schecter 1982, Smith and Lipsky 1993). Community, says Selznick, is a variable; "it can evolve out of special purpose institutions, but happens most readily when purpose is not very rigidly or narrowly conceived, but when participation is an important part of the individual's life" (Selznick as cited in Handler 1996:238). Organizations struggling to build communal relationships must maintain a commitment to governance structures that promote participation. This commitment, suggests Selznick "may or may not be altruistic; it may only reflect the need for cooperation" (Selznick cited in Handler 1996:239). Participation is the underpinning for the cocreation of social services or reciprocal relationships of exchange between staff and service users (Boyte and Kari 1996). Reciprocity requires that each party contributes to the exchange. Reciprocity, not equality of exchange, is crucial. The contributions may be unequal yet meet the requirements of reciprocity. Embedded in reciprocal exchanges is respect, interdependence, and a greater sharing of power. Thus, the organization must have a culture that emphasizes reciprocity if it is to have any hope of creating the trust necessary to effect a fuller engagement with and authentic participation in the life of the agency (Putnam 1995). As detailed in chapter 1, this kind of collaborative practice characterized the early settlement houses. Over time these dynamics may translate into a deepening identification and affiliation.

Selznick contrasts community with contract, which he characterizes as a relationship of limited obligations. "With community, mutuality extends beyond exchange to enduring bonds of caring and commitment. The transition is from reciprocity to solidarity" (Selznick as cited in Handler 1996:239). Clearly, there are strong opposing tendencies. The impulse in formal organizations toward hierarchical rather than horizontal relationships, for instance, assigns greater importance to order than to participation. This is the case not only for relationships between staff and community residents but also for those between administrators and line workers. As William Kahn states, "The extent to which caregivers are emotionally 'held' within their own organizations is related to their abilities to hold others similarly. . . . To be cared for is essential to the capacity to be caring (Kahn 1993b:2).

Members of the Dudley Street Neighborhood Initiative (DSNI) remarked that despite obstacles social solidarity can be built through formal organizations if mutual respect remains a cornerstone of the work.

> There is a sense that there is a growing relationship and the mistrust has subsided. . . . It's refreshing . . . we sit here and argue sometimes but when we come out . . . we're hugging. . . .
> DSNI is different. . . . People work in mutual respect. (It's) like a family and that is its strength. [We] created an equal playing field.
>   (Medoff and Sklar 1994:250)

Efforts to develop programs that intentionally build social networks are multiplying. Recently, several foundations expressed a common commitment to strengthen the social relationships within neighborhoods (Annie Casey Foundation 1993, 1997; Chapin Hall Center for Children 1997; Walsh 1997; Stone 1996; Wynn, Costello, Halpern et al. 1994; Hirota et al. 1997; Kellogg Foundation 1997; Mediratta 1995). In addition, HUD has issued RFPs that emphasize the need to connect housing and job creation with the development of social networks. The potential contribution of social services to community building, however, is too often minimized or even denied. Most dramatically, some authors have suggested that because social service agencies turn citizens into clients they are disempowering and undermining community-building processes (McKnight 1989; Boyte and Reissman 1986). This argument is not without merit. It is the contention of this work, however, that although complex and challenging, the project of integrating social service delivery and community-building practice in agency-based settings is both possible and already underway. The remainder of this chapter will be devoted to exploring program strategies, processes, and organizational norms associated with community building through the prism of concrete, agency-based examples.[4]

The leadership of an agency is central to the development of community-building work. Despite the pressures of contracting, many social service agencies successfully struggle to develop community-building forms of practice. Almost without exception, these initiatives and the concomitant higher morale of staff can be traced to agency leadership that is committed to a vision and understanding of social service work as an agent for change. Most important, such leadership is willing to struggle to translate its ideas into new practice approaches. Finally, the most effective leaders model the kind of practices they are struggling to create agency-wide in their daily encounters with staff and service users. In this way, the authenticity of their practice approach and integrity of their commitment is daily reinforced. As chapter 7 indicates, leadership is a decisive factor in promoting both resistance to present corporatizing trends and catalyzing alternative forms of practice. Such leadership and the agency culture it helps to create concretely reinforce the understanding that, although difficult, service work can still be a basis for building community and advancing social justice issues.

Recent community building initiatives have had a special significance for settlement houses. A number of settlement leaders currently attempt to address present constraints through a rekindling of their historic mission and practice (Chapin Hall Center for Children 1997; Hirota et al. 1997). The intensifying need for a community-building practice to bolster the increasingly fiscally driven and fragile relationships between settlements and neighborhood residents is described below.

> Today a great many external and internal pressures are at work changing the role of settlements in decisive ways, often undermining the link between a settlement and its neighborhood, weakening the call to social action. . . . Pivotal among these pressures is funding: settlements have become dependent on highly bureaucratized public social service agencies. . . . In order to survive economically, settlements have had to shift their focus from community to discrete groups of needy residents, bureaucratically defined. Yet as the limits of this approach have become increasingly apparent, settlements are devising strategies to recapture or enhance their traditional community building functions, even as they face significant public sector funding cuts, shrinking flexible resources and increasingly complex community problems.
>
> (Hirota and Ferroussier-Davis 1998:1)

The pressures of contracting and the struggle to develop a community-building practice extend beyond settlements to not-for-profit social service agencies in general. The community-building framework developed in the next sections of this chapter draws on this broader, richer experience. No agency applied all or even most of the themes of this practice framework. Rather, fragments of a community-building practice emerged from a variety of efforts and sources associated with specific program experiences. These fragments over time cohered into a practice framework (see table 8.1 for an overview of the dimensions of the practice framework. Each of these di-

TABLE 8.1 The Dimensions of a Community-Building Practice

Norms Building Toward Membership Relationship	Process Steps Relational Principles That Promote and Deepen Affiliation	Strategic Interventions Building Social Connection Through Service Activity
1. Engagement	1. Reciprocity	1. Voice, capacity building, and leadership development
2. Participation	2. Respect	2. Joint project and interdependence
3. Membership Relationship with agency/organization	3. Inclusiveness	3. Ritual, historic continuity, and shared meaning
4. Member relationship with the neighborhood or wider community	4. Accountability	4. Space and attachment to place
		5. Individual caregiving and the nurturing of emotional connection

mensions will be more fully explained in the subsequent sections of this chapter.) The framework is intended to codify and holistically represent interrelated practice elements that promote affiliation or membership relationships. Clearly, no single construct can be applied to the myriad of complex practice situations. As such, this framework should be applied flexibly and with the knowledge that elements may need to be added or deleted depending on the specific practice circumstances. Finally and perhaps paradoxically, this broad framework can be implemented only in fragments. It would be a mistake to imagine that this structure exists as a totality in any organization. Clearer understanding of the holistic fit between the many pieces of a community-building practice, however, may allow administrators and line workers to make more strategic and informed choices in gradually developing their community-building work. Joel Handler comments on the necessary early modesty of such initiatives.

Ways have to be explored that will restructure relationships to empower dependent clients. This requires changes in professional ideologies, re-designing reciprocal incentives, and providing resources to clients so that they can participate. Still one must proceed cautiously. The ex-amples that I have outlined are special and fragile. While they may indicate beginnings, it must not be forgotten that they exist in small corners of large-scale, hierarchical structures.   (Handler 1992:293)

Norms and Process of Community-Building Practice

The practice of community building or social capital formation is com-plex. At least three dimensions of this work have been identified in the literature. As was briefly noted earlier, norms such as reciprocity, respect, and inclusiveness are critical to building the trust necessary to promote social connections. Equality of respect, as Mansbridge suggests, "preserves . . . (or creates) respect and makes empathy easier" (Mansbridge as cited in Handler 1996:233). A community-building organization and its leadership need to imbue their daily work with a sensibility that creates a language, behavior, and attitude of respect. If, for instance, the staff talk about participation but leave little time for community residents to voice their opinions and dissent, then the discontinuity between what is said and what is experienced will undermine trust. Consistent with this point is Hasenfeld's definition of the client-worker relationship in human service organizations. He argues that at the core of the relationship between worker and client is trust, whereby the worker treats the client as a subject and not as an object (Hasenfeld 1987). The daily incorporation of such norms into practice is difficult and complex. Staff socialization to a professional ethos that emphasizes formal expertise, productivity demands, and bureaucratic impulses to control work processes conspires to limit commitment to more reciprocal and inclusive relation-ships with service users. There are no shortcuts to engendering connection, trust, or affiliation (Ewalt 1998; Falck 1984, 1989; Morgan 1995; Murphy and Choi 1993; McNeil 1995; Sergiovanni 1994; Schorr 1988; Stone et. al. 1996). Without a commitment and struggle to incorporate such norms into daily practice, community-building initiatives will have no substance and little meaning to neighborhood residents.

A second dimension of community-building practice is process; it is the basis upon which relationships are built. For the purposes of this discussion, it is the democratic means by which the democratic end of social solidarity is achieved. In any relationship-building project, "the concept of process has to be taken seriously" (Handler 1996:219). It is the contention of this analysis that four distinct stages of process are salient to community-building practice: engagement, participation, membership relationship with the agency, and membership relationship with the wider community. The remainder of this section will briefly describe each stage and identify difficulties associated with managing progress along this continuum.

Engagement

Engagement is critical to the process of building affiliation between community residents and service organizations. As noted earlier, in very poor communities, residents have experienced weakened neighborhood institutions and social networks (Wilson 1987, 1991; Putnam 1993a, 1995; Di-Rienzo 1995, 1996; Downton and Wehr 1991; Drucker 1994; Kuttner 1997; Kingsley and Wilson 1997; Stern et al. 1998). Unresponsive public and private agencies have also widened the gulf between neighborhood residents and key local institutions (Fabricant and Burghardt 1992; Naperstack and Dooley 1998; Walkowitz 1999; McKnight 1985, 1989). These dynamics promote a disengagement of service users from local agencies. Yet, the literature suggests that if citizens or residents are given the opportunity to participate, they will. As any tenant organizer or youth worker understands, opportunity to participate, though necessary, is not sufficient to promote a widening and deepening involvement. Participation remains an abstraction until service users are given a reason to invest their scarce resources of trust and time (Comer 1980; Dupper and Poertner 1998; Gulati and Guest 1990; Jackson et al. 1996; Jones and Silva 1991; Sashkin 1984; Webster-Stratton 1997). First, the distrust and consequent distancing that have accumulated over the years need to be addressed during the engagement stage of work. The false hope of a practice that leaps past engagement work to participation is described in the following passage.

One of the major problems we have in poor disadvantaged, urban communities is that we have "client communities." They're not producers of jobs, they're not producers of the solutions to their own problems partly because the system has created that. Poor and minority families in these communities are used to being clients in a public social service system. They are now being asked to be partners.

(Dupper and Poertner 1998:311)

What then are the qualities of workers and agencies most likely to stimulate community residents to begin to see service activities and staff in new ways? To begin with, the agency needs to create a disequilibrium, to get residents to reassess their assumptions and prior relationships with service agencies. This disequilibrium jars the service user into breaking with patterned perceptions and responses that promote distance (O'Connell 1988; Swartz 1995; Gulati and Guest 1990; Segal and Baumohl 1980, 1985; Berman 1991; Balsanak 1998; Minkler 1997; Morgan 1995, Reinelt 1994; Reinelt et al. 1995). Some part of a fuller engagement with service users is developed by welcoming and inviting them to take part in the life of the agency. Such welcoming can take many forms, but what remains constant is an effort on the part of the agency to facilitate relationships with staff, to respond to needs, and to listen to clients early on in the decision-making process. This may appear to be a simple recipe for client engagement, but as any line worker can attest, the translation of such guidelines into daily practice is quite complex. It is also important to reiterate that this and subsequent stages of work require clear expressions of the norms that were described earlier.

A process that sparks deepening affiliations must tend to the subjective as well as the objective needs of service users (Kahn 1993a). Warmth, expressions of commitment, and the risk of sharing parts of a private life or public history are but a few ways in which workers can help to transform service users early on from objects into the subjects of service encounters. From the very beginning of service delivery or this engagement stage, attention must be paid to converting distrust into trust. Only in this way will service users be prepared to give more and more of themselves to early service encounters and relationships. Further, engagement means not only interacting but seeing oneself in public, as a social being. It is for this reason that the IAF (Industrial Areas Foundation) does "one-on-ones" in which it seeks to get people to see themselves in public as members of a group or community rather than simply as isolated, private individuals (Fisher 1994).

Participation

Evidence of commitment on the part of agency leadership and line staff to maximize participation of service users is a cornerstone of building relationships and social capital. The work of participation occurs along at least two axes. Relatively formal encounters between staff and clients in the provision of services represents one pathway for promoting participation. In these meetings attention may be paid to questions regarding problems and needed services. Embedded in such processes is the intention to involve service users in decision making (Badding 1989; Arnstein 1969; Dachler and Wilpert 1978; Hirschman 1970; Mullender and Ward 1991; Pargament, Habib, and Antebi 1978; Ramey 1992; Valentine and Caponi 1989; Sviridoff and Ryan 1997). This cocreation of service, as Harry Boyte and Nancy Kari note, is at least one expression of more democratic agency decision making (Boyte and Kari 1996). This approach can have substantial consequences.

> I learned to be dependent on others making decisions for me. . . . I felt . . . that I deserved to be a throwaway. [This program] provided me with the opportunity to gain autonomy, select options, set boundaries and achieve a better quality of life.   (Jackson et al. 1996:176)

The agency may also provide opportunities for participation that are less directly associated with the provision of services tailored to specific individual needs. For instance, service users may participate in social events, advisory groups, or support activities structured to address collective aspirations. This type of participation expands the residents' relationships with the agency, which becomes a hub of vital communal activity and not just a service provider (Dupper and Poertner 1998; Swartz 1995; Jackson et al. 1996; Boyte and Kari 1996; Comer 1980; Carp 1981; DeLeon and Rosenthal 1989).

Participation, unlike engagement demands a deeper commitment on the part of the service user. The focus of practice here is not on gaining the attention of service users but on effecting a fuller involvement in both the processes of service provision and the broader currents of agency life. Increased trust and stronger bonds translate into a willingness to risk expressing one's opinions and into a greater sense of individual ownership of specific service projects. This last point is particularly important, as participation does not necessarily require identification with a collective project (Falck 1984, 1989). Rather, service users may recognize only individual benefits associated with greater participation. For instance, participation may help to create a more customized fit between a package of services and an individual's needs or provide a group forum for working through individual issues. One can participate in a group and not see oneself as an interdependent member. During this stage of the community-building process, trust in specific services as a basis for working through an individual's problems or issues will likely be built. Equally important, isolated relationships with workers and neighbors will take form. This stage of the community-building process remains focused on a more participatory albeit at times individualized mode of service consumption. Greater participation of community residents in service provision and programs, however, is essential to a developing sense of membership in regard to the agency.

A number of factors have been reported in the literature as barriers to the participation of service users. Two that are worth mentioning here are: (1) tokenism and (2) role strain. Too often consumers are asked to participate in ways that lack authentic meaning. The effort toward greater participation of service users may be sparked by new funding requirements or a narrow ideological commitment. Consequently, the agency may restrict participation in ways that undercut the development of authentic new roles and a greater say of residents in specific decisions. The initiatives may be experienced as more artifice than substance (Valentine and Caponi 1989). And the transition from one set of role expectations to another without sufficient preparation or lead time may produce tensions. Such strains may be compounded when "members are unsure of their individual roles and what is expected of them, or when they fail to recognize or acknowledge the scope or complexity of other members' roles" (Valentine and Caponi 1989:10). Participation is not only a complex concept but also represents at the very least a shift in power dynamics. If the agency has a commitment to a more inclusive participatory mode of decision making, then tokenism and role strain must be minimized. Otherwise, participatory initiatives will be experienced as an essentially meaningless and exploitative exercise (McNeil 1995). Such perceptions will derail the larger enterprise of community building and social capital formation.

Member Relationship to Agency or Program

The practice literature most frequently characterizes membership as both recognition and experience of interdependence with other members of a group (Jackson et al. 1996; Forte 1991; Salem, Seidman, and Rappaport 1988; Lieberman and Snowden 1993; Sergiovanni 1994; Falck 1989; Pollio, McDonald, and North 1996). Service users develop a "connection to something larger than themselves in a group experience" (Salem, Seidman, and Rappaport 1988:406). As Joan Laird reminds us, membership requires that individuals' participation be transformed in ways that "make the meanings of other persons behavior one's own through internalization. . . . What is observable are social interactions which include not only the interactions themselves but what these mean to participants" (Laird 1984:156). In some sense the group and its members become an extension of the self. As the individual identifies ever more strongly with the collective experience, a dynamic sense of ownership and belonging is reinforced (Gummer 1995; Walter 1997; Wallarstein, Sanchez-Merki, and Dow 1997; Zachary 1996, 2000; Minkler 1997; Delgado 1998b; Gardner 1992).

The transition to membership is perhaps most fully realized when the concept of exchange is redefined (Putnam 1995; Gardner 1992). The exchange benefits in the marketplace of investment and individual gain characterize the early stages of participation (Kanter 1982). Membership is distinctive in part because of reconfigured understandings of exchange that emerge over time, when exchange benefits are understood to occur not simply in the taking but also in the giving. As membership attachment takes root, the act of giving takes on a more complex meaning. Investment in the group is experienced as enhancing the individual. For example, this may be the case for parents who become highly involved in neighborhood schools. In the beginning, such participation may be focused on a narrow understanding of self-interest. Participation is keyed to benefits for their children. Over time, however, a broader commitment to change and a shifting understanding of benefits may emerge. The investment and payoff may come to be calculated on the basis of more collective benefits that strengthen the capacity of the community and agency to effect, for instance, the restoration of a physical plant or broad investment in professional training.

What promotes this more "cooperative spirit, sense of shared ownership and responsibility . . . or cohesive community within organizations or agencies?" Comer strongly emphasizes a decision-making climate in which "there has to be mutual respect and a willingness to listen" (Comer as cited in Handler 1996:237). More specifically, such an ownership or membership relationship is nurtured in organizations that practice strong democracy and where elements of face-to-face governance, reciprocal empathy, and equal respect are priorities (Handler 1996:237). These elements of democracy are synonymous with the norms of community building. Clearly, the parts of this practice discussion—engagement, participation, membership—are not self-contained but in dynamic interaction. Only by consistently applying or practicing the norms of community building can the trust and cooperative spirit necessary to transition to membership or collective relationships be built. Furthermore, membership identification is seeded through engagement and participation experiences. Once internalized, such experiences gradually redefine the boundaries and possibilities of relationships. If membership connections are to be built through social service programs, then the challenge of fostering reciprocal, inclusive, and respectful relationships must be faced (Delgado 1998a; Guttierez and Lewis 1997; Bailey 1992; Moore 1991; Tutunjian 1997; Winkle and Ward-Chene 1992; Zachary 1996). This challenge exists at the level of the organization, where a culture or climate is developed, and at that of the social service workers, where specific services are created. Leadership must be attentive to at least these two aspects of agency life to assure that even modest community-building initiatives will take root and flourish.

If service users are to become more fully invested in a joint agency effort, there must also be, as Mediratta suggests, a sense of efficacy among the residents involved in the community-building initiative (Mediratta 1995). Efficacy here refers to the personal transformation or growth of participants as they begin to experience their own growing leadership or other capacities. An essential aspect of this experience is a greater ability to change one's life by one's own efforts (Taub 1990). Much of the literature sees service delivery as ensnaring users in a structure of clientelism, which reduces self-reliance and alienates. We are proposing, however, that distributing resources in an atmosphere committed to community building helps residents become more self-reliant and empowered. In this process, resources in the form of services represent only a first step toward users' greater efficacy. Over time, they must see themselves as effective individuals and members of a public group if the complex and dynamic process of empowerment is to bear fruit. Deepening collective identification requires respectful, democratic processes as well as personal transformation of the individuals involved. This dynamic exchange, which simultaneously leads to individual gain and collective identification, is the essence of interdependent or membership relationships.

Broadening Communal Capacity and Identification

An especially critical task of community-building processes is to extend the user's web of relationships. The emergence of interorganizational coalitions and informal networks spanning all or most of the neighborhood may mark the transition to the final stage of community building, which results in a broader communal sense of identity and more political and economic clout (Chapin Hall Center for Children 1998; Hirota et al. 1997, 1998; Rubin 1993, 1994, 1996). It is necessary but not sufficient for agencies to build identification or membership relationships with services, programs, or organizations. If the process of building social capital stops at the level of the organization, then the larger neighborhood will be shortchanged.

To be sure, the temptation for many agencies will be to build insular organizational communities (Gardner 1992). Yet, the agency and its service users are nested in a larger community. The monopolization of such relationships does not maximize the potential contribution of the agency network to the revitalization of the neighborhood or building of the residents' social and political capacities. Equally important, the impulse toward hoarding social capital may be counterproductive. It can promote distrust as neighborhood residents interpret such behavior as self-interested and an expression of indifference to the needs of the larger community in which they live. Alternatively, to the extent that opportunities arise that enable an organization to improve the quality of life in surrounding neighborhoods or assist other agencies in their own community, social networks will grow.

This last step in the community-building process is especially critical because it reinforces the link between social and political capital. Strong local social networks and institutions provide a basis for entering the political process in the neighborhood with greater power. This is one reason that entrenched power blocs often discourage strong community organizations. They fear political opposition and alternatives (Fisher 1994). Such power can be used to affect decision making and in turn have greater influence over the flow of funds, access to resources, and the responsiveness of particular institutions to the circumstances and needs of service users (Gardner 1992; Lichterman 1995; Mullender and Ward 1991; Medoff and Sklar 1994; Boyte and Kari 1996; Pierre-Louis 1996; Pope 1990). It is therefore essential that community-building projects contribute to the formation of political capital. There is a context of resource and power deprivation that accounts in large measure for the downward spiral and isolation of very poor communities and individuals. To create local social capital and not nurture and use political capital can promote an almost exclusive reliance on self-help as a means of improving the community's circumstances. This approach impedes a more complex understanding of community problems and the necessary interventions. Analogously, it reduces the threat of struggle over resources and power. Community building stripped of political intention tacitly demands that neighborhoods solve their problems within the confines of present economic and power arrangements. As such, it represents an essentially conservative initiative. For community-building practice to achieve its full potential, the nexus between present political or power arrangements and communities' difficulties must be acknowledged (Cortes 1997). Through the community-building process and their own lived experience, residents come to understand that personal needs and community problems often are rooted beyond the neighborhood to the structural arrangements in society as a whole (Fisher and Shragge 2001). Although political initiatives, particularly in the beginning, may be very modest, they are essential to promoting a wider legitimacy for social service agencies and their community-building work. Only such linkages affirm the lived experience of poor service users who daily struggle with the subtle interpenetration of powerlessness and social isolation (Burghardt 1982).

Settlement houses have been particularly clear about the need to link projects for social capital formation to political change. While the conflicts associated with such work are not lost on settlement leadership, they understand its critical benefits.

> As settlements become more and more part of the government's social service system, reliant on it for revenue and destabilized by cutbacks, they face increasingly complex dynamics affecting . . . their ability to advocate for social justice and it may need to find new strategies for using the power of its community embeddedness . . . to leverage change and reform. . . . Identifying the common good and finding common ground within a larger social justice framework becomes a very complicated and dangerous task for the settlement, although it is one that can strengthen the community a great deal in the long run.
> (Chapin Hall Center for Children 1998:8, 9)

The specific stage of a communal relationship is not always easy to discern. For instance, wide participation may reveal a need to join but may also mask a very limited engagement with a program and its personnel. Alternatively, neighborhood residents' outwardly passive encounters with agency personnel may belie their readiness to risk more time and trust in forming relationships. Because specific signals can be misleading and calibrating the stage of relationship with the agency or program is often imprecise, assessments at any single point in time must be made with a healthy degree of skepticism. The more compelling evidence accumulates over time. Effective community building is a long-term process. Only by weighing evidence over time can practitioners develop more refined assessments of patterns and outcomes of affiliation.

Steps in the community-building process may be skipped, but not without cost. For instance, neighborhood issues and not identification of residents with the agency are often the starting point for initiatives intended to promote broader change. By skipping earlier stages, broad neighborhood concerns can be addressed immediately. This is important in an era of intensifying problems for very poor communities. Political mobilization builds communities. Helping to organize a protest with neighbors promotes both self-reliance and social solidarity. However, the benefits of a political mobilization that pays little, if any, attention to the development of social networks will likely be limited in the long term. The difficult and complex work of creating strong and expansive social networks must be undertaken precisely because it is critical to effective political organizing.

The process of community building does not follow a simple, linear trajectory. Relationships with an agency or program can progress as well as regress; service users may come to trust staff or rely on services that over time are weakened or disappear. These changes may be a consequence of unstable funding, the search for better paying jobs, or new demands on a staff member's time. Any one or a number of factors may prompt the transition from a membership relationship back to earlier stages of affiliation. Relationships have a life cycle that is not immune to decay. Consequently, practitioners and agencies must pay attention to service users moving back and forth across a spectrum of relationships. Practitioners also need to proceed cautiously because regression is not necessarily undermining to long-term relationships. It may effect a pause that reaffirms a sense of commitment or embeddedness in the life of an agency. Whatever the outcome, the process is not a simple or predictable one, and consequently practitioners must remain aware of the fluidity of relationships.

Does this mean that the process of building membership relationships must be given a consistent priority? Clearly, practice situations, particularly nowadays, can offer no such assurance. For example, the pressures under contracting to do more with less conflict with the need to develop social service community-building initiatives. However, the tendency not to struggle with the processes of community building in an era that primarily rewards increasingly narrow outcomes will be lethal to the social cohesion essential to effective service delivery and social change. In addition, a leadership that imagines that membership relationships can be created in the absence of authentic forms of participation is committed to little more than the superficial rather than the difficult substantive practice choices associated with agency-based community building. Resistance to new practice approaches is both predictable and inevitable, as with any kind of change initiative. Despite resistance, new forms of relationships can be nurtured if there is an authentic commitment to the struggle. Only in the back-and-forth between the intensifying constraints of privatization and the effort to purposefully extend the boundaries of social services will practice experimentation be grounded to practice circumstance. To separate an agency-based community-building agenda from such struggles and complex dynamics is to advance an idealized rather than a reality-based understanding of practice innovation.

A Third Dimension of Community-Building Practice: Strategic Intervention Through Service Activity

The work of community building also occurs along a third axis. The culture and process of community building are channeled through specific areas of service activity. These activities are structured to promote affiliation as a means of strengthening social networks and the individual functioning of service users. Each approach emphasizes a different form of connection, but all revolve around a common intention to connect the service user to an aspect of agency life. Over time, these new forms of attachment are expected to provide a basis for effective community building and social change in poor communities. The five strategic service activities that will be briefly described in this discussion include (1) voice as a means of joining individual capacity with leadership development, (2) joint projects and the promotion of interdependence, (3) ritual and the development of collective memory, (4) the use of space and attachment to place, and (5) caregiving and the nurturing of emotional connections. It is important to note that these are not mutually exclusive categories.[5] Clearly, each strategy makes an independent and overlapping contribution. For the purposes of analytic clarity, however, each approach will be discussed on the basis of its most distinctive contribution.

Moreover, strategies will be discussed in relationship to their contribution to specific stages of the community-building process. The development of community-building practice does not rely simply on the undifferentiated utilization of independent service strategies. On the contrary, the various dimensions of this framework are in dynamic interplay with each other. As was suggested earlier, the norms of community building must inform the development of every stage of the community-building process. Additionally, service strategies need to be differentiated on the basis of their contribution to engagement, participation, and membership relationship. The following discussion will explore the nexus between strategic service interventions and community building.

Voice, Capacity Building, and Leadership Development

The literature on community building consistently emphasizes the essential relationship between participatory democracy and the development of dense affiliative relationships. This point was made in the earlier discussion. One of the questions confronting practitioners is how their practice can be an instrument for such participatory decision making (Arnstein 1969). The task is complex because it requires that daily practice not simply provide narrow opportunities for the expression of voice but also encourages collaborative relationships between staff and service users. Collaboration implies not only partnership but the transformation of clients into leaders in the day-to-day life of the agency. As Paolo Freire notes:

> Man's ontological vocation . . . is to be a subject who acts upon and transforms his world, and in so doing moves toward ever new possibilities of fuller and richer life individually and collectively. The world to which he relates is not a static and closed order, a given reality which man must accept and to which he must adjust; rather, it is a problem to be used by man to create history. . . . Each man wins back his right to say his own word, to name the world.
>
> (Freire 1970:12–13)

Community, as John McKnight notes, is not built "with a focus on deficiencies and needs. Every community for ever and in the future will be built on the capacities and gifts of those who live there" (McKnight as cited in Boyte and Kari 1996:254). The project of agency-based community building requires that services be structured to transform the historic role of the client from that of an object to that of a subject in decision making (Moxley and Jacobs 1995). Yet, the assumption that all service users have an equal capacity to participate is specious. Leadership demands certain skills that may well be underdeveloped in oppressed communities and individuals. It is for this reason that a practitioner noted, "community building is about capacity building, giving residents the skills they need to have a place at the table with agency and other leadership used to getting things done alone" (Walsh 1997:25). Leadership may be encouraged and developed in programs primarily organized to enhance job market, educational, and emotional capacities. Furthermore, leadership development can be directly and systematically addressed through training programs. This discussion will initially focus on training strategies. Subsequently, specific opportunities for leadership development through the provision of services will be described.

Leadership training programs have been developed for parents of school-aged children, the elderly, the mentally disabled and for indigenous members of low-income neighborhoods (Zachary 1996, 2000; Vandenberg 1993; Kouzes and Posner 1988). Almost all of these initiatives, however, pay insufficient attention to the kinds of leadership that promote social capital or a sense of membership relationship. As Eric Zachary notes:

> The reality that most of the literature doesn't convey is that grass-roots leaders can be their own worst enemy. They have often internalized the dominant approach to leadership . . . which views leadership as convincing or telling people what is best for the group and as a status symbol deserving of special privileges. . . . The leader controls through threats, skill . . . and manipulation. In both versions power resides fundamentally in the leader. (Zachary 1996:70)

In volunteer associations, leaders who primarily employ force or manipulative strategies to get others to do what they are convinced should be done are likely to prompt others to exit from the relationship in one way or another (Hirschman 1970; Kouzes and Posner 1988; Zachary 1996). Clients will leave because norms that might bind them to the group are systematically violated by the leadership. These practices are reinforced by the demands and structures of contracting described in chapters 2 through 8 (Smith and Lipsky 1993). The "rank and file will experience a lack of respect, reciprocity and inclusiveness in such leadership and process." Relatedly, their capacity to develop voice, leadership role, or name need is muted at best and silenced at worst. Such experience may also provide a basis for "volunteers choosing to unvolunteer" (Vandenberg 1993). For volunteers this choice is rather simple and unencumbered. Critically, many grass-roots leaders have been socialized to a leadership style that does not fit their context (Zachary 1996). Equally important, this leadership approach is in conflict with the intention to build membership relationships.

On the other hand, a group-centered approach to leadership development maximizes opportunities for participation. This framework is structured to use skills, knowledge, and values to enable the group to determine what it wants to do, develop an action plan, and maintain a sense of solidarity or cohesion (Kahn 1993b; Kokopeli and Lakey n.d.; Vandenberg 1993). The purpose of the group-centered leader is to motivate people to get involved and to then facilitate participation in and ownership of the organization (Vandenberg 1993) The goal of such training is for "leaders to become members and members to become leaders" (Zachary 1996:73). Clearly, there is a consonance between this leadership development practice and the larger project of community building.

Group-centered leadership training facilitates skill development in areas such as managing meetings, delegating, public speaking, development of agendas, and interpretation of information. The training locates skills and skill development within a broader philosophy out of which community participants can grow. As Rubin and Rubin note, indigenous leadership needs to know not only what to do in certain circumstances but why to do it (Rubin and Rubin 1992). The interplay of skills and values is animated by strategic considerations about how one engages others and supports participation, the ability and willingness of a leader to critically reflect on strengths and deficits, and a vision or larger aspiration that informs and guides some part of the day-to-day work. It is not the intention of this discussion to offer a full explication of such training protocols or experiences. Rather, the purpose here is simply to briefly characterize a leadership development strategy that offers opportunities for the development of specific skills while simultaneously promoting broad participation and ownership in the decision-making process. These are dual requisites of any leadership training that has as its larger intention to build capacity and community. It should be noted that group-centered training approaches have been applied in settings ranging from schools to neighborhood-based social service organizations. A recent evaluation of a group-centered parent leadership training program in New York City documents statistically significant changes in participants' leadership skills and attitudes (Zachary 1996).

Leadership capacity can also be nurtured less directly in the process and exchange of service delivery. Unleashing this potential may well begin with a demystification of services. Often consumers are reluctant to participate because the nature of the service and the role of workers are masked in a language and process that may be experienced as incomprehensible. Explanations and choices may enable clients to voice their concerns or interests. This point is underscored by the director of an employment program in Boston, Massachusetts:

> A demystification of services is essential for a client-centered model of service delivery. A clear explanation allows clients to choose if and in what manner they want to participate . . . in what we have to offer thus increasing their power as consumers.   (Swartz 1995:86)

Art projects can help individuals unlock their voice and learn to trust it. Writing a story about a family experience, photographing neighborhood sites that have personal significance, or participating in the production of a play may enable individuals to develop skill and confidence. Art projects intended to build skill, voice, and leadership are increasingly abundant in programs offering a wide variety of services to the homeless, the aged, the mentally ill, and the unemployed, among others (Darrow and Lynch 1983; Freeman 1995; Swartz 1995; Hirsch 1998; New Settlement Apartments 1998). As Lowe suggests, art is a particularly powerful amplifier of voice for the most marginal and oppressed communities (Lowe 2000).

Fountain House, a program for mentally disabled adults, uses a clubhouse model of services to promote voice and leadership capacity. It has been suggested that "much like settlement houses of the past century, clubhouse communities are characterized by respect and equality among staff, attention to all aspects of each member's life with emphasis on the importance of work . . . and a focus on members' strengths and competencies" (Jackson et al. 1996:174). Consumers' voice or participation is central to every aspect of service provision at Fountain House. Capacity, leadership role, and voice are nurtured through the shared work of the house. Consumers' leadership role is woven into both service provision and agency governance. As Vorspan notes, members discover their capabilities by becoming valued contributors to the community. For many, this is a new experience (Vorspan 1992).

An employment training initiative for the mentally disabled called Rainbow Services, encouraged consumer voice in the governance of specific aspects of the program (Forte 1991). Administrators of the program indicated that giving consumers the opportunity to voice their grievances or participate in decision making helped democratize relationships between staff and consumers. Such exchanges also offered opportunities to learn about compromising and mediating and to test verbal as well as written skills. However, any governance structure must always weigh the benefits of consumer voice against the need to fulfill contracted service obligations. Aside from that, administrators may have to exercise a prerogative in decision making in particular moments and in regard to specific questions, i.e., threats to the community or financial crisis. The enterprise of community building is not necessarily about full equality in every area of agency/program operations but rather about enfranchisement through more opportunities to exercise voice and influence decision making.

School-based reform has been another arena for experimentation in the building of voice and leadership capacity. Over the past three decades James Comer has helped to convert 600 mostly inner city schools to "cooperative management in which parents, teachers and mental health counselors jointly decide policy and focus on building close-knit relationships with children and schools" (Dupper and Poertner 1998:309). The findings of this experiment confirm that the academic success of school children is contingent upon parents' active involvement. This fuller participation has enhanced the capacity of both parents and children. Parents have learned how to navigate school systems, advocate for change, and support aspects of classroom learning. The children, on the other hand, become more committed and active learners in response to the concerted efforts of parents and professionals to advance their academic capacity. Such partnerships and leadership roles are forged through specific training and the day-to-day practice of the schools. Venues for the exercise of voice are opened with teachers and principals and within the governance structure of the school.

Leadership role and enhanced capacity can also be nurtured in unexpected ways. For instance, a community support system for homeless women developed a dinner group to break the isolation of single room occupancy (SRO) residents and promote a sense of "self-mastery over the larger environment" (Berman-Rossi and Cohen 1988) Over a five-year period the group and service evolved as the women gradually asserted their independence from workers. This example subtly illustrates the relationship between the cultivation of voice, leadership, and capacity building.

> The members' overall pleasure with the group, their instinctive cautiousness in relationships with peers and authorities and their fear of losing something valuable, inhibited them from assertively dealing with the workers' power. . . . Rules and formal voting became vehicles for establishing order and helping the group move together. . . .

> The workers' definition of function shifted from a "doing for" to a "doing with" perspective as they gained confidence in the women's abilities to handle issues in their lives. The cooking group became a structure around which severely disabled women were able . . . to experience some new level of competence.
>
> (Berman-Rossi and Cohen 1988:75)

By offering consumers the opportunity to express their concerns, assume leadership roles, and develop various kinds of competence, the agency promotes opportunities for what Stern describes as the "reflexive construction of the self" (Stern 1998). Simply stated, this kind of service strategy and experience offers individuals a means for personal growth and redefinition. It can contribute to a wholesale redefinition of self-perception and promote a sense of empowerment. Most important, this is a personal empowerment nurtured by the group. It does not, however, necessarily effect a sense of collective or interdependent identity. It is rather the gift of the group to the individual. This point is critical because it locates this strategy in relationship to the stages of the community-building process. It may offer a transition to more collective identification if individuals recognize and internalize the contribution of the group to their personal growth. The primary work of this service strategy, however, is to build consumer participation.

This strategic intervention fosters participation through inclusion of consumers in program governance and capacity-building services. Capacity building critical to participation requires both enhanced skills and self-esteem. Skill development that builds greater self-esteem can also have the salutary effect of creating the emotional basis for participation. Voice, leadership role, and capacity building contribute independently and interactively to the empowerment of consumers. This creates the basis for increased involvement in the life of the agency and community.

Joint Project and Interdependence

Social services and the traditional culture of agencies tend to emphasize highly individualized forms of service. A fundamental assumption of such service provision is that individuals can build lives of independence without systematic attention being given by the worker or the agency to the development of a support network (Glazer 1993; O'Donnell, Michalak, and Ames 1998; Powell 1982; Thompson, Griffith, and Leaf 1990). On the other hand, community-building practice assumes that such independence can be achieved only through the active support of others. Social networks are considered essential not only to independent functioning but, perhaps more important, to improved utilization of service resources and the development of interdependent relationships.

Joint projects as means of fostering interdependent relationships are most salient to the membership stages of the community-building process. It is important to reiterate, however, that the building of communal connection is not a linear experience. Still, for collective identity to become internalized and solidify, service users must pass through earlier developmental stages of affiliation. This foundation experience is essential to the formation of a shared identity.

Collective identity forms through joint projects that consistently underscore the mutual dependence of members. A group's contributions to the completion of a work task, development of a skill, locating necessary health services, or stabilizing a specific behavior are a few examples of its potential significance to the individual. The other half of the equation of interdependence requires that the individual participant extend support to other group members. The mechanistic provision and acceptance of such support, however, is not sufficient to complete the transition to a more mutual or interdependent relationship. Emotional as well as cognitive recognition of the contribution of reciprocal exchange to individual well-being must be cultivated. It is in the intertwining of the individual with the group that a sense of interdependence is created and sustained. Thus, the transition to membership relationships in the larger project of community building requires that service users experience and internalize an understanding of interdependent relationships.

A sense of interdependence or group solidarity may also be marked by a shift from a contractual to a covenantal concept of relationships. A covenant is a promise or mutual commitment to serve a common purpose. In contrast to more instrumental contractual relationships of individual exchange, covenants

> involve intrinsically motivated efforts rather than earning something or getting somewhere. . . . The more strongly a person identifies with the collective entity . . . and feels valued and values the connection, the less that individual will rely on legal sanction to resolve difficulties . . . and the more he or she will be an active contributor to the community.   (Fong and Gibbs 1995:89)

Covenantal relationships have been developed by mutual aid support groups inside and outside of social service agencies (Gartner and Reissman 1982, 1984). An example of such a program is GROW, founded in Australia to aid in the recovery of former mental patients. This program is unique because it extends beyond weekly meetings to form a "community for living" (Salem, Seidman, and Rappaport 1988; GROW 1982). Formal structure (social gatherings, drop-in centers, assignments to see members) and informal networks combine to promote supportive relationships. The program has become a critical part of people's lives because each member is expected to be both a helper and receive help. It is in this reciprocity of exchange that relationships of interdependence have grown. This conception and practice did not emerge accidentally. Rather it evolved out of consistent attention to joining service experiences to larger purposes. Practitioners emphasized group forums in the provision of services and simultaneously encouraged and monitored reciprocal exchanges as central to the service process and intention.

The development of work teams also provides a basis for creating a common or shared identity. Clubhouse programs for the mentally disabled frequently organize members into work crews. Each team or work crew matches an individual's capacity with the required group tasks. The crew assumes collective responsibility for meeting, assembling supplies, dividing tasks, resolving problems, and completing the job on schedule. The success of each individual member is dependent on the performance of others. Collective planning, problem resolution mechanisms, and work site responsibilities reinforce the understanding that work can be successfully completed only through each individual's contributions to the group. Service staff have also used the vehicle of collective work activities to teach important lessons about compromise, responsibility, and the common purpose of membership relationships (Minkler 1997).

Interdependence can also be forged between small groups and a larger community. For instance, in San Francisco the Tenderloin Senior Outreach Project (TSOP) was organized to reduce the social isolation of residents of a hotel and to find solutions to common health problems (Minkler 1997). Residents used Freirian problem-posing processes to engage in a dialogue about shared problems and plans of action. The intention was to build cohesion in small groups while also tending to the larger, more political concerns of members. Early successes in improving access to sufficient and nutritious foods contributed to residents' feelings of control, competence, and collective ability to bring about change. Gradually, residents began to recognize and act on their interdependence and relationships to a larger community. The success of small groups regarding matters of nutrition led to discussions of crime and safety. Consequently, an interhotel coalition was formed. Coalition members started a safe house project and set up places of refuge identified by colorful posters where residents could go in times of emergency. Additionally, the mayor was persuaded to increase police patrols in the neighborhood. These measures contributed to an 18 percent reduction in the crime rate, a particular problem for elderly residents. Strong membership identification with small groups created the basis for broader affiliations and social action. The strength of the small groups contributed to the success of their wider coalition work. The essential point, however, is that interdependent relationships within small groups can be catalysts for wider change. Small successes, common concerns, and shared identity within small groups can reinforce insularity or provide the impetus for forays into and identification with a wider community (Minkler 1997:246).

In New York City, the United Community Centers (UCC), a settlement house, implemented HIV prevention work in a ten-block area of East New

York. The program relied on taxi drivers to promote awareness of HIV and AIDS and participate in the planning and implementation of activities (Hirota et al. 1997). UCC understood that the cab drivers were both an important target group for services and, perhaps more important, a conduit to other parts of the neighborhood. Many cab drivers were predisposed to joining the project because the agency had helped drivers settle an acrimonious strike and establish their own taxi association. Thus, the agency created reciprocity of exchange when it requested assistance. Over time, new forms of collaboration evolved. The agency helped drivers with a ticketing problem, and in turn they helped the neighborhood organize street fairs and implement crime prevention programs. This example is unique because it suggests that an agency's organizing projects can build partnerships with small business groups as well as with volunteer associations. Initially, the connection was limited to the agency and the taxi association. Eventually, however, new connections were established between these groups and the surrounding neighborhood. The relationships were nurtured gradually. The agency supported the taxi drivers without necessarily expecting anything in return either right away or in the long term. UCC helped to resolve a conflict because it was embedded in and identified with the neighborhood. Its action was more covenantal than instrumental. However, this act of solidarity created a basis for future collaboration and for the development of deepening and growing interdependent relationships (Hirota et al. 1997:10).

The work of the community-building practitioner must be to facilitate ever greater circles of social networks and membership relationships. This wider community work is critical for educating residents about the personal consequences of imbalances in power and resources. In this way, residents can come to a new understanding of shared political and economic circumstances and the need for solidarity and social action. Organizing initiatives, however, must remain attentive to both solidifying membership relationships and the array of tasks connected with concrete political or economic objectives (Staples 1997; Susser 1988; Burghardt 1982; Medoff and Sklar 1994; Naperstack and Dooley 1998). Too often organizing projects have undervalued the process requirements of promoting social connectedness between participants in their drive to achieve specific political outcomes. This imbalance ultimately undercuts the capacity of organizing work to create an enduring and substantial social base for present and future political work (Hirota and Ferroussier-Davis 1998:18). Relatedly, too often proponents of community building undervalue the importance of organizing initiatives in the formation of social networks and social solidarity. Community building is seen as separate from rather than as basic to organizing. But effective community organizing almost always includes a process that builds community. Some of the strongest bonds of social cohesion can be found in meetings, events, and actions that bring residents together to oppose a slumlord, clean up a vacant lot, confront a city department that ignores a neighborhood's needs, and so forth. The relationship between community organizing and community building is complex and multilayered. Without a commitment from leadership, a critical analysis, and an openness to conflict, community-building efforts will not lead to social solidarity and the formation of political capital. On the other hand, community organizing initiatives that do not have a commitment to extending and deepening social relationships will not capitalize in the long term on the inherent community-building potential of their work. To see the two, community building and community organizing, as separate is a misleading dualism. Finally, to imagine the relationship between the two as simply one of community building leading to community organizing, excluding the possibility of community organizing leading to and furthering community building, minimizes the complexity of both (Fisher and Shragge 2001).

Ritual, Historic Continuity, and Shared Meaning

Connections of meaning, belief, history, and commitment are critical to the building of community. They are often created and reinforced through ritualized events.

> Rituals or patterns of behavior engaged in by a group of people have deeply embedded and significant meanings as they are repeated over time. . . . These rituals not only . . . reinforce core beliefs but are a source of commitment and community. . . . Some even become bonded to these rituals.   (Downton and Wehr 1991:128)

The shared meanings of a community, "everything from its nursery tales and its legendary figures to its structure of law and custom are forever conveying messages of instruction and reinforcement. Its history speaks, its symbols speak" (Gardner 1992:23). It is in the nexus of ritual and shared meaning that some part of communal experience is built. Rituals repeated over time create a basis for historic memory. Kathleen Hirsch and Wendell Berry describe the contribution of ritualized storytelling to the formation of communal meaning and memory.

> We are the stories we tell one another, the myths we live by. So much of who we are comes from the stew of plots over which those before us have argued fiercely, shaded and shaped and simply come to claim. . . .

> What keeps us bound to one another is our pattern . . . to those who are wedded to place, even the smallest fillip is fodder for our common life. . . . It is our ongoing engagement to who we are as a community.
> (Hirsch 1998:192–193)

> In its cultural aspect, the community is an order of memories preserved consciously in instruction, songs and stories.
> (Wendell Berry, cited in Hirsch 1998:192)

Moreover, communities use rituals for ceremonies and celebrations to reaffirm the group identity, to recognize and reward exemplary members, and to provide bonding experiences (Gardner 1992). Ceremony and celebration are a source of various kinds of affirmation. To begin with, an event that is experienced by members as joyous enhances understanding that work, struggle, and responsibility, though essential to communal experience, are not sufficient. Celebration and fun are basic to the creation and renewal of relational connections. Such moments meet the need of members to experience each other at play as well as at work. Holiday celebration, birthday parties, Friday night dances, and regularly scheduled basketball or other games are but a few of the ways in which play can becomes a ritualized part of the life of a community. The accomplishments of community members offer specific reasons to celebrate. Repeated and public acknowledgments create incentives for others to strive for similar levels of performance. Finally, ritualized ceremonies, such as an agency welcoming, early morning songs in a school, or days of remembrance for notable local figures, can provide a basis for affirming the values or purposes of a community. Traditional agencies have used rituals in this way, but so can agencies and organizations committed to social change.

The creation of historicity or historic memory through storytelling is a device increasingly used in social service work; for example, it has been used by organizations serving people with AIDS (Walter 1997:76). Perhaps the most powerful tool for telling the story of the many people felled by the AIDS epidemic has been "the quilt." This craft form was a most unorthodox and compelling way to create connections to the many men and women who had been infected by and died from the AIDS virus. Separately, each patch signified, whether through word, symbol, or picture, the very personal and intimate costs of the epidemic. Woven together they conveyed a powerful collective story of struggle, loss, and grief. Most important, the ritualized storytelling of the quilt preserved the memory of those who had died while promoting connection among survivors. The New Settlement Apartments located in the Mount Eden Section of the Bronx has created a program, "Memories of Silence," that encourages elderly people to share their stories with others. This historical excavation is intended to unburden individual participants while simultaneously providing group members with powerful connections to a part of each other's past. It was agreed that initially the creative work of this project would not carry names or signatures. Dresser drawers were used to display personal letters, pictures, family albums, hats, or other treasured items. At a later point, each of the participants wrote a brief narrative on the meaning of the display and the exercise (New Settlement Apartments 1998).

The Elizabeth Coalition to House the Homeless has an event each year in which it celebrates and tells the story of Eddie Gray, a now deceased but once notable volunteer and renowned person in the community. The event is attended by formerly and presently homeless people, staff, volunteers, and family as well as friends. Through stories and a slide show Eddie Gray's relationship to the agency and the larger community is told. This annual event weaves the story of an exceptional volunteer into an organizational history. As such, relationships to the memory of a local activist promote an engagement and participation with the purpose and past of the agency (Fabricant and Burghardt 1998).

The ritual of retreat can also be used to maintain connection to a recent past. It allows participants who may be frustrated, drifting, or withdrawing to pause and reflect. This examination can help to highlight how historic commitments continue to have significance in the present. This intellectual and emotional understanding may also contribute to a reinvigorated commitment or renewal of relationship. The retreat is a device that can help to identify problems, chart new directions, and renew damaged relationships. Continuity of experience is often possible only because otherwise hostile or indifferent participants are reminded of their historic relationships and meaning to each other.

Ceremonies to affirm achievements have also been used to deepen attachment between an agency and service users. For example, graduation ceremonies have been instituted by agencies serving the mentally ill to mark achievement milestones of members (Fabricant and Smith 1997). Leadership training programs for parents of public school children have also developed graduation ceremonies to acknowledge accomplishments. Songs and speeches heighten the sense of formality of the ceremony and affirm the contribution of the program to individual as well as collective development. For many, the event is especially meaningful because it marks the first time they have graduated from a program of any kind or been publicly affirmed for an achievement (Zachary 1996).

Ritual gestures that affirm achievements are particularly important to very poor and oppressed groups. Knowledge of a history of oppression can motivate people to engage in public life and collective response, but too often their struggles and achievements remain invisible. Consequently, ceremonies or rituals can have unexpected and substantial meaning precisely because they fill a large void. The subjective experience of public acknowledgment may therefore elicit a degree of relational attachment for the unrecognized or underrecognized that is objectively out of proportion to the modesty of the event. Such a response, however, can only evolve from ceremonies that offer authentic expressions of appreciation for specific achievements. Conversely, ritualized events experienced as mechanistic, insincere, or obligatory are likely to have far less meaning.

As the previous illustrations suggest, rituals and collective memory can contribute to the formation of relationships across the full continuum of the community-building process. They do not offer an especially snug or dynamic fit with a particular stage of the process. From early engagement to participation through membership various forms of ritual can be used to deepen the meaning of relationships and promote the transition from one stage to the next. If ritual and collective memory are to be effective practice tools, however, they must be applied differentially. For instance, the rituals of engagement work, which builds early trust, will be markedly different in structure and expectation than a retreat organized to reaffirm collective identity. The promise of ritual and collective memory will be unlocked only by astute practitioners able to match specific tools with appropriate and opportune moments in the community-building process.

Space and Attachment to Place

The space people occupy can contain symbols and meanings closely associated with the experience of community (Hirsch 1998; Richter-Greer 1986; Segal and Baumohl 1985). For instance, a home can help to establish historic continuity as objects are associated with important people and moments. The physical attractiveness of a piece of land can be emotionally internalized (Berry 1993). The open spaces, lush greenery, unpolluted waterways of rural areas, for example, are frequently described in almost reverential terms by local people. For many these dimensions of rural life create deep attachments to the land and a specific place.

The potential connection between physical environment and people is instructive for social service agencies attempting to build social networks (Baker and Douglas 1990; Cohen and Phillips 1998; Ridgeway et al. 1994). An inviting environment is a powerful tool in promoting early forms of engagement between the agency and service users. Yet, too often this opportunity is squandered. On the basis of its state of disrepair or formality (few posters on the walls, desks and chairs arranged to separate service user and staff, and institutional green or gray colors), agency space can create a sense of estrangement and worthlessness (Swartz 1995; Fabricant and Burghardt 1992). Such spatial arrangement effectively relegates service users to the role of marginal strangers, an uninvited and not especially valued guest. Even the most effective community-building practitioners will have a difficult time overcoming these early, disengaging messages and experiences of place.

On the other hand, space has been used quite inventively by a number of agencies. A JOBS program in Boston used photographs and posters as a basis for creating an early connection between staff and service recipients. Politics and personal life were simultaneously conveyed through these images. The displays opened up new conversational possibilities.

Having radical and alternative posters side by side with family photographs promotes a culture where the unmentionable becomes mentionable, where politics and social change are constant companions, inseparable from the rest of people's lives—lives that are rich with music and art and family and promise (Swartz 1995).

This JOBS program also featured a 15-foot long and 10-foot high wall that functioned as a community message board. It enabled agency stakeholders to independently and imaginatively communicate with each other. Photographs, letters, newspaper columns, listings of program graduates, and announcements were some of the items pasted on the wall and arranged to form a collage. The wall became a place to share fears, name a personal history, announce the recent birth of a child, highlight recent policies that might help or hurt, or simply speak out. Part of the culture of the agency revolved around the creation and recreation of this space. The wall was visible upon first entering the agency. Consequently, it sparked initial conversation and activity between prospective trainees and agency staff. For both new and old trainees, the wall also represented a part of the physical space they, at least partially, owned. It promoted a different albeit modest beginning in reshaping understanding of the role of service users in the life of the agency.

Women in Need, a shelter for homeless women in New York City pays special attention to the development of living space that "conveys a sense of the value and worth of residents" (Fabricant 1988). Prints are hung on walls, rooms are painted in pastel colors, and beds are covered with spreads to create a space that is physically inviting. Services for the Underserved, an agency in New York City, is attentive to the physical environments of the apartments it makes available to the mentally disabled. The size of the living space and its state of repair offer tenants powerful messages about personal worth. Equally important, residents are given the power to decorate their living areas or to personalize the apartment and transform it into a home (Fabricant and Smith 1997; Ridgeway et al. 1994). Schools have also recreated their space. In one instance, it was observed that "it is obvious that in every aspect of the school, children are the focus and celebration. The office area is the first room one encounters when entering the building. This is no ordinary office. Rather than cold, impersonal furniture in an isolated area there are 'squishy' comfortable couches, area rugs, small chairs for children and puzzles and books at the end tables" (Sergiovanni 1994:179). In each of these agencies the medium of living space was perceived as a critical facilitator of the agency's relationships with residents. Attractive, personalized living space provides at least part of the basis for a deepened attachment to the agency once it is internalized by recipients as an active expression of regard or respect. This point is illustrated by the statement of a member of a clubhouse community.

As a member I chose the horticulture unit. I was responsible for maintaining plants. I was responsible for maintaining the plants throughout the clubhouse. This meant that I was responsible for keeping the clubhouse community beautiful and attractive. This made me feel . . . valued.   (Jackson et al. 1996:175)

Programs organized to be "community living rooms" also recreate and extend agency space. The intention is to provide a place where people can gather informally. The space may simply be a storefront with couches, a pool table, games, or a television set. Alternatively, a room may be transformed into a coffee house with magazines, books, a coffee machine, and a supply of doughnuts. Such space offers a basis for outreach, a very early stage of engagement, to groups as disparate as the homeless and teenage residents of a neighborhood. Community living rooms are often critical to engaging groups that are otherwise hard to reach. This informal or less structured service space, as Forte suggests, can become a second home. For groups like the homeless this space can provide both recreational services and access to critical material resources (Forte 1991; Smith and Brown 1992).

Community living rooms must be kept nondirected and informal. This is a particularly difficult charge for social service agencies organized to promote predictable outcomes through the provision of specific services. However, it is precisely the "openness" of this common space that offers a powerful medium for establishing and extending social relationships.

It is in this . . . nondirected space that the worker gains the most intimate knowledge of "clients" by listening to them describe their circumstance. . . . It is also in such settings that worker-client relationships can be formed gradually and candidly with minimal role distance interfering. Here unencumbered . . . with rituals that confirm clienthood, worker and client may become known to each other through a process of gradual disclosure. There is a further value to working with people in such a setting. To the extent that people have friends who provide them with support or to the extent that they can develop such relationship during the course of "hanging out" in the community living room workers can support these ties.

                                    (Segal and Baumohl 1980:113–114)

The relationship between safety and space is also salient to the building of communal relationships. For instance, neighborhood residents may avoid particular agencies during the evening or parts of the day because the surrounding area is considered threatening. An agency's reputation may in part turn on its efforts to build a safer neighborhood. A number of community development projects have tried, in partnership with residents, to reduce crime rates through block watches, educational campaigns, and rallies. These initiatives at best produce mixed results because of the resiliency and greater resources of various forms of black market or criminal trade. Of course, the capacity of any single agency or community group to affect a downturn in the neighborhood crime rate is limited. The push-pull between crime and safe space, however, remains a particularly critical and dangerous battleground for residents and organizers.

> During the summer, Urban Edge reinstated the "Take Back the Streets" marches and cookouts. . . . These activities along with the renovation of Walnut Park, were widely credited throughout the neighborhood with substantially reducing the previously flagrant drug activity of in the Walnut Park and School Street areas of the neighborhood. . . . Our field data also indicate that crime and drugs were still rampant in the neighborhood. Tenants knew where dealing occurred, and sometimes worked with police, but the situation remained largely unchecked.   (De Souza Briggs et al. 1995:74)

Agencies' experiments with space can also contribute to the formation of new neighborhoods. For instance, in Illinois, foster children, parents, and grandparents have been relocated to an abandoned air force base (Johnson 1996). This intervention is intended to redefine foster care as a community or neighborhood intervention. Both the individual foster parent and an extended network of foster grandparents share in the responsibility of working with each of the children. The web of relationships in the new neighborhood are nurtured by professional staff. The program is politically and socially conservative, organized to replicate relationships of an earlier era. However, the reinvention of foster care from an individualized to neighborhood service can also create the basis for new forms of social and political solidarity. Especially pertinent to this discussion, however, is the programmatic interplay between physical space and communal relationship.

On the grounds of a shuttered air force base here an old-fashioned close-knit Midwestern neighborhood has been created from scratch, right down to the stay-at-home moms and to the checker playing grandparents. . . .

The program pays one parent $18,000 dollars a year to stay home with the children. The group also recruited middle-aged and elderly grandparents who serve as "honorable grandparents." . . . Principal value comes in simply being a part of the lives of the children, playing ball, lending an ear and telling tall tales about the old days.

(Johnson 1996:1)

As this discussion has consistently suggested, the first stage of relationship between service user and program is highly sensitive to messages associated with physical space. Consequently, the configuration of a place is a particularly powerful strategic intervention for practitioners during the engagement phase of community building. The potential contribution of space to the project of community building, however, is not restricted to early engagement work. An agency's physical environment can also contribute to the formation of participatory and membership relationships. The community living rooms and the foster care experiment with neighborhood illustrate the latter point. Above all, an agency's space must be consistently designed and arranged in ways that convey respect and are inviting. It needs to be shared with service users whenever possible. They should be offered the opportunity to place an imprint on the space. Such influence can be as modest as picking a color or as substantial as claiming a wall. Finally, whenever possible, it must be organized to meet the basic needs of a community for safety and strengthened networks.

Individual Caregiving and the Nurturing of Emotional Connection

Caregiving is essential to the building of communal relationship. Various forms of care were described in earlier parts of this discussion. For instance, collective experiences in mutual support groups and ritual ceremonies of affirmation can offer emotional sustenance. Often, however, ritual and collective experience can be experienced as devoid of caregiving. These strategic interventions are enriched by, but do not necessarily require, such gestures or behaviors. Additionally, caregiving creates intimacy and attachments between people in private, small groups. Conversely, rituals and collective experiences are frequently public events involving substantial numbers of people. These forums may be experienced as a complement to, but not a substitute for, small group acts of caring that provide an emotional basis for communal relationship. Therefore, although overlapping with other strategic interventions, caregiving's distinctive character and contribution to the building of communal relationship merits independent attention.

As Noddings notes, caregiving is a witnessing of other's journey such that they experience themselves as joined, as seen and felt, as known, and as not alone. These are the core experiences of feeling cared for (Noddings 1984). Caregiving behavior emphasizes accessibility, inquiry, attention, validation, empathy, support, compassion, and consistency (Kahn 1993a). Perhaps most critically, caregiving is a balancing act of attachment to and detachment from others in regard to their growth and healing (Kahn 1993b). Often overlooked in professional practice is the need for detachment or space. Caring detachment provides at least part of the basis for achieving the confidence and competence of independence. Conversely, care seekers denied such space are likely to be assigned the more static and dependent role of client. In this regard, Marc Freedman describes the relational consequences of nonreciprocal forms of mentoring.

> While mentors often have to provide all the initiative early in the relationship as trust is being established and the relationship built, mentoring is a two-way street. Growth, benefits and struggles are present on both sides, and mentors who are able to convey they are there for mutual exchange—not to solve the problems of youth— stand the greatest chance of making a solid connection.
>
> (Freedman 1993:103)

Mentoring is an essential caregiving role for community-building practitioners. It simultaneously offers a basis for nurturing relationships, partnerships, and competence. Partnership, or the relinquishing of control, demands more, not less, emotional connection to the circumstances of those being assisted. The practice conflicts of caregiving mentorship in a welfare-to-work program are illustrated briefly below:

I see our role as being mentor to the women who aren't ready yet. We just can't say to them "get a job" we have to say "Here's where you can get training. Here's where you can get child care. Here's a GED class if you need it."   (De Souza Briggs et al. 1995:12)

We just give them a spark and some opportunity. Then you have many women who have some disability, depression, dysfunction. But when the . . . advocates reach out to them these women latch on to their coattails and get pulled along. Our role is in catalyzing productive relationships between responsible adults. . . . That's how you create community.   (Walsh 1997:75)

Advocacy is another practice medium that offers opportunities for caregiving. Too frequently, advocacy is practiced mechanistically or by the numbers. The advocate may recite specific laws or regulations and await a verdict. The sense of urgency or crisis is not conveyed in either the language or the behavior of the practitioner. Limited encounters, inconsistent follow-up, and passionless discourse suggest little commitment or emotional attachment. Advocates can only affect an emotional connection to the service recipient if their effort expresses a committed attention and empathy. At the very least, the behavior of the advocate must reflect the degree of difficulty, dislocation, or anxiety experienced by the care seeker. The worker's willingness to "walk the extra mile" by forcefully describing the service recipient's circumstances to decision makers, refusing to leave an agency until a matter is resolved, remaining on the phone until greater clarity is achieved regarding entitlement status, and/or independently engaging in follow-up work are but a few of the ways in which caregiving can be extended and experienced. Clearly, this kind of advocacy work may be increasingly difficult in service environments that demand more and more from workers. This tension, as the preceding chapters underscored, is real and growing. However, an empathically attentive advocacy often demands more presence from the practitioner than time. The message and reverberation of such advocacy is described by a member of a supportive living program for the mentally disabled.

I have had serious problems that demanded that staff really get to my situation quickly. If they hadn't, I don't know what would have become of me. I might have wound up on the streets. But they got the job done.

They cared enough to get the job done fast. They turned the situation around. They were real friends. I'll never forget what they did for me.
(Fabricant and Smith 1997:46)

Caregiving can also be extended through small acts of remembrance. Cards for a birthday or to wish a speedy recovery for someone recently hospitalized are small gestures of support, validation, and compassion (Nelsen 1980). Physical presence at such moments, for instance, a visit to a hospital, is also deeply appreciated. Each of these acts sends a message of witnessing other's journey such that they experience themselves as joined, as seen, as felt, as known and not alone (Noddings 1984). Such remembrances are powerful stimulants for enriching emotional connections between service providers and recipients.

When I got sick, staff made a big difference. I first got here and was sick and it was shocking you know people who hardly knew me and cared so much it shocked me. Because I couldn't believe it. They were calling in at the hospital on their way home, and then they would come in with something for me. . . . It wasn't natural. And then I found out when something is wrong or you have a need you can count on them. I wasn't alone and I tell you what I found, I had not just workers here but friends. Now I want to find a way to give something back to them. (Fabricant and Smith 1997:53)

Caregiving can also be built into the structure of a program. For instance, in Denver, Sharing Partners, a program for teen mothers, developed a baby store. Coupons were given and redeemed. To obtain commodities for the store, the program worked in alliance with local merchants who donated items. A week-long campaign culminated in "the world's largest baby shower with cakes games, streamers and a hand-knit sweater to be given by 'grandma Bea'" (Balsanak 1998).

In an agency serving homeless people, caregiving gestures of hospitality systematically attend to the early needs of residents. Upon entry into the Red Cross facilities for the homeless in New York City, residents are greeted with a basket of gifts. These gifts offer hospitality and specific forms of needed support (O'Connell 1988). Pre-intake inquiry assures a proper fit between family composition and basket content. For example, families with infants are given baby food, diapers, and wipes. This information is also used to create a living space that has an appropriate mix of beds and cribs for residents. Such greetings convey a message that families will not be managed as undifferentiated units but rather will be attended to on the basis of their distinctive needs and makeup. These practices can foster an early engagement between residents and staff. Women remarked that these gestures of caregiving took them by surprise and engendered an early, albeit still wary, trust.

Deepened forms of communal attachment require an emotional charge. Caregiving is perhaps the most critical means of creating and sustaining robust emotional relationships between members and their community. Conversely, the absence or minimization of caregiving will promote more sterile and formulaic community-building experiences. Caregiving, however, must balance the need of care seekers for attachment and detachment. As noted earlier, caring detachment contributes at least one of the ingredients, space, that is necessary for care seekers struggle toward independence.

Dilemma and the Evolution of a Community-Building Praxis

There can be no single blueprint for applying a community-building framework. What may apply in one situation or community may not work in another. The size, location, mission, and auspice of social service organizations will influence how to incorporate community building into an agency's practice. The work must be tailored to specific circumstances. Moreover, affiliation is a fluid process. The bonds between service users and an agency are subject to change. Turnover of key personnel, shifts in funding, the movement of community residents in and out of agency life, or their multiple commitments may affect the strength of relationships.[6] The variability and complexity of practice situations prompted Dennis Poole to remark that "there is little room for formula or cookie-cutter thinking in community-capacity building" (Poole 1998:375). Recognizing the uniqueness of and then creating an appropriate response to each local situation requires thoughtful judgment. What the preceding section offers is a framework for thinking about the practice of community building. It is an attempt to holistically represent the dynamic relationship between dimensions and subdimensions of a practice framework. But the framework must be adapted to the complexity, constraints, and opportunities of specific practice environments. Furthermore, it can be applied only in pieces to influence parts of agency life. To expect anything more is to underestimate the challenges and dilemmas of our contemporary privatized context and to overestimate the practice framework as an immediate corrective to present difficulties.

Corporatization and Community Building

Perhaps most fundamental, the intensifying demands and narrowed practice options of contracts promote a proletarianization of service work that conflicts with the building of relationships and community. As was documented in chapters 6 and 7, the contractual underpinnings of social services increasingly impair agencies' capacity to build relationships. Increased demands, less flexible structures for defining tasks and activities, and diminished supports restrict service encounters. Workers simply have less and less time to carry out expansive, increasingly proscribed responsibilities. Relatedly, the inventive energy, commitment to service work, attachment to agency, and reflective space necessary to promote membership relationships are less and less available. If staff are not cared for within agencies, if the structures that overburden and constrain service work are not transformed, their capacity to create communal experiences for consumers will be significantly limited.

Workers have to experience the agency as a community before they can internalize and recreate such a possibility for others. This is, of course, a difficult task for agency leadership presently struggling to meet new service quotas or demands. The expansive requirements of contracting and the diminished supports for institutional maintenance create pressures to centralize administrative decision making and make it more efficient. Greater emphasis on hierarchy or centralization of authority minimizes inclusiveness and reciprocity between administrators and their staff. These tendencies exacerbate the estrangement of staff from agency life. The service worker, like the client, is treated as a receptacle, to be filled with directives. Such circumstances only permit shallow relationships with the leadership of the agency as well as with day-to-day work requirements. Centralized decision making, detached, "efficient" service provision and disregard for the critical themes outlined in this chapter then also mark encounters between staff and consumers. This cycle is self-reinforcing and ultimately robs social service work of any possibility of promoting layers of membership relationships or social networks. This is increasingly the reality of service work in our contemporary political economy and a fundamental obstacle to effective practice.

Therefore, a primary challenge facing policy makers, funders, and bureaucrats is to create a contractual language and performance standards that balance the need for concrete, discrete, accountable services with the often more fluid, less quantifiable, dynamic processes necessary to promote affiliation. These aspects of service provision, though distinct, are not necessarily in conflict. Presently, however, contractual incentives emphasize a market logic of productivity. This market logic thwarts the potential core contribution of service agencies to the formation of social relationships. Relatedly, little if any attention has been paid to using contracts as a tool for promoting collective outcomes. As noted in chapter 1, there is a history of public and private support for community building and social change. The present withdrawal of support for these elements of practice must be corrected if not-for-profit social service agencies are to have the financial incentives necessary to more fully participate in the project of community building.

Risking for a More Inclusive, Capacity-Building Leadership

The culture of partnership and risk essential to agency community building must be established and reinforced through the practices of agency leadership. The dilemmas associated with community building can only be navigated by an agency leadership committed to and willing to risk for the development of membership relationships. The following anecdotes underscore this point.

> For those who seek the empowerment of the powerless, the basic point of instability, context and struggle is both one of hope that change can come and despair that there is no end. So much depends on dedicated leadership.   (Handler 1996:240)

> Leaders must recognize the difficulty of building community in a hostile environment and have "the gumption" to take up the challenge.
>   (Hirota and Ferroussier-Davis 1998:22)

A communal culture, however, cannot be invoked or invented unilaterally by agency leadership. Staff throughout the agency must be active participants in the reinvention of an agency's culture. Fundamental to the development of community-building practitioners will be an agency's investment in training. Efforts will need to be undertaken to create training modules that transmit some of the skills, sensibilities, and purposes of a community-building practice. This investment can represent a powerful signal of the agency's commitment to its staff and to the work of community building. It is important to reiterate, however, that such initiatives must be joined to aspects of administrative practice that model and reinforce community-building themes. The larger struggle of administrators, therefore, is to translate the simulation of training into palpable, grounded forms of support for the day-to-day work of building organizational citizenship. As noted earlier, such leadership is an essential feature of those agencies presently struggling to develop and implement community-building practices.

The transformation of an agency's work life also depends on staff developing a capacity to independently advance their own interests as workers. Although some administrators may recognize the need to promote organizational citizenship, many will not. Even the most respectful and inclusive administrators are removed from the day-to-day tensions and frustrations of line work. Consequently, the perceptions of staff and administration of pressing organizational needs may not coincide. For these and other reasons, social service workers' sense of inclusion or citizenship will in part depend on their capacity to collectively have a say in decisions. An independent union of social service staff, for example, offers the possibility—though not a guarantee—that quality of work life issues will be addressed. Within the larger labor movement such matters are often removed from discussion or negotiation in favor of bread-and-butter wage and benefit issues. If the project of community building or the quality of work life are to be given priority, then staff must incorporate such concerns into their negotiations with administrators. Clearly, in the best of all possible worlds, these negotiations should proceed within a collaborative framework that reinforces a sense of partnership between administrators and workers. It must also be recognized that areas of conflict will exist that are endemic to the distinctive roles of line staff and administrators. The best hope is that structures can be developed to permit the participation of different stakeholders and that over time authentic struggles to reinvent the organizational culture will be undertaken.

The Challenge of Difference Within and Between Communities

Encounters between white service providers and people of color often begin with an unstated subtext of distrust. Differences in culture, income, and experiences of oppression often combine to create very low expectations. The staff person may be perceived by the consumer as unlikely to know enough or care enough to make a difference. Clearly, race is a complex and critical issue for social service agencies interested in building partnership relationships. A number of the ingredients necessary for bridging differences and legitimate distrust are embedded in the structure of the community-building practices sketched in the preceding section. However, specific forms of knowledge and skill development will have to be incorporated into the training of community-building practitioners. Even in the best of circumstances this work will be difficult. It will require vigilant attention to cultural and racial differences. Trust will only be built with agencies and practitioners prepared to authentically struggle over the long haul. Perception, however, may be influenced by aspects of agency life not directly related to matters of race. For instance, the detached delivery of service or centralization of decision making described earlier may be interpreted as a sign of an agency's arrogance and indifference. Such experiences may in turn be viewed and filtered through a racial lens. As noted earlier, the interplay between race and distrust is complex. No single intervention can provide the magic bullet. Clearly, however, a community building practice should emphasize both partnership and the importance of difference. To bridge some part of this divide, people must revel in diversity and inclusion.[7] Otherwise community building becomes another means of restrictive "enclave consciousness" helpful only to some communities or some in a community but of little help to the broader project of building social cohesion, public life, and an empowered social solidarity (Fisher 1994).

Settlement Services, Community Building, and Social Change

The conversion of social networks into political capital poses particular challenges for social service agencies. The creation of social capital or networks offers opportunities to mobilize ever greater numbers of people to exert political pressure on decision makers. Agencies engaged in organizing must often challenge a public sector that provides critical funding. The tension for social service agencies between funding and political action is not new. What must be calculated by the agency, however, are the trade-offs, strategies, and tactics specific to particular kinds of organizing. The basic relationship of political work to community building must be integrated into a calculus of risks and returns. Different circumstances will dictate different responses. What remains unequivocal, however, is that the promise and risk of organizing must be incorporated into the practice of community-building agencies. Ultimately, any decision by a community-building agency to play it safe and not engage in political work will undercut its legitimacy with and contribution to disenfranchised communities.

A central dilemma for any strategy to build political capital is both the larger society's and community-building theorists' stance against conflict. The opposition of global capitalism to democratic conflict and its complimentary preference for building consensus reflects its desire for social peace and reduced social costs. Paradoxically, contemporary capitalism pushes people back into communities and away from oppositional strategies at the same time that global entities concentrate power and compete furiously with each other. Conflict and contestation are accepted practices in the global marketplace. The goal is to eliminate competitors and minimize the cost of competition. In terms of domestic or social matters, conflict and contestation are discouraged as costly and counterproductive: cooperation and consensus building are the only acceptable strategies and modes of operation. The same is true for the contemporary world of community organization. The process of community building, for example, is seen as one of building relationships. We agree in large measure. But our understanding of community building incorporates conflict and tensions, not simply cohesion and consensus building. That was the basis of our earlier point about the complex relationship between community organizing and community building. Organizing can also build community. Through social actions people come together, forge relationships, and build social as well as political capital. The examples of community building and leadership development presented earlier in this chapter, such as the efforts of seniors in the Tenderloin section of San Francisco and the work of DSNI in Boston, were initiated by organizers with both a conflict approach and a desire to build social cohesion and solidarity around a progressive agenda. Individual empowerment, leadership development, amplification of voice, and, more generally, community building often occur in struggle with those institutions and actors outside the community that are responsible for many of the ills of poor neighborhoods. Trust and relationships are built in community-organizing efforts such as those focusing on what Jane Mansbridge calls adversarial democracy. Despite contemporary pressures for depoliticized social processes that enable global capital to remain unaccountable to citizens and workers, a broad approach to community building that includes varied strategies for dealing with the powerlessness and problems besetting poor communities must be developed (Fisher and Shragge 2001).

In an age dominated by a highly conservative credo of corporatization that emphasizes social moderation and consensus strategy, agencies are faced with the dilemma of gaining support for community work open to conflict and oriented to political mobilization. Creating the internal and external resources for such initiatives, although increasingly difficult, remains possible. This work will be central to truly effective long-term change in poor and working-class communities. The structures of privatization that dominate both on the local and the global level must be challenged in order for the contemporary system of contracting and its definitions of human welfare to be sufficiently redefined to permit the project of social and economic justice to move forward.

The project of community building has both historic and present significance for settlements. It allows settlements to reclaim the practice work of promoting organizational citizenship and political change. In this way, settlements, and social service agencies in general, can perhaps most directly contribute to the renewal of poor communities. This will not occur over the short term. Rather, agency life and practice can only be transformed over the long haul. Small changes over time can accumulate and gradually reinvent the possibilities and purposes of social service work. As in the case of liberation theology, pastoral work in Latin America, civil rights activism in the South, or labor organizing in Western Europe, local networks serve as the basis of broad social movements. This requires patience, time, leadership, and a committed belief system. Broader political or social change must be built upon a foundation of painstaking, incremental work that fosters social networks, recreates organizations, and readies people for a time of greater progressive opportunity. There are no short cuts. Clearly, social service agencies cannot engage in this struggle alone. They will need to join with other groups and institutions struggling to invent approaches that promote citizenship. Agencies will also need to participate in a broader communal reimagining of a public life that includes greater access to resources. Only in this way can service agencies fulfill part of the early settlement promise and hope: service provision and social activism as gifts to and foundations of a just community.

Appendix: Methodology of the Qualitative Inquiry

Context

As noted in the analysis, a combination of monetary and political pressures caused many settlements to reexamine their fundamental mission, value commitments, program priorities, and practices. See table 1 for approximate summaries of the budget cuts experienced by the sample of agencies selected for this study. This self-examination was initially observed at both a settlement house retreat sponsored by UNH (United Neighborhood Houses) and during meetings at several of the houses over an extended period of time. It was therefore felt that this was a particularly propitious moment to more systematically and rigorously explore the intersection between environmental turbulence and the changing culture in the settlements and more generally not-for-profit social service agencies.

A purposive sample of settlement houses in New York City was selected for this inquiry. Special attention was given to leadership in order to uncover exemplary strategies for coping with environmental changes. The study was conducted between March 1995 and March 1996. During that period ninety-nine interviews were conducted. Among the respondents were executive, associate, site, and program directors of ten settlement houses. See table 2 for a more detailed explication of the individual respondents' job title, agency affiliation, and substantive work. Agencies are identified by a letter and respondents by a number to assure confidentiality.

TABLE 1 Fiscal and Staff Cuts Reported to External Evaluation Team*

Settlement House	Program	Dollar Cuts	Staff Cuts
A	Youth Programs	$48,000	2
B	Teen Program Child Sexual Assault Parent-child	$100,000 (combined)	7
C	State/Local initiative Youth Services HDP Senior Services	$80,000 50% 20% 10%	37
D	Youth Programs	$9,000	
E	Teen Vocational Counseling Housing Assistance (restored)	$25,000 $10,000	1
F	Department of Youth Services ACD Performing Arts	50% 3% continuous	1–7
G	OASAS Substance Abuse Probation Arts	2% $50,000 $700,000	7
H	Senior Services Credit Union Day Care Youth Services Substance Abuse	2–3% 3% $175,000 $240,000	1
I	Homeless Arts Youth	$70,000 3–5% $240,000	1
J	High School	$25,000	1

This is a highly imprecise accounting that is derived from snapshot and often impressionistic reporting of agency administrators.

*Full-time employees.

Sampling Strategy

Alternative strategies were considered in the selection of houses. To begin with, we examined archival materials to explore each settlements' historic connection to a tradition of innovation, community involvement, and progressive programming. More specifically, materials were reviewed from the Wagner School of Public Administration's archival project on New York City settlements. Additionally, a mix of settlements was selected with some having roots that extend back to the nineteenth century and others having been established only recently. See table 3 for founding dates of each of the houses selected for the study. Next, using the most recent data, we considered house size, population, and range of programs. The sampling strategy emphasized maximum variation. The intention was to develop a sample that captured differences in the universe of New York City settlements. See table 4 for a depiction of house size. Finally, we considered the house's current reputation for leadership and innovation as the sample was built.

As noted earlier, ninety-nine respondents or employees of settlements were interviewed. For each of the ten houses, every executive director, associate director, and program director was interviewed for the study. Moreover, site directors of some satellite programs were included in the study sample. Finally, two maintenance people were interviewed because it was determined that their job tenure and insight made them key respondents. It should be noted that interviewing concentrated on three job types—executive, associate, and program directors. The majority of respondents (sixty-seven) were program directors. This was a strategic decision. It was determined that this subset of employees had both administrative and direct practice responsibilities. The study's interest in the changing culture and practice of social services was particularly consonant with this group of employees' breadth of social service experiences.

Interview Guide

The interview guide was divided into four sections. They included: (1) budget cuts; (2) consequences of budget cuts; (3) activities undertaken in response to cuts and; (4) proactive measures introduced by agency or programs. The structured guide identified specific prompts and questions to be raised during the course of each interview. See table 5 for a sample copy of the Executive Director Interview Guide. The format for the Program Director Interview Guide was only slightly modified to elicit information specific to the program. Over time the structure of the interview guide changed.

TABLE 2 Respondent Job Title and Agency Affiliation

Settlement House Letter and Respondent Number	Job Title of Respondent
A1	Assistant Executive Director
A2	Program Director
A3	Program Director
A4	Program Director
A5	Program Director
A6	Program Director
A7	Program Director, Head Start
A8	Program Director, Day Care
A9	Program Director, Youth Services
A10	Program Director, Alcoholism
A11	Executive Director
B1	Executive Director
B2	Program Director, Child Sexual Assault
B3	Program Director, Parents & Children/ Teen Parents
B4	Program Director, Senior Services
B5	Program Director, Youth Services
B6	Associate Executive Director
B7	Program Director, College Selection
B8	Program Director, Head Start
B9	Associate Director, Fiscal and Contr. Manag.
C1	Executive Director
C2	Associate Director
C3	Program Director, Housing Eviction
C4	Maintenance
C5	Program Director, Youth Outreach
C6	Program Director, Youth Employment
C7	Program Director, Adult Day Services
C8	Program Director, Senior Services
C9	Program Director, Youth Services
C10	Program Director, Data
C11	Program Director, OPTIONS
C12	Program Director, Homeless Services
C13	Associate Director
C14	Associate Assistant
C15	Program Director, Pre-School

TABLE 2 Respondent Job Title and Agency Affiliation (*continued*)

Settlement House Letter and Respondent Number	Job Title of Respondent
D1	Executive Director
D2	Executive Program Director
D3	Program Coordinator, Youth Leadership Training
D4	Program Director, Senior Services
D5	Program Director, Vocational and Educational
D6	Program Director
D7	Coordinator
D8	Director, Senior Citizens Center
D9	Director, Community Center
D10	Program Director, Community Center
D11	Project Director, Fork Road
D12	Program Director, Youth Leadership Training
E1	Executive Director
E2	Associate Director Program
E3	Program Director, Homeless Services
E4	Associate Director, Financial
E5	Director, Program Development
E6	Director, Older Adult Services
E7	Program Director, Administrative Services
E8	Program Director, Youth and Family
E9	Program Director, Community Services & Information
E10	Program Director, After School
F1	Executive Director
F2	Associate Executive Director
F3	Program Director, Alcohol and Substance Abuse
F4	Program Director, Performing Arts
F5	Program Director, Foster Care
F6	Program Director, Camp
F7	Mental Health/Consultation
F8	Program Director, Teen Parenting
F9	Program Director, College Bound

TABLE 2 Respondent Job Title and Agency Affiliation (*continued*)

Settlement House Letter and Respondent Number	Job Title of Respondent
G1	Executive Director
G2	Executive Director
G3	Executive Director
G4	Associate Director
G5	Deputy Director, Substance Abuse Services
G6	Program Director, Counseling Center
G7	Program Director, Substance Abuse Services
G8	Director, Child Safety
G9	Program Director, Senior Mental Health
G10	Program Director, Theater
G11	Director of Development
H1	Executive Director
H2	Associate Executive Director
H3	Program Director, Child Care
H4	Maintenance
H5	Program Director, Credit Union
H6	Program Director, Senior Services
H7	Program Director, Adult Education
H8	Program Director, Mental Health
I1	Executive Director
I2	Associate Director
I3	Program Director, Youth
I4	Program Director, Senior Companion
I5	Program Director, Homeless Services
I6	Program Director, Mental Health Services
I7	Program Director, Mental Health
J1	Executive Director
J2	Social Worker to High School
J3	Program Director, Home Care
J4	Program Director, After School
J5	Program Director, Family Day Care

TABLE 3 Date Settlement House Was Founded

Settlement House	Date
D	1891
I	1893
E	1894
H	1895
J	1897
A	1898–1902
G	1902
F	1937
B	1974
C	1975

TABLE 4 Size of Settlement House as Measured by Number of Part-Time and Full-Time Employees

Size	Settlement House
100–199 (or<200)	B E J C
200–299 (or<300)	G A
300–399 (or<400)	D
400–499 (or<500)	F
>500	H I

New lines of questioning were developed in response to emerging themes or data. For instance, the interplay between changes in public entitlement (Medicaid, Medicare, AFDC, etc.) and agency worklife surfaced as a critical theme during the course of the inquiry.

Five interviewers were hired in February 1995. Training materials were developed and a series of training sessions initiated. Additionally, briefing

TABLE 5 Interview Guide

Executive Director Assistant

OPENING STATEMENT: We are in the midst of state and city budget cuts which have led to funding reductions for social services. We would like to talk to you about the effect of these cuts on your house. We are particularly interested in how they have impacted your Human Resource Development Activities.

AGENCY:_____

POSITION:_____

A. Budget Cuts

1. Can you identity program areas that have experienced substantial financial cuts?

PROMPT: [let's start with the largest]

2. What was the magnitude of the cuts?

PROMPT: please include: city, state, and federal sources; also size by program area; specific program areas such as aging, mental health, youth, etc.

3. What have been the immediate consequences for staff?

PROMPT: salary, salary cuts, size, deployment, health benefits.

PROMPT: did you use any Settlement House Resource Development Project's services during this time (e.g., resume workshops)

B. Immediate Consequences

4. What has been the impact on staff?

PROMPT: morale - [staff conflicts, all work satisfaction measures, absenteeism, lateness, turnover, part-time staff, etc.]

5. What has been the impact on your agency?

PROMPT: information/communication; objective working condition [caseload, security, support staff]

PROMPT: has your programming been affected [amount of service, frequency of service, types of service, service mix.]

C. Agency Processes and Response

6. What planning activities have been undertaken to plan for future cuts?

7. To what extent has staff been involved in planning the agency's response to these cuts?

PROMPT: meetings, time devoted to it, planning, budget reviews, etc.

8. Has your agency done anything to recruit, maintain, or develop staff in this difficult period?

TABLE 5 Interview Guide (*continued*)

PROMPT: has your experience with the Settlement House Resource Development Project (SHRDP) influenced your HRD work?

9. In this process, what values were most central to guiding your actions?

PROMPT: for example, was preserving jobs more important than other considerations? Any value conflicts?

D. *Proactive Initiatives*

10. What has your agency done to develop new programs during this period?

PROMPT: collaborative work with other agencies.

11. In what ways, if any, has the fiscal environment led to new fund-raising activity?

12. In what ways, if any, has the fiscal environment led to political and social action?

13. In what ways, if any, has the fiscal environment affected your relationship with your board?

14. Have the cuts had an impact on your ability to fulfill the mission of your settlement?

15. Have there been other consequences associated with cuts that you would like to mention?

---

sessions were held with interviewers individually and collectively. These briefing sessions enabled the principal investigators to discern emerging themes more rapidly, respond to breaks in the data collection process (unavailable respondents, questions or prompts that failed to elicit anticipated responses, etc.), and fine-tune the data collection skills of the interviewers. The interviewers were students in the City University of New York's doctoral programs in sociology and social welfare and in the master's program in social work at Hunter College. Each of the student interviewers was responsible for reaching program directors. Executive directors and associate directors were contacted and interviewed by the project director. All interviews were tape-recorded and transcribed. Ninety-nine interviews were completed generating over 2,000 pages of transcription. The transcripts were entered and stored in Martin (a software program structured to expedite the analysis of qualitative data). Initially, the interviews were organized by questionnaire topic and later by theme and/or category derived from an evolving content analysis of the data.

Data Analysis

The data analysis proceeded through a three-stage process. In the first stage, line-by-line analysis of the transcript was initiated. Early provisional categories were developed both during and after data collection. This open coding over time yielded the core categories of the inquiry. As these core categories surfaced, axial coding was introduced. The axial coding focused on fleshing out the deeper structure or subcategory elements of core analytic themes. Finally, selective coding was introduced to create narrative linkage between otherwise disparate category and subcategory elements of the analysis.

During initial stages of the process, coding sheets were developed that enumerated early themes and subthemes of the analysis. Over time these themes were reassembled into more enduring core, and subsidiary or sub-categoric elements of the analysis. In the final stages of the analysis a twenty-seven page outline of the narrative structure about which the data cohered was developed. This outline linked specific strips of data (anecdote location was symbolized) with particular themes or subtheme. Data analysis was con-ducted over an approximate two-year period.

Notes

Introduction

1. The principles of best business practices can be traced back to Taylorism. Their intention is to create structures that heighten productivity and divide work. The focus is exclusively on the production of individual "goods." Collective goods, like meeting social needs or developing social networks or clubs, are simply not in the field of vision of such a framework.

2. There is no consensus regarding the devolution or weakening of community. For instance, Nicholas Lehman argues that new forms of community on the Internet and among suburban moms (soccer clubs, gourmet clubs, etc.) indicate changes in the form but not a loss of strength of community (Lehman 1996). Skocpol views the crisis in the formation of social capital as a consequence of the change in character of voluntary organizations. She suggests that these organizations no longer emphasize horizontal ties or membership interaction but rather vertical structures in which participants send money to a central cadre of paid lobbyists (Skocpol and Fiorina 2000). On the other hand, Wills suggests that there is no crisis of social capital or network (Wills 2000). This analysis accepts the basic proposition of Wilson, Putnam, and others that the social ties that define community and help residents, especially in very poor neighborhoods, have been seriously weakened. The connections between poor people and the neighborhoods in which they live have become more tenuous for a variety of reasons. While we disagree about the causes of this development and certainly about its resolution, this argument and the body of data that supports it informs all aspects of this book's analysis and recommendations.

3. Robert Putnam notes that an impressive and growing body of literature suggests that civic connection helps make us healthy, wealthy, and wise (Putnam 2000).

4. Too often, however, the focus tends to be on informal community organizations and not on community-based social service organizations. This book offers a partial corrective.

5. The literature on settlement houses is almost exclusively devoted to their historic contribution to poor communities and the profession of social work. In the 1970s Bert Beck broke with this pattern and developed an article for the *Encyclopedia of Social Work* that provided an update on settlements (Beck 1977). Beck, who at the time was director of the Henry Street settlement house, argued on the basis of existing literature that settlements had evolved into organizations little different from any other community-based multiservice agency. Judith Trolander's work (1987, 1991) also traces settlements through the early 1980s. A primary intention of this book is to provide a detailed update of settlement life.

6. For a full description of the study sampling strategy and guide see the appendix.

7. The authors recognize the impact of these bureaucratic trends on, for instance, community-building initiatives. This is addressed in the concluding chapter in an extended discussion of the dilemmas associated with implementing a community-building practice framework.

8. Throughout we have applied the concept of community very broadly. It is not the purpose of this discussion to engage in a debate about the definition and the meaning of community. Like Lowe (2000), I use Hillery's (1955) clarification of community as "a social group inhabiting a common territory and having one or more additional ties. . . . Common territory is a neighborhood demarcated by by geographic boundaries. Common ties are interconnected or cohesive social relationships. . . . Community sentiment represents the social fact of community at the neighborhood level; community sentiment is the subjective measure of positive feelings that group members have for each other and the community" (Lowe 2000:360; Hillery 1955:31).

1. The Settlement House in Context

1. Putnam is not alone in asserting the contemporary relevance of the settlement experience. See also Harkavy and Puckett (1994), Husock (1992), Brieland (1990), and Stivers (1995).

2. In a review of Lasch-Quinn's (1993) more local study, Hirsch (1994) emphasizes the importance of contextualizing the history of settlement houses in the major events and developments of the era.

3. For a nuanced treatment of the relationship between professionalism, class, and gender, see Walkowitz (1990 and 1999). For more information on the critical role of gender in the development of social work, see Chambers (1986). Cham-

bers (2000) points out that there was a persisting focus on professionalism in social work, not one tied to a specific decade or context. There was concern with professional education, professional organization, definition of membership, wrestling with differing strategies of service delivery, and so forth.

4. Schlesinger (1986) includes a discussion of the history and variety of the historical cycles model. We find his own interpretation deterministic and, curiously, apolitical, in that he tends to ignore or downplay the elements of political economy, power, and democratic conflict.

5. In the early years of social work tension grew between those who saw social work as a cause, who were committed to social reform and grounded in the values of social justice, and those who saw it as a function, who were committed to development of a profession grounded in disciplined practice and a knowledge base. Settlements were associated more with the former; most of the rest of social work, especially casework practitioners, with the latter.

6. The history and analysis of financial and administrative structures relies heavily on the primary and secondary literature related to the larger social settlements. As this book focuses on New York City, so does this study of settlement financing and administration emphasize settlements, such as Henry Street and Greenwich House and United Neighborhood Houses, the collective organization of New York settlements. But it also relies on the extensive literature related to Hull-House in Chicago as well as on the secondary accounts of social settlements in general. Because of the absence of material on the subject, it was difficult to piece together a history of settlement house financing and administration based on the larger and more notable settlement houses, let alone include the much less accessible financial and administrative records of smaller and more obscure ones. Chambers (2000) points out that in the many settlement collections he has surveyed, budget materials are largely missing.

7. For example, head worker Mary Simkhovitch only briefly mentions funding in her autobiography, *Neighborhood: My Story of Greenwich House* (1938). Occasional asides appear: expenses for the first year, including rent, totaled $2,800. There were no salaries; everyone paid his or her own way. The first check came from "the elder Mrs. J Pierpont Morgan," whom Simkhovitch describes as someone "whose interest in people had always been keen, as was attested by her excellent personal management and improvement of the tenement dwellings she owned" (Simkhovitch 1938:102). Likewise, there's little mention of financing by Helen Hall (1971), the head worker at Henry Street Settlement after Lillian Wald, in her autobiography, *Unfinished Business* in Neighborhood and Nation, despite the fact that she cultivated support from the influential Morgenthau, Wagner, and Lehman families (Chambers 2000).

8. Moreover, settlements relied heavily on their boards for fund-raising, many of which were quite stable and self-perpetuating. Trolander writes, "Membership

on these boards almost always implied financial obligations. Members were chosen mainly because of their ability to give or their ability to get others to give. Indeed the emphasis on fund-raising overshadowed other functions of the boards in New York and Chicago" (Trolander 1975:50).

9.   Fund-raising was complicated by the fact that this was still an age before a national income tax and before nonprofit statutes identifying the settlement houses as tax exempt. Settlement houses in the early years even paid some local and state taxes as incorporated organizations (Lohmann 1991).

10.   Of course, there are exceptions to this general historical model at almost every turn. Despite the conservatism of the 1920s, Chambers (2000) notes the experience of a black settlement in Minneapolis, led by a powerful and effective African-American woman, that served as a safe haven for the efforts of A. Phillip Randolph to organize Pullman Porter workers in the Twin Cities.

11.   For an interpretation that discusses the more social and activist orientation of Freudian psychology in Vienna, see Danto (1998, 2000).

12.   Wald felt the withdrawals of funds from Henry Street were almost always about her political and social positions. As she wrote, "we have had agonizing experiences of help given and then withdrawn. It would seem worth recording that the reason has never been disapproval of the work, but rather criticism of the head worker" (Wald 1934:119).

13.   For additional information on the financing of social settlements and other nonprofit service organizations, see Huntley (1935). One noteworthy point is that the percentage of settlement house funding from foundations fell from a high in 1910 of 27.9 percent of total funding to a negligible 1.9 percent in 1929. Apparently the settlement houses had fallen out of favor and other institutions, such as hospitals, had replaced them.

14.   Despite such overarching trends of bureaucracy and formalization, settlement workers interviewed in 1927–28, asked what they liked about their jobs, emphasized autonomy and creative freedom (Walkowitz 1999). In part, this may be because of the expansion of support for recreational and educational services during the economic prosperity of the late 1920s, and in part because the pressures of bureaucratization and formalization were only just developing and not yet impacting workers at the ground level.

15.   Chambers (1963) proposes that the National Federation of Settlements and some key settlement leaders began to revive the reform impulse in the late 1920s, addressing the inequities of that decade and laying the groundwork for settlement-led social change efforts during the Depression.

16.   A similar phenomenon for settlement houses occurred much earlier in Great Britain. By 1910 there were fewer than fifty British settlements, largely because of the development and policies of the Labour Party. The goals of the settle-

ments were thought to be better addressed through more centralized means (Skocpol 1992).

17. Most of them had affiliations with either Henry Street and Christadora House in New York City or Hull-House in Chicago.

18. Whereas Trolander (1987:5) thinks "The significance and impact of settlements houses has probably fluctuated more than their numbers," it seems their overall numbers nationally had changed by the 1930s as well. In the first twenty-five years, Wald asserted, settlements doubled their numbers every five years. In 1910 Woods and Kennedy (1911) reported there were 413 settlements. But after 1914 the growth stopped and remained unchanged for fifteen years (Wald 1934). Curiously, for 1928 Kennedy, Farra, et al. (1935) reported 600–800 settlements. Kennedy (1932) repeats the estimated figure. An NFS study in the 1930s reported approximately 230 settlements (Wenocur and Reisch 1989). Trolander totals 202 in 1936 based on membership in the NFS, UNH, and the Chicago Federation of Settlements. The huge discrepancy in the Kennedy studies seems the result of his including sectarian and religious settlements in the count.

19. This was a significant amount of money. The $30,000 per year Jane Addams donated to and raised from friends for Hull-House is worth about $374,000 today. Calculation is based on data from the Consumer Price Index from the Bureau of Labor Statistics web site (see //stats.bls.gov/CPIhome.htm). It was calculated that $30,000 \times$ (CPI in 2000/CPI in 1935) $= 30,000 \times 12.4572 = \$374,015$. On average, prices have risen over ten times since then. The authors would like to thank Janet Kohlhase for her help in this matter.

20. With preparation for and then entry into World War II, settlements were hit hard by funding cuts, declining interest, and personnel shortages as men and women, staff and volunteers, went into the military and defense work.

21. Social work leaders began to think it had to scrap its interest in social action if it wanted greater recognition as a legitimate and important profession (Wenocur and Reisch 1989). Labor unions were being told something similar. If they wanted to be brought into the mainstream of American life, if they wanted decent wages and working conditions, they should get rid of the social change component that characterized the Congress of Industrial Organizations, and, most of all, they should get rid of the "radicals" who were raising larger issues about class and race inequities in American society (Fried 1996; Lynd and Lynd 1981).

22. New York City settlements were able to secure state and local funds to take the place of the Lanham Act, funding day care at thirty-nine settlements, but only through 1947 (Trolander 1987).

23. There are countless examples of activity in the 1950s that counter the stereotype of the era as a conservative time, see Carter (1983). In addition, consider the

origins of the civil rights movement, both in terms of judicial reforms occurring in Washington, D.C., and of grassroots activism in places like Montgomery, Alabama, and Little Rock, Arkansas. Likewise, in social work there were progressive efforts to broaden the profession and counter its narrowing in terms of method and research (Fisher 1999). But most of these efforts, especially in social work, were seen as running against the grain or as exceptions that proved the rule of a relatively quiescent and conservative period.

24. Later on, Berry, always of generous spirit and deeply committed to the cause of social and economic justice, reflected that settlements should have tried to work more closely with the student movements of the time, see Berry (1999).

25. In both public-focused and private-focused eras most politics in the United States is contested in the middle between political parties that are roughly similar and tied to the dominant political economy. In private-focused eras, however, the range of politics and claims extends from liberalism on the Left all the way to the reactionary Right—including religious fundamentalists and right-wing extremists who seek to turn the clock back to some prior era in the hopes of restoring a more hierarchical and less egalitarian and democratic society. That is why in a private-focused era such as the current one, people are careful not to be associated with the "L-word," because being a liberal appears as the most radical left position in the contemporary debate. In such contexts, liberals and their organizational embodiments, such as the settlements oriented toward social action, operate on the fringes of society. The middle of the road is occupied by conservative leaders, ideas, and programs largely uncritical of society or capitalism. In public-focused eras, such as the 1960s, the range of political debate and policy initiatives extends from conservative politics on the right, such as Barry Goldwater, to groups on the radical left, such as SDS (Students for a Democratic Society), SNCC (Student Nonviolent Coordinating Committee), the Black Panthers, and socialist and anarchist parties. These groups on the left seek a fundamental transformation of that system, through nonviolence or violence. In these eras liberal politicians end up being in the middle of the road, and liberal programs, such as those of the social settlements, are not only part of the political discourse, but their issues and solutions become the center of political discussions and policy initiatives. They are no longer a fringe organization as in private-focused eras, but appear as splendid alternatives to the much more threatening radicalism of the Left. In this way, liberal programs benefit from heightened social struggle and leftist activism. For example, in the conservative 1950s Saul Alinsky and Martin Luther King Jr. were seen as radical threats. When politics moved left in the 1960s, including the appearance of more radical alternatives such as Malcolm X and rioting in the streets of major cities, both Alinsky and King looked much more acceptable, if still not part of the mainstream. To their credit, Alinsky and King moved left

during the decade, with King, for example, becoming a major supporter of the antiwar movement. But it was no accident that King, a pariah for a decade, had become, by mid-decade, recipient of *Time* magazine Man of the Year award and the Nobel Peace Prize. Likewise, Alinsky's efforts, largely ignored in the 1950s and marginalized in the early 1960s, began to receive a good deal of attention and support after the urban riots. Social welfare programs can play a similar if unintended role. In private eras it is not essential or even appropriate to fund social reforms. But settlements and social welfare programs in general become much more attractive to potential supporters as a moderate alternative in more public-focused and public-challenging eras.

26. The decade began with few changes in financing for settlements. Henry Street started a program in 1956 to improve relations between parents and children through working with parents and home visits. They continued to seek funds from private donors for such work. In 1961 the Vincent Astor Foundation gave $1 million to UNH, which coordinated efforts for settlements in New York City, to be used by nine settlements over a three-year period to implement the Henry Street approach (Hall 1971; Trolander 1987).

27. Leftist critics were appalled that the War on Poverty revived the settlements, but settlements did not receive funding because they were favored institutions. They were favored institutions in the years before 1918 but not in the 1960s. Rather, in the 1960s they received funding because they were well-situated in poor communities, they had a history of work involving community participation, youth, and poverty issues, and there was so much money available. MFY ended up being the model program for the Office of Economic Opportunity, which ran the War on Poverty. It proposed a new model of social action and community organizing for attacking poverty. MFY proposed to get the poor involved in neighborhood organizations to identify their own problems and employ whatever strategies and tactics were necessary. Settlements had engaged in social action in the past but tended to be more top-down (with settlement leaders advocating for the poor) and incremental consensus-builders rather than confrontational with those in power. Nevertheless, funding for settlements was now available in a qualitatively as well as quantitatively different way than it had ever been before.

28. As Smith and Lipsky (1993:55) describe this novel feature of the 1967 Social Security Act, "These amendments contained a novel provision that allowed states to increase social services by obtaining from the federal government triple the amount contributed by public or private sources. A nonprofit could 'donate' $25,000 to the state and receive a public match of $75,000 for a total contract amount of $100,000."

29. The expansion of Medicaid and Medicare meant indirect contract support for settlements as nonprofits get reimbursement for individual services. These were

different from direct contracted services, where the nonprofit gets paid without intermediary for aggregate services. But both reflect increased public-sector support for settlement work and represent two aspects of the new contract system. The New Deal delivered services only through public sector agencies. The Great Society transformed social welfare in the United States by directly and indirectly giving public funding to nonprofits, through aggregate contracts and individual reimbursements.

30.   In addition, there were many other programs that expanded public-sector interest in and expenditure on social welfare needs, many of which affected settlement programs and funding: the amendments in 1962 to the Social Security Act, the 1963 Community Mental Health Centers Act, and a generally steep increase in funding for discretionary programs and demonstration grants (Smith and Lipsky 1993).

31.   Also in 1965 the Housing and Urban Development (HUD) Act began a Neighborhood Facilities Program, which meant significant funding for rehabilitation and new construction of neighborhood centers.

Chapter 2: Privatization, Contracting, and Nonprofits Since 1975

1.   The years ahead were clearly going to be difficult for American business. If sacrifices were to be made, the members of the elite business roundtable proposed, they should not be made by those at the top of society. Profits or corporate salaries, the highest in the world, should not be cut (Boyte 1980; Fisher 1994).

2.   The top economic groups flourished to such an extent that being a millionaire, the epitome of wealth twenty years before, was dubbed "meaningless" by one conservative commentator. By the end of the decade there were some 100,000 "decamillionaires," those with wealth above $10 million (Phillips 1990:4). These were the symbols of the decade's economic success.

3.   Consider the fact that in 1995 alone, at the beginning of the economic improvement, AT&T fired 40,000 workers, IBM laid off 60,000 workers, and Sears, GM, and Boeing terminated 50,000, 70,000, and 28,000 workers respectively (Boggs 2000).

4.   The number of settlement houses and neighborhood centers increased during the decade. In 1991 the United Neighborhood Centers of America (UNCA), established in 1979 to succeed the National Federation of Settlements (NFS), was both reorganized and revitalized. Contributing houses grew from 52 in 1992 to 150 in 1994, with the potential of more than 800 neighborhood centers nationwide (Smith 1995).

5.   Sclar (2000) also focuses on the relationship between privatization and contracting. But his definition of privatization is narrower ("initiatives to introduce

market relationships into the bureaucratic production of public services," p. 3) than ours. Moreover, his range of privatized public services is broader than ours, but includes few social services.

6. For those with fewer resources, opportunities to address the problems decline. Instead, they see a shortage of adequate and sufficient housing for the working class, working-class poor, and homeless; less available and adequate public services in the areas of health, education, and welfare; and a declining sense of safety and security on the streets (Fisher and Kling 1993).

7. While the broad strategy of privatization includes contracting to for-profit providers, we focus our attention on the not-for-profit sector of which settlements are a part.

8. As noted in the first chapter, nonprofit voluntary organizations, such as social settlements, from the outset preferred to be funded by private-sector contributions. In the first decades they seemed immune to tensions between sources of funding, on the one hand, and settlement life, goals, policies, programs, and services, on the other. But this honeymoon with financial supporters lasted only as long as the intersection between the very public context of the Progressive Era and the reform work of settlements. Once the social ferment receded in the 1920s and social settlements were no longer seen or needed as "spearheads of reform," funding issues, as noted earlier in chapter 1, became critical.

9. Smith and Lipsky offer some of the best data on POSC expenditures, but even these figures underestimate the total because they exclude both federal and state allocations for programs such as Medicaid and Medicare.

10. As Peat and Costley (2000:21) emphasize, "there has been rapid growth in the privatization of community-based social services over the past quarter century."

11. Load-shedding refers to the transfer of work previously carried out by public agencies to organizations and institutions in the private sector.

12. Curiously, however, the success of the nonprofit sector does not discredit the private, for-profit sector. Privatization policy, with its inherent attack on government and anything associated with the public sector, makes it seem as though the success of the nonprofit sector derives from developments in and the support of the more efficient and effective private sector (Wagner 2000).

13. Panetta was also not enamored of funding the contracting system to the tune, in 1993, of $103 billion.

14. It should be noted that government funding sources are generally no more demanding in terms of requirements than United Way or most large private donors (Kramer 1994). The difference is the extent to which government has become a dominant source of funding, thus making it the most significant influence in shaping and reshaping the voluntary sector.

15. In a very different way, but in similar terms, economist Burton Weisbrod (1988:168) speaks of nonprofits as a "hidden" part of the economy.

16. In Massachusetts in the mid-1980s, because wages for workers in nonprofit agencies were much lower than wages for comparable workers in the public sector, nonprofits had difficulty finding or retaining staff and were forced to leave positions open or fill them with employees from temporary agencies (Smith and Lipsky 1993).

17. As noted above, dependence of service providers on the contracting system can burden nonprofits with added expenses and programs. Agencies develop staff and programs to deliver the contracted services, but when government cuts funds, as happened dramatically in the early 1980s and again in the mid-1990s, agencies not only have fewer resources, but they are often pressured into sustaining the defunded programs.

18. In a sense agencies become more political with contracting, lobbying politicians, encouraging legislation, advocating for the interests of their organization. Informally, they must cozy up to political officials and bureaucrats just as they are expected to wine and dine CEOs, bankers, realtors, and the like in their local area to secure grants and donations (Wagner 2000).

19. He is not alone in his critique (Etzioni 1993, 1995; Elshtain 1994; Bellah, Madsen, Sullivan, et al. 1985). Communitarian philosophy is an increasingly attractive ideological alternative to free-market anarchy, especially for those interested in social cohesiveness and the development of a stronger civil society. Most communitarian analysis understands that context heavily determines the opportunities and supports for community building (Putnam 1996, 2000; Elshtain 1994; Etzioni 1995). But most communitarian analysis rarely identifies the decline of civil life as resulting from the new privatized global economy (Fisher 1996). Others argue that the new political economy promotes different values, politics, and policies that shatter community (Boggs 2000; Sassen 1994; Smith and Feagin 1987; Feagin 1998; Brecher and Costello 1994; Fisher and Karger 1997), undermine public life (Boggs 2000; Bauman 1998; Sandel 1988), weaken attachment to place (Delgado 1994; Bauman 1998; Kling 1993; Fainstein and Fainstein 1974; Smith and Feagin 1987), and, most important, subvert the ability of citizens to do something about this (Amin 1990; Montgomery 1995; Boggs 1986; Fisher and Kling 1993).

Chapter 3: Fiscal Instability: Rewriting the Contract

1. See the appendix for agency and respondent identifying information. Respondents and agency names are protected to assure confidentiality. Therefore, each settlement house has been assigned a letter and each respondent a number. The appendix offers information regarding the size and budget cuts of the settlements included in the sample. The role of each respondent is also identified. For instance, the hierarchical position (executive, associate, site, program directors) and program or responsibility (elderly, after-school program, mental

health, etc.) of each staff member is provided. The sample was composed of one hundred staff from ten houses across New York City. The sampling strategy and rationale are also discussed.

Chapter 7: Navigating the Current Fiscal Turbulence While Struggling to Chart a Social Services Future

1. The potential conflicts between organizing neighborhood residents to advance collective interests and developing for-profit corporate enterprises (see preceding section) was not considered by the respondents or raised by the interviewers.

Chapter 8: From Corporatized Contracting to Community Building

1. As was noted in chapter 3, public contracts are wrapped around grants made directly to programs and individual entitlements (SSI, Medicare, etc.), which trigger reimbursement.
2. The two dimensions of transformed labor include ideological (conception) and technical (execution) proletarianization (Larson 1980; Derber 1982). Ideological proletarianization represents loss of control over the goals and social purposes of one's work. Alternatively, the loss of control over the process itself (the means) can be called technical proletarianization. Contracting contributes to both the technical and ideological proletarianization of social service work.
3. For the purposes of this discussion social network and affiliation will be used interchangeably. The language of network and affiliation will be used to describe a first stage of relationship to a group. The group may be joined but identification with collective purpose is undeveloped. Social solidarity represents the transition to firmer forms of collective or communal identity. Finally, social solidarity can spawn a political activism intended to advance group interests.
4. The framework presented in the next section of this chapter was derived from published and unpublished literature. Unpublished sources were primarily identified through discussions with foundation personnel, staff of the United Neighborhood Houses (an umbrella organization for settlement houses), and key practitioners. This multipronged search was intended to identify publications and agencies that focused on the practice of community building. A number of organizations with disparate interests in, for instance, mental illness, education, job training, health, housing, or multiservice delivery, yet sharing a common practice commitment to building membership relationships with service users were identified through the literature search. These agency experiences provide the basis for an illustrative guideline for the subsequent discussion on community-building practice.

5. For instance, ritualized events or ceremonies substantially overlap with joint projects. However, rituals are distinctive because in their form (awards at acknowledgment ceremonies), scheduling (holidays), participants (Sunday dinner for family and friends), and even use of language (liturgy at a church service) connection is fostered through repetition. The conscious reenactment of parts of an experience over time helps to establish reference points for a collective memory. Alternatively, joint project strategies more frequently emphasize time-limited and variable activities. Consequently, their contribution to promoting collective memory is less central than their contribution to the development of experiences of interdependence.

6. In fact, lowering the flame of network relationships may represent a healthy choice to pause, reflect upon, and integrate recent experiences. The developmental cycle of relationships often requires that members be able to enter and exit to extend and reclaim parts of themselves. Exit is not necessarily irreversible or hostile and can be strongly associated with renewal. The development of organizational citizenship or membership relationships is not linear. It is marked by progression and regression. Such renewal, however, depends on network members and staff remaining attentive to changing patterns of relationships and on their working to meet the needs of both the group and the individual.

7. Historically, communal identification has been a source of insularity or exclusivity. Therefore, local or community processes must be joined to values promoting inclusiveness if the larger purposes of community building are to be achieved. The effort to build inclusive local communities, however, will be tested by other impulses. For instance, can long-term members of the agency community continue to welcome people who may be different? Will the structure of an agency remain sufficiently flexible to rework practices that may have welcomed or included past members but are not as responsive to more recent cohorts of service users? In general, can the agency and its stakeholders continue to welcome new members even as they have an ever greater investment in the agency as it exists presently? These tendencies toward exclusion are powerful. What will distinguish community-building agencies, however, is a value base and structure that fosters inclusion and struggles with the associated conflicts. In this regard, Handler reminds us, "Reforms based on shared values or a sense of ownership, while touted as promoting excellence, in a prior age, they remind us, promoted intolerance and exclusivity, and even today, are used by the religious right to seize control of local schools. What is important is how social values and individual commitments become manifest in the organization of the school" (Handler 1996:224).

References

Abramovitz, Mimi. 1986. The Privatization of the Welfare State: a Review. *Social Work*. 31 (4): 257–65.

———. 1993. Should all social workers be educated for social change? *Journal of Social Work Education* 29:6–11, 17–18.

Addams, Jane. 1902. *Democracy and Social Ethics*. New York: Macmillan.

———. [1910] 1999. *Twenty Years at Hull-House*. Reprint, Boston: St Martins.

———. 1930. *The Second Twenty Years at Hull-House*. New York: Macmillan.

Alcaly, Roger, and David Mermelstein, eds. 1977. *The Fiscal Crisis of American Cities: Essays on the Political Economy of Urban America with Special Reference to New York*. New York: Vintage.

Amin, Samir. 1990. *Transforming the Revolution: Social Movements and the World-System*. New York: Monthly Review Press.

Anderson, Elijah. 1990. *Streetwise: Race Class and Change in the Urban Community*. Chicago: University of Chicago Press.

Andrews, Janice L. 1990. Female social workers in the second generation. *Affilia* 5 (2): 46–59.

Andrews, Janice, and Michael Reisch. 1997. Social work and anticommunism: A historical analysis of the McCarthy era. *Journal of Progressive Human Services* 8 (2): 29–47.

Annie Casey Foundation. 1993. *Rebuilding Communities: A Neighborhood Reinvestment Strategy*. Baltimore, Md.: Annie Casey Foundation.

———. 1997. *The Next Five Years*. Baltimore, Md.: Annie Casey Foundation.

Arenson, Karen. 1995. Gingrich's welfare vision ignores reality, charities say. *New York Times*, June 4, p. 1.

Arnstein, Sherry. 1969. A ladder of citizen participation. In *Journal of the American Institute of Planners* 35 (4): 216–224.

———. 1972. Maximum feasible manipulation. *Public Administration Review* 32:377–389.

Aronowitz, Stanley. 2000. *The Knowledge Factory: Dismantling the Corporate University and Creating True Higher Learning.* Boston, Mass.: Beacon Press.

Aronowitz, Stanley, and William DiFazio. 1994. *The Jobless Future: Sci Tech and the Dogma of Work.* Minneapolis, Minn.: University of Minnesota Press.

Aspen Institute. 1997. *Voices from the Field: Learning from the Early Work of Comprehensive Community Initiative.* Washington, D.C.: The Aspen Institute.

Austin, David. 1983. The flexner myth and the history of social work. *Social Service Review* 57:357–377.

———. 1986. *A History of Social Work Education.* Austin: University of Texas Press.

Badding, Nancy. 1989. Client involvement in case recording. *Social Casework* 70 (9): 539–548.

Bailey, Darlyne. 1992. Organizational change in a public school system: The synergism of two approaches. *Social Work in Education* 14 (2): 94–105.

Baker, Frank, and Charlene Douglas. 1990. Housing environments and community adjustment of severely mentally ill persons. *Community Mental Health Journal* 26 (6): 497–505.

Balsanak, Judy. 1998. Addressing at-risk pregnant women's issues through community, individual, and corporate grassroots efforts. In *Community Building: Renewal, Well-Being, and Shared Responsibility*, ed. Patricia Ewalt, Edith Freeman, and Dennis Poole, 411–419. Washington, D.C.: NASW Press.

Bannister, Robert. 1979. *Social Darwinism.* Philadelphia: Temple University Press.

Barbuto, Domenica. 1999. *American Settlement Houses and Progressive Social Reform: An Encyclopedia of the American Settlement Movement.* Phoenix: Oryx Press.

Barnekov, Timothy, Robin Boyle, and Daniel Rich. 1989. *Privatism and Urban Policy in Britain and the United States.* New York: Oxford University Press.

Barnet, Richard J. 1994. Lords of the global economy. *The Nation*, December 19, pp. 754–757.

Bauman, Zygmunt. 1998. *Globalization: The Human Consequences.* New York: Columbia University Press.

Beck, Bertram M. 1976. Settlements in the United States: Past and future. *Social Work* 21 (4): 268–272.

———. 1977. Settlements and community centers. In *Encyclopedia of Social Work*, ed. Turner et al., 1262–1266. Washington, D.C.: NASW.

Bellah, Robert, Richard Madsen, William Sullivan, et al. 1991. *The Good Society.* New York: Knopf.

Bellah, Robert, Richard Madsen, William Sullivan, et al.1985. *Habits of the Heart: Individualism and Commitment in American Life*. New York: Harper & Row.

Berman, Ellen. 1991. Fostering community in the South Bronx: Social support as an alternative to foster care. Ph.D. diss., City University of New York.

Berman-Rossi, Toby, and Marcia Cohen. 1988. Group development and shared decision making working with homeless mentally ill women. *Social Work with Groups* 11 (4): 63–74.

Berry, Margaret. 1986. *One Hundred Years on Urban Frontiers: The Settlement Movement, 1886–1986*. New York: United Neighborhood Centers of America.

———. 1999. Service and cause: Both sides of the coin. In *Reflections on Community Organization: Enduring Themes and Critical Issues*, Jack Rothman, ed., 106–122. Itasca, IL.: Peacock.

Berry, Wendell. 1993. *Sex, Economy, Freedom, and Community*. New York: Pantheon.

Blakely, Edward, and Mary Snyder. 1997. *Fortress America: Gated Communities in the United States*. Washington, D.C.: Brookings Institution Press.

Blau, Joel. 1999. *Illusions of Prosperity: America's Working Families in an Age of Economic Insecurity*. New York: Oxford University Press.

Block, Fred, Richard Cloward, Barbara Ehrenreich, and Frances Fox Piven. 1987. *The Mean Season: The Attack on the Welfare State*. New York: Pantheon.

Bloomberg, Lynn, James Meyers, and Marc T. Braverman. 1994. The importance of social interaction: A new perspective on social epidemiology and social risk factors and social health. *Social Health Quarterly* 4:447–463.

Bluestone, Barry, and Bennett Harrison. 1982. *The Deindustrialization of America*. New York: Basic Books.

Boggs, Carl. 1986. *Social Movements and Political Power*. Philadelphia: Temple University Press.

———. 2000. *The End of Politics: Corporate Power and the Decline of the Public Sphere*. New York: Guilford Press.

Bookchin, Murray. 1992. *From Urbanization to Cities*. London: Cassell.

Boris, Eileen. 1992. The settlement movement revisited: Social control with a conscience. *Reviews in American History* 20:216–221.

Bowles, Samuel, David Gordon, and Thomas Weiskopff. 1990. *After the Wasteland: A Democratic Economics for the Year 2000*. Armonk, NY: Sharpe.

Boyte, Harry. 1980. *The Backyard Revolution*. Philadelphia: Temple University Press.

———. 1989. *Commonwealth: A Return to Citizen Politics*. New York: Free Press.

———. 1992. The pragmatic ends of popular politics. In *Habermas and the Public Sphere*, ed. Craig Calhoun, 109–135. Boston: MIT Press.

Boyte, Harry, and Nancy Kari. 1996. *Building America: The Democratic Promise of Public Work*. Philadelphia: Temple University Press.

Boyte, Harry, and Frank Riessman, eds. 1986. *The New Populism: The Politics of Empowerment*. Philadelphia: Temple University Press.

Bradley, Bill. 1995. Civil society and the rebirth of our national community. *The Responsive Community* 5:4–10.

Brager, George. 1999. Agency under attack: The risks, demands, and rewards of community activism. In *Reflections on Community Organization: Enduring Themes and Critical Issues*, ed. J. Rothman, 57–74. Itasca, IL: Peacock.

Brecher, Jeremy, and Tim Costello. 1994. *Global Village or Global Pillage: Economic Reconstruction from the Bottom Up*. Boston: South End Press.

Brecher, Jeremy, John Brown Childs, and Jill Cutler, eds. 1993. *Global visions: Beyond the New World Order*. Boston: South End Press.

Breines, Winifred. 1982. *Community Organization and the New Left, 1962–1968*. New York: Praeger.

Breton, Margaret. 1989. Liberation theology, group work, and the right of the poor and oppressed to participate in the life of the community. *Social Work with Groups* 12 (2): 5–18.

Brieland, Donald. 1990. The Hull-House tradition and the contemporary social worker: Was Jane Addams really a social worker? *Social Work* 35 (2): 134–138.

Bruno, Frank J. 1948. *Trends in Social Work, 1874–1956: A History Based on the Proceedings of the National Conference of Social Work*. New York: Columbia University Press.

Bryan, Mary Lynn McCree, and Allan Davis, eds. 1990. *One Hundred Years at Hull-House*. Bloomington, IN: Indiana University Press.

Burghardt, Steve. 1982. *The Other Side of Organizing*. Cambridge, Mass: Schenkman Publishers.

Business Week. 20 November 1995. Rewriting the social contract. http://www.businessweek.com/1995/47/b34511.htm.

Carp, Joel. Winter 1981. Youth's need for social competence and power: The community-building model. *Adolescence* 16 (64): 935–951.

Carson, Clayborne. 1982. *In Struggle: SNCC and the Black Awakening of the 1960s*. New York: Oxford University Press.

Carson, Mina, 1990. *Settlement Folk: Social Thought and the American Settlement Movement, 1885–1930*. Chicago: University of Chicago Press.

Carter, Paul. 1975. *The Twenties in America*. Arlington Heights, Ill.: Harlan-Davidson.

———. 1983. *Another Part of the Fifties*. New York: Columbia University Press.

Chafe, William. 1980. *Civilities and Civil Rights: Greensboro, North Carolina, and the Black Struggle for Freedom*. New York: Oxford University Press.

Chambers, Clarke A. 1963. *Seedtime of Reform: American Social Service and Social Action, 1918–1933*. Minneapolis: University of Minneapolis Press.

———. 1986. Women in the creation of the profession of social work. *Social Service Review* 60 (1): 1–33.

———. 1992. Uphill all the way: Reflections on the course and study of welfare history. *Social Service Review* 66:492–504.

———. September 30, 2000. Personal communication with author.

Chambers, Clarke A., and Andrea Hinding. 1968. Charity workers, the settlements, and the poor. *Social Casework* 49:96–101.

Chapin Hall Center for Children. 1997. *Settlement Houses and Community Building.* Chicago: The United Neighborhood Houses.

Chapin Hall Center for Children. 1998. *Settlement Houses Today: Their Community-Building Role.* Chicago: The United Neighborhood Houses.

Chapman, Gary. 2000. Public interest will be served in our new Gilded Age. *Houston Chronicle*, April 9, p. 4C.

Chaskin, Robert, and Mark Joseph. 1995. *The Ford Foundation Neighborhood Initiative: Moving Toward Implementation.* Chicago: Chapin Hall.

Clark, Kenneth. 1965. *Dark Ghetto: Dilemmas of Social Power.* New York: Harper and Row.

Cloward, Richard, and Richard Elman. 1973. Advocacy in the ghetto. In *How We Lost the War on Poverty*, ed. Marc Pilisuk and Phyllis Pilisuk, 121–135. New Brunswick, NJ: Transaction Books.

Cloward, Richard, and Frances Fox Piven. 1972. *The Politics of Turmoil.* New York: Pantheon.

———. 1999. Disruptive dissensus: People and power in the industrial age. In *Reflections on Community*, ed. Jack Rothman, 165–193. Itasca, Ill. Peacock.

Cohen, Carol, and Michael Phillips. 1998. Building community: Principles for social work practice in housing settings. In *Community Building: Renewal, Well-Being, and Shared Responsibility*, ed. Patricia Ewalt, Edith Freeman, and Dennis Poole, 239–251. Washington, D.C.: NASW Press.

Cohen, Joshua, and Joel Rogers. 1995. *Associations and Democracy.* New York: Verso.

Cohen, Mitchell, and Dennis Hale, eds. 1966. *The New Student Left: An Anthology.* Boston: Beacon Press.

Cohen, Sheldon, and S. Leonard Syme. 1985. *Social Support and Health.* New York: Academic Books.

Coit, Stanton. 1974. *Neighborhood Guilds: An Instrument of Social Reform.* New York: Arno Press.

Colborn, Fern M. 1955. *Tomorrow: Guide for Planning Settlements and Community Buildings.* New York: Whiteside.

Coleman, James. 1990. *The Foundations of Social Theory.* Cambridge, Mass.: Belknap Press.

Coleman, James, and Thomas Hoffer. 1987. *Public and Private Schools: The Impact on Community.* New York: Basic Books.

Comer, James. 1980. *School Power: Implications of an Intervention Program.* New York: Free Press.

Cortes, Ernesto. 1997. The IAF and education reform: Organizing citizens for change. Unpublished paper.

Crocker, Ruth H. 1992. *Social Work and Social Order: The Settlement Movement in Two Industrial Cities, 1889–1930.* Urbana: University of Illinois Press.

Crunden, Robert M. 1982. *Ministers of Reform: The Progressives' Achievement in American Civilization, 1889–1920.* New York: Basic Books.

Dachler, Peter, and Bernhard Wilpert. 1978. Conceptual dimensions and boundaries of participation in organizations: A critical evaluation. *Administrative Science Quarterly* 23 (March): 1–39.

Dailey, Wilda. 1974. Professionalism and the public dollar. *Social Casework* 55 (7): 428–434.

Danto, Elizabeth. 1998. The ambulatorium: Freud's free clinic in Vienna. *International Journal of Psychoanalysis* 79:287–300.

———. 2000. Sex, class, and social work: Wilhelm Reich's free clinics and the activist history of psychoanalysis. *Psychoanalytic Social Work* 7:55–72.

Darrow, Nancy, and Mary Lynch. 1983. The use of photography activities with adolescent groups. *Social Work with Groups* 6 (1): 77–84.

Davis, Allen F. 1967. *Spearheads for Reform: The Social Settlements and the Progressive Movement, 1890–1914.* New Brunswick: Rutgers University Press.

Davis, Allen F., and Mary Lynn McCree. 1969. *Eighty Years at Hull-House.* New York: Quadrangle Books.

Davis, Mike. 1992. *City of Quartz.* New York: Vintage.

Deegan, Mary Jo, ed. 1991. *Women in Sociology.* New York: Greenwood Press.

De Leon, George, and Mitchell Rosenthal. 1989. Treatment in residential therapeutic communities. In *Treatments of Psychiatric Disorders*, ed. Toksoz B. Karasu, 2:1380–1396. Washington, D.C.: American Psychiatric Press.

Delgado, Gary. 1994. *Beyond the Politics of Place: New Directions for Community Organizing in the 1990s.* Oakland, Ca.: Applied Research Center.

———. 1998. *Beyond the Politics of Place: New Directions for Community Organizing in the 1990s.* Oakland, Ca: Applied Research Center.

Delgado, Melvin. 1998a. Role of Latina-owned beauty parlors in a Latino community. In *Community Building: Renewal, Well-Being, and Shared Responsibility*, ed. Patricia Ewalt, Edith Freeman, and Dennis Poole, 82–9. Washington, D.C.: NASW Press.

———. 1998b. Strengths-based practice with Puerto Rican adolescents: Lessons from a substance abuse prevention program. In *Community Building: Renewal, Well-Being, and Shared Responsibility*, ed. Patricia Ewalt, Edith Freeman, and Dennis Poole, 213–224. Washington, D.C.: NASW Press.

Demone, Harold Jr., and Margaret Gibelman, eds. 1989. *Services for Sale: Purchasing Health and Human Services.* New Brunswick, NJ: Rutgers University Press.

Derber, Charles. 1982. *Professionals as Workers: Mental Labor in Advanced Capitalism.* Beston: Hall.

De Souza Briggs, Xavier, and Elizabeth Mueller with Mercer Sullivan. 1997. *From Neighborhood to Community: Evidence on the Social Effects of Community Development.* New York: Community Development Research Center, New School for Social Research.

DiRienzo, Harold. 1995. Beyond the melting pot: Preserving culture, building community. *National Civic Review* 84 (1): 5–15.

———. October 1996. Community building: A program for settlement houses. Memo. New York: Parodenick Foundation.

Dowd, Douglass. 1974. *The Twisted Dream: Capitalist Development in the United States.* Cambridge: Winthrop.

Downton, James, and Paul Wehr. 1991. Peace movements: The role of commitment and community in sustaining member participation. *Research in Social Movements, Conflict, and Change* 13:113–134.

Drake, St. Clair. 1966. *Race Relations in a Time of Rapid Social Change.* New York: National Federation of Settlements and Neighborhood Centers.

Drucker, Peter. 1994. The age of social transformation. *The Atlantic Monthly*, November, 53–80.

Dupper, David, and John Poertner. 1998. Public schools and the revitalization of impoverished communities: School-linked family resource centers. In *Community Building: Renewal, Well-Being, and Shared Responsibility*, ed. Patricia Ewalt, Edith Freeman, and Dennis Poole, 316–330. Washington, D.C.: NASW.

Edin, Katherine, and Laura Lein. 1997. *Making Ends Meet: How Single Mothers Survive Welfare and Low-Wage Work.* New York: Russell Sage Foundation.

Ehrenreich, John. 1985. *The Altruistic Imagination: A History of Social Work and Social Policy in the United States.* New York: Cornell University Press.

Eisenstein, Zillah. 1998. *Global Obscenities.* New York: New York University Press.

Elshtain, Jean. 1994. *Democracy on Trial.* New York: Basic Books.

Etzioni, Amitai. 1993. *The Spirit of Community: Rights, Responsibilities, and the Communitarian Agenda.* New York: Crown.

———, ed. 1995. *New Communitarian Thinking: Persons, Virtues, Institutions, and Communities.* Charlottesville: University of Virginia.

Evans, Sara. 1979. *Personal Politics: The Roots of Women's Liberation in the Civil Rights Movement and the New Left.* New York: Random House.

Ewalt, Patricia. 1998. The revitalization of impoverished communities. In *Community Building: Renewal, Well-Being, and Shared Responsibility*, ed. Patricia

Ewalt, Edith Freeman, and Dennis Poole, 3–5. Washington, D.C.: NASW Press.

Fabricant, Michael. 1985. The industrialization of social work practice. *Social Work* 30 (5): item 503.

———. 1988. Empowering the homeless. *Social Policy* 4:44–55.

Fabricant, Michael, and Steve Burghardt. 1992. *The Welfare State Crisis and the Transformation of Social Service Work*. Armonk, NY: Sharpe.

———. 1998. Rising from the ashes of cutback, political warfare, and degraded services: Community building as a template for recreating the welfare state. In *Towards More Democracy in Social Services*, ed. Gaby Flosser and Hans-Uwe Otto, 325–336. Berlin: de Gruyter.

Fabricant, Michael and Michael Smith. 1997. *An Evaluation of the Starrett City Program for the Mentally Disabled: Building Community through Social Services*. New York: Services for the Underserved.

Fainstein, Norman, and Susan Fainstein. 1974. *Urban Political Movements*. Englewood Cliffs, NJ: Prentice Hall.

Falck, Hans. 1984. The membership model of social work. *Social Work* 29 (2): 155–160.

———. 1989. The management of membership: Social work group contributions. *Social Work with Groups* 12 (3): 19–32.

Feagin, Joe. 1988. *Free Enterprise City: Houston in Political-Economic Perspective*. New Brunswick, NJ. Rutgers University Press.

———. 1998. *The New Urban Paradigm: Critical Perspectives on the City*. Lanham, MD: Rowman and Littlefield.

Ferguson, Thomas. 1995. *Golden Rule, the Investment Theory of Party Politics, and the Logic of Money-Driven Political Systems*. Chicago: University of Chicago Press.

Fisher, Robert, 1994. *Let the People Decide*. 2d ed. New York: Twayne.

———. 1996. Social services and community in the new private city. *Urban Affairs Review* 31 (4): 554–561.

———. 1999. Speaking for the contribution of history: Context and the origins of the social welfare history group. *Social Service Review* 73 (2): 191–217.

Fisher, Robert, and Joseph Kling. 1991. Popular mobilization in the 1990s: Prospects for the new social movements. *New Politics* 3 (winter): 71–84.

———. 1993. *Mobilizing the Community: Local Politics in the Era of the Global City*. Newbury Park, CA.: Sage.

Fisher, Robert, and Howard Karger. 1997. *Social Work and Community in a Private World: Getting Out in Public*. New York: Longman.

———. 2000. The context of social work practice. In *Handbook of Social Work Direct Practice*, ed. Paula Alan Meares and Charles Garvin, 5–22. Thousand Oaks, CA.: Sage.

Fisher, Robert, and Peter Romanofsky, eds. 1981. *Community Organization for Urban Social Change: A Historical Perspective.* Westport, CT: Greenwood Press.

Fisher, Robert, and Eric Shragge. 2001. Challenging community organizing: Facing the 21st century. *Journal of Community Practice* (forthcoming).

Fong, Lillian, and Jewelle Gibbs. 1995. Facilitating services to multicultural communities in a dominant cultural setting: An organizational perspective. *Administration in Social Work* 19 (2): 1–10.

Forte, James. 1991. Operating a member-employing therapeutic business as part of an alternative mental health center. *Health and Social Work* 16 (3): 213–233.

Franklin, Donna L. 1986. Mary Richmond and Jane Addams: From moral certainty to rational inquiry in social work practice. *Social Service Review* 60 (4): 504–525.

Freeman, Edith. 1995. Honoring children's narratives. *Social Work in Education* 17 (4): 202–206.

Freedman, Marc. 1993. *The Kindness of Strangers: Adult Mentors, Urban Youth, and the New Volunteerism.* San Francisco: Jossey Bass.

Fried, Albert, ed. 1996. *McCarthyism: The Great American Red Scare: A Documentary History.* New York: Oxford University Press.

Friedman, Milton. 1962. *Capitalism and Freedom.* Chicago: University of Chicago.

Freire, Paolo. 1970. *The Pedagogy of the Oppressed.* New York: Seabury.

Gardner, John. 1992. *Building Community.* Palo Alto, CA.: Leadership Studies Center of the Independent Sector.

Galbraith, John K. [1958] 1998. *The Affluent Society.* New York: Houghton, Mifflin.

Gans, Herbert J. 1962. *The Urban Villagers: Group and Class in the Life of Italian-Americans.* New York: Free Press.

———. 1964. Redefining the settlements' function for the War on Poverty. *Social Work* 9 (4): 3–12.

Gartner Audrey, and Frank Riessman. 1982. Self-help and mental health. *Hospital and Community Psychiatry* 33:631–635.

———. 1984. *The Self-Help Revolution.* New York: The Human Science Press.

Ghere, Richard. 1981. Effects of service delivery variations on administration of municipal human service agencies: The contract approach versus agency implementation. *Administration in Social Work* 5 (1): 65–78.

Gibelman, Margaret. 1995. Purchasing Social Services. In *Encyclopedia of Social Work 19th Edition,* ed. Richard Edwards, 1998–2007. Silver Springs, MD: National Association of Social Workers.

———. 1998a. Introduction. In *The Privatization of Human Services: Case Studies in the Purchase of Services,* ed. Margaret Gibelman and Harold Demone Jr., 2:1–18. New York. Springer.

———. 1998b. Theory, practice, and experience in the purchase of services. In *The*

Privatization of Human Services: Policy and Practice Issues, ed. Margaret Gibelman and Harold Demone Jr., 1:1–51. New York: Springer.

Gibelman, Margaret, and Harold Demone Jr. 1989. The evolving contract state. In *Services for Sale: Purchasing Health and Human Services*, ed. Demone and Gibelman, 17–58. New Brunswick, NJ: Rutgers University Press.

———, eds. 1998a. *The Privatization of Human Services: Policy and Practice Issues*. Vol. 1. New York: Springer.

———, eds. 1998b. *The Privatization of Human Services: Case Studies in the Purchase of Services*. Vol. 2. New York: Springer.

Gilder, George. 1981. *Wealth and Poverty*. New York: Basic Books.

Gimpel, James. 1995. *Legislating Revolution: The Contract with America in Its First 100 Days*. New York: Addison-Wesley.

Gittell, Marilyn, and Teresa Shtob. 1980. Changing women's roles in political volunteerism and reform of the city. *Journal of Women in Culture and Society* 5 (3, suppl.): 567–578.

Glazer, Lisa. 1993. Making connections. *City Limits* 43 (2): 18–21.

Goldstein, Howard. 1993. Government contracts are emasculating boards and turning charities into agents of the state. *Chronicle of Philanthropy*, July 13, p. 41.

Goss, Kristin. 1993. A crisis of credibility for America's nonprofits. *Chronicle of Philanthropy*, June 15, p. 1

Gottdiener, Mark. 1986. *Cities in Stress*. Newbury Park, CA: Sage.

Gough, Ian. 1979. *The Political Economy of the Welfare State*. London: Macmillan Press.

Greider, William. 1992. *Who Will Tell the People*. New York: Simon and Schuster.

Gronbjerg, Kirsten. 1990. Poverty and nonprofit organizational behavior. *Social Service Review* 64 (2): 208–243.

Grossman, James. 1991. *Land of Hope: Chicago, Black Southerners, and the Great Migration*. Chicago: University of Chicago Press.

GROW. 1982. *The Program of Growth to Maturity*. Sydney, Australia: GROW Publications.

Gulati, Padi, and Geoffrey Guest. 1990. The community-centered model: A garden-variety approach or a transformation of community practice. *Social Work* 35 (1): 63–68.

Gummer, Burton. 1995. Which side are you on? Current perspectives on member identification with the organization. *Administration in Social Work* 19 (2): 81–99.

Guttierez, Lorraine, and Edith Lewis. 1997. Education, participation, and capacity building in community organizing with women of color. *Community Organizing and Community Building for Health*, ed. Meredith Minkler, 216–229. New Brunswick NJ: Rutgers University Press.

Habermas, Jürgen. 1989. *The Structural Transformation of the Public Sphere*. Boston: Harvard University Press.

Hall, Helen. 1971. *Unfinished Business in Neighborhood and Nation*. New York: Macmillan.

Hall, Peter D. 1992. Teaching and research of philanthropy, voluntarism, and non-profit organizations: A case study of academic innovation. *Teacher's College Record* 93 (3): 403–435.

Halpern, Robert. 1995. *Rebuilding the Inner City: A History of Neighborhood Initiatives to Address Poverty in the United States*. New York: Columbia University Press.

Hammack, David, ed. 1998. *Making the Nonprofit Sector in the United States: A Reader*. Bloomington: Indiana University Press.

Handler, Joel. 1992. Dependency and discretion. In *Human Services as Complex Organizations*, ed. Yeheskel Hasenfeld, 276–297. Newbury Park, Cal.: Sage.

———. 1996. *Down From Bureaucracy: The Ambiguity and Privatization of Empowerment*. Princeton New Jersey: Princeton University Press.

Hardina, Donna. 1991. Purchase of service contracting for job training: Fostering collaboration or conflict between government and nonprofit organizations? *Proceedings of the Association for Research on Nonprofit Organizations and Voluntary Action*. Pullman, Wash.: ARNOVA.

Hargrove, Gordon P. 1993. Neighborhood center perspectives on community service learning. *Equity and Excellence in Education* 26 (2): 35–40.

Harkavy, Ira, and John Puckett. 1994. Lessons from Hull-House for the contemporary urban university. *Social Service Review* 68:299–319.

Harrington, Michael. [1962] 1963. *The Other America: Poverty in the United States*. Baltimore: Penguin.

Harney, Stefan, and Frederick Moten. 1998. Doing academic work. In *Chalk Lines: The Politics of Work in a Managed University*, ed. Randy Martin, 154–180. Durham, N C: Duke University Press.

Hasenfeld, Yeheskel. September 1987. Power in social work practice. *Social Service Review* 61 (3): 469–483.

———. 1992. Theoretical approaches to human service organizations. In *Human Services as Complex Organizations*, ed. Yeheskel Hasenfeld, 24–44. Newbury Park, CA: Sage.

Hawkins, Gaynell. 1937. *Educational Experiments in Social Settlements* New York: American Association for Adult Education.

Hays, Samuel. 1957. *The Response to Industrialism, 1885–1914*. Chicago: University of Chicago Press.

Helfgot, Joseph H. 1981. *Professional Reforming: Mobilization for Youth and the Failure of Social Science*. Lexington, MA: Lexington Books.

Herrick, John M. 1970. A holy discontent: The history of the New York City social settlements in the interwar era, 1919–1941. Ph. D. diss., University of Minnesota.

Hillery, George. 1955. Definitions of community: Areas of agreement. *Rural Sociology* 20:111–123.

Hillman, Arthur. 1960. *Neighborhood Centers Today.* New York: National Federation of Settlements and Neighborhood Centers.

Hirota, Janice, Prudence Brown, and Nancy Martin. 1998. *Building Community: The Tradition and Promise of Settlement Houses.* Chicago: Chapin Hall Center for Children.

Hirota, Janice, Prudence Brown, William Mollard, and Hannah Richman. 1997. *Pathways to Change: Settlement Houses and the Strengthening of Community.* Chicago: Chapin Hall Center for Children.

Hirota, Janice, and Odile Ferroussier-Davis. 1998 *Putting Ideas to Work: Settlement Houses and Community Building.* Chicago: Chapin Hall Center for Children.

Hirsch, Arnold. 1994. Unsettling settlements. *Reviews in American History* 22:480–485.

Hirsch, Kathleen. 1998. *A Home in the Heart in the City: A Woman's Search for Community.* New York: North Point Press.

Hirschman, Albert. 1970. *Exit, Voice, and Loyalty: Responses to Firms, Organization, and States.* Cambridge, MA: Harvard University Press.

Hofstadter, Richard. 1948. *The American Political Tradition.* New York: Knopf.

———. 1944. *Social Darwinism in American Thought.* Philadelphia: Lippincott.

Holden, Arthur C. 1922. *The Settlement Idea: A Vision of Social Justice.* New York: MacMillan.

Horwitt, Sanford D. 1990. *Let them Call Me Rebel: Saul Alinsky, His Life and Legacy.* New York: Knopf.

Huntley, Kate. 1935. *Financial Trends in Organized Social Work in New York City.* New York: Columbia University Press.

Husock, Howard. 1990. Fighting poverty the old-fashioned way. *Wilson Quarterly* 14 (spring): 79–91.

———. 1992. Bringing back the settlement house. *Public Interest* no. 109 (fall): 53–72.

———. 1993. Bringing back the settlement house: Settlements see poor people as citizens, not clients. *Public Welfare* 51 (4): 16–25.

Jackson, Robert, Dorothy Purnell, Stephan Anderson, and Bradford Sheafor. 1996. The clubhouse model of community support: An emerging opportunity for social work education. *Journal of Social Work Education* 32 (2): 173–180.

Jansson, Bruce. 1989. The political economy of monitoring: A contingency perspective. In *Services for Sale: Purchasing Health and Human Services,* ed. Harold Demone Jr. and Margaret Gibelman, 343–359. New Brunswick, NJ: Rutgers University Press:

————. 2000. *The Reluctant Welfare State.* Pacific Grove, CA: Brooks/Cole.

Jason, Leonard. 1997. *Community Building: Values for a Sustainable Future.* Westport, CT: Praeger.

Johnson, Dirk. 1996. Program creates community for foster care.*The New York Times,* April 1, p. A-1.

Jones, Bernie, and Juliette Silva. 1991. Problem solving, community building and systems interaction: An integrated practice model for community development. *Journal of the Community Development Society* 22 (2): 1–21.

Judd, Dennis, and Michael Parkinson. 1990. *Leadership and Urban Regeneration.* Newbury Park, CA: Sage.

Kahn, William. 1993a. Caring for the caregivers: Patterns of organizational caregiving. *Administrative Science Quarterly* 38:539–563.

————. 1993b. Facilitating and undermining organizational change: A case study. *The Journal of Applied Behavioral Science* 29 (1): 32–55.

Kanter, Rosabeth Moss. 1982. Dilemmas of managing participation. *Organizational Dynamics* (summer): 5–27.

Kalberg, Stephen. 1975. The commitment to career reform: The settlement movement leaders. *Social Service Review* 49 (4): 608–628.

Karger, Howard. June 1981. Burnout as alienation. *Social Service Review* 55:270–283.

————. 1986. Phyllis Wheatley House: A history of the Minneapolis black settlement house, 1924–1940. *Phylon* 47 (1): 79–90.

————. 1987a. *The Sentinels of Order: A Study of Social Control and the Minneapolis Settlement House Movement, 1915–1950.* Lanham: University Press of America.

————. 1987b. Minneapolis settlement houses in the not-so-roaring 20s: Americanization, morality, and the revolt against popular culture. *Journal of Sociology and Social Welfare* 14 (2): 89–110.

————. 1988. *Social Workers and Labor Unions.* New York: Greenwood Press.

————. 1994. Is privatization a positive trend in social services: No. In *Controversial Issues in Social Policy,* ed. Howard Karger and James Midgley, 110–116. Boston: Allyn and Bacon.

Karger, Howard, and David Stoesz. 1998. *American Social Welfare Policy.* New York: Longman.

Katz, Michael. 1986. *In the Shadow of the Poor House.* New York: Basic Books.

Katz, Michael. 1989. *The Undeserving Poor.* New York: Pantheon.

Kellogg Foundation. 1997. *Community Voices: A National Demonstration Project for Local Visionary Models.* Battle Creek, MI: Kellogg Foundation.

Kendall, Katherine. 2000. *Social Work Education: Its Origins in Europe.* Alexandria, VA: Council on Social Work Education.

Kennedy, Albert. 1932. Social Settlements. *Encyclopedia Britannica.* 14th ed., 903–904. New York: Encyclopedia Britannica.

Kennedy, Albert, Kathryn Farra, et al. 1935. *Social settlements in New York City: Their Activities, Policies, and Administration.* New York: Columbia University Press.

Kennedy, David. 1999. *Freedom from Fear: The American People in Depression and War, 1929–1945.* New York: Oxford University Press.

Kettner, Paul, and Lawrence Martin. 1985. Purchase of service contracting and the declining influence of social work. *Urban and Social Change Review* 18 (2): 8–11.

———. 1986. Making decisions about purchase of service contracting. *Public Welfare* 44 (4): 30–37.

———. 1990. Purchase of service contracting: Two models. *Administration in Social Work* 14 (1): 15–30.

———. 1993a. Purchase of service contracting in the 1990s: Have expectations been met? *Journal of Sociology and Social Welfare* 20:89–103.

———. 1993b. Performance, accountability, and purchase of service contracting. *Administration in Social Work* 17 (1): 61–79.

———. 1996a The impact of declining resources and purchase of service contracting on private nonprofit agencies. *Administration in Social Work* 20 (3): 21–38.

———. 1996b. Performance contracting in the human services: An initial assessment. *Administration in Social Work* 19:47–61.

———. 1996c. Purchase of service contracting versus government service delivery: The views of state human service administrators. *Journal of Sociology and Social Welfare* 23:107–119.

———. 1998. Accountability in purchase-of-service contracting. In *The Privatization of Human Services: Policy and Practice Issues,* ed. Margaret Gibelman and Harold Demone Jr., 1:183–204. New York: Springer.

Kiely, Kathy. 1995. Gingrich celebrates GOP agenda on TV. *Houston Post,* April 8, p. A1.

Kingsley, G. Thomas, and James O. Wilson. August 1997. *Civil Society, the Public Sector, and Poor Communities.* Washington, D.C.: Urban Institute.

Kirschner, Don. 1986. *The Paradox of Professionalism: Reform and Public Service in Urban America, 1900–1940.* Westport, CT: Greenwood.

Kling, Joseph. 1993. Complex society/complex cities: New social movements and the restructuring of space. In *Mobilizing the Community,* ed. Robert Fisher and Joseph Kling, 28–51. Newbury Park, CA: Sage.

Kogut, Alvin. 1972. The settlements and ethnicity, 1890–1914. *Social Work* 17:99–108.

Kokopeli, B., and G. Lakey. n.d. *Leadership for Change: Toward a Feminist Model.* Santa Cruz, CA: New Society Publishers.

Kolko, Gabriel. 1976. *Main Currents in Modern American History*. New York: Harper and Row.

Kouzes, James, and Barry Posner. 1988. *The Leadership Challenge: How to get Extraordinary Things Done in Organizations*. San Francisco: Jossey Bass.

Kramer, Ralph. 1969. *Participation of the Poor: Comparative Case Studies in the War on Poverty*. Englewood Cliffs, NJ: Prentice Hall.

———. 1981. *Voluntary Agencies in the Welfare State*. Berkeley: University of California Press.

———. 1985. The future of the voluntary agency in a mixed economy. *Journal of Applied Behavioral Science* 21 (4): 377–391.

———. 1989. From voluntarism to vendorism: An organizational perspective on contracting. In *Services for Sale: Purchasing Health and Human Services*, ed. Harold Demone Jr. and Margaret Gibelman, 97–112. New Brunswick, NJ: Rutgers University Press.

———. 1994. Voluntary agencies and the contract culture: Dream or nightmare? *Social Service Review* 68 (1): 33–60.

Kramer, Ralph, and Bart Grossman. 1987. Contracting for social services: Process management and resource dependencies. *Social Service Review* 61 (1): 32–55.

Kraus, Allen. 1980. *The Settlement House Movement in New York City, 1886–1914*. New York: Arno Press.

Kraus, Allen, and Ajay Chaudry. 1995. The settlement house initiative: Merging Headstart and day care in New York. *Public Welfare* 53 (4): 34–43, 52.

Kravitz, Sanford. 1969. The community action program: Past, present, and future. In *On Fighting Poverty*, ed. James Sundquist, 52–69. New York: Basic Books.

Kretzman, John, and John McKnight. 1993. *Building Communities from the Inside Out: A Path Toward Finding and Mobilizing a Community's Assets*. Chicago: Institute for Policy Research, Northwestern University.

Kuttner, Robert. 1991. *The End of Laissez-Faire: National Purpose and the Global Economy After the Cold War*. New York: Knopf.

———. 1992. The splitting of America. *Boston Globe*, May 18. In *The Organizer Mailing*, July 6, p. 1.

———. [1996] 1997. *Everything for Sale: The Virtues and Limits of Markets*. New York: Knopf.

Laird, Joan. 1984. Sorcerers, shamans, and social workers: The use of ritual in social work practice. *Social Work* 29 (2): 123–130.

Landers, Susan. 1998. Settlement houses survive and thrive. *NASW News* (January): 93.

Larson M. 1980. Proletarianization and educated labor. *Theory and Society* 9:560–568.

Lasch, Christopher. 1978. *The Culture of Narcissism*. New York: Norton.

———. 1991. *True and Only Heaven*. New York. Norton.

———. 1997. Sexual division of labor: The decline of civic culture and the rise of the suburbs. In *Women and the Common Life: Love, Marriage, and Feminism*, ed. Elisabeth Lasch-Quinn, 93–120. New York: Norton.

Lasch-Quinn, Elisabeth. 1993. *Black Neighbors: Race and the Limits of Reform in the American Settlement House Movement, 1890–1945*. Chapel Hill: University of North Carolina Press.

Lemann, Nicholas. 1991. *The Promised Land: The Great Black Migration and How it Changed America*. New York: Knopf.

———. 1996. Kicking in groups: Acceptance of R. D. Putnam's views concerning the decline of civic virtue. *Atlantic Monthly*, April, 3.

Leiby, James. 1978. *A History of Social Welfare and Social Work in the United States*. New York: Columbia University Press.

Leuchtenburg, William. 1995. *The FDR Years*. New York: Columbia University Press.

Levitan, Sar. 1969. *The Great Society's Poor Law*. Baltimore: Johns Hopkins University Press.

Lichterman, Paul. 1995. Piecing together multicultural community: Cultural differences in community building among grassroots environments. *Social Problems* 42 (4): 513–533.

Lieberman, Morton, and Lonnnie Snowden. 1993. Problems in assessing prevalence and membership characteristics of self-help group participants. *The Journal of Applied Behavioral Science* 29 (2): 166–179.

Lindenberg, Sidney J., and Ruth E. Zittel. 1936. The settlement scene changes. *Social Forces* 14:559–566.

Lipsitz, George. 1988. *A Life in the Struggle: Ivory Perry and the Culture of Resistance*. Philadelphia: Temple University Press.

Lipsky, Michael. 1980. *Street Level Bureaucracy*. New York: Russell Sage Foundation.

Loavenbruck, Grant, and Paul Keys. 1987. Settlements and neighborhood centers. *Encyclopedia of Social Work*. 18th ed., 556–561.

Logan, John, and Todd Swanstrom, eds. 1990. *Beyond the City Limits: Urban Policy and Economic Restructuring in Comparative Perspective*. Philadelphia: Temple University Press.

Lohmann, Roger. 1991. The administration of Hull-House. Presentation to the Social Welfare History Group, Council of Social Work Education, annual planning meeting. New Orleans.

Lowe, Seana. 2000. Creating community: Art for community development. *Journal of Contemporary Ethnography* 29 (3): 357–386.

Lubove, Roy. 1975. *The Professional Altruist: The Emergence of Social Work as a Career, 1880–1930*. New York: Atheneum.

Lundblad, Karen S. 1995. Jane Addams and social reform: A role model for the 1990s. *Social Work* 40 (5): 661–669.

Lynd, Alice, and Staughton Lynd. 1981. *Rank and File: Personal Histories of Working Class Organizers.* Princeton: Princeton University Press.

Manser, Gordon. 1974. Further thoughts on purchase of service. *Social Casework* 53:335–340.

Marks, Emily M. 1993. Settlement houses today: A public-private collaboration. *Public Welfare* 51 (4): 24–25.

———. 1998. Introduction. In *Building Community: The Tradition and Promise of Settlement Houses,* ed. Janice Hirota, Prudence Brown, and Nancy Martin, 1–2. Chicago: Chapin Hall Center for Children.

Marris, Peter, and Martin Rein. 1967. *Dilemmas of Social Reform: Poverty and Community Action in the United States.* New York: Atherton.

Martin, Randy, ed. 1998. *Chalk Lines: The Politics of Work in the Managed University.* Durham and London: Duke University Press.

Mattson, Kevin. 1998. *Creating a Democratic Republic: The Struggle for Urban Participatory Democracy During the Progressive Era.* University Park, PA: Pennsylvania University Press.

McGovern, Patricia. 1989. Protecting the promise of community-based care. In *Services for Sale: Purchasing Health and Human Services,* Harold Demone Jr. and Margaret Gibelman, 251–280. New Brunswick, NJ: Rutgers University Press.

McKenzie, Evan. 1994. *Privatopia: Homeowners Associations and the Rise of Residential Private Government.* New Haven: Yale University Press.

McKnight, John. 1985. A reconsideration of the crisis of the welfare state. *Social Policy* 16 (1): 27–30.

———. 1989. Do no harm: Policy options that meet human needs. *Social Policy* 20 (1): 6–15.

———. 1995. *The Careless Society: Community and Its Counterfeits.* New York: Basic Books.

McNeil, Larry. 1995. The soft arts of organizing. *Social Policy* 26 (2): 16–22.

Mead, Walter Russell. 1991. Recession obsession blurs economic decay. *Houston Chronicle,* April 21, p. 1E.

Mediratta, Kavitha. 1995. *Community Building Approaches: A Survey of Strategies and an Agenda for Future Work.* New York Rockefeller Foundation.

Medoff, Peter, and Holly Sklar. 1994. *Streets of Hope: The Fall and Rise of an Urban Neighborhood.* Boston: South End Press.

Melvin, Patricia M. 1987. *The Organic City: Urban Definition and Neighborhood Organization, 1880–1920.* Lexington: University of Kentucky Press.

Minkler, Meredith. 1997. Community organizing among the elderly poor in San Francisco's Tenderloin District. In *Community Organizing and Community Building for Health,* ed. Meredith Minkler, 244–259. New Brunswick NJ: Rutgers University Press.

Miller, Zane L. 1981. The role and concept of neighborhood in American cities. In

Community Organization for Urban Social Change, ed. Robert Fisher and Peter Romanofsky, 3–32. Westport, Conn: Greenwood Press.

Milward, H. Brinton. 1994. Nonprofit contracting and the hollow state. *Public Administration Review* 54 (1): 73–77.

Miringoff, Marc, and Marque-Luisa Miringoff. 1999. *The Social Health of the Nation: How America is Really Doing*. New York: Oxford University Press.

Mollenkopf, John. 1992. *A Phoenix in the Ashes: The Rise and Fall of the Koch Coalition in New York City Politics*. Princeton: Princeton University Press.

Montgomery, David. 1995. What the world needs now. *The Nation*, April 3, pp. 461–463.

Moore, Thom. 1991. The African-American church: A source of empowerment, mutual help, and social change. *Prevention in Human Services* 10 (1): 147–165.

Morgan, Sandra. 1995. It was the best of times: Emotional discourse in the work cultures of feminist health clinics. In *Feminist Organizations: Harvest of the Women's Movement*, ed. Myra Marx Ferree and Patricia Yancey Martin, 234–247. Philadelphia, PA: Temple University Press.

Moxley, David, and Dennis Jacobs. 1995. The role of animation as a program development strategy. *Administration in Social Work* 19 (1): 1–13.

Moynihan, Daniel. 1969. *Maximum Feasible Misunderstanding: Community Action in the War on Poverty*. New York: Free Press.

Mullender, Audrey, and David Ward. 1991. Empowerment through social action group work: The self-directed approach. *Social Work with Groups* 14 (3/4): 125–140.

Mulroy, Elizabeth, and John Cragin. 1994. Training future community-based managers: The politics of collaboration in a turbulent urban environment. *Journal of Teaching in Social Work* 9:17–35.

Murphy, John, and Jung Min Choi. 1993. Decentering social relations. In *Open Institutions: The Hope for Democracy*, ed. John Murphy and Dennis Peck, 160–176. Westport, CT: Praeger.

Murray, Charles. 1984. *Losing Ground*. New York. Basic Books.

Naperstack, Arthur, and Dennis Dooley. 1998. Countering urban disinvestment through community-building initiative. In *Community Building: Renewal, Well-Being, and Shared Responsibility*, ed. Patricia Ewalt, Edith Freeman, and Dennis Poole, 6–16. Washington, D.C.: NASW Press.

Nelsen, Judith. September 1980. Support: A necessary condition for change. *Social Work* 25 (5): 388–393.

Netting, Ellen, and Steve McMurtry. 1994. Will privatization destroy the traditional nonprofit sector? Yes. In *Controversial Issues in Communities and Organizations*, ed. Michael Austin and John Lowe, 159–164. Boston: Allyn and Bacon.

Newfield, Christopher. 1998. Recapturing academic business. In *Chalk Lines: The*

Politics of Work in the Managed University, ed. Randy Martin, 69–102. Durham, NC: Duke University Press.

New Settlement Apartments. 1998. Packet of materials on community-building service strategy. Bronx, New York: New Settlement Apartments.

New York Times. 1992. Editorial, May 6, p. A18.

Noddings, Nel. 1984. *Caring: A Feminine Approach to Ethics*. Berkeley, CA: University of California Press.

O'Connor, James. 1973. *The Fiscal Crisis of the State*. New York: St. Martin's Press.

O'Connell, Mary. 1988. *The Gift of Hospitality: Opening the Doors of Community Life to People with Disabilities*. Chicago: Center for Urban Affairs and Policy Research, Northwestern University.

O'Donnell, Sandra. 1996. Urban African-American community development in the Progressive Era. *Journal of Community Practice* 2 (4): 7–26.

O'Donnell, Julie, Elizabeth Michalak, and Ellen Ames. 1998. Inner-city youths helping children: After-school programs to promote bonding and reduce risk. In *Community Building: Renewal, Well-Being, and Shared Responsibility*, ed. Patricia Ewalt, Edith Freeman, and Dennis Poole, 191–201. Washington, D.C.: NASW Press.

Offe, Claus. 1981. The attribution of public status to interest groups: Observations on the West German case. In *Organizing Interests in Western Europe: Pluralism, Corporatism, and the Transformation of Politics*, ed. Suzanne Berger, 123–158. Cambridge: Cambridge University Press.

Pacey, Lorene. M., ed. 1950. *Readings in the Development of Settlement Work*. New York: Association Press.

Pargament, Kenneth, Miriam Habib, and David Antebi. 1978. Community participation in mental health. *Social Casework* 59 (10): 597–604.

Pierre-Louis, Francois. April 15, 1996. Community capacity building and school reform. Unpublished paper, CUNY Graduate Center, New York.

Peat, Barbara, and Costley, Dan. 2000. Privatization of social services: Correlates of contract performance. *Administration in Social Work* 24 (1): 21–38.

Pells, Richard. 1994. *The Liberal Mind in a Conservative Age: American Intellectuals in the 1940s and 1950s*. Middletown, Conn.: Wesleyan University Press.

Peterson, Jon. 1965. From social settlement to social agency: Settlement work in Columbus, Ohio, 1898–1958. *Social Service Review* 40 (March): 191–208.

Peterson, Paul, and David Greenstone. 1977. Racial change and citizen participation: The mobilization of low-income communities through community action. In *A Decade of Federal Antipoverty Programs: Achievements, Failures, and Lessons*, ed. Robert Haveman, 241–278. New York: Academic Press.

Phillips, Kevin. 1990. *The Politics of Rich and Poor: Wealth and the American Electorate in the Reagan Aftermath*. New York: Harper.

Philpott, Thomas L. 1978. *The Slum and the Ghetto: Neighborhood Deterioration and Middle-Class Reform, Chicago, 1880–1930.* New York: Oxford University Press.

Piven, Frances F., and Richard Cloward. 1971. *Regulating the Poor: The Functions of Public Welfare.* New York: Pantheon.

———. 1977. *Poor People's Movements: Why They Succeed, How They Fail.* New York: Pantheon.

———. 1982. *The New Class War: Reagan's Attack on the Welfare State and its Consequences.* New York: Pantheon.

Polenberg, Richard. 2000. *The Era of Franklin Delano Roosevelt, 1933–1945.* New York: St. Martin's Press.

Pottick, Kathleen. 1989. Jane Addams revisited: Practice theory and social economics. In *Group work with the poor and Oppressed,* ed. Judith A. B. Lee, 11–26. Binghamton, N.Y.: Haworth Press.

Poole, Dennis, and Mary Van Hook. 1998. Retooling for community health partnerships in primary care and prevention. In *Community Building: Renewal, Well-Being, and Shared Responsibility,* ed. Patricia Ewalt, Edith Freeman, and Dennis Poole, 407–410. Washington, D.C.: NASW Press.

Pollio, David, Sharon McDonald, and Carol North. 1996. Combining a strength-based approach and feminist theory in group work with persons on the streets. *Social Work with Groups* 19 (3–4): 5–20.

Pope, Jackie. 1990. Women in the welfare rights struggle: The Brooklyn welfare rights struggle. In *Women and Social Protest,* ed. Guide West and Rhoda Blumberg, 57–74. New York: Oxford University Press.

Poole, Dennis. 1998. Building community capacity to promote public and social health: Challenges for universities. In *Community Building: Renewal, Well-Being, and Shared Responsibility,* ed. Patricia Ewalt, Edith Freeman, and Dennis Poole, 375. Washington, D.C.: NASW Press.

Potts, Marilyn. 1998. Social support and depression among older adults living alone: The importance of friends within and outside of a retirement community. In *Community Building: Renewal, Well-Being, and Shared Responsibility,* ed. Patricia Ewalt, Edith Freeman, and Dennis Poole, 252–272. Washington, D.C.: NASW Press.

Powell, Thomas. 1983. The use of self-help groups as supportive reference communities. In *Agency-Based Social Work,* ed. Harold Weissman, Irwin Epstein, and Andrea Savage, 97–109. Philadelphia, PA: Temple University Press.

Powell, Walter W., and Rebecca Friedkin. 1987. Organizational change in nonprofit organizations. In *The Nonprofit Sector: A Research Handbook,* ed. Walter W. Powell, 180–194. New Haven: Yale University Press.

Putnam, Robert. 1993a. *Making Democracy Work: Civic Traditions in Modern Italy.* Princeton, NJ: Princeton University Press.

———. 1993b. The prosperous community: Social capital and public life. *The American Prospect* 13:35–42.

———. 1995. Bowling alone, revisited. *The Responsive Community* 5:18–35.

———. 1996. The strange disappearance of civic America. *American Prospect* 24 (winter): 22–38.

———. 2000. *Bowling Alone: The Collapse and Revival of American Community.* New York: Simon and Schuster.

Quandt, Jean. 1970. *From the Small Town to the Great Community.* New Brunswick, NJ: Rutgers University Press.

Ramey, John. 1992. Group work practice in neighborhood centers today. *Social Work with Groups* 15(2/3): 193–206.

Readings, Bill. 1996. *The University in Ruins.* Cambridge, MA: Harvard University Press.

Reed, Adolph, ed. 1999. *Without Justice for All: The New Liberalism and Our Retreat from Racial Equality.* Boulder, CO: Westview Press.

Regan, Paul S. 1998. Purchase of service and fostered failure: A Massachusetts case study. In *The Privatization of Human Services: Case Studies in the Purchase of Services,* ed. Margaret Gibelman and Harold Demone Jr., 2: 79–96. New York. Springer.

Reich, Robert. 1997. *Locked in the Cabinet.* New York: Vintage.

———. 2001. *The Future of Success.* New York: Knopf.

Reichert, Kurt. 1977. The drift toward entrepreneurialism in health and social welfare. *Administration in Social Work* 1:123–133.

Reinders, Robert C. 1982. Toynbee Hall and the American settlement movement. *Social Service Review* 56 (1): 39–54.

Reinelt, Claire. 1994. Fostering empowerment building community: The challenges for state-funded feminist organizations. *Human Relations* 47 (6): 685–705.

———. 1995. Moving into the terrain of the state: The battered women's movement and the politics of engagement. In *Feminist Organizations: Harvest of the Women's Movement,* ed. Myra Marx Ferree and Patricia Yancey Martin, 84–104. Philadelphia, PA: Temple University Press.

Richter, Barbara, and Martha Ozawa. 1983. Purchase of service contracts and the function of private agencies. *Administration in Social Work* 7 (1): 25–37.

Richter-Greer, Nora. 1986. *The Search for Shelter.* Washington, D.C.: American Institute of Architects.

Ridgeway, Priscilla, Alexa Simpson, Friedner Wittman, and Gary Wheeler. 1994. Homemaking and community building: Notes on empowerment and place. *Journal of Mental Health Administration* 21 (4): 407–418.

Romanofsky, Peter. 1978a. Hull-House association. In *Social Service Organizations,* ed. Peter Romanofsky, 351–357. Westport, CT: Greenwood Press.

———. 1978b. National federation of settlements and neighborhood centers. In

Social Service Organizations, ed. Peter Romanofsky, 533–540. Westport, CT: Greenwood Press.

Rose, Elizabeth. 1994. From sponge cake to hamentashen: Jewish identity in a Jewish settlement house, 1885–1952. *Journal of American Ethnic History* 13:3–23.

Roth, Bennett. 2000. Poverty rates plunge as incomes surge. *Houston Chronicle*, September 27, p. 1.

Rothman, Sheila M. 1973. Other people's children: The day care experience in America. *The Public Interest* 30 (winter):11–27.

———. 1978. *Woman's Proper Place*. New York: Basic Books.

Rubin, Herbert. 1993. Community empowerment within an alternative economy. In *Open Institutions: The Hope for Democracy*, ed. John Murphy and Dennis Peck, 100–121. New York: Praeger.

———. 1994. There aren't going to be any bakeries here if there is no money for jelly rolls: The organic theory for community-based development. *Social Problems* 41 (3): 401–424.

———. 1996. Being a conscience and a carpenter: Interpretations of a community-based development. Unpublished paper. Carbondale, IL.

Rubin, Herbert, and Irene Rubin. 1992. *Community Organization and Development*. New York: MacMillan.

Rudney, Gabriel. 1987. The scope and dimensions of the nonprofit sector. In *The Nonprofit Sector: A Research Handbook*, ed. Walter W. Powell, 55–64. New Haven: Yale University Press.

Ryan, Mary. 1992. Gender and public access: Women's politics in nineteenth-century America. In *Habermas and the Public Sphere*, ed. C. Calhoun, 259–288. Boston: MIT Press.

Salem, Deborah, Edward Seidman, and Julian Rappaport. 1988. Community treatment of the mentally ill: The promise of mutual-help organizations. *Social Work* 33 (5): 403–408.

Salamon, Lester. 1987a. Of market failure, voluntary failure, and third-party government: Toward a theory of government-nonprofit relations in the modern welfare state. *Journal of Voluntary Action Research* 16:29–49.

———. 1987b. Partners in public service: The scope and theory of government-nonprofit relations. In *The Non-profit Sector: A Research Handbook*, ed. Walter W. Powell, 99–117. New Haven: Yale University Press.

Salamon, Lester, and Alan Abramson. 1982. *The Federal Budget and The Nonprofit Sector*. Washington, D.C.: Urban Institute.

Salamon, Lester, J. C. Musselwhite Jr., and C. J. de Vita. 1986. Partners in public service: Government and the nonprofit sector in the welfare state, in *Institute Philanthropy, Voluntary Action, and the Public Good*, ed. Independent Sector, Inc., and United Way, 3–38. Washington, D.C.: Independent Sector.

Sampson, Robert, Stephan Raudenbush, and Felton Earls. 1997. Crime: A multilevel study of collective efficacy. *Science*, August 15, 918–924.

Sandel, Michael. 1996. *Democracy's Discontent*. Cambridge, MA: Harvard University Press.

———. 1988. Democrats and community. *New Republic*, February 22, pp. 20–23.

Santiago, Letty. 1972. From settlement house to antipoverty program. *Social Work* 17 (4): 73–78.

Sashkin, Marshall. 1984. Participative management is an ethical imperative. *Organizational Dynamics* 12:4–22.

Sassen, Saskia. 1994. *Cities in a World Economy*. Thousand Oaks, CA: Pine Forge Press.

Savas, Edward S. 1982. *Privatizing the Public Sector: How to Shrink Government*. Chatham, N.J.: Chatham House.

Schecter, Susan. 1982. *Male Violence: The Visions and Struggles of the Battered Women's Movement*. Boston: South End Press.

Schlesinger, Arthur Jr. 1986. *The Cycles of American History*. Boston: Houghton, Mifflin.

Schorr, Lisbeth. 1997. *Within our Reach: Breaking the Cycle of Disadvantage*. New York: Doubleday.

Schor, Juliet. 1999. Foreword to *Shifting Fortunes: The Perils of the Growing American Wealth Gap* (http://www.stw.org/html/shifting_fortunes_report.html).

Schor, Julia. 1999. *The Overspent American: Upscaling, Downshifting, and the New Consumer*. New York: Harper Perennial.

Schram, Sanford. 2000. *After Welfare: The Culture of Postindustrial Social Policy*. New York: New York University Press.

Schwartz, Joel. 1983. The New York City rent strikes of 1963–1964. *Social Service Review* 57:544–564.

Sclar, Elliott D. 2000. *You Don't Always Get What You Pay For: The Economics of Privatization*. Ithaca, NY: Cornell University Press.

Scudder, Vida. 1900. Settlement past and future. In *Readings in the Development of Settlement Work*, ed. Lorene M. Pacey, 69–73. New York: Association Press.

Segal, Steven, Carol Silverman, and Tanya Temkin. 1993. Empowerment and self-help agency practice for people with mental disabilities. *Social Work* 38 (6): 705–712.

Segal, Steven, and Jim Baumohl. 1980. Engaging the disengaged: Proposals on madness and vagrancy. *Social Work* 25 (5): 358ff.

———. 1985. The community living room. *Social Casework* 66 (2): 111–116.

Sennett, Richard. 1974. *The Fall of Public Man*. New York: Norton.

———. 1990. *The Conscience of the Eye*. New York: Norton.

Sergiovanni, Thomas J. 1994. *Building Community in Schools*. San Francisco: Jossey Bass.

Shapiro, Edward S. 1978. Robert A. Woods and the settlement house impulse. *Social Service Review* 52 (2): 215–226.

Sharkansky, Ira. 1980. Policymaking and service delivery on the margins of government: The case of contractors. *Public Administration Review* 40 (2): 116–123.

Sidel, Ruth. 1986. *Women and Children Last: The Plight of Poor Women in Affluent America.* New York: Penguin.

Simkhovitch, Mary K. 1938. *Neighborhood: My Story of Greenwich House.* New York: Norton.

Simon, Barbara L. 1994. *The Empowerment Tradition in American Social Work: A History.* New York: Columbia University Press.

———. 1998. CUSSW and settlement houses: Yesterday, today, and tomorrow. Unpublished presentation, Columbia University School of Social Work Centennial Celebration (July 12): 1–15.

Simonsen, William, and Mark Robbins. 2000. *Citizen Participation in Resource Allocation.* Boulder, CO: Westview.

Singer, Daniel. 1999. *Whose Millennium: Theirs or Ours?* New York: Monthly Review Press.

Sites, William. 1997. The limits of urban regime theory: New York City under Koch, Dinkins, and Giuliani. *Urban Affairs Review* 32 (4): 536–557.

Sklar, Kathryn Kish. 1995. *Florence Kelley and the Nation's Work.* New Haven: Yale University Press.

Skocpol, Theda. 1992. *Protecting Soldiers and Mothers: The Political Origins of Social Policy in the United States.* Cambridge, MA: The Belknap Press of Harvard University Press.

Skocpol, Theda, and Morris P. Fiorina. 2000. *Civic Engagement in American Democracy.* Washington, D.C.: Brookings Institution Press.

Skocpol, Theda, and Richard Leone. 2000. *The Missing Middle: Working Families and the Future of Social Policy.* New York: Norton.

Smith, Barbara L. 1991. Taking structure seriously: The learning community model. *Liberal Education* 77 (2): 6.

Smith, Helen, and Hilary Brown. 1992. Defending community care: Can normalization do the job? *British Journal of Social Work* 22 (6): 685–693.

Smith, Michael, and Joe Feagin. 1987. *The Capitalist City: Global Restructuring and Community Politics.* London: Blackwell.

Smith, Neil. 1998. Giuliani time: The revanchist 1990s. *Social Text* 57:1–20.

Smith, Rolland F. 1995. Settlements and neighborhood centers. *Encyclopedia of Social Work*, 19th ed., 2129–2135.

Smith, Steven R., and Michael Lipsky. 1993. *Nonprofits for Hire: The Welfare State in the Age of Contracting.* Cambridge, MA: Harvard University Press.

Smith, Steven Rathgeb, and Deborah A. Stone. 1988. The unexpected consequences of privatization. In *Remaking the Welfare State: Retrenchment and Social Policy in America and Europe*, ed. Michael K. Brown, 232–252. Philadelphia: Temple University Press.

Sorkin, Michael, ed. 1992. *Variation on a Theme Park: The New American City and the End of Public Space*. New York: Noonday Press.

Soule, Frederick J. 1947. Settlements and neighborhood houses. In *Readings in the Development of Settlement Work*, ed. Lorene Pacey, 321–330. New York: Association Press.

Spann, Robert M. 1977. Public vs. private provision of government services. In *Budgets and Bureaucrats: The Sources of Government Growth*, ed. Thomas Borcherding, 71–89. Durham, N.C.: Duke University Press.

Specht, Harry, and Mark Courtney. 1994. *Unfaithful Angels: How Social Work has Abandoned its Mission*. New York: Free Press.

Stanford, Michael. 1994. *A Companion to the Study of History*. Oxford: Blackwell.

Staples, Lee. 1997. Selecting and cutting the issue. In *Community Organizing and Community Building for Health*, ed. Meredith Minkler, 175–194. New Brunswick, NJ: Rutgers University Press.

Starr, Paul. 1987. *The Limits of Privatization*. Washington, D.C.: Economic Policy Institute.

Steinberg, Richard. 1987. Nonprofit organizations and the market. In *The Nonprofit Sector: A Research Handbook*, ed. Walter W. Powell, 118–138. New Haven: Yale University Press.

Stern, Mark. 1998. The end of Progressivism: Paradigmatic shifts and social welfare. In *Towards More Democracy in Social Services*, ed. Gaby Flosser and Hans-Uwe Otto, 19–42. Berlin: de Gruyter.

Still, Bayrd. 1974. *Urban America*. Boston: Little, Brown.

Stivers, Camilla. 1995. Settlement women and bureau men: Constructing a usable past for public administration. *Public Administration Review* 55 (6): 522–529.

Stone, Clarence. July 17, 1995. Linking civic capacity and human capital formation. Unpublished paper. College Park, Md.

Stone, Rebecca, ed. 1996. *Core Issues in Comprehensive Community Building Initiatives*. Chicago: Chapin Hall Center for Children at the University of Chicago.

Stuart, Paul H. 1992. The Kingsley House extension program: Racial segregation in a 1940s settlement program. *Social Service Review* 66 (1): 112–120.

Suarez, Ray. 1999. *This Old Neighborhood: What We Lost in the Great Suburban Migration, 1966–1999*. New York: Free Press.

Sullivan, Maura. 1993. Social work's legacy of peace: Echoes from the early 20th century. *Social Work* 38 (5): 513–520.

Susser, Ida. 1988. Working-class women, social protest, and changing ideologies. In *Women and the Politics of Empowerment*, ed. Ann Bookers and Sandra Morgan, 257–271. Philadelphia, PA: Temple University Press.

Sviridoff, Mitchell, and William Ryan. 1997. Community-centered family service. *Families in Society* 78 (2): 128–138.

Swartz, Sue. 1995. Community and risk in social service work. *Journal of Progressive Human Services* 6 (1): 73–92.

Taub, Richard. 1990. *Nuance and Meaning in Community Development.* The New York Community Development Research Center, Graduate School of Management and Urban Policy. New York: The New School of Social Research.

Thompson, Kenneth, Ezra Griffith, and Philip Leaf. 1990. A historical review of the Madison model of community care. *Hospital and Community Psychiatry* 41 (6): 625–634.

Thompson, Edward P. 1971. Anthropology and the discipline of historical context. *Midland History* 3:41–55.

Tilly, Charles. 1990. Down and out in the city: Examining the roots of urban poverty. *Dollars and Sense* 12:155.

Tobin, Eugene. 1988. From Jane Addams to Saul Alinsky. *Reviews in American History* 16 (3): 117–124.

Trattner, Walter I. 1999. *From Poor Law to Welfare State: A History of Social Welfare in America.* New York: Free Press.

Trolander, Judith Ann. 1973. The response of settlements to the Great Depression. *Social Work* 18 (5): 92–102.

———. 1975. *Settlement Houses and the Great Depression.* Detroit: Wayne State University Press.

———. 1982. Social change: Settlement houses and Saul Alinsky, 1939–1965. *Social Service Review* 56 (3): 346–365.

———. 1987. *Professionalism and Social Change: From the Settlement House Movement to Neighborhood Centers, 1886 to the Present.* New York: Columbia University Press.

———. 1991. Hull-House and the settlement movement: A centennial reassessment. *Social Service Review* 17:410–424.

Tsanoff, Corrine. 1958. *Neighborhood Doorways.* Houston: Neighborhood Centers Association of Houston and Harris County.

Tusiani, Bea. 1995. Rosemary Kelly Giugliano: When social service organizations are under budget scalpel. *New York Times*, January 22, 13LI, p. 2.

Tutunjian, Noelle. May 1997. A vision toward a community-building social work practice. Unpublished paper. New York: Hunter College School of Social Work.

Tyson, Katherine. 1995. *New Foundations for Scientific Social and Behavioral Research: The Heuristic Paradigm.* Boston: Allyn & Bacon.

Uchitelle, Louis. 1999. Rising incomes lift poor out of poverty. *New York Times*, October 1, section A, p. 20.

———. 2000. Lonely bowlers, unite: Mend the social fabric. *New York Times*, May 6, section B, p. 11.

Valentine, Mary Beth, and Pat Capponi. 1989. Mental health consumer participation on boards and committees: Barriers and strategies. *Canada's Mental Health* 37 (2): 8–12.

Vanderberg, Lela. 1993. Leaders' perspectives on neighborhood organizing leadership: The motivation-participation-ownership triangle. Ph.D. diss., Michigan State University.

Vorspan, Robby. 1992. Why work works. *Psychosocial Rehab Journal* 16 (2): 23–27.

Wagner, David. 2000. *What's Love Got to Do With It: A Critical Look at American Charity.* New York: New Press.

Wald, Lillian. 1934. *Windows on Henry Street.* Boston: Little, Brown.

———. 1971. *The House on Henry Street.* New York: Dover Publications.

Walkowitz, Daniel. 1990. The making of a feminine professional identity: Social workers in the 1920s. *American Historical Review* 95:1051–1075.

———. 1999. *Working with Class: Social Workers and the Politics of Middle-Class Identity.* Chapel Hill: University of North Carolina Press.

Wallach, William. 1978. Henry Street settlement urban life center. In *Social Service Organizations*, ed. Peter Romanofsky, 345–351. Westport, CT: Greenwood Press.

Wallarstein, Nina, Victoria Sanchez-Merki, and Lily Dow. 1997. Freirian praxis in health education and community organizing: A case study of an adolescent prevention program. In *Community Organizing and Community Building for Health*, ed. Meredith Minkler, 195–215. New Brunswick, NJ: Rutgers University Press.

Walsh, Joan. 1997. *Stories of Renewal: Community Building and the Future of Urban America.* New York: The Rockefeller Foundation.

Walter, Cheryl. 1997. Community-building practice: A conceptual framework. In *Community Organizing and Community Building for Health*, ed. Meredith Minkler, 68–87. New Brunswick, NJ: Rutgers University Press.

Warner, Sam Bass Jr. 1968. *The Private City: Philadelphia in Three Periods of Growth.* Philadelphia: University of Pennsylvania Press.

———. 1972. *The Urban Wilderness: A History of the American City.* New York: Harper and Row.

Webster-Stratton, Carolyn. 1997. From parent training to community building. *Families in Society* 78 (2): 156–171.

Wedel, Kenneth. 1974. Contracting for public assistance social services. *Public Welfare* 32 (1): 57–62.

Wedel, Kenneth, and Nancy Chess. 1989. Monitoring strategies in purchase of service. In *Services for Sale: Purchasing Health and Human Services*, ed. Harold

Demone Jr. and Margaret Gibelman, 360–370. New Brunswick, N.J.: Rutgers University Press.

Weil, Marie. 1996. Community building: Building community practice. *Social Work* 41 (5): 481–498.

Weinstein, James. 1968. *The Corporate Ideal in the Liberal State, 1900–1918*. Boston: Beacon Press.

Weisbrod, Burton. 1988. *The Nonprofit Economy*. Cambridge, MA: Harvard University Press.

Wenocur, Stanley, and Michael Reisch. 1989. *From Charity to Enterprise: The Development of American Social Work in a Market Economy*. Urbana: University of Illinois Press.

Whitman, Craig. 1995. Heading toward normal: Deinstitutionalization for the mentally retarded client. *Marriage and Family Review* 21 (1–2): 51–63.

Wiebe, Robert. 1967. *The Search for Order, 1877–1920*. New York: Oxford University Press.

Wieman, Donald, and Robert Dorwart. 1998. Evaluating state mental health care reform: The case of privatization of state mental services in Massachusetts. In *The Privatization of Human Services: Policy and Practice Issues*, ed. Margaret Gibelman and Harold Demone Jr., 1:53–78. New York: Springer.

Wills, Gary. July 17, 2000. Putnam's America. *The American Prospect* 11 (16): 97.

Wilson, William J. 1999. *The Bridge Over the Racial Divide*. Berkeley: University of California Press.

Wilson, Julius. 1987. *The Truly Disadvantaged*. Chicago: University of Chicago Press.

——. 1991. Another look at the truly disadvantaged. *Political Science Quarterly* 106 (4): 639–656.

Winkle, Curtis, and Douglas Ward-Chene. 1992. Power, social support, and HIV-related service use: The roles of community and homelessness. *Journal of Health and Social Policy* 4 (2): 47–70.

Wolch, Jennifer, and Andrea Akita. 1989. The federal response to homelessness and its implications for American cities. *Urban Geography* 10:62–85.

Wolch, Jennifer. 1990. *The Shadow State: Government and the Voluntary Sector in Transition*. New York: The Foundation Center.

Wolpert, Julian. 1993. *Patterns of Generosity in America: Who's Holding the Safety Net?* New York: Twentieth Century Fund Press.

Woods, Robert A., and Albert J. Kennedy. 1911. *Handbook of Settlements*. New York: Charities Publications Committee.

Wynn, Joan, Joan Costello, Robert Halpern, and Harold Richman. 1994. *Children, Families, and Community: A New Approach to Communities*. Chicago: The Chapin Hall Center at the University of Chicago.

Zachary, Eric. 1996. Grassroots leadership training: A case study to join theory and method. Ph.d. diss., City University of New York.

———. 2000. Grassroots leadership training: A case study to integrate theory and method. *Journal of Community Practice* 7 (1): 71–93.

Zurcher, Louis A., and Alvin E. Green. 1969. *From Dependency to Dignity: Individual and Social Consequences of a Neighborhood House.* New York: Behavioral Publications.

Index

rejection of, 34–35; settlements in,
7, 39, 53, 54; as threat, 48
Social Darwinism, 24
Social Diagnosis (Richmond), 35
Social feminism, 28
Social investment, 18, 20, 21, 22, 53;
cyclical theory of, 16
Social issues, public distancing from,
66–67
Social networks, 2, 5, 6, 7, 12, 242,
243, 244, 246, 258, 285, 311n3;
building, 248; building through
planned intervention, 243–45; in
community building, 270–72;
converted into political capital,
288–89; and independence, 267–
68; necessary to political
organizing, 259–60; physical
environment and, 276; in poor
communities, 252–53;
strengthening, 260–61
Social policy: federal, 77–78; history
of, 19–20; responsibility for, 72,
73
Social problems, 39, 48, 67, 73, 74;
business and, 72; cause of, 33, 64;
caused by poverty, 43; in
conservative eras, 56;
individualization of, 3, 4, 64, 240–
41; privatization and, 11, 70;
public/private, 24
Social reform, 15, 36, 38, 309n8; in
cycles of history, 19–20; financial
support for, 22; funding, 51,
307n25; history of, 16–17; 1960s,
55; rejection of, 33, 35; repression
of, 19; settlement houses and, 38,
39, 48–49, 53, 56, 89
Social responsibility, shift in, 39,
100–01
Social Security, 41, 43, 79, 185–86

Social Security Act of 1935, 41;
amendments, 57, 58, 61, 76,
308n30
Social service agencies: contract
volatility, 101–12; collaboration
among, 227–29; community
building, 258–59; culture of, 240–
41, 249; member relationship to,
255–57; partnerships among, 215–
16; settlements transformed into,
51, 52; smaller, unable to compete,
92, 115–16; and social capital,
244–45; welcoming services users,
253
Social Service Block Grant program,
77
Social service ethic, 237–38
Social services, 8, 9, 12, 27, 35, 41, 53;
change in meaning of, 236–37;
change in nature of, 168–69;
community-based, 6–7; controlling
demand for, 169–75; demand for,
79; devolution of responsibility for,
to states, 112–14; disinvestment in,
116–18; effect of contracting on,
84–86; fiscal turbulence and future
of, 198–230; funding, 51, 52–53,
77, 80–81, 103–12; instability of,
116–18; inventing future for, 214–
30; marketing, 205–06; paperwork
and quality of, 195–97; political
and social action in defense of,
207–15; privatization of, 179–81;
quality and content, 193–95, 196;
rationing, narrowing, redefining,
168–197; redefining concrete
dimensions of, 192–96; redefining
quality of, 186–96; reducing supply
of, 174–78; responsibility for, 78;
rollback in core, 194–96; shifting
conception of, 6, 203–04; staffing